PREFACE

The experiment of publishing this Bibliography as a companion volume to the second edition of my Jurisprudence, was encouraging enough to prompt a repetition. In this edition there are, of course, many additional references to contributions which have appeared since the last publication, but it has also been necessary to eliminate other references which have been superseded or have become obsolete through change. The significant new feature is the addition of indices. Pressure of time made it impossible to prepare indices when this volume was first published; but opportunity has now been taken to provide these.

The present edition can stand completely on its own; but with a bibliography of this size a breakdown of the references into appropriate topics and sub-topics is preferable to straightforward alphabetical lists. The most convenient arrangement, from my point of view, is still that adopted in the textbook, but there is no magic in arrangement as such, and the various headings and sub-headings set out here should be, in any case, self-explanatory.

Jurisprudence is a subject which embraces a diversity of opinions. It is therefore important that scholars should be put on the track of material rather than just be told what to know. With that end in view this compilation seeks to provide the means whereby the reader can steep himself in many different aspects of each topic. The references given here are not exhaustive, but they do include a good deal of the relevant material written in the English language and such as will furnish pointers to other important sources of information, especially Continental. Within these limits an effort has been made to present as many different points of view and shades of opinion as possible and the policy, in cases of doubt, has been to include rather than to exclude.

Mere lists of references, however arranged and divided, tend to be somewhat daunting. Accordingly, indication has been given of what each reference is about so as to inform the prospective reader what to expect and to enable him to decide whether or not a particular reference is what he wants. This, it is hoped, will prevent an unnecessary waste of time and might also assist in the selection and planning of one's own reading. This last consideration is particularly important in the case of undergraduates, who have all too little time at their disposal; and it is hoped that some of them, at any rate, might be helped and encouraged to read more widely than they would otherwise have done.

Preface

Finally, I must record heartfelt thanks to my wife and daughter, Julia, for the prolonged sacrifice of their own concerns in order to help with the indices. In this exacting task their patience and devotion to the job often outlasted my own.

October, 1969   R.W.M. DIAS

CONTENTS

ABBREVIATIONS

The following is a table of the abbreviations used for legal and other periodicals referred to in this Bibliography

A.J.C.L.	American Journal of Comparative Law
A.J.I.L.	American Journal of International Law
A.J.S.	American Journal of Sociology
Am. B.A.J.	American Bar Association Journal
Am. J.L.H.	American Journal of Legal History
Am. L.R.	American Law Review
Am. Pol. Sc. R.	American Political Science Review
Ann. L.R.	Annual Law Review
Aust. L.J.	Australian Law Journal
B.L.R.	Boston Law Review
Br. J.C.	British Journal of Criminology
Br. Tax. R.	British Tax Review
Brook. L.R.	Brooklyn Law Review
B.S.A.L.R.	Butterworths South African Law Review
B.Y.I.L.	British Yearbook of International Law
Calif. L.R.	Californian Law Review
Can. B.J.	Canadian Bar Journal
Can. B.R.	Canadian Bar Review
Cape L.J.	Cape Law Journal
C.I.L.S.A.	Comparative and International Journal of Southern Africa
C.L.J.	Cambridge Law Journal
C.L.P.	Current Legal Problems
Col. L.R.	Columbia Law Review
Corn. L.Q.	Cornell Law Quarterly
Crim. L.R.	Criminal Law Review
D.L.J.	Duke Law Journal
F.L.R.	Fordham Law Review
Geo. L.J.	Georgetown Law Journal
Geo. Wash. L.R.	George Washington Law Review
Harv. L.R.	Harvard Law Review
How. J.	Howard Journal
I.C.L.Q.	International and Comparative Law Quarterly
I.J.E.	International Journal of Ethics
I.L.Q.	International Law Quarterly
Ill. L.Q.	Illinois Law Quarterly
Ill. L.R.	Illinois Law Review
I.L.T.	Irish Law Times
Iowa L.R.	Iowa Law Review
Ir. Jur.	Irish Jurist
Ir. Jur. (N.S.)	Irish Jurist (New Series)
J.A.L	Journal of African Law
J.B.L.	Journal of Business Law

Abbreviations

J.C.L.	Journal of Comparative Legislation
J. Comm. P.S.	Journal of Commonwealth Political Studies
J. Cr. L.	Journal of Criminal Law
J.L.E.	Journal of Legal Education
J.L. Pol. S.	Journal of Legal and Political Sociology
J.P.J.	Justices of the Peace Journal
J.P.L.	Journal of Public Law
J.S.P.T.L. (N.S.)	Journal of the Society of Public Teachers of Law (New Series)
Jur. R.	The Juridical Review
Jur. S. (N.S.)	The Juridical Review (New Series)
Kansas L.R.	University of Kansas Law Review
Ken. L.J.	Kentucky Law Journal
L.C.P.	Law and Contemporary Problems
Legal Exec.	Legal Executive
L.J.	Law Journal
L.Q.R.	Law Quarterly Review
L.S. Gaz.	Law Society Gazette
L.T.	Law Times
Malaya L.R.	Malaya Law Review
McGill L.J.	McGill Law Journal
Melb. U.L.R.	Melbourne University Law Review
Mich. L.R.	Michigan Law Review
Minn. L.R.	Minnesota Law Review
Miss. L.R.	Missouri Law Review
M.L.R.	Modern Law Review
Nat. L.F.	Natural Law Forum
New L.J.	New Law Journal
N.I.L.Q.	Northern Ireland Law Quarterly
N.Y.L.Q.R.	New York Law Quarterly Review
N.Y.U.L.R.	New York University Law Review
N.Z.U.L.R.	New Zealand Universities Law Review
Os. H.L.J.	Osgoode Hall Law Journal
P.A.	Public Administration
P.A.S.	Proceedings of the Aristotelian Society
P.L.	Public Law
Pol. S.	Political Studies
Pol. Sc. Q.	Political Science Quarterly
Rhod. L.J.	Rhodesian Law Journal
Rutgers L.R.	Rutgers Law Review
S.A.L.J.	South African Law Journal
Scand. S.L.	Scandinavian Studies in Law
S.L.T.	Scottish Law Times
Sol. Jo.	Solicitors' Journal
Sol. Q.	The Solicitor Quarterly
Southern Calif. L.R.	Southern California Law Review
Stan. L.R.	Stanford Law Review
Syd. L.R.	Sydney Law Review

Abbreviations

Tasm. L.R.	Tasmanian Law Review
Tor. L.J.	Toronto Law Journal
Trans. Gro. S.	Transactions of the Grotius Society
Tran. Jur. S.	Transactions of the Juridical Society
Tul. L.R.	Tulane Law Review
U. Br. Col. L.R.	University of British Columbia Law Review
U.C.L.R	University of Chicago Law Review
U.G.L.J.	University of Ghana Law Journal
U. Pa. L.R.	University of Pennsylvania Law Review
U. Wes. Aus. A.L.R.	University of Western Australia Annual Law Review
Vand. L.R.	Vanderbilt Law Review
Vir. L.R.	Virginia Law Review
Wash. L.R.	Washington Law Review
W. Vir. L.Q.	West Virginia Law Quarterly
Yale L.J.	Yale Law Journal

G E N E R A L

The Scope of Jurisprudence

1. STONE, J. <u>Legal System and Lawyers' Reasonings</u>, (Stevens & Sons, Ltd., 1964), Introduction and chaps. 1 and 5, pp. 162-185: the broad scope of jurisprudence requires that theorising about law should be conducted with the aid of the wisdom of predecessors. The subject cannot be brought within any one philosophy. In chapter 1 the function of language and logic is explained. Words have many meanings and there is no one proper meaning for all people and all purposes. Law is an instrument for achieving certain social purposes. But before its teleology and sociology can be discussed, the nature of the instrument needs to be elucidated. This involves analysis for which logic is employed. The analytical method of approach, its uses and limits are explained. Definition is considered in chapter 5. No definition is likely to prove acceptable, nor will it be adequate for all purposes. A definition is only a mnemonic: what is important is the exposition which it calls to mind. The purpose and function of a definition of ''law'' are discussed, and the matters, which jurists have thought to require clarification, are indicated.

2. COWEN, D.V. ''An Agenda for Jurisprudence'' (1964), 49 Corn. L.Q. 609: the questions are posed: are there any significant questions of a jurisprudential character? in what sense are they ''significant''? which of them are most urgent? and how may these be effectively taught? In the light of these questions a six-point scheme of study is outlined and discussed.

3. PATTERSON, E.W. <u>Jurisprudence</u>, (The Foundation Press, Inc., 1953), Part I: the three chapters comprising this part are important in that they address themselves to various questions relating to the scope of modern jurisprudence, to problems of meaning and of approach. Chapter 2, which includes a discussion of semantics, is especially noteworthy.

4. KANTOROWICZ, H.U. and PATTERSON, E.W. ''Legal Science - a Summary of its Methodology'' (1928), 28 Col.L.R., 679: the nature of scientific study in general is examined in · detail. With reference to legal science, the authors point out its wide coverage. A good many of the technical matters dealt with anticipate what is to be found in this book and its companion text book, but may be read here as indicating the scope of modern jurisprudence.

1. ISAACS, N. "The Schools of Jurisprudence" (1917-18), 31 Harv.
    L.R., 373: this is a good and profiting account of the
    various "schools" of jurisprudence and what each is aiming
    to do. Each has a valuable part to play.

2. BRYCE, J. Studies in History and Jurisprudence, (Oxford,
    1901), chap. 12: the metaphysical, analytical, historical
    and comparative methods of approach are examined. Of these
    the historical is said to be the most profitable. The parts
    played by all four methods are considered and it is con-
    tended that the historical method should be used in
    presenting the other three.

3. ALLEN, C.K. Legal Duties, (Oxford, 1931), chap. 1: various
    matters concerning the nature and purpose of jurisprudential
    study are discussed. It is made clear that the author
    favours general jurisprudence and regards jurisprudence as
    an inductive discipline.

4. POUND, R. Jurisprudence, (West Publishing Co., 1959), I,
    chap. 1: the different senses in which the word
    "jurisprudence" has been used are explained. The divisions
    into analytical, historical, philosophical and sociological
    jurisprudence are examined in so far as these constitute
    different methods of approach.

5. BENTHAM, J. An Introduction to the Principles of Morals and
    Legislation, in Works, (ed. J. Bowring, William Tait & Sons,
    1843), I, chap. 19 Sect. 2: Bentham originates the well-
    known division into "expositorial jurisprudence", explaining
    what the law is, and "censorial jurisprudence", the critical
    examination of the law in the light of what it ought to be.

6. AUSTIN, J. Lectures on Jurisprudence, (5th ed., R. Campbell,
    John Murray, 1885), II, pp. 1071-91: the general basis of
    approach is advocated. Austin lists the topics common to
    what he calls "the ampler and maturer systems." The study
    of jurisprudence brings in the study of legislation. The
    value of studying jurisprudence and Roman law is also con-
    sidered. See also W.J. BROWN: The Austinian Theory of Law,
    (John Murray, 1906), chap. 7; and J. AUSTIN: The Province of
    Jurisprudence Determined and the Uses of the Study of
    Jurisprudence, (ed. H.L.A. Hart, Weidenfeld & Nicholson,
    1954), and see also Hart's Introduction.

7. EASTWOOD, R.A. and KEETON, G.W. The Austinian Theories of Law
    and Sovereignty, (Methuen & Co., Ltd., 1929), pp. 1-6: this
    gives a brief account of the nature of jurisprudential study
    and its different varieties. It is a simplified introduction
    to the principal doctrines of Austin.

1. THORNE, C. "Concerning the Scope of Jurisprudence" (1901), 35 Am.L.R., 546: this is a protest against the adoption in America of the analytical positivism of Austin. This, it is urged, though valuable, should only provide an introduction.

2. DOWDALL, H.C. "The Present State of Analytical Jurisprudence" (1926), 42 L.Q.R. 451: analytical jurisprudence, it is said, satisfies few. The reasons for this, and the best way of re-organising the study of legal philosophy and analytical jurisprudence are considered.

3. LIGHTWOOD, J.M. The Nature of Positive Law, (Macmillan & Co., 1883), chap. 1: it is open to each writer to treat law from different points of view and to select his own department in it. Jurisprudence includes ideas and principles of the law and their improvement. After a discussion of general and particular jurisprudence, the author considers the claims of what he calls "applied jurisprudence".

4. CLARK, E.C. History of Roman Private Law, (Cambridge University Press, 1914), II, chap. 1: the nature of jurisprudence is discussed generally in relation to its use in legislation and legal education. Towards the end there is also a discussion of its relation to the study of Roman law.

5. JENKS, E. The New Jurisprudence, (John Murray, 1933), chaps. 2-3: this discussion, along traditional lines, deals with the analytical, historical, comparative and critical methods. Chapter 1 gives the author's views on the material covered by jurisprudential study.

6. HOLLAND, T.E. The Elements of Jurisprudence, (13th ed., Oxford, 1924), chap. 1: jurisprudence is defined as "the formal science of positive law." Various applications of the term are considered and rejected as "improper". Holland himself recognises only general jurisprudence.

7. POLLOCK, F. Essays in Jurisprudence and Ethics, (Macmillan & Co., 1882), chap. 1: this is partly a comment on Holland's Elements of Jurisprudence (supra), whose views are considered and criticised. Pollock's own views about the scope of the subject appear only indirectly.

8. BUCKLAND, W.W. Some Reflections on Jurisprudence, (Cambridge University Press, 1945), chaps. 1 and 6: the first chapter deals primarily with what Austin meant by jurisprudence as being "the philosophy of positive law". It is pointed out that his theories about the nature of law and sovereignty are only a prologue to a study of jurisprudence. In chapter 6 particular and general jurisprudence are considered. It is

pointed out that advocates of the general approach do not
adhere to it in their treatment.

1. BUCKLAND, W.W. "Difficulties of Abstract Jurisprudence"
   (1890), 6 L.Q.R. 436: this is a critical discussion of the
   claim of certain English writers on jurisprudence to construct a universal philosophy of law. Holland's position,
   in particular, is subjected to attack.

2. BROWN, W.J. The Austinian Theory of Law, (John Murray, 1906),
   Excursus F: this is a lengthy and interesting inquiry into
   the methods of pursuing jurisprudential study. The relation
   between them is set out in a table (p. 369). Brown's own
   preference is discussed towards the end, namely, particular
   or "national" jurisprudence.

3. HALL, J. Studies in Jurisprudence and Criminal Theory,
   (Oceana Publications, Inc., 1958), chaps. 1-2, 6 and 8: the
   dichotomy between particular and general jurisprudence and
   between nominalists and realists is considered with reference to jurisprudence and criminal law. Chapter 2 is perhaps
   the most important, for it contains a plea for what is
   called "integrative jurisprudence" i.e., one which would
   combine facts, ideas and evaluations. See also J.HALL:
   "Integrative Jurisprudence" in Interpretations of Modern
   Legal Philosophies, (ed. P. Sayre, Oxford University Press,
   New York, 1947), chap. 14. Chapters 6 and 8 are of general
   interest.

4. HALL, J. "Concerning the Nature of Positive Law" (1948-49),
   58 Yale L.J., 545: a purely formal study of positive law is
   inadequate. The author pleads that the study should widen
   its scope so as to include past and present experience and
   standards.

5. SALMOND, J.W. Jurisprudence, (7th ed. by J.W. Salmond; 12th
   ed. by P.J. Fitzgerald, Sweet & Maxwell, Ltd., 1966) chap.
   1: this should be taken as a standard discussion of the
   nature of jurisprudence. Comments on it are contained in
   Chapter 1 of R.W.M. Dias on Jurisprudence, (3rd ed., 1970)

6. JOLOWICZ, H.F. Lectures on Jurisprudence, (ed. J.A. Jolowicz,
   The Athlone Press, 1963), Introduction: the difficulties in
   the way of giving an explanation of what "jurisprudence"
   means are indicated. As between particular and general
   jurisprudence, the author's own preference for the latter
   is indicated. He also discusses and rejects any attempt to
   divide the study into analytical, historical etc.

7. GRAY, J.C. The Nature and Sources of the Law, (2nd ed., R. Gray,

The Macmillan Co., New York, 1921) chap. 7: the
traditional approaches to jurisprudential study are
explained and the views of certain writers are criticised.
The discussion is still a useful one.

1. DEL VECCHIO, G. Philosophy of Law, (trans. T.O.Martin, The
   Catholic University of America Press, 1953), chap. 1: a
   distinction is drawn between the "science of law", which is
   particular, and the "philosophy of law", which is universal.
   The latter comprises logical, phenomenological and
   deontological aspects. The relation between the philosophy
   of law and other disciplines and the use of the deductive
   and inductive methods are explained.

2. SNYDER, O.C. Preface to Jurisprudence, (The Bobbs-Merrill Co.,
   Inc., 1954), I, chaps. 1-2: various aspects of
   jurisprudential study are considered, as well as the kind
   of art and proficiency that constitutes skill in the law.
   The different approaches to the subject of jurisprudence
   are outlined. Chapter 2 makes it clear that only particular
   jurisprudence is being dealt with and explains why.

3. KEETON, G.W. The Elementary Principles of Jurisprudence, (2nd
   ed., Pitman & Sons, Ltd., 1949), chap. 1: the different
   "types" of jurisprudence are surveyed generally and discussed.

4. POLLOCK, F. "The History of Comparative Jurisprudence" (1903),
   5 J.C.L. (N.S.), 74: the inter-relation between the
   historical and comparative methods of approach is examined.
   The article traces the evolution of the comparative method
   from Roman times onwards.

5. VINOGRADOFF, P. Collected Papers, (Oxford, 1928), II,
   chaps. 10-11, 16: the first of these chapters pleads for
   the historical approach to jurisprudential study. The next
   chapter points out that the 20th century has witnessed
   events that have dispelled the complacent sway of analytical
   positivism. There is now a preoccupation with social problems.
   In the last chapter it is pointed out that analytical
   positivism is inadequate. The new sociological approach
   involves historical study.

6. GUPTA, A.C. "The Method of Jurisprudence" (1917), 33 L.Q.R.
   154: this is primarily a plea that the study of jurisprudence
   should include ethical and sociological phenomena. It
   constitutes an answer to Brown's critique of Duguit.

7. SETHNA, M.J. "The True Nature and Province of Jurisprudence
   from the Viewpoint of Indian Philosophy" in Essays in
   Jurisprudence in Honor of Roscoe Pound, (ed. R.A.Newman,

The Bobbs-Merrill Co., Inc., 1962), 99: the study of
jurisprudence should combine analytical, historical,
philosophical and, above all, sociological and functional
study. Sociological jurisprudence and the sociology of law
are distinguished and the work of the supporters of each is
outlined. Particular attention is devoted to Pound's
contribution.

1. WURZEL, K.G. "Methods of Juridical Thinking" in Science of
   Legal Method. Select Essays by Various Authors, (trans.
   E.Bruncken and L.B.Register, Boston Book Co., 1917),
   pp. 389-96: law is said to have been the first of the
   social sciences.

2. GOODHART, A.L. "An Apology for Jurisprudence" in
   Interpretations of Modern Legal Philosophies, (ed. P.Sayre,
   Oxford Universities Press, New York, 1947), chap. 12:
   jurisprudence, or legal philosophy, fulfils a useful
   function by explaining the elements of a concept such as
   law. The author considers certain ideas that have been put
   forward about law and also proffers his own.

3. WOLHEIM, R. "The Nature of Law" (1954), 2 Pol.S., 128: the
   problems that have been encountered in defining "Law" are
   considered and the methods of its elucidation are critically
   appraised. Inquiry into the nature of law includes the
   question of its validity, development and function.

4. CAIRNS, H. "Philosophy as Jurisprudence" in Interpretations
   of Modern Legal Philosophies. (ed. P.Sayre, Oxford
   University Press, New York, 1947), chap. 4: there has been,
   and is, an extensive cross-fertilization between science
   and philosophy, but only a one-way fertilization between
   science and the social disciplines. The role of philosophy
   in jurisprudence is considered at length.

5. RADBRUCH, G. "Anglo-American Jurisprudence through Continental
   Eyes" (1936), 52 L.Q.R. 530: in presenting the development
   of Anglo-American jurisprudence a constant comparison is
   made with Continental thought. This article is helpful in
   obtaining a broad view of jurisprudential thought.

6. JONES, J.W. "Modern Discussions of the Aims and Methods of
   Legal Science" (1931), 47 L.Q.R. 62: this is a general
   survey of the views of certain modern writers. It is of
   interest as showing the kind of problems that confront
   jurists.

7. SUMMERS, R.S. "Legal Philosophy Today - an Introduction", in
   Essays in Legal Philosophy, (ed. R.S.Summers, Basil

Blackwell, Oxford, 1968), 1: the scope and methods of modern legal philosophy are outlined. As to scope, it is concerned with conceptual analysis and conceptual revision; as to method, there is now a keener awareness of certain errors. Some of the reasons for the revived mutual interest between lawyers and philosophers in their respective subjects are explained.

1. HART, H.L.A. "Philosophy of Law and Jurisprudence in Britain (1945-52)" (1953), 2 A.J.C.L., 355: this gives a survey of the trends in Britain and assesses their significance.

2. COWAN, T.A. "Legal Pragmatism and Beyond" in Interpretations of Modern Legal Philosophies, (ed. P. Sayre, Oxford University Press, New York, 1947), chap. 7: the progress of jurisprudential thought from the Middle Ages to the present is repidly surveyed. The article concludes with remarks on the future shape of the study.

3. CAMPBELL, A.H. "A Note on the Word 'Jurisprudence'" (1942), 58 L.Q.R., 334: there has been a transition from the old-fashioned meaning of "jurisprudence" as practical wisdom to that of the nature of law. The different meanings attached to the word by various authors are set out in order.

4. LEFROY, A.H.F. "Jurisprudence" (1911), 27 L.Q.R. 180: the article aims at delimiting the word usefully. In the course of the discussion the views of Austin and Holland as to the meaning of "jurisprudence" are critically considered.

5. SALMOND, J.W. "The Names and Nature of the Law" (1899), 15 L.Q.R. 367: this is of general interest. Various meanings and synonyms for the terms "law" and "right" are considered.

6. WIGMORE, J.H. "The Terminology of Legal Science" (1914-15), 28 Harv.L.R. 1: the suggested terminology is of general interest. More important are the different types of study which they are designed to signify. The author particularly advocates the study of what ought to be law.

Aims of Legal Education

7. COOK, W.W. "Scientific Method and the Law" (1927), 13 Am.B.A.J., 303: the case-method has turned out good legal technicians, but are they scientifically trained? Contemporary scientific developments show that too much reliance has been placed on deduction and induction. A new approach to law-teaching is necessary. It should introduce students to the new methods of science, to observing the structure and function of society, analysing existing law,

studying the actual operation of law and enlisting the
co-operation of other social sciences.

1. BODENHEIMER, E. Jurisprudence, (Harvard University Press,
    1962), pp. 343-46: the need is stressed for training in
    social problems. It requires a knowledge of national and
    world history, political theory, economics and philosophy.
    A lawyer should be a person of culture and breadth of
    understanding.

2. COHEN, M.R. Reason and Law, (The Free Press, Glencoe, 1950),
    chap. 5: the point is developed that it is important to
    have a wide coverage in jurisprudence beyond mere technical
    proficiency. Reference might also be made to chapter 1 on
    methods of approach.

3. POUND, R. "Do We Need a Philosophy of Law ?", (1905) 5
    Col.L.R. 339; Jurisprudence in Action, (Baker, Voorhis &
    Co., Inc., 1953), 389: the plea is that law students
    should be trained in the social, political and legal
    philosophy of the time. In the past the common law used to
    be looked to as the bulwark of the individual. Now it tends
    to be frowned upon because it champions individual rights
    at the expense of society.

4. COOK, W.W. "The Utility of Jurisprudence in the Solution of
    Legal Problems" in Lectures on Legal Topics, (The
    Macmillan Co., New York, 1928), p. 338: conceptual tools
    need to be analysed in order that their adequacy may be tested
    tested. This paper contains an examination of the concept
    of "right", which will be dealt with in a later chapter.

5. LLOYD, D. The Idea of Law, (Penguin Books, Ltd., A 688, 1964),
    chap. 12: concepts exist as ideas and not as concrete
    entities. This appears to make law a kind of game. Although
    there are resemblances between law and games, there are
    important and significant differences. Although concepts are
    creations of law, they have a vitality and a creative
    element of their own. A rigid conceptualism has its dangers,
    but concepts are useful in many ways.

6. RHEINSTEIN, M. "Education for Legal Craftsmanship" (1944-45),
    30 Iowa L.R. 408: the mere mechanical manipulation of legal
    concepts is rightly deplored. But concepts are very
    important.

7. HOHFELD, W.N. Fundamental Legal Conceptions as Applied in
    Judicial Reasoning, (ed. W.W. Cook, Yale University Press;
    London: Humphrey Milford, 1923), chap. 8: this address was
    delivered in 1914. It constitutes a plea to law schools to

train students, not merely to be practitioners, but to play
a full part in a developing society.

1. SAMEK, R.A. "The Dynamic Model of the Judicial Process and the
    Ratio Decidendi of a Case" (1964), 42 Can. B.R. 433: towards
    the end of the article the point is made that legal concepts
    are not fixed, but "open-ended". The analysis of concepts
    should take this into account.

2. SIMPSON, A.W.B. "The Analysis of Legal Concepts" (1964) 80
    L.Q.R. 535: the analysis of concepts on the basis simply of
    the logical function of words or sentences is said to be
    unfruitful. Instead it is suggested that there should be an
    investigation into the way in which the meaning of legal
    terms both diverges from and is related to their non-legal
    meaning. Attention should be paid to explaining how, when,
    why and with what consequences this comes about.

3. KELLY, D.St.L. "Legal Concepts, Logical Functions and
    Statements of Facts" (1968) 3 Tasm.L.R. 43: the author
    defends Professors Hart and Ross against A.W.B. Simpson's
    criticisms. It is alleged that the latter misunderstands
    what they said. In the course of the demonstration there is
    a discussion of the function of words.

For discussions on the place and uses of Jurisprudence in legal
education, see the following contributions to (1948-49), 1 J.L.E.:

4. HALL, J. "Introductory Remarks", p. 475: the reasons why
    jurisprudence has won popularity for itself are considered,
    and various suggestions are made as to its teaching.

5. NORTHROP, F.S.C. "Jurisprudence in the Law School Curriculum",
    p. 482: teaching in jurisprudence is considered in the
    light of the legal needs of contemporary society and the
    ability of the subject to train people to cope with them.
    This theme is developed in the light of the factors which
    make contemporary society unique. The solution is said to
    lie in a jurisprudence rooted in a natural law philosophy.

6. FULLER, L.L. "The Place and Uses of Jurisprudence in the Law
    School Curriculum", p. 495: this considers what should be
    taught, how, at what point in the law school course, and why
    teach jurisprudence at all. See also L.L. FULLER: "What the
    Law School can Contribute to the Making of Lawyers", p. 189.

7. GOODHART, A.L. "The Vocational Teaching of Law" (1950),
    1 J.S.P.T.L.(N.S.), 333: the remarks towards the end of
    the address are of especial interest. The vocational
    importance of jurisprudential study is pointed out.

1. BROWNE, D. "Reflections on the Teaching of Jurisprudence"
    (1953), 2 J.S.P.T.L.(N.S.), 79: this is an interesting
    address on the best way in which jurisprudential teaching
    might be revised. What it aims at accomplishing and the
    best methods of achieving its ends are dealt with.

2. HARVEY, C.P. "A Job for Jurisprudence" (1944), 7 M.L.R. 42;
    W.B. KENNEDY: "Another Job for Jurisprudence" (1945), 8
    M.L.R. 18; C.P. HARVEY: ibid., 236: this is a hard-hitting
    disputation. Harvey complains of the fruitlessly academic
    approach of traditional law-teaching and advocates a more
    realistic approach to social problems. The other references
    are to Kennedy's reply and Harvey's rejoinder.

3. STREET, H. "Law and Administration: Implications for University
    Legal Education" (1953), 1 Pol.S.97: although this is not
    concerned specifically with jurisprudential teaching, the
    purpose of the address is to demonstrate the importance of
    teaching law in relation to finance, psychology, economics,
    history, politics, sociology, etc.

4. CLARK, E.C. "Jurisprudence: its Uses and its Place in Legal
    Education" (1885), 1 L.Q.R. 201: this is of interest as
    indicating the old fashioned approach and how much wider
    the subject is today. Only general and comparative
    jurisprudence are thought to be worth considering.

5. BROWN, W.J. "The Purpose and Method of a Law School" (1902),
    18 L.Q.R. 78, 192: the discussion concerns legal education
    in general. The point is made that lawyers need to be
    educated in the widest sense, and the value of legal history
    and philosophy towards this end is touched on.

6. BROWN, W.J. "Jurisprudence and Legal Education" (1909), 9 Col.
    L.R., 238: although this article was written at a time when
    the state of jurisprudence was different from what it is
    now, it is still useful in suggesting some of the points
    that jurisprudential study should cover and what instruction
    in it should seek to achieve.

7. REICH, C.A. "Towards a Humanistic Study of Law" (1964-65) 74
    Yale L.J. 1402: stress is laid on the need for relating the
    teaching of law to life in its varied aspects.

Problems of Language and Definition

8. WILSON, J. Language and the Pursuit of Truth, (Cambridge
    University Press, 1956): this is a simplified, short and
    highly rewarding introduction to semantics. The section on
    "verification" deserves special attention (pp. 51-55).

1. WILLIAMS, G.L. "Language and the Law" (1945), 61 L.Q.R. 71,
   179, 293, 384; (1946), 62 L.Q.R. 387: the meaning of words
   is examined and the lessons to be drawn from the analysis
   are applied iconoclastically to various legal doctrines.
   (See, however, for corrective, J. WISDOM: Philosophy and
   Psycho-Analysis, (Blackwell, Oxford, 1957), pp. 249-54).

2. WILLIAMS, G.L. "International Law and the Controversy
   Concerning the Word 'Law'" in Philosophy, Politics and
   Society, (ed., P. Laslett, Blackwell, Oxford, 1956), chap.
   9: the author pursues his analysis of meaning by examining
   the famous dispute between the followers of Austin and the
   international lawyers as to the "proper" meaning of the
   word "law".

3. FARNSWORTH, E.A. "'Meaning' in the Law of Contracts" (1966-
   67) 76 Yale L.J. 939: this article discusses semantic
   problems of interpretation. The distinction between
   "interpretation" and "construction" is considered in
   relation to meaning in general and contracts in particular.

4. STOLJAR, S.J. "The Logical Status of a Legal Principle"
   (1952-53), 20 U.C.L.R., 181: certain fallacies in legal
   thinking are exposed. In the course of the discussion
   (pp. 197-211) different types of definition are explained.
   This is a useful article both as to the nature of legal
   conceptions and the judicial process.

5. DEWEY, J. How We Think, (D.C. Heath & Co., 1909), chaps.
   8-11: chapters 9-11 deal generally with meaning,
   understanding, concrete and abstract thinking and
   comparisons between empirical and scientific thinking.
   Chapter 8 is particularly important for lawyers, dealing
   as it does with the decisional process.

6. SMITH, J.C. "The Unique Nature of the Concepts of Western
   Law" (1968) 46 Can.B.R. 191: legal concepts are linguistic
   constructs. Language forms the ideas with which one
   approaches problems. Primitive systems evolve concepts
   which are more factual than Western concepts. The latter
   were evolved in Classical Roman Law and adopted into the
   common law.

7. SMITH, J.C. "Law, Language, and Philosophy" (1968) 3 U.Br.
   Col.L.R. 59: this gives a review of the different attitudes
   towards language function that underlie the works of well-
   known legal philosophers from ancient times to the present.
   Much of this material is also relevant in later contexts.

8. COOK, W.W. "'Facts' and 'Statements of Fact'" (1936-37),

4 U.C.L.R., 233: this is a most interesting analysis of the
difficulties surrounding the conception of a "fact" for
legal purposes. It is also indirectly relevant to the
question of the approach to study. For further discussions,
see W.W. COOK: "Statements of Fact in Pleading under the
Codes" (1921), 21 Col.L.R. 416; N. ISAACS: "Judicial Review
of Administrative Findings" (1921), 30 Yale L.J. 781; "The
Law and the Facts" (1922), 22 Col.L.R. 1; H.C. DOWDALL:
"Pleading 'Material Facts'" (1929), 77 U.Pa.L.R. 945;
C. MORRIS: "Law and Fact" (1941-42), 55 Harv.L.R. 1303;
J.B. THAYER: Preliminary Treatise on the Law of Evidence,
(Sweet & Maxwell, Ltd., 1898), chap. 5.

1. LAMONT, W.D. The Principles of Moral Judgment, (Oxford, 1946),
   pp. 15-20: this might be of some indirect relevance.
   "Observable facts" in ethics differ from those of physical
   sciences. An explanation is given of what is meant by the
   application of the "scientific method" in ethics.

2. ROBINSON, R. Definition, (Oxford, 1954): this is the best and
   most convenient account of definition. The various types and
   their functions are examined in detail.

3. KANTOROWICZ, H.U. The Definition of Law, (ed. A.H. Campbell,
   Cambridge University Press, 1958), especially chaps. 1-2:
   this short work was to have been the prologue to a larger
   project which never materialised owing to the author's
   death. The process of constructing the most useful definition
   of law for the purpose of the projected work is demonstrated
   stage by stage.

4. BENTHAM, J. Theory of Fictions, (2nd. ed., C.K. Ogden,
   Routledge & Kegan Paul, Ltd., 1951), Introduction and
   pp. 75-104: Bentham's account of the function of definition
   is remarkable for its modernity and insight into linguistic
   problems. As Ogden observes in his detailed introduction,
   Bentham is entitled to rank among the foremost linguistic
   philosophers.

5. HART, H.L.A. "Definition and Theory in Jurisprudence" (1954),
   70 L.Q.R. 37: the technique of definition here advocated is
   that of explaining the term in question in the context of a
   characteristic proposition rather than in isolation, and to
   explain the conditions under which the proposition is true.

6. HART, H.L.A. The Concept of Law, (Oxford, 1961), pp. 13-17:
   this gives a brief account of the difficulties and the part
   played by definition in elucidating the meaning of the word
   "law".

1. AUERBACH, C.A. "On Professor Hart's Definition and Theory in Jurisprudence" (1956), 9 J.L.E. 39: Hart's suggested method of elucidating legal terms is criticised in detail. It is alleged that a definition which ignores the purpose or justification or origin of a legal or political institution cannot illumine the meaning of that institution.

2. HALL, J. Studies in Jurisprudence and Criminal Theory, (Oceana Publications, Inc., 1958), pp. 113 et seq.; 125-30: various weaknesses in Hart's method of elucidating legal terms are pointed out. The difficulties and problems encountered in defining the word "law" are also examined. In another paper this author surveys the developments that have taken in American legal thought and he proceeds to consider three different functions which definition performs in jurisprudential thought.

3. HALL, J. "Analytic Philosophy and Jurisprudence" (1966) 77 Ethics, 14: to elucidate terms by seeing how they are used is inadequate, because there are different levels of discourse, which have different significance and functions. One should elucidate the word "punishment" not by asking how it is used, but by relating it to voluntary conduct, social harm, causation; and also by bringing that set of interrelations into the larger pattern of the interrelation of principles, doctrines and rules.

4. LUMB, R.D. "On a Modern Approach to Jurisprudence" (1960), 5 Jur.R. (N.S.) 143: Hart's technique of definition is explained and examined, and it is alleged to be inadequate.

5. BODENHEIMER, E. "Modern Analytical Jurisprudence and the Limits of its Usefulness" (1955-56), 104 U.Pa.L.R., 1080: this takes issue with Hart's technique. It is alleged that Hart's technique would mean the abandonment of analytical jurisprudence.

6. SIMPSON, A.W.B. "The Analysis of Legal Concepts" (1964) 80 L.Q.R. 535, 541 et seq., 553 et seq.: Hart's distinction between statements of fact and statements of conclusions is investigated and criticised.

7. HART, H.L.A. "Analytical Jurisprudence in Mid-twentieth Century: a Reply to Professor Bodenheimer" (1957), 105 U.Pa.L.R. 953: in this the objections raised by Bodenheimer are dealt with.

8. DICKERSON, F.R. "Statutory Interpretation: Core Meaning and Marginal Uncertainty" (1964) 29 Miss. L.R. 1: there is no irreconcileable antinomy between the "core and penumbra"

theory of meaning and the "context and purpose" theory. The usage of each speech community determines the core and penumbral meanings with varying degrees of definiteness even when words are taken in isolation. Context and purpose help to select the meaning in the instant case out of the range of potential meanings. This important study has repercussions in statutory interpretation and the Positivist-Naturalist controversy.

1. DICKERSON, F.R. The Fundamentals of Legal Drafting (Little, Brown & Co., 1965): the whole of this book, especially chapters 3 and 7, is important to those concerned with the problems of meaning. In Chapter 3 it is pointed out that a legal document is a communication, involving an author, an audience, an utterance and a context. The significance of the last and the principal diseases of language are examined with particular care. Chapter 7 deals with types of definition and the forms they should assume. The part that definition plays in communication should be borne constantly in mind.

2. WILLIAMS, G.L. "The Definition of Crime" (1955), 8 C.L.P., 107: the opening part deals generally with definition. The whole article is of interest as bearing on the problem of definition.

3. POUND, R. "Law and the Science of Law in Recent Theories" (1933-34), 43 Yale L.J. 525: different persons mean different things when talking of law. This point is developed with reference to five leading jurists of modern times.

4. STONE, J. and TARELLO, G. "Justice, Language and Communication" (1960-61), 14 Vand.L.R., 331: this is a long and difficult investigation into the function of language in the respective spheres of law and justice.

5. MORRIS, C. How Lawyers Think, (Harvard University Press, 1938), chaps. 7-9: definitions depend upon classification. The method of dealing with meaning by "extension" (all instances covered) and "intension" (significance) is also discussed. The latter two chapters deal respectively with a comparison between deductive and inductive logic and with theory and reasoning.

6. MORRIS, C. Signs, Language and Behaviour, (Prentice-Hall, Inc., 1946): this is of general interest, and might be referred to for an analysis of meaning.

7. PROBERT, W. "Law and Persuasion: the Language Behaviour of

Lawyers" (1959-60), 108 U.Pa.L.R. 35: language studies
should be harnessed in a constructive way to progress in
law. This article is concerned with the emotive function of
many legal terms.

1. OLIVECRONA, K. "Legal Language and Reality" in Essays in
   Jurisprudence in Honor of Roscoe Pound, (ed. R.A. Newman,
   The Bobbs-Merrill Co., Inc., 1962), 151, at pp. 169-91:
   after posing the problem of understanding the concept
   "right", the question is approached through the function of
   language. Some words, e.g., "right", do not refer to any
   thing, they are "hollow" words. They serve as tools of
   thought and speech.

2. KENDAL, G.H. "The Role of Concepts in the Legal Process"
   (1962), 1 U.Br.Col.L.R. 617: the law has to be capable of
   dealing with the changes that are taking place in the world
   of ideas. The function of concepts is approached through an
   examination of meaning.

3. SMITH, G.H. "Of the Nature of Jurisprudence and of the Law"
   (1904), 38 Am.L.R. 68: accurate definition is said to be
   of the essence of success in moral and legal sciences. The
   confused definitions of "law" are examined. A definition of
   "jurisprudence" is offered and its implication considered.

4. SMITH, G.H. "Logic, Jurisprudence and the Law" (1914), 48
   Am.L.R. 801: the first part deals in outline with logic
   and in this connection the mental processes involved in
   reasoning are examined. In the second part the author seeks
   to demonstrate that much of the difficulty concerning
   "jurisprudence" and "law" is caused by the neglect of
   logical principles, especially with reference to definition.

5. PATON, G.W. A Text-Book of Jurisprudence, (3rd ed.,
   D.P. Derham, Oxford, 1964), chap. 3: the complexities of
   definition are set out and the different approaches to it
   are considered.

6. LLOYD, D. Introduction to Jurisprudence, (2nd ed., Stevens
   & Sons, Ltd., 1965), chaps. 1-2: the first chapter deals
   with the method of science and how far this can be applied
   to law. Social studies cannot aspire to hypotheses of such
   uniformity and generality as the physical studies. The
   second chapter contains a discussion of the function and
   dangers involved in definition.

7. TAMMELO, I. "Sketch for a Symbolic Juristic Logic" (1955-56),
   8 J.L.E. 277: it is alleged that the traditional ways of
   legal thinking are no longer apt. Accordingly, in this

article the author attempts to work out a new "symbolic logic".

1. FITZGERALD, P.J. "Law and Logic" (1964) 39 Notre Dame Lawyer, 570: Law and science are not alike in several respects. Law suffers from both semantic and syntactic ambiguities in its language. The question how far the use of logic in laying down and applying law will help is considered.

2. CASTBERG, F. Problems of Legal Philosophy, (2nd ed., Oslo University Press; Allen & Unwin, Ltd., 1957), chaps. 1-2: different types of jurisprudential study are listed in the first chapter and explained. The opening of the second chapter is particularly important in that it discusses the approach to the study. The fact that a concept of law is given a priori is denied, but it is conceded that the notion of validity has an a priori element.

3. COHEN, M.R. "Law and Scientific Method" in Law and Social Order, (Harcourt Brace & Co., 1933), 184, 219: the scientific teaching of law is important. By the scientific method is signified the hypothetico-deductive method. The starting point does not consist of certainties, but of guesses which may not be free from error.

4. COHEN, M.R. Reason and Nature, (Kegan Paul, Trench, Trubner & Co., Ltd., 1931), chap. 1 sect. 3; Part III: this is of general interest and deals with the part played by reason in the social sciences. Chapter 1 draws attention to the need for hypothesis to guide observation.

5. POPPER, K.R. Poverty of Historicism, (Routledge & Kegan Paul, 1957), pp. 139-40: it is argued that the method of science and certainly the most fruitful method for social studies is that of proceeding by hypothesis and verification. It is stressed that the hypothesis should only be provisional.

6. POPPER, K.R. "Philosophy of Science" in British Philosophy in Mid-Century, (ed. C.A. Mace, Allen & Unwin, Ltd., 1957), 135, at pp. 177-79: the author goes on to make the point that falsifiability and refutability is the criterion of the scientific status of a theory. It is also stated that people are born with certain "expectations" or "knowledge" which are prior to all observation.

7. CAIRNS, H. The Theory of Legal Science, (The University of North Carolina Press, 1941), especially chaps. 1, 6 and 10: jurisprudence is defined as a function of disorder. It is accepted as axiomatic that all theories of society have to begin with certain unprovable assumptions which cannot be

tested conclusively. Hence the method is that of hypothesis and verification. A hypothesis which fails to stand up to verification should be modified or rejected.

1. CAIRNS, H. Legal Philosophy from Plato to Hegel, (John Hopkins Press, 1949), chaps. 1 and 15: interest in classical philosophies of the ancient thinkers has revived. The method of study is that of proceeding by hypothesis and verification.

2. COOK, W.W. "The Logical and Legal Bases of the Conflict of Laws" (1923-24), 33 Yale L.J. 457: the opening part is of interest for it firmly rejects the a priori method in favour of the experimental method of hypothesis and verification.

3. ROSS, A. On Law and Justice, (Stevens & Sons, Ltd., 1958), chap. 1: the scope of jurisprudence is dealt with in outline. Doctrinal and sociological studies are regarded as useful, but ethical inquiry is rejected. It is suggested that the nature of law should be approached with the aid of a "tentative orientation of the nature of legal phenomena" to be followed by a more detailed investigation.

4. ROSS, A. Directives and Norms, (Routledge & Kegan Paul, Ltd., 1968), chaps. 1-3, 6: the author distinguishes between indicative and directive speech, and classifies the latter into eight types. Fictions and "deontic logic" are also dealt with.

5. KEYSER, C.J. "On the Study of Legal Science" (1928-29), 38 Yale L.J., 413: the function and structure of mathematical and scientific propositions are contrasted. The subject-matter of law, as a branch of science, is human behaviour, i.e., judicial decisions. The possibility of applying the mathematical method to legal science is explored.

6. KORKUNOV, N.M. General Theory of Law, (trans. W.G. Hastings, The Boston Book Co., 1909), sects. 3-4: what are called the "encyclopaedic" and "a priori" methods are considered and rejected.

7. For general philosophical discussions on the problems of meaning the following might be consulted: C.K. OGDEN and I.A. RICHARDS: The Meaning of Meaning, (10th ed., Routledge & Kegan Paul, Ltd., 1949); L. WITTGENSTEIN: Tractatus Logico-Philosophicus, (Routledge & Kegan Paul, Ltd., 1922); The Blue and Brown Books, (Blackwell, Oxford, 1958); Philosophical Investigations, (trans. M. Anscombe, Blackwell, Oxford, 1953); A. KORZYBSKI: Science and Sanity, (2nd ed., The International Non-Aristotelian Library Publishing Co., 1941); M. BLACK:

Language and Philosophy, (Cornell University Press, 1949),
chaps. 3, 5, 6, 8 and 10; S. CHASE: The Power of Words,
(Phoenix House, Ltd., 1955); The Tyranny of Words, (5th ed.,
Methuen & Co., Ltd., 1943); J. WISDOM: Philosophy and Psycho-
Analysis, (Blackwell, Oxford, 1957), pp. 36, 149, 248;
A.J. AYER: Language, Truth and Logic, (Gollancz, Ltd., 1946);
G. RYLE: The Concept of Mind, (Hutchinson's University Library,
1949); H.H. PRICE: Thinking and Experience, (Hutchinson's
University Library, 1953); L.F. VINDING KRUSE: The Foundations
of Human Thought, (trans. A. Fausbøll and I. Lund, Einar
Munksgaard, Copenhagen, 1949); J.O. URMSON: Philosophical
Analysis, (Oxford, 1956); British Philosophy in Mid-Century,
(ed. C.A. Mace, Allen & Unwin, Ltd., 1957); The Revolution in
Philosophy, (Macmillan & Co., Ltd., 1956); R. Von MISES:
Positivism, (Harvard University Press, 1951); J.R. WEINBERG:
An Examination of Logical Positivism (Routledge and Kegan Paul,
Ltd., 1936); Logic and Language, (ed. A.G.N. Flew, Blackwell,
Oxford, 1955), I and II; C.S. LEWIS: Studies in Words,
(Cambridge University Press, 1960); W. EMPSON: The Structure of
Complex Words, (Chatto & Windus, 1952).

The Temporal Approach

1. DIAS, R.W.M. "Legal Politics: Norms behind the Grundnorm"
   (1968) 26 C.L.J. 233: legal institutions do not exist just
   for a moment, but endure over periods of time, just as
   human beings do not exist just for a moment. There are thus
   two time-frames, the present time-frame and the enduring
   time-frame. When considering any phenomenon (legal or
   otherwise) in the latter time-frame all factors that are
   involved in the idea of endurance become an integral part of
   the concept of it as an enduring thing.

2. HURST, J.W. Justice Holmes on Legal History (The Macmillan
   Co., New York; Macmillan, Ltd., London, 1964): every legal
   order has a dimension in time, which determines its
   character, impact and direction. Historiacal perspective
   brings out aspects not revealed by mere logical analysis,
   the dimensions being "sequence" and "context". The approach
   is very similar to the one outlined above, but does not
   develop in the same direction.

3. TAYLOR, R. "Law and Morality" (1968) 43 N.Y.U.L.R. 611:
   towards the end of the article the author comes close to a
   temporal approach. Considerations of morality, he says, do
   not come in except in relation to "law" regarded as an
   activity, in which case the end to be achieved becomes
   relevant.

THE CRITERIA OF IDENTIFICATION

1. SALMOND, J.W. <u>Jurisprudence</u>, (12th ed. by P.J. Fitzgerald, Sweet & Maxwell Ltd., 1966), chap. 3: the important distinction is made between "legal" sources, those which give to a rule the quality of "law", and "historical" sources, those from which the content of a rule may be derived. He also makes the crucial point that the rule that statutes are law is ultimate.

2. AUSTIN, J. <u>Lectures on Jurisprudence</u>, (5th ed., R. Campbell, John Murray, 1885), II, pp. 510-550: on his theory of law, the sovereign is the source of law in the sense that it is his authority which imparts to a rule the quality of being "law". After a lengthy and somewhat confusing discussion of "written" and "unwritten" law, it emerges that in all cases the "source" is the sovereign and the term "law" is applicable to whatever proceeds from him directly or indirectly. There is also discussion of some of the other meanings of "source".

3. HART, H.L.A. <u>The Concept of Law</u>, (Oxford, 1961), chaps. 5, 6 and pp. 246-247: a "rule of recognition" is required by which to identify "primary" rules. The "rule of recognition" is ultimate because there is no other rule providing a criterion for its validity. It is simply accepted for use in this way. At pp. 246-247 he defends Salmond against Allen's criticism.

4. HART, H.L.A. "Legal and Moral Obligation" in <u>Essays in Moral Philosophy</u>, (ed. A.I. Melden, University of Washington Press, 1958), 82: rules are identified as valid by reference to a superior criterion of validity.

5. PATON, G.W. <u>A Text-book of Jurisprudence</u>, (3rd ed. D.P. Derham, Oxford, 1964), chap 6: this is a brief discussion of "source" of law with reference to the criterion of validity.

6. CROSS, A.R.N. <u>Precedent in English Law</u>, (2nd ed. Oxford, 1968), chap. 5: this is a discussion of the different meanings of "source" and of the views of Austin, Salmond and Gray. At pp. 207-211 he defends Salmond and points out that the "ultimate rules" are "law" because they are accepted as such.

7. BODENHEIMER, E. <u>Jurisprudence</u>, (Harvard University Press, 1962), pp. 269-272: these pages contain a discussion of sources and the adoption of a distinction between "formal" and "non-formal" sources.

20 The Criteria of Identification

1. OLIVECRONA, K. Law as Fact, (Einar Munksgaard, Copenhagen; Humphrey Milford, 1939; reprinted by Wildy & Sons, Ltd., 1962), chap. 2 passim: when a rule is promulgated through certain media it acquires a psychological pressure, which is why it is accepted as law.

2. CARDOZO, B.N. The Growth of the Law, (Yale University Press, 1924), chap. 2: he makes the point that the term "law" is applicable not only to what has actually been recognised by courts, but that there is a stage before adjudication when it acquires this character.

3. HOLLAND, T.E. The Elements Jurisprudence, (13th ed., Oxford, 1924), chap. 5: this gives a general discussion of the various meanings of the term "source".

4. KEETON, G.W. The Elementary Principles of Jurisprudence, (2nd ed., Isaac Pitman & Sons, Ltd., 1949), chap. 5: this gives a brief account of the different meanings of "source" and draws attention to the distinction between "binding" and "persuasive" sources.

5. KOCOUREK, A. An Introduction to the Science of Law, (Little, Brown & Co., Boston, 1930), pp. 155-158, 185-191: an account is given of the different meanings of "source" with emphasis on "official sources", i.e. rule-making by the organs or agencies of the state, as distinguished from "unofficial sources".

6. ALLEN, C.K. Law in the Making, (7th ed., Oxford, 1964), pp. 268-285: he rejects Salmon's distinction between "legal" and "historical" sources; but he is only using the term source in the sense of the origin of a rule without allowing for the other, and it is submitted, more important sense.

7. GRAY, J.C. The Nature and Sources of the Law, (2nd ed., R. Gray, The Macmillan Co., New York, 1921), pp. 84, 123-125, 308-309: he distinguishes between "law" and "sources of law" on the basis that "law" is only what the courts propound. Therefore, even a statute is not "law", but only a source of law. Such a view is opposed to that adopted by most lawyers.

8. FRANK, J.N. Law and the Modern Mind, (Stevens & Sons, Ltd., 1949), pp. 121-125, 269-271: he pursues the same line as Gray to an even greater extreme.

9. ROSS, A. On Law and Justice, (Stevens & Sons, Ltd., 1958), chap. 1, pp. 11-18, chap. 2, chap. 3, pp. 75-78, and pp. 101 et seq.: he proceeds on the basis that the test of

the validity of law is the likelihood of application by the
courts. Sources are thus all the factors which influence
the judge's formulation of a rule. Statute is, however,
"law" because of the high degree of probability that a
court will apply it.

1. HART, H.L.A. "Scandinavian Realism", [1959], C.L.J. 233,
   especially pp. 236-240: he criticises Ross. To a judge, law
   is valid not because of the likelihood that he will apply
   it; he will apply it because it is law. What judges need is
   a rule of recognising "law".

2. HUGHES, G.B.J. "The Existence of a Legal System" (1960),
   35 N.Y.U.L.R. 1001, at pp. 1010-23: certain critical
   observations are made on the views of Hart and Ross.

P R E C E D E N T

1. CROSS, A.R.N. Precedent in English Law, (2nd ed., Oxford, 1968): this is the most convenient general account of this topic, and might be regarded as the most up-to-date standard work.

2. ALLEN, C.K. Law in the Making, (7th ed., Oxford, 1964), chaps. 3-4: this is another standard work which gives the origin and nature of judicial precedent and a general account of precedent in Roman and Continental law.

Nature of Precedent

3. GRAY, J.C. The Nature and Sources of the Law, (2nd ed., R. Gray, Macmillan Co., New York, 1921), pp. 200-216: brief account of precedent in Roman, German, French, Scots and English law.

4. SALMOND, J.W. "The Theory of Judicial Precedents", (1900), 16 L.Q.R., 376; Jurisprudence, (12th ed., P.J. Fitzgerald, Sweet & Maxwell, Ltd., 1966), chap. 5: these are both general accounts of precedent, its authority and classification.

5. HODGINS, F.E. "The Authority of English Decisions", (1923), 1 Can.B.R. 470, at pp. 475-478: the reasons for the authority of judicial decisions in England are discussed by a Canadian judge.

6. WILLIAMS, E.K. "Stare Decisis", (1926), 4 Can.B.R., 289: this is a general comparison of the position in England and Canada.

7. SNYDER, O.C. Preface to Jurisprudence, (Bobbs-Merrill Co., Inc., 1954), Part III, chapter 3, pp. 412-415: this gives a general introduction and a brief discussion of the basis of stare decisis.

8. WINDER, W.H.D. "Precedent in Equity", (1941), 57 L.Q.R. 245: the development of equity from broad principles to precedent is outlined.

9. YALE, D.E.C. Lord Nottingham's Chancery Cases, (73 Selden Society, 1954), I, Introduction, Part II: this is a valuable account of the development of precedent in equity.

10. GARDNER, J.C. Judicial Precedent in Scots Law, (W. Green & Sons Ltd., Edinburgh, 1936), chaps. 1-4: the extent to which stare decisis operates in England, France and Scotland, and

its development are discussed.

1. SMITH, T.B, The Doctrine of Judicial Precedent in Scots Law,
   (W. Green & Sons, Ltd., 1952): evolution of stare decisis
   in Scots Law and the extent of English influence is dealt
   with.

2. WALTON, F.P. "The Relationship of the Law of France to the
   Law of Scotland" (1902), 14 Jur.R. 17: the gulf is growing
   between the two systems since Scots Law is increasingly
   becoming a case-law system.

3. WALKER, D.M. "A Note on Precedent", (1949), 61 Jur.R., 283:
   it is pointed out that the bulk of citations in Scottish
   Courts comes from 20th. century cases.

4. SAFFORD, A. "The Creation of Case Law under the National
   Insurance and National Insurance (Industrial Injuries)
   Acts", (1954), 17 M.L.R. 197: this is of general interest
   as showing how a body of case-law grows up.

Historical Development

5. PLUCKNETT, T.F.T. A Concise History of the Common Law,
   (5th ed. Butterworth & Co. Ltd., 1956), Part III, chapter
   5: this is a convenient and highly instructive account.

6. ALLEN, C.K. Law in the Making, (7th ed., Oxford, 1964),
   pp. 187-235: this gives a general and fairly detailed
   historical account.

7. ELLIS LEWIS, T. "History of Judicial Precedent", (1930), 46
   L.Q.R. 207, 341; (1931), 47 L.Q.R. 411; (1932), 48 L.Q.R.
   230: a detailed account of the development down to 1765
   will be found in these articles.

8. HOLDSWORTH, W.S. A History of English Law, (Methuen & Co.,
   Ltd.,), II, pp. 188-192 (Glanvil); 235-236 (Bracton);
   525-556 (Year Books); V, pp. 355-378; VI, pp. 551-624:
   this is useful for referring to different aspects of the
   development.

9. WINFIELD, P.H. The Chief Sources of English Legal History,
   (Harvard University Press, 1925), chap. 7: a good account
   of the development of reports and reporting.

10. MORAN, C.G. The Heralds of the Law, (Stevens & Sons, Ltd.,
    1948), chaps. 1-4: a historical account of law reporting
    is provided.

1. POLLOCK, F. <u>A First Book of Jurisprudence</u>, (6th ed.,
   Macmillan & Co., Ltd., 1929), chap. 5, Part II: a historical
   account of law reports is given with hints on how to find
   authorities; chap. 6, down to p. 331, deals with the
   evolution of <u>stare decisis</u>: (the rest of the chapter is now
   out of date).

2. DANIEL, W.T.S. <u>The History and Origin of 'The Law Reports</u>",
   (William Clowes & Sons, Ltd., 1884): a detailed, documented
   account of the introduction of the Law Reports by one who
   played a leading part.

3. "ALEPH-ZERO", "The Incorporated Council of Law Reporting -
   the History and Development of the Law Reports", (1958), 55
   L.S.G., 483: a brief and very general account.

4. WALLACE, J.W. <u>The Reporters</u>, (4th ed., F.F. Heard, Boston,
   1882): this gives a detailed account of the early reports
   and it is a very useful source of information as to
   particular reporters.

5. PLUCKNETT, T.F.T. "The Place of the Legal Profession in the
   History of English Law", (1932), 48 L.Q.R., 328: this is
   principally an account of the Year Books.

6. SIMPSON, A.W.B. "The Circulation of Yearbooks in the Fifteenth
   Century", (1957), 73 L.Q.R. 492: a further study of the
   Year Books.

7. SIMPSON, A.W.B, "Keilway's Reports, temp. Henry VII and
   Henry VIII", (1957), 73 L.Q.R. 89: a particular set of
   reports is discussed.

8. WAMBAUGH, E. <u>The Study of Cases</u>, (2nd ed., Boston, 1894),
   chaps. 10 and 11: these provide a general account of reports
   and digests.

9. POLLOCK, F. "Judicial Records", in <u>Essays in the Law</u>,
   (Macmillan & Co., Ltd., 1922), chap. 9: the distinction is
   explained between the record and a report of a case and the
   importance of the former.

<u>Law Reporting</u>

10. WINFIELD, P.H. "Early Attemps at Reporting Cases", (1924),
    40 L.Q.R. 316: this might be consulted for a short account
    of the reporting methods in some Year Book cases.

11. LINDLEY, N. "The History of the Law Reports", (1885), I L.Q.R.
    137: W.T.S. Daniel's book (<u>supra</u>) is reviewed, and there is

also a critical discussion, <u>inter alia</u>, of the subject-
matter of reports, mode of reporting and time and form of
publication.

1. HEMMING, G.W. "The Law Reports" (1885), I L.Q.R. 317: some of
   the difficulties confronting a reporter are explained; (it
   is in answer to some of Lord Justice Lindley's criticisms,
   <u>supra</u>).

2. MEWS, J. "The Present System of Law Reporting", (1893), 9
   L.Q.R. 179: this is a discussion of reportable and
   unreportable cases, with criticisms of the present system
   and suggestions for reform.

3. EVANS, F. "Law Reporting: a Reporter's View", (1904), 20 L.Q.R.
   88: this was written before some modern series began, but
   portrays the atmosphere in which reporters work.

4. HOLDSWORTH, W.S. "Law Reporting in the Nineteenth and
   Twentieth Centuries", in <u>Essays in Law and History</u>, (Oxford,
   1946), p. 284: this provides a general account of law
   reporting.

5. POLLOCK, F. "English Law Reporting", in <u>Essays in the Law</u>,
   (Macmillan & Co., Ltd., 1922), chap. 10: an account is given
   of modern reporting and the function of an editor based on
   his own experience.

6. POLLOCK, F. "Government by Committees in England", in <u>Essays
   in the Law</u>, (Macmillan & Co., Ltd., 1922), chap. 4, pp. 137-
   139: a brief account of the working of the Incorporated
   Council of Law Reporting will be found in these pages.

7. BURROWS, R. "Law Reporting", (1942), 58 L.Q.R. 96: the
   function of a law reporter in modern times is discussed.

8. <u>REPORT OF THE LORD CHANCELLOR'S COMMITTEE ON LAW REPORTING</u>:
   (1940): also found in summarised form in D. and G. FORD,
   A Breviate of Parliamentary Papers, 1940-1954, p. 451; and
   in C.G. MORAN, <u>The Heralds of the Law</u>, chap. 9: a review of
   the history and nature of law reports. The Committee reject
   any radical reform.

9. O'SULLIVAN, R. "On Law Reporting", (1940-41), 4 M.L.R. 104:
   this is a discussion of the Report of the Lord Chancellor's
   Committee (<u>supra</u>).

10. MORAN, C.G. <u>The Heralds of the Law</u>, (Stevens & Sons, Ltd.,
    1948), chaps. 5-10: the present system of law reporting is
    discussed, together with its problems and suggestions for

improvement.

1. PARKER, C.F. "Law Reporting and the Revision of Judgments",
    (1955), 18 M.L.R. 496: this is a note on the extent to
    which judges alter their judgments in the process of
    revision.

The Assessment of Reports

2. ROGERS, S. "On the Study of Law Reports", (1897), 13 L.Q.R.
    250, 256 et seq.: this gives hints on how to read reports
    and a general account of their educational value.

3. WAMBAUGH, E. The Study of Cases, (2nd ed., Boston, 1894),
    chap. 5, sect. 1: this contains a discussion of factors
    relevant to assessing the weight of a case.

4. RAM, J. The Science of Legal Judgment, (2nd ed., J. Townshend,
    Baker, Voorhis & Co., New York, 1871), chap. 13: this
    contains a useful assessment of the worth of certain old
    reports.

5. MORAN, C.G. The Heralds of the Law, (Stevens & Sons, Ltd.,
    1948), chap. 8: this contains many sidelights on the
    problems of using cases.

Authority of the Deciding Tribunal Some of the works referred to
    below include discussions of the Court of Criminal Appeal,
    which was abolished by the Criminal Appeal Act 1966 (c.31),
    and of the rule that the House of Lords is bound by its own
    decisions, which was abolished by the Practice Statement
    (Judicial Precedent), [1966] 2 All E.R. 77; [1966] 1 W.L.R.
    1234.

6. ALLEN, C.K. Law in the Making, (7th ed., Oxford, 1964), pp.
    236-257: this provides an account of the different courts
    with detailed discussion of some of the questions that have
    arisen. The parts dealing with the now defunct Court of
    Criminal Appeal and the House of Lords binding itself are
    out of date.

7. SALMOND, J.W. Jurisprudence: (12th ed., P.J. Fitzgerald,
    Sweet & Maxwell, Ltd., 1966), pp. 158-174: a detailed
    account of the hierarchy of courts with especial attention
    to the rule (now abolished) that the House of Lords binds
    itself and an examination of the Rule of Young's case will
    be found.

8. CROSS, A.R.N. Precedent in English Law, (2nd ed., Oxford,
    1968), chap. 3: this account of the hierarchy of courts is

not as complete in detail as Salmond or Allen; chap. 4 has
a discussion of the exceptions to stare decisis; chap. 8
concerns mainly the question of judicial legislation and
prospective overruling.

1. WILLIAMS, G.L.   Learning the Law, (8th ed., Stevens & Sons
    Ltd., 1969), pp. 89-91: a brief, general account of the
    position is provided.

2. HOOD PHILLIPS, O.   A First Book of English Law, (5th ed., Sweet
    & Maxwell Ltd., 1965), Part I: this is a very convenient
    and readable account of all the tribunals.

3. KIRALFY, A.K.R.   The English Legal System, (4th ed., Sweet &
    Maxwell, Ltd., 1967), pp. 98-110: the hierarchy of courts
    is dealt with in outline, and also the evolution of the
    doctrine of stare decisis.

4. PATON, G.W.   A Text Book of Jurisprudence, (3rd ed.,
    D.P. Derham, Oxford, 1964), chap. 8, sect. 45: a brief
    account of the hierarchy of courts is given.

5. MIGNAULT, P.B.   "The Authority of Decided Cases", (1925), 3
    Can.B.R. 1: this includes (at pp. 2-9) a review of the
    position in England, and a contrast with the position in
    France and in Quebec.

6. LAIRD, D.H.   "The Doctrine of Stare Decisis", (1935), 13 Can.
    B.R. 1: the working of the doctrine in the courts of
    England and Canada is described.

7. ABRAHAM, H.J.   The Judicial Process (New York and Oxford Univ.
    Press, 1962), chap. 6: the book as a whole deals with an
    analysis of the courts of the United States, Britain and
    France. A section of this chapter is concerned with the
    organisation of courts in Britain. Some of the points have
    since been altered by legislation.

Particular Courts

8. ALLEN, C.K.   "Road Traffic Precedents", (1956), 72 L.Q.R. 516:
    this shows the difficulties confronting magistrates when
    decisions of the Divisional Court conflict.

9. WINDER, W.H.D.   "The Rule of Precedents in the Criminal Courts",
    (1941), 5 J.Cr.L. 242: the Court of Criminal Appeal,
    Divisional Court and the High Court are compared with
    reference to the working precedent. (The Court of Criminal
    Appeal has since been abolished).

1. WINDER, W.H.D. "Divisional Court Precedents", (1946), 9 M.L.R. 257: this is a general account.

2. STONE, O.M. "Stare Decisis in the Divisional Court", (1951), 14 M.L.R. 219: a note on the position.

   The work of the Court of Criminal Appeal was transferred to the Criminal Division of the Court of Appeal by statute in 1966. The following discussions are still relevant to the working of that Division.

3. NOTE: "Judicial Precedents in Criminal Law", (1958), 22 J.C.L. 155: this is a general discussion of the position.

4. SEABORNE-DAVIES, D. "The Court of Criminal Appeal: the First Forty Years", (1951), 1 J.S.P.T.L. (N.S.), 425: the working of the Court is surveyed and critically assessed.

5. GODDARD, R. "Working of the Court of Criminal Appeal", (1952), 2 J.S.P.T.L. (N.S.), 1: the day to day work of the Court is recounted.

6. WILLIAMS, G.L. "Bigamy and the Third Marriage", (1950), 13 M.L.R. 417, at pp. 418, 419: a short discussion of the power of the Court of Criminal Appeal to overrule itself will be found at these pages.

7. ANONYMOUS, "Exceptions to the Rule of Stare Decisis" (1958), 92 I.L.T. 131: the Rule in Taylor's case is considered together with the earlier position.

8. PARKER, H.L. "The Criminal Division of the Court of Appeal" (1969) 46 Law Guardian 11: The Riddell Lecture to the Institute of Legal Executives by the Lord Chief Justice is published in an abridged form. Lord Parker outlines the origin of the abolition of the Court of Criminal Appeal and the transfer of its work to the Criminal Division of the Court of Appeal, the principal differences between the Civil and Criminal Divisions and the altered powers of the latter. He also considers the present state of criminal appeals.

9. EVERSHED, F.R. The Court of Appeal in England, (London, 1950): a general account. See also F.R. EVERSHED: "The Work of Appellate Courts" [1962], 36 Aust.L.J., 42.

10. COHEN, L.L. "Jurisdiction, Practice and Procedure of the Court of Appeal", (1951), 11 C.L.J., 3: this is a general account of the working of the Court, including a discussion of whether it should be a final court of appeal.

1. ASQUITH, C. "Some Aspects of the Work of the Court of Appeal",
   (1950), I J.S.P.T.L. (N.S.), 350: the first part deals with
   the history of the Court and an account of its day to day
   work. In the latter part there is special reference to the
   problems raised by the Rule in Young's case.

2. GOODHART, A.L. "Precedents in the Court of Appeal", (1947),
   9 C.L.J. 349: this contains introductory remarks on the
   rule in the House of Lords (since abolished), followed by
   a detailed discussion and criticism of the Rule in Young's
   case.

3. GOODERSON, R.N. "Young v. Bristol Aeroplane Co. Ltd.", (1950),
   10 C.L.J. 432: this deals principally with the first two
   exceptions to the Rule, including a reply to Goodhart.

4. MASON, G.F.P. "Stare Decisis in the Court of Appeal", (1956),
   19 M.L.R. 136: the Rule in Young's case is examined in the
   light of subsequent cases.

5. MEGARRY, R.E. "Fair Wear and Tear and the Doctrine of
   Precedent", (1958), 74 L.Q.R. 33: a short but illuminating
   discussion of the first exception to the Rule in Young's
   case.

6. MEGARRY, R.E. "Precedent in the Court of Appeal: How Binding
   is 'Binding'?", (1958), 74 L.Q.R. 350: a further discussion
   of the first exception.

7. MONTROSE, J.L. Note in (1954), 17 M.L.R. 462: on the incuria
   exception.

8. E.K. "Judgments per incuriam and the Doctrine of Precedent",
   (1955), 72 S.A.L.J., 404: a short note on this exception.

9. NOTE: in (1946), 62 L.Q.R. 110, 210: this illustrates
   difficulties of the Rule in Young's case.

10. CROSS, A.R.N. "Stare Decisis in Contemporary England" (1966)
    82 L.Q.R. 203: since 1948 there has been a relaxation of
    the rigidity of stare decisis. This has come about because
    of a more liberal interpretation of the exceptions to
    Young's case and·the invention of possible new exceptions,
    and also to a narrower conception of what precisely is
    binding in a case.

11. STEVENS, R. "The Final Appeal: Reform of the House of Lords
    and Privy Council, 1867-1876" (1964) 80 L.Q.R. 343: during
    these years appeals to the House of Lords were abolished
    but restored in three years. The political factors that

were involved are traced in detail.

1. BLOM-COOPER, L.J. and DREWRY, G.R. "The House of Lords:
   Reflections on the Social Utility of Final Appellate
   Courts" (1969) 32 M.L.R. 262: the question whether a two-
   tier appeal system is desirable or not might be approached
   by looking at the position elsewhere. But hasty inferences
   should not be drawn from the situations in other countries;
   a great many social and other factors need to be taken into
   account. After a brief review of nine Commonwealth and
   other countries, the conclusion is that House of Lords does
   a useful function.

2. du PARCQ, H. "The Final Court of Appeal", (1949), 2 C.L.P.,
   1: a historical account is given of some of the changes in
   the working of the House of Lords.

3. DIAS, R.W.M. "Precedents in the House of Lords - a Much
   Needed Reform" [1966] C.L.J. 153: the abolition by means of
   a practice statement of the rule that the House is bound by
   its own decisions is considered. Attention is drawn to the
   need to give effect to a doctrine of prospective overruling.

4. LEACH, W.B. "Revisionism in the House of Lords: the Bastion of
   Rigid Stare Decisis Falls" (1967) 80 Harv.L.R. 797: the
   origin of the rule that the House should be bound, how far
   this was approved by the profession and the manner of its
   overthrow are set out. The possibilities of adopting a
   doctrine of prospective overruling are touched on.

5. ANONYMOUS, "Stare Decisis" (1967) 101 I.L.T. 61: this is a
   note commenting on the House of Lords' Practice Statement.

6. ANONYMOUS, "The Force of Precedent" (1966) S.L.T. 157: the
   binding character of stare decisis is reviewed from a
   Scottish point of view and winds up with the Practice
   Statement in 1966.

7. St. JOHN, E. "Lords Break from Precedent: an Australian View"
   (1967) 16 I.C.L.Q. 808: one at least of the factors behind
   the Lords' pronouncement may have been the progressive
   revolt of Australian courts against being bound by British
   decisions. But this, it is suggested, only triggered a gun
   already loaded.

8. ANONYMOUS, "Precedent" (1967) 131 J.P. & L.G.R. 595: a brief
   comment on the Lords' Practice Statement.

9. JONES, T.C. "The Implications of the New Doctrine of Stare
   Decisis in the Irish Supreme Court" (1967) 101 I.L.T. 281,

291, 301, 311, 321: consideration is given to the way in
which the new flexibility introduced by an Irish decision
in 1965 and the Practice Statement of the House of Lords
in 1966 is likely to affect advocacy, law-teaching and
judicial law-making.

1. BIRNBAUM, H.F. "Stare Decisis vs. Judicial Activism. Nothing
   Succeeds like Success" (1968) 54 Am.B.A.J. 482: this
   considers the Practice Statement of the House of Lords, and
   reviews the question whether the old rule that the House
   was bound by its decisions was one of law or practice and
   what effect the Practice Statement has. This leads to a
   consideration of the legislative function of courts in
   Britain and America.

2. HALDANE, R.B. "The Work for the Empire of the Judicial
   Committee of the Privy Council", (1921), I C.L.J. 143: this
   is useful as showing what the position used to be.

3. RANKIN, G. "The Judicial Committee of the Privy Council",
   (1939-41), 7 C.L.J. 2: this carries the review of the
   Committee's work further than the previous article.

4. NORMAND, W.G. "The Judicial Committee of the Privy Council -
   Retrospect and Prospect", (1950), 3 C.L.P., 1: the modern
   position is discussed.

5. McWHINNEY, E. Judicial Review in the English-speaking World,
   (2nd ed., University of Toronto Press, 1960), chap. 3: this
   considers the work of the Privy Council, including at p. 55
   a discussion of the Council not binding itself.

6. McWHINNEY, E. "Legal Theory and Philosophy of Law in Canada"
   in Canadian Jurisprudence. The Civil Law and Common Law in
   Canada (ed. E. McWhinney, The Carswell Co., Ltd., Stevens
   & Sons, Ltd., 1958), 1: the positivist role played by the
   Judicial Committee in Canada until 1949 is deplored,
   especially the attitude that judges do not make law. The
   problems facing the Canadian Supreme Court in pursuing a
   creative role in a heterogeneous community are considered.

7. PALLEY, C. "The Judicial Committee of the Privy Council as
   Appellate Court - the Southern Rhodesian Experience" [1967]
   P.L. 8: the Privy Council, it is alleged, tends to approach
   written constitutions with British notions of sovereignty.
   Two of its decisions are analysed and criticised on this
   basis.

8. MARSHALL, H.H. "The Judicial Committee of the Privy Council:
   a Waning Jurisdiction" (1964) 13 I.C.L.Q. 697: the growth

and decline of Privy Council jurisdiction is recounted at
some length. See also N. BENTWICH: "The Jurisdiction of the
Privy Council" (1964) 114 L.J. 67.

1. MENZIES, D. "Australia and the Judicial Committee of the
    Privy Council" (1968) 42 A.L.J. 79: the author traces the
    work of the Privy Council from the background to s.74 of
    the Constitution. On the whole, it is said, the Privy
    Council has served Australia well.

2. MARSHALL, H.H. "The Binding Effect of Decisions of the
    Judicial Committee of the Privy Council" (1968) 17 I.C.L.Q.
    743: decisions of the Privy Council bind the courts of the
    country from which the appeals are launched. In this paper
    the author discusses how far they are binding in other
    countries.

3. The following cases might be consulted as illustrating the
    attitude of different tribunals: Metropolitan Police District
    Receiver v. Croydon Corporation, [1956] 2 All E.R. 785;
    Monmouthshire County Council v. Smith, [1956] 2 All E.R. 800;
    on appeal, [1957] 2 Q.B. 154; [1957] 1 All E.R. 78;
    Huddersfield Police Authority v. Watson, [1947] K.B. 842;
    [1947] 2 All E.R. 193; R. v. Taylor, [1950] 2 K.B. 368; [1950]
    2 All E.R. 170; Young v. Bristol Aeroplance Co., Ltd., [1944]
    K.B. 718; [1944] 2 All E.R. 293; Practice Statement (Judicial
    Precedent), [1966] 2 All E.R. 77; [1966] 1 W.L.R. 1234;
    Ibbralebbe v. R., [1964] A.C. 900; [1964] 1 All E.R. 251.

On the question whether rules of precedent are rules of "law", the
following might be referred to:

4. SALMOND, J.W. Jurisprudence: (12th ed., P.J. Fitzgerald,
    Sweet & Maxwell, Ltd., 1966), pp. 159-161.

5. CROSS, A.R.N. Precedent in English Law, (2nd ed., Oxford,
    1968), chap. 7, especially pp. 209-211.

6. SIMPSON, A.W.B. "The Ratio Decidendi of a Case and the
    Doctrine of Binding Precedent" in Oxford Essays in
    Jurisprudence, (ed. A.G. Guest, Oxford, 1961), pp. 150-155.

7. MEGARRY, R.E. "Decisions by Equally Divided Courts as
    Precedents", (1954), 70 L.Q.R. 318; G.L. WILLIAMS,
    "Decisions by Equally Divided Courts", ibid. p. 469;
    R.E. MEGARRY, ibid. p. 471.

The Ratio Decidendi

Terminology

1. MONTROSE, J.L. "The Language of, and a Notation for, the Doctrine of Precedent", (1951-53), 2 Ann.L.R., 301, 504: this suggests a terminology which might help to avoid the prevailing confusion.

2. MONTROSE, J.L. "Judicial Law Making and Law Applying", (1956), B.S.A.L.R., 187: a further examination of certain phrases.

3. MONTROSE, J.L. "Ratio Decidendi and the House of Lords", (1957), 20 M.L.R. 124-126: this discusses the ambiguity of the expression "ratio decidendi".

Determining the Ratio Decidendi

4. WILLIAMS, G.L. Learning the Law (8th ed., Stevens & Sons, Ltd., 1969), pp. 72-85: a concise account is given of the whole question, emphasising the point that the principle of a case alters with interpretation.

5. STONE, J. "The Ratio of the Ratio Decidendi", (1959), 22 M.L.R. 597: a distinction is drawn between the "descriptive" and "prescriptive" ratio decidendi. There is no one ratio in a case.

6. STONE, J. Legal System and Lawyers' Reasonings, (Stevens & Sons, Ltd., 1964), chaps. 7-8: the syllogistic form of a judgment is exposed. Judges nearly always have a choice. The judicial process is "a continuous creative adaptation of the law to changing social conditions".

7. SAMEK, R.A. "The Dynamic Model of the Judicial Process and the Ratio Decidendi of a Case" (1964) 42 Can. B.R. 433: the concept of ratio decidendi belongs to a static model of the judicial process, as opposed to a dynamic model. The concept of binding ratio decidendi stems from a failure to distinguish between the two models, from the identification of the judicial process with authoritative pronouncements rather than with reason, justice and social policy, and from the ambiguity of the phrase itself. The task of the judge on a dynamic model is to decide disputes by setting standards. On this view authority is not contrasted with justice etc. Authority is itself "open-textured" and is continually expanding, contracting and reforming.

8. LLEWELLYN, K.N. The Bramble Bush, (New York, 1930), chaps. 3 and 4: this stresses the point that the ratio decidendi

depends on subsequent interpretation.

1. FRANK, J.N. "What Courts Do in Fact", (1932), 26 Ill.L.R.,
   645: the difficulty of achieving certainty, how facts are
   viewed by courts and the complications introduced by
   plural opinions in appellate courts are surveyed at length.

2. GOODHART, A.L. "Determining the Ratio Decidendi of a Case" in
   Essays in Jurisprudence and the Common Law, (Cambridge
   University Press, 1931), chap. 1: this examines how the
   ratio decidendi is to be determined. It consists of the
   decision based on the material facts as found by the judge.

3. GOODHART, A.L. "The Ratio Decidendi of a Case", (1959), 22
   M.L.R. 117: the original thesis is restated.

4. GOODERSON, R.N. "Ratio Decidendi and Rules of Law", (1952),
   30 Can.B.R., 892: this replies to Goodhart's thesis and
   defends the traditional view that ratio decidendi is the
   principle of law necessary for the decision.

5. SIMPSON, A.W.B. "The Ratio Decidendi of a Case and the
   Doctrine of Binding Precedent" in Oxford Essays in
   Jurisprudence, (ed. A.G. Guest, Oxford, 1961), chap. 6:
   this includes a discussion of the distinction between
   "defining" and "determining" the ratio decidendi.

6. DERHAM, D.P. "Precedent and the Decision of Particular
   Questions", (1963), 79 L.Q.R. 49: there is a difference
   between the binding-ness of the decision in a case and of
   the principle behind it.

7. SNYDER, O.C. Preface to Jurisprudence, (Bobbs-Merrill Co.,
   Inc., 1954), Part III, chap. 3, pp. 420-426: an explanation
   of ratio decidendi is given and attention is drawn to the
   court's discretion in selecting material facts.

8. RAM, J. The Science of Legal Judgment, (2nd ed. J. Townshend,
   Baker, Voorhis & Co., New York, 1871), chaps. 3, 5, 14-17:
   this is of general interest; it deals with principle and
   dicta, appellate decisions, distinguishing decisions on
   particular facts and of decisions in new situations.

9. WAMBAUGH, E. The Study of Cases, (2nd ed., Boston, 1894),
   chap. 2: here will be found the famous test of ratio
   decidendi, namely, to reverse the proposition in question
   and to see whether this would affect the decision: (note:
   this test can only apply to cases with a single principle).
   Chap. 3: deals with cases involving several questions.

1. OLIPHANT, H. "A Return to Stare Decisis", (1928), 14 Am.
   B.A.J., 71, 107, 159: the well-known suggestion is made
   that the ratio decidendi may be constructed out of the
   decision, not necessarily out of what the judge has said.

2. CROSS, A.R.N. Precedent in English Law, (2nd ed., Oxford,
   1968), pp. 35-80: this examines the question of ratio
   decidendi and summarises the various views.

3. SALMOND, J.W. Jurisprudence, (12th ed., P.J. Fitzgerald,
   Sweet & Maxwell, Ltd. 1966), pp. 174-183: a general account.

4. PATON, G.W. A Text-book of Jurisprudence, (3rd ed., D.P.
   Derham, Oxford, 1964), chap. 8, sect. 45: this gives an
   account of ratio decidendi in the light of recent analyses
   of the problems.

5. LLOYD, D. Introduction to Jurisprudence, (2nd ed., Stevens &
   Sons, Ltd., 1965), pp. 373-378: there is no one method of
   ascertaining the ratio decidendi.

6. VINOGRADOFF, P. Common-sense in Law, (3rd ed., H.G. Hanbury,
   Oxford University Press, 1959), chap. 7: this general
   account demonstrates (at pp. 138 et seq.) how a series of
   later cases may expand or modify the original decision.

7. WRIGHT, R.A. "Precedents", (1943), 8 C.L.J. 118, 138 et seq.:
   some of the difficulties of finding the ratio decidendi are
   pointed out.

8. FRIEDMANN, W. Legal Theory, (5th ed., Stevens & Sons, Ltd.,
   1967), pp. 468-474: this discusses distinguishing
   techniques.

9. FRIEDMANN, W. "Stare Decisis at Common Law and under the
   Civil Law of Quebec", (1953), 31 Can.B.R., 723, 731-740:
   the difficulties of finding the ratio decidendi and the
   flexibility inherent in the doctrine of stare decisis are
   discussed.

10. SMITH, T.B. The Doctrines of Judicial Precedent in Scots Law,
    (W. Green & Sons, Ltd., 1952), chap. 4: precedent is
    examined from the Scottish point of view. Scots Law has a
    broader approach to the question of ratio decidendi than
    English Law.

The following references are to a debate on ratio decidendi,
which is primarily useful in so far as it clarifies the
attitudes of the various participants:

1. MONTROSE, J.L. "Ratio Decidendi and the House of Lords", (1957), 20 M.L.R., 124, 587.

2. SIMPSON, A.W.B. "The Ratio Decidendi of a Case", (1957), 20 M.L.R. 413: (1958), 21 M.L.R. 155; (1959), 22 M.L.R. 453.

3. GOODHART, A.L. "The Ratio Decidendi of a Case", (1959), 22 M.L.R. 117.

4. To complete this controversy, reference to the article by J. STONE, "The Ratio of the Ratio Decidendi" (1959), 22 M.L.R. 597, is essential.

Problems Connected with Ratio Decidendi

5. CROSS, A.R.N. Precedent in English Law, (2nd ed., Oxford, 1968), pp. 86-101: this gives a detailed account of some of the major problems.

6. GOODHART, A.L. "The 'I think' Doctrine of Precedent: Invitors and Licensors" (1950), 66 L.Q.R. 374: the view that where a judge gives two reasons for his decision, both should be regarded as being the ratio decidendi, is critically examined.

7. MEGARRY, R.E. "Precedent in the Court of Appeal: How Binding is 'Binding'?" (1958), 74 L.Q.R. 350: this demonstrates that the Court of Appeal rejected one of two grounds which it had previously given for a decision.

8. MONTROSE, J.L. "Ratio Decidendi and the House of Lords", (1957), 20 M.L.R. pp. 126 et seq.: the problems arising out of Walsh v. Curry are considered.

9. Notes by J.C.H.M., R.E.M. and J.A. COUTTS in (1948), 64 L.Q.R. 28, 29, 193, 454, 463.

10. COUTTS, J.A. Note in (1950), 71 L.Q.R. 24: the difficulty of extracting the ratio decidendi when there is more than one issue and the judges differ is considered.

11. PATON, G.W. and SAWER, G. "Ratio and Obiter Dictum in Appellate Courts", (1947), 63 L.Q.R. 461: this is a penetrating discussion of some of the problems.

12. WRIGHT, R.A. "Precedents", (1943), 8 C.L.J. pp. 127-129: some of the major difficulties are reviewed.

13. HONORÉ, A.M. "Ratio Decidendi: Judge and Court", (1955),

71 L.Q.R. 196: this is discussion of _Fellner_ v. _Minister of the Interior_, 1954(4) S.A. 523 (A.D.)

1. GOODERSON, R.N. Note in (1955), 33 Can.B.R., 612: this, too, is a discussion of _Fellner's_ case.

2. R.E.M.: Note in (1950), 66 L.Q.R. 298: this discusses the effect of disagreement among judges in appellate courts and briefly compares the English and Scots practice.

3. ASQUITH, C. "Some Aspects of the Work of the Court of Appeal", (1950), 1 J.S.P.T.L. (N.S.), 350: in the latter part there is a discussion of the problems of _ratio decidendi_ in tribunals with multiple opinions.

4. STONE, O.M. "Appeals and the Doctrine of Precedent", (1951), 14 M.L.R. 493: this case-note shows the difficulties of determining what is _ratio_ and what is _dictum_.

5. A.M.: "Ratio Decidendi in Appellate Courts", (1949), 23 Aust. L.J., 355: a short note on the difficulty of extracting the _ratio decidendi_ when judges give different reasons.

6. BERMAN, H.T. The Nature and Functions of Law, (The Foundation Press, Inc., 1958), 282-374: extracts are given from Llewellyn and Levi and, more important, extracts from selected American cases, followed by questions based on each as to the reasoning in it. There are also a brief comparison with Continental doctrines and a history of _stare decisis_.

7. The following cases and judgments are useful examples of judicial technique: Lord ATKIN and Lord MACMILLAN in _Donoghue_ v. _Stevenson_, [1932] A.C. 562; BRAMWELL, L.J., in _Household Fire Insurance Co._ v. _Grant_ (1879), 4 Ex.D.216; SCOTT, L.J., in _Haseldine_ v. _C.A. Daw & Son, Ltd._, [1941], 2 K.B. 343; [1941], 3 All.E.R. 156; DENNING, J., in _Central London Property Trust, Ltd_, v. _High Trees House, Ltd._, [1947], K.B. 130; [1956], 1 All.E.R. 256; DENNING and ASQUITH, L.JJ., in _Candler_ v. _Crane Christmas & Co._, [1951], 2 K.B. 164; [1951], 1 All.E.R. 426; Lord MACDERMOTT in _Walsh_ v. _Curry_, [1955], N.I. 112; _Scruttons Ltd._ v. _Midland Silicones, Ltd._, [1962], A.C. 446; [1962], 1 All.E.R.1. _Rylands_ v. _Fletcher_ (1868), L.R. 3 H.L. 330; DENNING, L.J. in _Broom_ v. _Morgan_, [1953] 1. Q.B. 597; [1953] 1 All.E.R. 849; Viscount SIMONDS and Lord REID in _Davie_ v. _New Merton Board Mills, Ltd._, [1959] A.C. 604; [1959] 1 All.E.R. 346; _Fellner_ v. _Minister of the Interior_, 1954 (4) S.A. 524 (A.D.); _Hedley Byrne & Co., Ltd._ v. _Heller & Partners, Ltd._, [1964] A.C. 465; [1963] 2 All.E.R. 575.

Obiter Dicta

1. CROSS, A.R.N. Precedent in English Law, (2nd ed., Oxford,
   1968), pp. 80-86: a general account is given of the position
   of dicta.

2. MONTROSE, J.L. "The Language of, and a Notation for, the
   Doctrine of Precedent", (1951-53), 2 Ann.L.R. 325 et seq.:
   this gives, inter alia, explanation of obiter dicta.

3. RAM, J. The Science of Legal Judgment, (2nd ed. J. Townshend,
   Baker, Voorhis & Co., New York, 1871), chap. 5, especially
   pp. 102-107: this gives a general account and an estimate
   of the weight of various types of dicta.

4. SLESSER, H. The Judicial Office and Other Matters,
   (Hutchinson & Co., Ltd., 1942), a general account.

5. See also the discussion of Bell v. Lever Bros., By P.A. LANDON:
   (1935), 51 L.Q.R. 650; T.H. TYLOR: (1936), 52 L.Q.R. 27;
   C.J. HAMSON: (1937), 53 L.Q.R. 118.

6. R.E.M.: Note in (1944), 60 L.Q.R. 222: this draws attention to
   the suggested distinction between "obiter dicta" and
   "judicial dicta".

Logic in the Judicial Process

7. GUEST, A.G. "Logic in the Law", in Oxford Essays in Jurisprudence, (ed. A.G. Guest, Oxford, 1961), chap. 7: the
   function of logic in law is explained and certain
   misconceptions are dispelled.

8. TREUSCH, P.E. "The Syllogism", in J. Hall, Readings in
   Jurisprudence (Bobbs-Merrill Co., Inc., 1938), p. 539: this
   provides a useful account of the terminology and nature of
   syllogistic reasoning with reference to case-law, as well
   as a demonstration of certain fallacies.

9. COHEN, M.R. "The Place of Logic in the Law", (1916-17), 29
   Harv.L.R. 622: logic is valuable in testing conclusions
   derived from given premises. It is the latter that need to
   be examined. "Facts" are not as rigid and principles not as
   flexible as supposed.

10. SMITH, G.H. "Logic, Jurisprudence and the Law", (1914), 48
    Am.L.R., 801, at pp. 802-818: this is a general account
    of logic and terminology.

11. COFFEY, P. "The Science of Logic: II, pp. 153-157" in J. HALL:

Readings in Jurisprudence, (The Bobbs-Merrill Co., Inc.
1938), p. 561: this discusses analogy and syllogism.

1. LLOYD, D. "Reason and Logic in the Common Law", (1948), 64
   L.Q.R. 468: this is a discussion of the uncertainty of the
   terms used in legal propositions and of the nature of
   syllogistic reasoning.

2. JENSEN, O.C. The Nature of Legal Argument, (Oxford, 1957),
   Part I: deductive and inductive reasoning in law are
   considered, and there is a demonstration of certain misconceptions about logic.

3. STOLJAR, S.J. "The Logical Status of a Legal Principle",
   (1952-53), 20 U.C.L.R., 181: the various logical processes
   involved in legal reasoning are considered and stress is
   laid on the function of values, the "logic of attitudes".

4. HART, H.L.A. "Positivism and the Separation of Law and Morals",
   (1957-58), 71 Harv.L.R., 593, 606: logic has its limitations
   in that it does not prescribe the interpretation of terms.

5. STONE, J. "Reason and Reasoning in Judicial and Juristic
   Argument", in Legal Essays. A Tribute to Frede Castberg,
   (Universitets-forlaget, 1963), 170: much trouble has been
   caused by using formal logic to reach conclusions which it
   cannot yield. The decisional process is subjected to acute
   analysis.

6. STONE, J. Legal System and Lawyers' Reasonings, (Stevens &
   Sons, Ltd., 1964), pp. 35-41, chaps. 7 and 8: semantically
   a judgment cannot possess any one meaning, and not even
   computers will help in finding what is not there. Judges
   nearly always have a choice as to how they decide because
   there may be no exclusive premise from which to reason, or
   the premise itself may be imprecise in a number of ways.
   These "categories of illusory reference" are explained in
   detail. A case yields a number of potentially binding
   rationes. Precedents serve to present a review of social
   contexts comparable to the present, the rules thought
   suitable and the kind of results that follows the
   application of one rule or another. Where choice exists
   judges may or may not be aware of their responsibility in
   making acceptable decisions. These involve questions of
   justice and sociology. Arguments about justice and social
   facts are a basis for justifying and testing decisions. In
   this way rhetorical reasoning fits the judicial process
   better than syllogistic reasoning.

7. JONES, T.C. "Stone on Lawyers' Logic: Twenty Years On" (1965)

31 Irish Jur. 21: this is principally a critique of J.
Stone's Legal System and Lawyers' Reasonings in the light
of developments since his earlier book in 1946.

1. HOERNLĒ, R.F.A. Review of Science of Legal Method: Select
   Essays by Various Authors, (1918), 31 Harv.L.R., 807: what
   is often condemned as bad logic is the bad selection of
   premises.

2. TAMMELO, I. "Sketch for a Symbolic Juristic Logic", (1955-56),
   8 J.L.E., 277, 300: some fallacies in legal reasoning are
   dealt with, but in the context of a rather special system
   of symbols.

Methods of Reasoning

3. MORRIS, C. How Lawyers Think, (Harvard, 1938), especially
   chaps. 3-5, 8: a careful analysis is given of the deductive
   and inductive processes, showing that their application is
   attended by special problems.

4. DEWEY, J. How We Think, (D.C. Heath & Co., 1909), chap. 8:
   the thought processes behind giving a judicial decision are
   examined. The selection of facts and relevant principles
   and the decision based on them is first explained. Then the
   shaping of the ideas leading to the judgment is
   investigated. These are tentatively formed with reference
   to their fitness for resolving the problem. "Meaning" is
   used as a tool of judgment.

5. DEWEY, J. "Logical Method and Law", (1924), 10 Corn,L.Q. 17:
   the logic of the judicial process is that of finding a
   reason for the decision already reached.

6. POUND, R. "The Theory of Judicial Decision", (1922-23), 36
   Harv.L.R., 640, 802, 940: the last section is particularly
   important, analysing as it does the various steps in giving
   a decision.

7. CARDOZO, B.N. The Nature of the Judicial Process, (Yale
   University Press, 1921): this is a classic exposition by a
   famous American Judge of the various factors that are
   involved, principally analogy, history, custom and sociology.

8. CORBIN, A.L. "The Judicial Process Revisited: Introduction"
   (1961-62) 71 Yale L.J. 195: this is mainly an appreciation
   of Judge Cardozo, but there are comments on certain aspects
   of his thesis.

9. Van VOORHIS, J. "Cardozo and the Judicial Process Today"

(1961-62), 71 Yale L.J. 203: growth since 1921 has been
marked by a greater emphasis on sociological jurisprudence,
the expansion of administrative law and vast increase in
legislation. Some of the developments are reviewed in the
light of Judge Cardozo's work.

1. STEIN, P. "Justice Cardozo, Marcus Terentius Varro and the
   Roman Juristic Process" (1967) 2 Ir. Jur.(N.S.) 367: three
   of Cardozo's four methods of legal development are reflected
   in the work of the Roman grammarian Varro, viz., analogy,
   custom and history ("nature"). Analogical reasoning was
   introduced into law by Labeo.

2. FRIENDLY, H.J. "Reactions of a Lawyer - Newly made Judge"
   (1961-62), 71 Yale L.J. 218, especially pp. 229 et seq.:
   how do judges in fact judge ? Intuition needs to be trained
   by experience. The judge's personal beliefs as to the
   desirability of a certain result is relevant, but it is
   kept in a subordinate place.

3. LLEWELLYN, K.N. "The Normative, the Legal, and the Law-jobs:
   the Problem of Juristic Method" (1939-40), 49 Yale L.J.
   1355: beneath all doctrines lie problems which are a proper
   study for social disciplines. The jobs of the law are the
   disposal of trouble-cases, which is a "garage-repair" type
   of job; preventive channelling of conduct and expectations
   so as to avoid trouble; and to legitimise authoritative
   action.

4. LLEWELLYN, K.N. The Common Law Tradition. Deciding Appeals
   (Little, Brown & Co., 1960): the author takes issue with
   those who deny predictability in the judicial process.
   There is "reckonability", which is based on a judge's
   selection of the right rule for the case in hand guided
   by his "situation-sense". This "situation-sense" is the
   product of the whole inherited culture and craft of the law.
   Judicial discretion is not exercised at large, but is
   conditioned in a predictable way.

5. CLARK, C.E. and TRUBEK, D.M. "The Creative Role of the Judge:
   Restraint and Freedom in the Common Law Tradition" (1961-
   62), 71 Yale L.J. 255: this article is principally a
   criticism of K.N. Llewellyn's Common Law Tradition and it
   comes down firmly on the side of Cardozo's thesis, and is
   in fact one of a series of articles on Cardozo. Llewellyn
   saw an objective factor in guiding judges so that they are
   not free to do as they wish. This thesis is criticised on
   the ground that Llewellyn underplays the subjective element,
   and that the failure to take account of the subjective
   element will lead to a failure to achieve what Llewellyn

seeks to achieve, namely, predictability.

1. ALLEN, C.K. "Precedent and Logic", (1925), 41 L.Q.R. 329:
   this discusses the process of deciding a case: (to some
   extent this account has been superseded by Law in the
   Making, chap. 3.

2. LEVI, E.H. An Introduction to Legal Reasoning, (Chicago,
   1948): legal reasoning has a logic of its own. He discusses
   this with reference to case-law and statute-law.

3. POLLOCK, F. "The Science of Case-law" in Essays in Jurisprudence and Ethics, (Macmillan & Co., 1882), p. 237: this
   seeks to show the analogies between the method of natural
   scientists and common lawyers, and particularly the process
   employed by the latter in dealing with novel situations.

4. WASSERSTROM, R.A. The Judicial Decision, (Stanford University
   Press, 1961), chaps. 2-3, 7: these discuss criticisms of
   the deductive theory, showing that many of them stem from
   misconceptions of the function of logic. The judicial
   process is a process of justification, not of discovery.
   This should be a "two-level procedure of justification",
   i.e., the decision deduced from the most desirable rule.

5. DWORKIN, R.M. "Does Law have a Function? A Comment on the
   Two-level Theory of Decision" (1964-65), 74 Yale L.J. 640:
   Professor Wasserstrom's thesis is criticised on the ground
   that the assumptions underlying it make it valueless. These
   are said to be that there is some unique goal or function
   which a legal system should serve, that judicial decision
   should involve calculation of the sort discussed, and the
   absence of legislative rules.

6. MORRIS, C. "Peace Through Law: the Role and Limits of Judicial
   Adjudication" (1960-61) 109 U. Pa. L.R. 218: a judicial
   decision is "rational" only when supported by acceptable
   rational grounds. Judicial rationality is a work of art. It
   should satisfy those who have to live with it as being the
   right answer to the problem, but the judge should also keep
   within his role.

7. FRANK, J.N. "What Courts Do in Fact", (1932), 26 Ill.L.R.,
   645: this points out the difficulty of attaining certainty
   because of the uncertainty of "facts"; and that the decision
   often precedes the explanation.

8. FRANK, J.N. Law and the Modern Mind, (Stevens & Sons, Ltd.,
   1949), chaps. 12, 14: the judge begins with a vaguely formed
   conclusion and then finds premises to support it. The

decision is the result of the judge's personal experience
during the hearing. See also J.N. FRANK: Courts on Trial,
(Princeton, 1950), chaps. 19, 20, 23.

1. ADLER, M.J. "Law and the Modern Mind: a Symposium. Legal
   Certainty", (1931), 31 Col.L.R., 91: the parties to a
   dispute so marshal their authorities as to establish the
   premises from which the desired conclusion will follow
   logically. The judge has to choose.

2. OLIPHANT, H. and HEWITT, A. "Introduction" to From the
   Physical to the Social Sciences: Introduction to a Study of
   Economic and Ethical Theory, (trans. H. Green) in J. HALL,
   Readings in Jurisprudence, (Bobbs-Merrill Co., Inc., 1938),
   p. 355: this is a discussion of the deductive and inductive
   methods, showing that the selection of premises depends on
   the choice between different interests.

3. AUBERT, V. "Structure of Legal Thinking" in Legal Essays, A
   Tribute to Frede Castberg, (Universitetsforlaget, 1963), 41:
   there is a difference in the thinking process involved in
   practical and juristic work. The former, as a decisional
   process, differs from scientific thought in that it proceeds
   by comparison.

4. COOK, W.W. "The Logical and Legal Bases of the Conflict of
   Laws", (1924), 33, Yale L.J., 457: the premises of a
   syllogism must be constructed before the deduction is
   performed.

5. GREEN, L. "The Duty Problem in Negligence Cases", (1928), 28
   Col.L.R., 1014, at pp. 1019-1022: he makes the point that a
   judicial opinion is a justification in words of a judgment
   already passed.

6. ROBINSON, E.S. Law and Lawyers, (The Macmillan Co., New York,
   1935), chap. 8: the psychological processes behind the
   giving of judicial decisions are examined. The expressed
   reasons serve to persuade the judge himself and others of
   the correctness of his original conclusion. Although the
   mental operations of a judge are his own, yet his acceptance
   or rejection of them is governed by his estimate of the
   opinions of others.

7. DICKINSON, J. "Legal Rules and their Function in the Process
   of Decision", (1931), 79 U.Pa.L.R., 833: this stresses the
   importance of arguing from rules even though discretion may
   enter into the process. See also "Legal Rules, their
   Application and Elaboration", ibid., p. 1052: "aplication"
   means employing a rule to decide a case; "elaboration" means

the creation of a new rule to fill a gap. These processes
are examined in detail, with particular attention to the
finding of similarities and dissimilarities.

1. SEIDMAN, R.B. "The Judicial Process Reconsidered in the Light
    of Role-theory (1969) 32 M.L.R. 516: there is a difference
    between "clear" and "trouble" cases. In the former, there
    is a rule at hand and the facts fall clearly within the
    inner core of the categories specified by the rule; in the
    latter one or other of these conditions is lacking. The
    judge's tasks differ too. In "clear" cases he is applying
    a pre-existing rule; in "trouble" cases he makes a rule ex
    post Facto.

2. LEVY, B.H. Cardozo and Frontiers of Legal Thinking, (New York,
    1938), pp. 39-63, 86-96: the judicial method is neither
    exclusively deductive nor inductive. The judge reaches a
    conclusion and then proceeds to justify it.

3. KEETON, G.W. and LLOYD, D. (edd.): in The British Commonwealth.
    The Development of its Laws and Constitutions, (Stevens &
    Sons, Ltd., 1955), 1, pp. 15-19: a succinct account of the
    extent of judicial discretion is provided.

4. LLEWELLYN, K.N. Jurisprudence. Realism in Theory and Practice,
    (Chicago, 1962), chap. 6: it is the use that judges make of
    precedents that is important, and this is guided by outside
    considerations.

5. VON MEHREN, A.T. The Civil Law System: Cases and Materials,
    (Prentice-Hall, Inc., 1957), chap. 16, especially at pp.
    821-822: a decision is the accomodation of two or more
    interests, and this is not purely mechanical.

6. POWELL, T.R. "The Judiciality of Minimum-wage Legislation",
    (1923-24), 37 Harv.L.R., 545: this gives a demonstration of
    how the personal views of judges dictated their attitude
    towards a legislative enactment.

7. WISDOM, J. "Gods", in Philosophy and Psycho-Analysis, (Oxford:
    Blackwell, 1957), 149, at pp. 157-158: in some types of
    cases the reasoning consists of viewing the facts one way
    and another so as to be able to perceive similarities and
    dissimilarities to past cases.

8. WISDOM, J. "Philosophy, Metaphysics and Psycho-Analysis" in
    Philosophy and Psycho-Analysis, (Oxford: Blackwell, 1957),
    pp. 248-254: a still more forceful presentation of the same
    point as above.

1. LLOYD, D. Introduction to Jurisprudence, (2nd ed., Stevens &
    Sons, Ltd., 1965), pp. 382-384: this stresses the same
    point as Wisdom (supra), and points out that judicial
    reasoning has a logic of its own.

2. CASTBERG, F. Problems of Legal Philosophy, (2nd ed., Oslo
    University Press; Allen & Unwin, Ltd., 1957), chap. 3,
    especially sects. 2-3: this draws attention to the
    insufficiency of logic in legal thinking which involves the
    subsumption of cases under normative propositions.

3. JØRGENSEN, S. "Argumentation and Decision" in Liber Amicorum
    in Honour of Professor Alf Ross, (Copenhagen, 1969), 261:
    To Ross the crucial problems are: What is law? and What
    does it mean to say that law is valid? Only "is" statements
    can be verified. Valid law is a normative ideology that
    animates a judge. It is pointed out that Ross does not
    tackle the question how the judge himself arrives at his
    ideas of valid law. Various processes of decision-making are
    then discussed.

4. FRANK, J.N. "Mr. Justice Holmes and Non-Euclidean Thinking",
    (1932), 17 Corn.L.Q. 568: premises should be selected
    according to their correspondence with observable phenomena
    or utility.

5. AUSTIN, J. Lectures on Jurisprudence, (5th ed. R. Campbell,
    J. Murray, 1885), II, Excursus on Analogy, pp. 1001-1020:
    analogical reasoning and the use of the syllogism are
    explained.

6. VINOGRADOFF, P. Common-Sense in Law, (3rd ed., H.G. Hanbury,
    Oxford University Press, 1959), chap. 7, pp. 132 et seq.:
    the syllogistic form of reasoning and the use of analogy
    are explained.

7. HAMMOND, W.G. "Appendix G to Legal and Political Hermeneutics",
    pp. 276-280 in J. HALL, Readings in Jurisprudence, (Bobbs-
    Merrill Co., Inc., 1938), 568: the limits of analogical
    reasoning are examined.

8. FREUND, E. "Interpretation of Statutes", (1917), 65 U.Pa.L.R.,
    207: use of analogy in the interpretation of statute is
    considered.

9. ALLEN, C.K. Law in the Making, (7th ed. Oxford, 1964), pp.
    285-311: this is a general account of the working of legal
    induction.

10. PATON, G.W. A Text-Book of Jurisprudence, (3rd ed., D.P. Derham

Oxford, 1964), chap. 8 sect. 43: the operation of syllogistic and inductive reasoning is discussed.

1. LLEWELLYN, K.N. The Bramble Bush, (New York, 1930), chap. 5,
    pp. 67-73: this gives an account of the inductive process
    in constructing premises.

2. O'SULLIVAN, R. "On Law Reporting", (1940-41), 4 M.L.R. 104,
    pp. 107 et seq.: this discusses how cases were decided
    before the evolution of stare decisis and alleges that the
    inductive method is without foundation in history or
    authority.

3. MAYO, L.H. and JONES, E.M. "Legal-policy Decision Process:
    Alternative Thinking and the Predictive Function" (1964-65)
    33 The Geo. Wash. L.R. 318: lawyers should now learn to
    think in terms of process rather than formulae, the movement
    of events as well as the relevance of formulae. In a very
    long article the structure and working of a Basic Decisional
    Model are set out and explained.

4. HIGGINS, R. "Policy Considerations and the International
    Judicial Process" (1968) 17 I.C.L.Q. 58: the distinction,
    well-known in International Law, between "legal" and
    "political" disputes is critically examined. The idea that
    a judge has simply to apply the law as he finds it is not
    applicable to international adjudication any more than it
    is to municipal adjudication. A decision at International
    Law requires concern with the policy alternatives, including
    the interests of the parties and also of the world community.
    The judge's task is a choice between alternatives, and the
    assessment of extra-legal considerations is part of the
    legal process.

5. Law and Philosophy. A Symposium, (ed. S. Hook, New York,
    University Press, 1964), Part III: this is of very general
    interest only. The various contributions touch on some
    aspects of the judicial process, but none are penetrating.

6. The following cases may be consulted as illustrating judicial
    technique: Armstrong v. Strain, [1951] 1 T.L.R. 856; affirmed,
    [1952] 1 K.B. 232; [1952] 1 All E.R. 139; Donoghue v. Stevenson,
    [1932] A.C. 562; Hedley Byrne & Co., Ltd. v. Heller & Partners,
    Ltd., [1964] A.C. 465; [1963] 2 All E.R. 575; Haley v. London
    Electricity Board, [1965] A.C. 778; [1964] 3 All E.R. 185;
    Myers v. Director of Public Prosecutions, [1965] A.C. 1001;
    [1964] 2 All E.R. 881; South Pacific Co. v. Jensen (1917), 244
    U.S. 205; Morgan v. Fear, [1907] A.C. 425; Fibrosa Spolka
    Akcyjna v. Fairbairn Lawson Combe Barbour, Ltd., [1943] A.C.
    32; [1942] 2 All E.R. 122; Holmes v. Director of Public

Prosecutions, [1946] A.C. 588; [1946] 2 All E.R. 124; Foakes
v. Beer (1884), 9 App. Cas. 605; Searle v. Wallbank, [1947]
A.C. 341; [1947] 1 All E.R. 12; Leathley v. J. Fowler & Co.,
Ltd., [1946] K.B. 579; [1946] 2 All E.R. 326.

Judges Making Law

1. CARTER, J.C. "The Ideal and the Actual in the Law", (1890),
   24 Am.L.R., 752: the view that law is custom and that the
   task of the judges is to discover it is supported.

2. CARTER, J.C. Law: Its Origin, Growth and Function,
   (G.P. Putnam's Sons, 1907), pp. 65 et seq.: an elaboration
   of the above.

3. AUSTIN, J. Lectures on Jurisprudence, (5th ed. R. Campbell,
   J. Murray, 1885), II, pp. 628-647: this is a detailed
   demonstration of how judges make law as contrasted with
   legislation.

4. FRANK, J.N. Law and the Modern Mind, (Stevens & Sons, Ltd.,
   1949), pp. 32-37, and Appendix I: explanations are offered
   of the orthodox view that judges do not make law, with
   especial reference to the desire for a "father-symbol".

5. LEVY, B.H. Cardozo and Frontiers of Legal Thinking, (New York,
   1938), pp. 39-46: this is a discussion of the law-making
   function of judges with an investigation into the reasons
   for the orthodox theory.

6. VON MEHREN, A.T. The Civil Law System: Cases and Materials,
   (Prentice-Hall, Inc., 1957), chap. 16, sects. 3-4: this
   provides an excellent account of four situations in which
   judges do make law and the factors affecting this function.

7. GRAY, J.C. The Nature and Sources of the Law, (2nd ed.,
   R. Gray, Macmillan Co., New York, 1921), chap. 9: this is
   a critical discussion of the orthodox view. The conclusion
   is that judges do make law.

8. POUND, R. "The Theory of Judicial Decision", (1922-23), 36
   Harv.L.R., 802: judicial attitudes depend on current
   philosophies and the orthodox theory was influenced by the
   analytical and historical theories of law.

9. POUND, R. An Introduction to the Philosophy of Law, (Yale
   University Press, 1922), pp. 100-129: interpretation of
   law shades into law-making and law-applying.

10. POUND, R. Jurisprudence, (West Publishing Co., 1959), IV,

chap. 20, especially sect. 115: law-making inevitably
enters into the process of law-applying.

1. COHEN, M.R. "The Process of Judicial Legislation", (1914),
    48 Am.L.R., 161: this challenges the Blackstonian theory
    by showing how judges make law even when purporting to find
    it.

2. FULLER, L.L. "What Motives give rise to the Historical Legal
    Fiction?" in Recueil d'Etudes sur les Sources du Droit en
    l'Honneur de F. Geny, (Lib. du Recueil Sirey, 1934) II,
    157: why do judges introduce new doctrine under the
    linguistic cover of the old? Various possible reasons are
    considered.

3. DICKINSON, J. "Legal Rules and their Function in the Process
    of Decision", (1931), 79 U.Pa.L.R., 833: a new rule is
    created when there is a choice and a balance has to be
    effected between the rules themselves.

4. CARDOZO, B.N. The Growth of the Law, (Yale University Press,
    1924), chap. 5: this is a demonstration of how essential
    the creative function is.

5. LEFROY, A.H.F. "Judge-made Law", (1904), 20 L.Q.R., 399:
    different types of judge-made law are discussed.

6. LEFROY, A.H.F. "The Basis of Case-law", (1906), 22 L.Q.R. 293:
    the judicial function in cases primae impressionis is
    considered.

7. CARPENTER, C.E. "Court Decisions and the Common Law", (1917),
    17 Col.L.R., 593: the theory that judges do not make law is
    inconsistent with the origin and growth of the law, besides
    operating unjustly.

8. CLARKE, S.B. "What may be Done to Enable the Courts to Allay
    the Present Discontent with the Administration of Justice",
    (1916), 50 Am.L.R., 161: a general attack is launched on
    stare decisis and on the law-making power of judges.

9. HALL, R.S. "Do Courts make Laws and should Precedents Command
    the Obedience of Lower Courts?", (1917), 51 Am.L.R., 833:
    this is a defence of the present system against S.B. Clarke's
    attack, (supra). The law-making power of the courts is
    important and necessary.

10. LLEWELLYN, K.N. The Common Law Tradition. Deciding Appeals
    (Little, Brown & Co., 1960): the Bar has lost confidence in
    the Supreme Court because of the lack of "reckonability".

This book is a powerful answer to this charge and seeks to show that there is "reckonability" notwithstanding the creative element. It derives from the judges' "situation-sense" for each dispute, which is a product of calculable factors.

1. JENKS, E. "English Civil Law" (1916-17), 30 Harv.L.R., 1, at pp. 13-19: the extent of judicial law-making and its significance are reviewed.

2. ALLEN, C.K. Law in the Making, (7th ed., Oxford, 1964), pp.302-311: judges do make law, but in a different sense from the way in which the legislature does so.

3. LAMBERT, E. "Codified Law and Case Law: their Part in Shaping the Policies of Justice" in Science of Legal Method: Select Essays by Various Authors, (trans. E. Bruncken and L.B. Register, Boston Book Co., 1917), chap. 9, sects. 6-9: the orthodox doctrine is a fiction, for judges do make law.

4. EVERSHED, F.R. "The Judicial Process in Twentieth Century England" (1961), 61 Col.L.R. 761: the judicial function of today is contrasted with that in the past, and also compared with the function in America. Law being a social structure it has to be applied to novel social conditions. Thus the creative function of the judges involves what Cardozo calls the Method of Sociology. This point is illustrated with reference to various branches of the law. At the end some relaxation of stare decisis in the highest tribunal is urged.

5. DIPLOCK, K. "The Courts as Legislators", Presidential Address to the Holdsworth Club, 1965: the courts by the very nature of their functions have to act as legislators. Because of the doctrine of stare dicisis in every judgment a court speaks as to the future as to the past. Creation of new machinery is for Parliament; the regulation of human relations within that framework is for the courts. Three criticisms of judge-made law and desirable changes in judicial attitude are considered.

6. WRIGHT, R.A. Legal Essays and Addresses, (Cambridge University Press, 1939), Preface, pp. xvi-xx: change is accomplished by a perpetual erosion of the authorities.

7. SNYDER, O.C. Preface to Jurisprudence, (Bobbs-Merrill Co., Inc., 1954), Part III, chap. 3, pp. 415-418; 426-438: this is a discussion of the basis of the orthodox theory and of how the judges do make law.

1. FRIEDMANN, W. <u>Legal Theory</u>, (5th ed., Stevens & Sons, Ltd.
    1967), chap. 32: this is a general discussion in the
    context of precedent as a whole.

2. FRIEDMANN, W. "Legal Philosophy and Judicial Lawmaking" (1961)
    61 Col.L.R. 821: the need for judicial creativeness is
    discussed from various points of view.

3. LLOYD, D. <u>The Idea of Law</u>, (Penguin Books, Ltd., A 688, 1964),
    chap. 11: judicial independence is important. The traditional
    view that judges do not make law is unreal in view of the
    part played by value-judgments. Logic alone cannot resolve
    problems, and there is a limit to the use of analogy. The
    binding force of precedent is discussed in general terms and
    contrasted with the position in Civil Law jurisdictions.

4. LLOYD, D. <u>Introduction to Jurisprudence</u>, (2nd ed., Stevens &
    Sons, Ltd., 1965), pp. 378-381: a general account of judges
    making law is provided.

5. LLOYD, D. in <u>The British Commonwealth</u>. <u>The Development of its
    Laws and Constitutions</u>, G.W. Keeton and D. Lloyd (edd.)
    (Stevens & Sons, Ltd., 1955), I, pp. 23-24: a brief summary
    of judicial law-making.

6. VINOGRADOFF, P. <u>Common-Sense in Law</u>, (3rd ed., H.G. Hanbury,
    Oxford University Press, 1959), chap. 7, pp. 147 <u>et seq.</u>:
    the retroactive operation of precedent is discussed.

7. CARDOZO, B.N. <u>The Nature of the Judicial Process</u>, (Yale
    University Press, 1921), chap. 4: the retroactivity of
    precedent may not be such a hardship in practice as it
    might appear.

8. WIGMORE, J.H. Editorial Preface: "The Judicial Function", in
    <u>Science of Legal Method</u>: <u>Select Essays by Various Authors</u>,
    (trans. E. Bruncken and L.B. Register, Boston Book Co.,
    1917), pp. xxxvii-xxxviii: the suggestion is advanced that
    overruling should operate for the future.

9. FREEMAN, R.H. "The Protection Afforded against the Retro-
    active Operation of an Overruling Decision", (1918), 18
    Col.L.R., 230: this is an inquiry into the extent to which
    American courts seek to minimise the retroactivity of
    precedent.

10. Von MOSCHZISKER, R. "<u>Stare Decisis</u> in the Courts of Last
    Resort", (1923-24), 37 Harv.L.R., 409: difficulties of
    Wigmore's suggestion (<u>supra</u>) are considered.

1. KOCOUREK, A. "Retrospective Decisions and Stare Decisis and a Proposal", (1931), 17 Am.B.A.J., 180: the draft is given of a proposed statute to enable a superior court to apply a principle to the instant case and to overrule it for the future.

2. CARDOZO, B.N. "Jurisprudence" in Selected Writings of B.N. Cardozo, (ed. M.E. Hall, 1947), pp. 35-36: the suggestion that overruling should operate prospectively and not retrospectively is supported.

3. LEVY, B.H. "Realist Jurisprudence and Prospective Overruling" (1960-61), 109 U. Pa. L.R., 1: a readier acceptance of realist jurisprudence would have enabled prospective over- ruling to be more widely used. The Blackstonian doctrine obscures the distinction between deciding the instance case and laying down a rule for the future. This article contains a full account of the history of prospective overruling in America down to 1961.

4. SNYDER, O.C. Preface to Jurisprudence, (Bobbs-Merrill Co., Inc., 1954), Part III, chap. 3, pp. 418-419: prospective overruling is supported.

5. KEETON, R.E. "Creative Continuity in the Law of Torts" (1961- 62), 75 Harv. L.R., 463, at pp. 486 et seq.: prospective and retrospective overruling in the law of torts is considered.

6. FRIEDMANN, W. "Limits of Judicial Lawmaking and Prospective Overruling" (1966) 29 M.L.R. 593: it is indisputable that judges do make law. If so, it is necessary to consider the limits of their lawmaking function. In this connection the operation of prospective overruling, in criminal and civil cases, is considered.

7. LEACH, W.B. "Divorce by Plane-Ticket in the Affluent Society - with a Side-Order of Jurisprudence" (1966) 14 Kansas L.R., 549: prospective overruling would remove the vested interest objection to judicial reform. All courts, civil and criminal, should have the option to give "prospective only" application to overruling decisions. This point is considered in connection with a detailed and amusing study of a divorce case. (See also W.B. LEACH, "Revisionism in the House of Lords: the Bastion of Rigid Stare Decisis Falls" (1967) 80 Harv. L.R. 797; R.W.M. DIAS, "Precedents in the House of Lords - a Much Needed Reform" [1966] C.L.J. 153).

8. ANONYMOUS. "Prospective Overruling and Retroactive Application in the Federal Courts" (1961-62), 71 Yale L.J. 907:

the declaratory theory of precedent is considered in detail
with reference to the constitutional doctrines of the
United States. The conclusion is that it should be left to
a later court to decide whether or not to give retroactive
effect to a new rule enunciated by a previous court. Such
a decision should be reached after a consideration of the
criteria relevant to the purpose of the new rule and to the
effective and equitable operation of the legal system.

1. MISHKIN, P.J. "Foreword: The High Court, the Great Writ, and
   the Due Process of Time and Law" (1965-66) 79 Harv.L.R. 56:
   the rejection of the Blackstonian myth that judges only
   declare what is law does not dispense with other good
   reasons for giving judicial decisions retroactive operation.
   The question is discussed with reference to leading America
   cases.

2. STONE, J. Social Dimensions of Law and Justice, (Stevens &
   Sons, Ltd., 1966), pp. 658-667: the question of
   prospectivity and retrospectivity is discussed in relation
   to judicial institutions as instruments of legal ordering.

Factors Affecting the Weight of Precedents

3. RAM, J. The Science of Legal Judgment, (2nd ed., J. Townshend,
   Baker, Voorhis & Co., New York, 1871), sects. 2-3: this
   gives an account of the factors which would increase or
   reduce the value of a precedent.

4. WAMBAUGH, E. The Study of Cases, (2nd ed., Boston, 1894),
   chap. 5: a detailed account is given of the various
   considerations that affect the assessment of the value of
   a case.

5. ANONYMOUS. "The Aged Precedent" [1965] S.L.T. 53: when may a
   court upset a long-established precedent? Nine factors
   that may prevent overruling are set out. There is also a
   useful review of a considerable number of cases in which
   the question has been considered.

Pros and Cons of Stare Decisis

6. MULLINS, C. In Quest of Justice, (John Murray, 1931), chaps.
   3-6: these provide an excellent discussion of the precedent
   system and the pros and cons.

7. GOODHART, A.L. "Precedent in English and Continental Law",
   (1934), 50 L.Q.R., 40: detailed consideration is given to
   the various arguments for stare decisis.

1. HOLDSWORTH, W.S. "Case Law", (1934), 50 L.Q.R., 180: this is
   a defence of stare decisis on the ground that much of the
   criticism has been exaggerated.

2. GOODHART, A.L. "Case Law - a Short Replication", (1934), 50
   L.Q.R., 196: a reply to Holdsworth.

3. ALLEN, C.K. "Case Law: an Unwarrantable Intervention", (1935),
   51 L.Q.R., 353: while in no way minimising the defects of
   stare decisis he comes down in support of it.

4. HOLDSWORTH, W.S. "Precedents in the Eighteenth Century",
   (1935), 51 L.Q.R., 441: a short reply to Allen.

5. AUSTIN, J. Lectures on Jurisprudence, (5th ed., R. Campbell,
   J. Murray, 1885), II, pp. 647-660: seven objections to
   judge-made law are presented in detail.

6. WASSERSTROM, R.A. The Judicial Decision, (Stanford University
   Press, 1961), chap. 4: this contains a detailed discussion
   of the pros and cons.

7. RADIN, M. "Case Law and Stare Decisis: Concerning
   Präjudizienrecht in Amerika" (1933) 33 Col.L.R. 199: this
   is a review of a book by Llewellyn. Stare decisis is the
   doctrine that a prior decision is followed, not because it
   is thought to be right, but simply because it is a prior
   decision. Most of the reasons in support are either a form
   of estoppel or based on the need for certainty. As courts
   actually handle, it turns out to be an instrument capable
   of a great many variations.

8. WRIGHT, R.A. "The Common Law in its Old Home", in Legal
   Essays and Addresses, (Cambridge University Press, 1939),
   pp. 341-345: the objections that stare decisis leads to
   uncertainty and voluminous law reports are over-estimated.

9. OLIPHANT, H. "A Return to Stare Decisis", (1928), 14 Am.B.A.
   J., 71, 107, 159: this advocates a study of social
   structure, a re-classification of law and a study of the
   non-vocal behaviour of judges.

10. WIGMORE, J.H. Editorial Preface: "The Judicial Function", in
    Science of Legal Method: Select Essays by Various Authors,
    (trans. E. Bruncken and L.B. Register, Boston Book Co.,
    1917), pp. xxxvi-xlii: stare decisis is considered with
    reference to equality, stability and certainty.

11. VON MOSCHZISKER, R. "Stare decisis in the Courts of Last
    Resort", (1923-24), 37 Harv.L.R., 409: the function of

stare decisis is considered and the conclusion is that,
properly used, it is useful.

1. McKEAN, F.G. "The Rule of Precedents", (1928), 76 U.Pa.L.R.,
    481: in the course of a general account he considers the
    extent of such flexibility as there is.

2. WADE, H.W.R. "The Concept of Legal Certainty. A Preliminary
    Skirmish", (1940-41), 4 M.L.R., 183: certainty in relation
    to justice is considered.

3. KOCOUREK, A. An Introduction to the Science of Law, (Little,
    Brown & Co., 1930), pp. 165-85: the doctrine of stare
    decisis is discussed in outline but somewhat special
    attention is paid to the requirement of certainty.

4. FULLER, L.L. "American Legal Realism", (1934), 82 U.Pa.L.R.,
    429: the traditional exclusion of social and other such
    considerations promotes uncertainty. A code is more
    susceptible to extension than case-law.

5. MARSH, N.S. "Principle and Discretion in the Judicial Process",
    (1952), 68 L.Q.R. 226: this gives consideration to stare
    decisis in relation to certainty and flexibility.

6. CARDOZO, B.N. The Nature of the Judicial Process, (Yale
    University Press, 1921), chap. 4: adherence to precedent
    should be the rule, but this should be relaxed in the light
    of experience.

7. CARDOZO, B.N. The Growth of the Law, (Yale University Press,
    1924) chap. 1: this is a discussion of certainty with the
    warning that it should not be allowed to prevent growth.

8. POLLOCK, F. "Judicial Caution and Valour", (1929), 45 L.Q.R.
    293: the problem of interpretation is to hold a balance
    between an excess of caution and an excess of valour.

9. SCHMITTHOFF, C.M. "The Growing Ambit of the Common Law",
    (1952), 30 Can.B.R., 48: this is indirectly relevant in
    that it shows how case-law has tended to relax so as to
    produce just and reasonable decisions.

10. JACKSON, R.H. "Decisional Law and Stare Decisis", (1944),
    30 Am.B.A.J., 334: although stare decisis is relaxed in
    America, it is of value because of the certainty that it
    imparts. Attention is also drawn to the difficulty caused
    by the growing bulk of case-law.

11. SPRECHER, R.A. "The Development of the Doctrine of Stare

Decisis and the Extent to which it should be Applied",
(1945), 31 Am.B.A.J., 501: there is a careful evaluation in
the second part of the various arguments for and against the
doctrine.

1. DOUGLAS, W.O. "Stare Decisis", (1949), 49 Col.L.R., 735:
    stare decisis represents a desire for security as the world
    grows more insecure. There is a suggestion that overruling
    should include overruling of "All the cases in the same
    genus as the one which is repudiated, even though they are
    not before the court".

2. GOLDSCHMIDT, H.W. English Law from a Foreign Standpoint,
    (Pitman & Sons, Ltd., 1937), chap. 2, sects. 3-4: English
    law is favourably compared with Continental systems. The
    English system does achieve certainty and flexibility.

3. GERLAND, H.B. "The Operation of the Judicial Function in
    English Law" in Science of Legal Method: Select Essays by
    Various Authors, (trans. E. Bruncken and L.B. Register,
    Boston Book Co., 1917), chap. 8, sects. 5-9: this considers
    the advantages and disadvantages of stare decisis, the
    latter outweighing the former. (Note: Gerland is said to
    have moved in favour of precedent later: H.W. Goldschmidt,
    English Law from a Foreign Standpoint, pp. 38-39).

4. RANDALL, H.J. "Case-law on the Continent", (1919), 35 L.Q.R.,
    101: this is a critical review of Science of Legal Method,
    especially the criticisms of the English system by
    H.B. Gerland, (supra).

5. POLLOCK, F. A First Book of Jurisprudence, (6th ed., Macmillan
    Co., Ltd., 1929), pp. 348-349: the need for consistency as
    the justification for stare decisis is accepted. On the
    whole this is achieved.

6. McLOUD, J.W. "The Value of Precedents", (1894), 28 Am.L.R.,
    218: this stresses the value of precedents as preserving
    past wisdom.

7. GOODHART, A.L. "Case Law in England and America", in Essays
    in Jurisprudence and the Common Law, (Cambridge University
    Press, 1931), chap. 3: the American system is moving away
    from stare decisis and the reasons for this are given.

8. COOPER, T.M. "The Common Law and the Civil Law - a Scot's
    View", (1950), 63 Harv.L.R., 468, 472: consistency should
    not be blind imitation. Stare decisis cannot keep the law
    abreast of social needs.

1. CROSS, A.R.N. "Recent Developments in the Practice of
   Precedent - the Triumph of Common Sense" (1969) 43 Aust.L.
   J. 3: the Australian High Court has refused to follow
   rulings of the House of Lords, the House of Lords has
   refused to be bound by its own rulings, and the Privy
   Council has upheld the view of the Australian High Court.
   While applauding these developments, certain cautions need
   to be observed. Their implications on the status of <u>stare
   decisis</u> are also considered.

2. LLOYD, D. in G.W. KEETON and D. Lloyd (edd.) <u>The British
   Commonwealth</u>. <u>The Development of its Laws and Constitutions</u>,
   (Stevens & Sons, 1955), I, pp. 24-26: this gives a brief
   evaluation of the Common Law system.

3. GOODHART, A.L. "Reporting the Law", (1939), 55 L.Q.R., 29:
   this draws attention to the growing volume of case-law and
   suggestions for dealing with it.

4. STONE, O.M. "Knowing the Law", (1961), 24 M.L.R. 475: this is
   a review of the difficulties of finding the law.

5. CARDEN, P.T. "Loose Leaf Law Reports", (1910), 26 L.Q.R., 75:
   this is interesting as a suggestion that would reduce bulk,
   cost and time.

6. SINGLETON, W.E. "Loose Leaf Law Reports", (1910), 26 L.Q.R.,
   156: the above idea is approved with modifications.

7. BORCHARD, E.M. "Some Lessons from the Civil Law", (1916), 64
   U.Pa.L.R., 570: this includes a criticism of <u>stare decisis</u>
   as having outlived its usefulness.

8. TRUMBULL, L. "Precedent versus Justice", (1893), 27 Am.L.R.,
   321: <u>stare decisis</u> trains people to be followers rather
   than leaders.

9. GARRISON, L.M. "Blind Adherence to Precedent", (1917), 51 Am.
   L.R., 251: a former judge is quoted as stressing the danger
   of losing sight of principle.

10. MacCORMICK, D.N. "Can <u>Stare Decisis</u> be Abolished?" [1967] Jur.
    R. 197: the doctrine originated in the idea that precedents
    were declaratory of the common law. With the collapse of
    that fiction, the judges were slow to avow that they do
    legislate. A decision is justified by showing that it is in
    accordance, or not in conflict, with authority; that it is
    desirable; or by using analogies. The effect of abolishing
    <u>stare decisis</u> is considered in relation to these. Although
    it would no longer be necessary to justify a decision with

reference to authority, it should remain sufficient to do
so.

1. WALKER, D.M. "Reform, Restatement and the Law Commissions"
    [1965] Jur.R. 245, 256-262: reform of stare decisis is
    advocated in connection with the proposed overhaul of Scots
    law by the Scottish Law Commission.

2. COOPER, H.H.A. "Ratio Decidendi" (1968) 118 New L.J. 1180: a
    short, but incisive plea that the Law Commission should
    consider the question of ratio decidendi. Practitioners
    have no time to bring their tools up to date, and it is
    distressing to find academic lawyers professing uncertainty.

Comparison with other Systems

3. LIPSTEIN, K. "The Doctrine of Precedent in Continental Law
    with Special Reference to French and German Law", (1946),
    28 J.C.L. (3rd Ser. Pt. III), p. 34: the reasons why
    Continental systems did not develop stare decisis are
    investigated.

4. ENSOR, R.C.K. Courts and Judges in France, Germany and
    England, (Oxford University Press, 1933), chap. 4: this is
    a general account of the position of the judge, with
    particular attention to the need for the English judge to
    be skilled in finding the law in precedent.

5. DAVID, R. and De VRIES, H.P. The French Legal System, (New
    York, 1958), chap. 4: this shows that in practice the
    French and Common Law systems do not differ very much.

6. SILVING, H. Sources of Law (Wm.S. Hein & Co., Inc., New York,
    1968), ""Stare Decisis" in the Civil and in the Common Law",
    p. 83: in Civil law countries the function of case-law is
    to demonstrate by means of examples the operation of statute.
    A combination of code and case-law is desirable, because
    both have advantages. Statute economises in wording, but is
    beset by semantic limitations; case-law is wasteful in its
    volume, but can amplify statutory provisions. The discussion
    of case-law includes most of its problems, e.g., ratio
    decidendi.

7. GUTTERIDGE, H.C. Comparative Law, (Cambridge University Press,
    1949), chap. 7: this is a discussion of the main differences
    between Common Law and Continental systems and how case-law
    is used on the Continent.

8. ROSS, A. On Law and Justice, (Stevens & Sons, Ltd., 1958),
    pp. 84-91: the position in Common Law and Continental

countries is similar in practice, but there is a difference
in approach due principally to the influence respectively
of judges and jurists.

1. LAWSON, F.H. Negligence in the Civil Law, (Oxford University
   Press, 1950), pp. 231-235: this is a note on the structure
   and procedure of the French courts, the form of a French
   report and the authority of case-law in France.

2. LAMBERT, E. and WASSERMAN, M.J. "The Case Method in Canada
   and the Possibilities of its Adaptation to the Civil Law",
   (1929), 39 Yale L.J., 1: in the course of this discussion
   it is pointed out that case-law is an important part of the
   practical application of law in civil law systems.

3. ANCEL, M. "Case Law in France", (1934), 16 J.C.L. (3rd Ser.)
   1: this examines how case-law has emerged in France and the
   position which it now occupies.

4. GARDNER, J.C. Judicial Precedent in Scots Law, (W. Green &
   Sons, Ltd., 1936), chap. 5: the position in France and
   England is considered with reference to Amos, Ancel,
   Goodhart and Holdsworth.

5. FRIEDMANN, W. Legal Theory, (5th ed., Stevens & Sons, Ltd.,
   1967), chap. 33: the differences between the Common Law
   and Continental systems have been exaggerated and they have
   been narrowed. Other differences have now grown up.

6. COHN, E.J. "Precedents in Continental Law", (1935), 5 C.L.J.,
   366: this shows the bad effects until 1935 of the German
   provision giving binding effect to decisions of the "Plenum",
   the United Divisions. (See substantially the same provision:
   Gerichtsverfassungsgesetz, 1950, 136, I-III).

7. DEÁK, F. "The Place of the 'Case' in the Common and Civil
   Law", (1933-34), 8 Tul.L.R., 337: case-law in its wider
   sense (not stare decisis) is discussed.

8. HENRY, R.L. "Jurisprudence Constante and Stare Decisis
   Contrasted", (1929), 15 Am.B.A.J., 11: this is an
   unfavourable comparison of stare decisis when contrasted
   with the doctrine of Jurisprudence Constante of Civil Law.

9. MARSH, N.S. "Deduction and Induction in the Law of Torts: a
   Comparative Approach", (1950-51), 33 J.C.L., (3rd series,
   Part III), 59: general principles on the Continent require
   a great deal of elaboration by case-law, while there are
   general principles to some extent in English law.

1. VON MEHREN, A.T. The Civil Law System: Cases and Materials,
    (Prentice-Hall, Inc., 1957), chap. 16: this is a comparative
    discussion of the nature of the problems concerning judicial
    decisions in American, French and German law.

2. SCHLESINGER, R.B. Comparative Law: Cases, Text, Materials,
    (2nd ed., The Foundation Press, Inc., Brooklyn, 1959),
    pp. 287-322: notes and questions with illustrative material
    of the operation of precedents are provided.

3. LLOYD, D. Introduction to jurisprudence, (2nd ed., Stevens &
    Sons, Ltd., 1965), pp. 369-373: this is a general comparison
    of precedent in the Common Law and on the Continent.

4. KOTZÉ, J.G. "Judicial Precedent", (1917), 34 S.A.L.J., 280;
    (1918), 144 L.T., 349: this is a discussion of the authority
    of precedent in Roman Law and early Roman-Dutch Law. South
    Africa has adopted stare decisis but not quite as rigidly as
    English law.

5. KAHN, E. "The Rules of Precedent Applied in South African
    Courts", (1967) 84 S.A.L.J., 43, 175, 308: the evolution and
    operation of precedent in Southern Africa from the old Dutch
    authorities down to the present is set out in detail. The
    doctrine has not been as rigid as in Britain.

6. MIGNAULT, P.B. "The Authority of Decided Cases", (1925), 3 Can.
    B.R., 1: comments thereon at pp. 109, 138, 349: a brief
    review is given of the position in England and France and
    then a more detailed account of the position in Quebec.

7. FRIEDMANN, W. "Stare Decisis at Common Law and under the Civil
    Law of Quebec", (1953), 31 Can.B.R., 723: Canadian courts
    have adopted the main features of English practice. Even in
    Quebec there is a closer approach to it than to the French
    doctrine.

8. MacGUIGAN, M.R. "Precedent and Policy in the Supreme Court"
    (1967), 45 Can.B.R., 627: this article reviews in detail the
    attitude towards stare decisis in Canada since the abolition
    of appeals to the Privy Council and the likely effect of the
    overthrow by the House of Lords of the doctrine of binding-
    ness with regard to themselves.

9. DAVIDSON, C.G. "Stare Decisis in Louisiana", (1932-33), 7 Tul.
    L.R., 100: this shows how stare decisis has been adopted.

10. IRELAND, G. "The Use of Decisions by United States Students of
    Civil Law", (1933-34), 8 Tul.L.R., 358: this gives account
    of how decisions are used in civilian systems.

1. WALTON, F.P. "The Relationship of the Law of France to the
   Law of Scotland", (1902), 14 Jur.R., 17: this draws
   attention to the growing gulf between the two systems since
   Scots Law is increasingly becoming a case-law system.

2. GARDNER, J.C. "A Comparison of the Doctrine of Judicial
   Precedent in American Law and in Scots Law", (1940), 26 Am.
   B.A.J., 774: the position in the two countries is summarised
   and it is shown that the Scots practice is more flexible
   than the English.

3. WALKER, D.M. "A Note on Precedent", (1949), 61 Jur.R., 283:
   this gives a demonstration that the bulk of cases quoted in
   Scots courts come from this century.

4. BROWN, L.N. "The Sources of Spanish Civil Law", (1956), 5
   I.C.L.Q., 364: this explains the nature and the position of
   "legal doctrine".

Codification

5. POUND, R. Jurisprudence, (West Publishing Co., 1959), III,
   chap. 19: the question of codification is reviewed fully.

6. AUSTIN, J. Lectures in Jurisprudence, (5th ed., R. Campbell,
   J. Murray, 1885), II, pp. 660-680: Austin supports
   codification and considers the French and Prussian codes.

7. FRANK, J.N. Law and the Modern Mind, (Stevens & Sons, Ltd.,
   1949), chap. 17: a code cannot dispense with judge-made law.

8. CALVERT, H. "The Vitality of Case-law under a Criminal Code",
   (1959), 22 M.L.R., 621: codification does not dispense with
   case-law or with the necessity for it.

9. LLOYD, D. "Codifying English Law", (1949), 2 C.L.P., 155: this
   discusses the possibility of codifying English Law.

10. LLOYD, D. in The British Commonwealth. The Development of its
    Laws and Constitutions, G.W. KEETON and (edd.) (Stevens &
    Sons, Ltd., 1955), I, pp.34-35: a summary of the above.

11. WRIGHT, R.A. "The Common Law in its Old Home", in Legal Essays
    and Addresses, (Cambridge University Press, 1939), pp. 338-
    341: this points out the difficulties that arise even with
    codified law, and that codification is not a universal
    panacea.

12. SALMOND, J.W. "The Literature of the Law", (1922), 22 Col.L.R.,
    197: this includes a discussion of the possibility of

codifying the Common Law.

1. FULLER, L.L. "American Legal Realism", (1934), 82 U. Pa.L.R.,
   429, at pp. 438-442: the development of the Common Law is
   inhibited by the absence of "doctrinal bridges"; a code
   would provide these.

2. BEST, W.M. "Codification of the Laws of England", (1856),
   Trans. Jur.S., 209: the principle of codification is unsound,
   amendment and consolidation is preferable.

3. CHALMERS, M.D. "An Experiment in Codification", (1886), 2 L.Q.
   R., 125: this considers the arguments against codification
   in the light of the Bills of Exchange Act, 1882.

4. CHALMERS, M.D. "Codification of Mercantile Law", (1903), 19 L.
   Q.R., 10: a continuation of the above thesis.

5. DOWDALL, H.C. "Suggestions for the Codification of the Law of
   General Average", (1895), 11 L.Q.R., 35: a draft of the
   proposed Code with explanatory notes.

6. STONE, H.F. "Some Aspects of the Problem of Law Simplification",
   (1923), 23 Col.L.R., 319: this gives consideration to the
   question of codification and argues for a restatement of the
   law.

7. GRUEBER, E. "Holtzendorff's Encyclopädie", (1885), 1 L.Q.R.,
   62: the possibility of a codification of English Law on the
   lines of "Holtzendorff" is explored.

8. AMOS, M.S. "The Code Napoleon and the Modern World", (1928),
   10 J.C.L., (3rd Ser.), 222: this a of general interest as
   providing some account of the operation of the Code in
   France and elsewhere.

9. SCARMAN, L.G. "Codification and Judge-made Law. A problem of
   Co-existence", (University of Birmingham, Faculty of Law,
   1966): the establishment of the Law Commission is a historic
   event. The Chairman of the Law Commission considers the task
   ahead of them and the creative task the judiciary will have
   to play under a codified system.

10. SMITH, T.B. "Unification of Law in Britain: Problems of Co-
    ordination", [1967] The Jur. Rev., 97: following the estab-
    lishment of the Law Commission, the problems of unification
    are considered at three different levels, national, regional
    and universal.

L E G I S L A T I O N

1. MAITLAND, F.W. The Constitutional History of England, (Cambridge University Press, 1908), pp. 251-275, 281-288, 297-301, 330-336, 381-382: this is quite the best account of the historical struggle between Parliament and the prerogative for supreme legislative authority.

2. DICEY, A.V. The Law of the Constitution, (10th ed., by E.C.S. Wade; London, Macmillan & Co., Ltd., 1961), chaps. 1 and 13: the classic exposition of Parliamentary supremacy is to be found in these chapters, including the contention that Parliamentary sovereignty favours the rule of law and vice versa.

3. WADE, E.C.S. Introduction to A.V. Dicey, The Law of the Constitution, (supra), pp. xxxiv-xcvi: this is an essential corrective to and a modernisation of Dicey's views. There is a full discussion of the relationship between Parliament and the courts with the conclusion that the courts cannot control legislative procedure. There is also a discussion of the position in Commonwealth countries.

Development and Nature of Sovereignty

4. ALLEN, C.K. Law in the Making, (7th ed., Oxford, 1964), pp. 426-469: this is a general account, including a discussion of possible limitations on the power of Parliament, the scope and duration of legislation, and an explanation of "codifying" and "consolidating" statutes.

5. McILWAIN, C.H. The High Court of Parliament and its Supremacy, (Yale University Press, 1910), chaps. 2, 3 and 5: the part played by the idea of a "fundamental law" in early times is recounted, and how Parliamentary sovereignty developed. He stresses that originally the legislative functions of the "High Court of Parliament" were not distinct from its judicial functions, and demonstrates that the evolution of the current doctrine of Parliamentary sovereignty was the unhistorical result of strife, not of growth.

6. BARRACLOUGH, G. "Law and Legislation in Medieval England", (1940), 56 L.Q.R., 75: this points out that the developments between the 13th and 15th centuries ultimately determined the issue in the struggle for legislative power. It is when certain processes came to be reserved for different types of royal activities that it became possible to distinguish between the legislative, judicial and executive functions.

1. WINFIELD, P.H. The Chief Sources of English Legal History, (Harvard University Press, 1925), pp. 71-74, 84 et seq.: this account of ancient statutes shows how the judges as well as the Council and Parliament occasionally had a hand in their making.

2. LUCAS, W.W. "The Co-operative Nature of English Sovereignty", (1910), 26 L.Q.R. 54, 247, 349: this detailed inquiry, beginning with Teutonic and Anglo-Saxon times, shows that the king never had ruled entirely on his own.

3. HOLDSWORTH, W.S. A History of English Law, (Methuen & Co., Ltd.,), II, pp. 435-446: this gives an account of how the idea developed that the king should consult others when legislating, and the results of this development are considered.

4. HOLDSWORTH, W.S. Sources and Literature of English Law, (Oxford, 1925), chap. 2: he makes the important point that although in medieval times the law was regarded as being fundamental, there was never a doctrine that Parliament could not alter the law; the most that lawyers might do was to disregard an Act which violated fundamental law. He also shows how originally the manner and form of legislating was uncertain, and how in the 14th and 15th centuries these began to be clarified; and the effect of this development is considered.

5. MARSHALL, G. Parliamentary Sovereignty and the Commonwealth, (Oxford, 1957), chap. 5: this gives a detailed historical review of the doctrine of Parliamentary sovereignty and the limitations thereon.

6. PLUCKNETT, T.F.T. Statutes and their Interpretation in the First Half of the 14th Century, (Cambridge University Press, 1922), chaps. 4 and 6: in the first of these chapters there is an inquiry how far the common law was regarded as fundamental law; in the second there is an account of how courts might ignore statutes, but not hold them void.

7. PLUCKNETT, T.F.T. "Bonham's Case and Judicial Review", (1926-27), 40 Harv.L.R., 30: this demonstrates how COKE, C.J. in Bonham's case misrepresented the authorities. These show that statutes had been ignored rather than held void. There is also a detailed account of the extent to which later judges claimed the power of review.

8. PLUCKNETT, T.F.T. A Concise History of the Common Law, (5th ed., Butterworth & Co., Ltd., 1956), pp. 318-325: 330-333: these pages provide a valuable general account of the

position of legislation from the earliest times, and of
the judicial attitude towards it.

1. THORNE, S.E. "Dr. Bonham's Case", (1938), 54 L.Q.R. 543:
    this is a detailed discussion of the case to show that
    COKE, C.J., was perhaps only refusing to follow a statute
    which was absurd on the face of it on the ground of
    repugnancy. His authorities certainly supported no doctrine
    of a higher law by virtue of which statutes could be held
    void.

2. THORNE, S.E. Introduction to A Discourse upon the Exposition
    & Understanding of Statutes, with Sir T. Egerton's Additions,
    (Huntington Lib., 1942), pp. 85-92: Bonham's case is further
    discussed and the disappearance of the medieval idea is
    outlined.

3. GOUGH, J.W. Fundamental Law in English Constitutional History,
    (Oxford, 1955), chaps. 3 and 6: this discussion of Bonham's
    case seeks to show that to "adjudge a statute void" meant
    only to interpret it strictly so that the case falls
    outside it. In the second chapter there is an account of
    the development of Parliamentary sovereignty in the 17th
    century.

4. LEWIS, J.U. "Sir Edward Coke (1552-1633): His Theory of
    'Artificial Reason' as a Context for Modern Basic Legal
    Theory" (1968) 84 L.Q.R. 330: COKE'S assertion in Bonham's
    Case that the common law can control Acts of Parliament
    when they go against common right and reason was more than
    rhetoric. It reflects his idea of law as a rational ordinance
    commanding obedience by virtue of being reasonable and hence
    just.

5. HAVIGHURST, A.F. "The Judiciary and Politics in the Reign of
    Charles II", (1950), 66 L.Q.R. 62, 229; "James II and the
    Twelve Men in Scarlet", (1953) 69 L.Q.R. 522: both these
    discuss the attitude of the judges during the Restoration
    period.

6. KEETON, G.W. "The Judiciary and the Constitutional Struggle,
    1660-1688", (1962) 7 J.S.P.T.L. (N.S.), 56: the judges,
    though not subservient, upheld the prerogative, but even
    they were not prepared to support all James II's claims.
    (See also G.W. KEETON, "Judge Jeffreys as Chief Justice of
    Chester, 1680-83", (1961) 77 L.Q.R. 36).

7. LEDERMAN, W.R. "The Independence of Judiciary", (1956) 34 Can.
    B.R., 769, 1139: the first part traces the relation between
    the Crown and the judges from early times down to the

present. The second part deals with the position in Canada.

1. BLACKSTONE, W. Commentaries on the Laws of England, (16th ed. 1825), I, pp. 90-91, 160-161: although he talks of statute being void if it is impossible, absurd or contrary to reason, he adds that he knows of no power to control it. He also makes the point that the consent of the King, Lords and Commons are all necessary to constitute a valid statute.

2. STEPHEN, J.F. Commentaries on the Laws of England, (21st ed., L.C. Warmington, Butterworth & Co., Ltd., 1950), III, pp. 288-291: this is a brief discussion of what the sovereignty of Parliament means and how it might become a danger to the supremacy of law.

3. MacDERMOTT, J.C. Protection from Power under English Law, (Stevens & Sons, Ltd., 1957), chap. 3: there is no fundamental rule to which the British Parliament has to conform. There is a discussion of how the dangers consequent upon this might be controlled.

4. QUEKETT, A.S. "The Action of Parliamentary Sovereignty upon Local Government", (1919), 35 L.Q.R. 163: this is only of general interest as showing how Parliament has recast executive action in this sphere.

5. BARTLETT, C.A.H. "The Sovereignty of the People", (1921), 37 L.Q.R. 497: this is a general discussion of the influence of the people on the origin of sovereignty: (cf. the doctrine of mandate).

6. CORWIN, E.S. "The 'Higher Law' Background of American Constitutional Law", (1928-29), 42 Harv.L.R., 149, 365: higher law from an American point of view is discussed.

7. McILWAIN, C.H. Constitutionalism and the Changing World, (Cambridge University Press, 1939), chaps. 2-3: sovereignty is a juristic concept and has no application outside law. This is a general discussion, which includes the views of a wide range of writers.

8. COHEN, H.E. Recent Theories of Sovereignty, (University of Chicago Press, 1937): the views of various modern writers are considered. At the end of the book the contradictory tendencies today and the future of theories on sovereignty are touched on.

9. GIERKE, O. Political Theories of the Middle Age, (trans. F.W. Maitland, Cambridge University Press, 1900), chaps. 5, 6, and pp. 92-93: the germ of sovereignty arose in the

12th century. The idea of popular sovereignty in State and
Church is traced, and beginnings of modern sovereignty are
touched on at the end.

1. MERRIAM, C.E. History of the Theory of Sovereignty since
    Rousseau, (The Columbia University Press, 1900): this is a
    useful reference work. The theories of various writers are
    considered, and the general development of ideas on
    sovereignty is considered at the end.

2. POLLOCK, F. An Introduction to the History of the Science of
    Politics, (Macmillan & Co., 1895), chap. 4: doctrines of
    sovereignty are considered in the course of a discussion of
    political theory.

On the points raised in the Prince of Hanover's case, the following
might be consulted:

3. PARRY, C. Note on the Decision at First Instance in [1955]
    C.L.J. 142: attention is drawn to the possible effect of
    the Royal Marriages Act, 1772.

4. NOTE in (1956), 72 L.Q.R. 5: this comments on the Court of
    Appeal's decision.

5. FARRAN, C.D'O. "An Unusual Claim to British Nationality",
    (1956), 19 M.L.R. 289: the Court of Appeal's decision is
    approved.

6. PARRY, C. "Further Considerations upon the Prince of Hanover's
    Case", (1956), 5 I.C.L.Q., 61: the questions involved in
    the Court of Appeal's decision are examined in detail.

7. SMITH, T.B. "British Nationality and the Union of 1707",
    (1956), S.L.T. 89: this note on the Court of Appeal's
    decision, draws attention to the possible effect on the
    Act of Anne of the Act of Union, 1707.

8. SMITH, T.B. Studies Critical and Comparative, (W. Green &
    Son, Ltd., 1962), pp. 24-27: this is a brief discussion of
    the question in the light of the decision in the House of
    Lords.

9. MITCHELL, J.D.B. "The Unimportance of the Case of Prince
    Ernest", (1957), 20 M.L.R. 270: this note on the decision
    of the House of Lords discusses principally what influence
    the Act of Union, 1707, would have had on the case, and
    the effect of disregarding the question.

10. PARRY, C. Note on the Decision of the House of Lords in [1957]

C.L.J. 1.

Limits on Parliamentary Sovereignty

1. MARSHALL, G. Parliamentary Sovereignty and the Commonwealth, (Oxford 1957); chaps. 2-4: these chapters contain a discussion of the Austinian idea of sovereignty, with special reference to illimitability of sovereign power; the power of judicial review, including the rule as to manner and form of legislating and the enrolled bill rule.

2. BENTHAM, J. A Fragment on Government, in Works, (ed. J. Bowring, William Tait, Edinburgh, 1843), I, p. 283 et seq: this is a comment on Blackstone; but he makes the important point that the supreme governor's authority is indefinite unless limited by express convention. Any excess of it would not then be acceptable. He also makes the point that to say that legislation could be held void is to give a controlling power to the judiciary.

3. JENNINGS, W.I. The Law and the Constitution, (5th ed., University of London Press, Ltd., 1959), chap. 4: this includes a discussion of the conclusiveness of the Parliamentary roll and the argument that the legislature can bind itself to observe a particular manner and form for legislating.

4. WADE, H.W.R. "The Basis of Legal Sovereignty", [1955] C.L.J. 172: this develops the argument that Parliament cannot bind itself to observe a particular manner and form for legislating because of the unalterable rule that the courts will always apply the latest statute.

5. JENNINGS, W.I. Parliament, (2nd ed., Cambridge University Press, 1957), chap. 1: this gives a general introduction to the authority of a statute and of the influence of public opinion on Parliament.

6. HOOD PHILLIPS, O. Constitutional and Administrative Law, (4th ed., Sweet & Maxwell, Ltd., 1967), chap. 3: a brief history of the doctrine of Parliamentary supremacy is provided, and the point made that it is based on recognition by the people and the courts. There is also a discussion of the limitations on Parliament's power, both from a practical point of view and also with regard to subject-matter and the manner and form of legislating.

7. KEIR, D.L. and LAWSON, F.H. Cases in Constitutional Law, (4th ed., Oxford, 1954), pp. 1-8: this is a general account. Elsewhere in the book are extracts from the Bilston

Corporation case, <u>Bradlaugh</u> v. <u>Gossett</u>, <u>Harris</u> v. <u>Minister</u>
<u>of the Interior</u> and from the Statute of <u>Westminster</u>.

1. HEUSTON, R.F.V. "Sovereignty" in <u>Oxford Essays in Jurispru-</u>
   <u>dence</u>, (ed. A.G. Guest, Oxford University Press, 1961),
   chap. 7: the rules regulating the composition and functioning of the sovereign are anterior to it. The courts may
   question the validity of a statute on grounds of composition
   or procedure, but not on the area of statutory power.

2. HART, H.L.A. <u>The Concept of Law</u>, (Oxford, 1961), chaps. 4, 6
   and pp. 144-150: this book should be read as a whole; but
   relevant to the present topic the point is made that legislative authority rests on the acceptance of a rule giving
   the sovereign the right to give orders and that this is an
   ultimate rule. Requirements as to manner and form are not
   limitations on sovereign power. There is also some discussion
   of Commonwealth problems and how far Parliament can be bound.

3. SIDGWICK, H. <u>Elements of Politics</u>, (2nd ed., Macmillan & Co.,
   Ltd., 1897), p. 627: sovereign power may be unlimited in
   the sense that there is no law which it cannot alter. But
   the very structure of a supreme legislature may limit its
   competence, and it may also be so limited by conditions
   determining its procedure.

4. FULLER, L.L. <u>The Morality of Law</u>, (Yale Unviersity Press, 1964)
   pp. 113-17: parliamentary supremacy is considered with special
   reference to Dicey's classic discussion of it. The point is
   also made that parliament only attains its superior position
   by subjecting itself to the law of its own internal procedure.

5. GRAY, J.C. <u>The Nature and Sources of the Law</u>, (2nd ed.,
   R. Gray, The Macmillan Co. of New York, 1921), pp. 74 <u>et</u>
   <u>seq</u>., 152-158, 161-170, 189-197: where sovereignty is
   vested in a collection of people, such persons are combined
   for action according to rules and will be obeyed only while
   they act in accordance with them. There is also a general
   discussion of the nature of statute and whether publication
   is a constitutive fact. The last section deals with
   desuetude and unrepealability.

6. BRYCE, J. <u>Studies in History and Jurisprudence</u>, (Oxford, 1901),
   I, pp. 206-207: this argues that even an Act of Parliament
   which embodies the constitution in a fundamental statute can
   itself be repealed.

7. POLLOCK, F. <u>A First Book of Jurisprudence</u>, (6th ed., Macmillan
   & Co., Ltd., 1929), Part II, chap. 3: this is an orthodox
   exposition of Parliamentary sovereignty, including a

distinction between legal sovereignty and political power.

1. LASKI, H.J. A Grammar of Politics, (4th ed., Allen & Unwin,
   Ltd., 1938), chap. 2: the evolution of the modern state is
   analysed historically and there is a discussion of the
   limitations that exist on sovereignty and need for these.

2. DODD, W.F. "Political Safeguards and Judicial Guarantees",
   (1915), 15 Col.L.R.. 293: the various ways in which the
   Judiciary controls legislation in the United States are
   discussed.

3. DODD, W.F. "Judicially Non-enforceable Provisions of
   Constitutions", (1932), 80 U.Pa.L.R., 54: this contains a
   discussion of the limitations relating to manner and form
   and those embodied in the text of a constitution as applied
   in the United States.

4. McWHINNEY, E. Judicial Review in the English-speaking World,
   (2nd ed., University of Toronto Press, 1960), chaps. 2, 6
   and 10: this general account begins with Dicey's view of
   the limits on Parliamentary power; and there is also a
   discussion of Parliamentary sovereignty and the role of the
   judiciary.

5. ROSS, A. On Law and Justice, (Stevens & Sons, Ltd., 1958),
   pp. 78-84: an enactment has force of law only if it has
   been made in conformity with the proper procedure and within its sphere of competence. A change in the ultimate
   authority is a purely social-psychological fact lying outside the province of the law.

6. SALMOND, J.W. Jurisprudence, (12th ed., P.J. Fitzgerald,
   Sweet & Maxwell, Ltd., 1966), pp. 115-130: a general account
   is given of legislation.

7. MIDDLETON, K.W.B. "Sovereignty in Theory and Practice", (1952),
   64 Jur.R., 135: the question what is meant by sovereignty is
   discussed and the conclusion is reached that sovereignty is
   not inconsistent with control by law. It is inconsistent
   with legal subordination to someone else.

8. GILMOUR, D.R. "The Sovereignty of Parliament and the European
   Commission of Human Rights" [1968] P.L., 62: the European
   Convention on Human Rights has the effect of subordinating
   Acts of Parliament to judicial review according to a set of
   international norms. The working of this is considered in
   relation to a set of decisions concerning the Iron and Steel
   Act 1967.

1. BROTHWOOD, M. "Parliamentary Sovereignty and U.K. Entry",
   (1968), 118 New L.J., 415: membership of the Common Market
   will involve modification of present ideas of Parliamentary
   supremacy. The nearest parallel is said to be the position
   of Parliament with regard to the Dominions after the
   Statute of Westminster 1931.

2. Legal and Constitutional Implications of United Kingdom
   Membership of the European Communities, (H.M. Stationary
   Office, 1967, Cmnd. 3301): the various institutions of the
   European Community and the differences between regulations,
   directives, recommendations and opinions are explained.
   Importance attaches to paras. 22-23, which discuss the
   implications of Community law which has direct internal
   effect. It is said that such law will have internal effect
   by virtue of an enabling Act of Parliament.

Judicial Review

3. LLOYD, W.H. "Pylkington's Case and its Successors", (1921),
   69 U.Pa.L.R., 20: this discusses how far the observance
   of the requirements of a statute may be insisted upon by
   the courts and how far the enrolment of a statute is
   conclusive.

4. ROSTOW, E.V. "The Democratic Character of Judicial Review",
   (1952-53), 66 Harv.L.R., 193: the power of judicial review
   is essential. He examines the matter primarily from the
   American angle.

5. ABRAHAM, H.J. The Judicial Process, (New York and Oxford
   University Press, 1962), chaps. 7-9: the power of the
   Supreme Court of the United States to declare Acts void is
   explained, the arguments for and against it are set out,
   and the part which such a power should play is considered.
   This account is useful in providing a contrast with the
   position in Great Britain.

6. LOVELL, C.R. "The Growth of Judicial Review in the United
   States", (1955), B.S.A.L.R., 107: it is maintained that
   the power of review in America had no constitutional basis
   and developed apart from the Constitution because it was
   inherent in the form of government.

7. DIETZE, G. "America and Europe - Decline and Emergence of
   Judicial Review", (1958), 44 Vir.L.R., 1233; reprinted in
   (1959), 76 S.A.L.J., 398: this historical account shows
   how the power of judicial review is essential to the
   freedom of the individual.

1. HAINES, C.G. "Judicial Review of Legislation in Canada", (1914-15) 28 Harv.L.R., 565: judicial review in Canada and America is considered historically. This comparative examination is especially interesting on the view taken of the function of the Judicial Committee of the Privy Council.

2. CAHILL, F.V. Judicial Legislation, (The Ronald Press Co., New York, 1952), chap. 3: the power of judicial review in America is explained in detail.

3. BARNETT, J.D. "External Evidence of the Constitutionality of Statutes", (1924), 58 Am.L.R., 88: this considers, with reference to America, how the courts inform themselves as to the facts behind the law.

4. DICKINSON, J. Administrative Justice and the Supremacy of Law in the United States, (Harvard University Press, 1927), especially chaps. 2, 4 and 5: this is of general interest as showing the position in America.

5. FINKELSTEIN, M. "Judicial Self-limitation", (1923-24), 37 Harv.L.R., 338; "Further Notes on Judicial Self-limitation" (1925-26), 39 Harv.L.R., 221: the reluctance of judges themselves to interfere in "political questions" is investigated.

6. GRANT, J.A.C. "Judicial Control of Legislative Procedure in California", (1948-49), 1 Stan.L.R., 428: this is of general interest. It deals with the situation that arose in California in 1925 when the courts declined to challenge a statute on the ground that it was for the legislature to determine whether a bill had been properly passed or not.

Problems Involving the Union with Scotland and Ireland

7. MARSHALL, G. "What is Parliament? The Changing Concept of Parliamentary Sovereignty", (1954), 2 Pol.S., 193: MacCormick's case is considered in the light of the position as regards the Commonwealth. The Parliament which can legislate for the United Kingdom is not the Parliament which, after the Statute of Westminster, can legislate for the Dominions. Similarly, the United Kingdom Parliament is not the body that can alter the Treaty of Union.

8. MARSHALL, G. "Parliamentary Supremacy and the Language of Constitutional Limitation", (1955), 67 Jur.R., 62: Parliamentary supremacy is discussed with reference to the composition of legislative bodies and methods of functioning.

1. MIDDLETON, K.W.B. "New Thoughts on the Union between England and Scotland", (1954), 66 Jur.R., 37: Lord Cooper's dicta in MacCormick's case are considered in detail, together with the hypothesis on which the Treaty of Union is to be regarded as a fundamental law.

2. SMITH, T.B. "Two Scots Cases", (1953), 69 L.Q.R. pp. 512-516: this section deals with MacCormick's case and considers whether Parliament is competent to alter the Treaty of Union.

3. SMITH, T.B. British Justice: the Scottish Contribution, (Stevens & Sons, Ltd., 1961), pp. 201-213: this considers possible fallacies underlying both the Scots and English attitudes towards the Treaty of Union. The Union is more than a treaty and more than ordinary legislation.

4. SMITH, T.B. "The Union of 1707 as Fundamental Law", (1951) P.L. 99; Studies Critical and Comparative, (W. Green & Son, Ltd., Edinburgh, 1962), chap. 1: this considers the unique nature of the Treaty and the power of the courts when a statute violates its terms.

5. SMITH, T.B. The United Kingdom, (Stevens & Sons, Ltd., 1955), pp. 641-650: these pages give a brief account of the significance and implications of the Union and a short discussion of MacCormick's case.

6. DICEY, A.V. and RAIT, R.S. Thoughts on the Scottish Union, (Macmillan & Co., Ltd., 1920), pp. 19-23, 242-243: Dicey here modifies to some extent the extreme position which he had adopted previously on the sovereignty of Parliament.

7. ANSON, W.R. "The Government of Ireland Bill and the Sovereignty of Parliament", (1886), 2 L.Q.R. 427: it is argued that the Bill amounted to an impairment of the sovereignty of Parliament.

8. JOHNSTON, W.J. "The English Legislature and the Irish Courts", (1924), 40 L.Q.R. 91: this is of general interest. It consists of a historical account of the relations between the two bodies.

Problems Involving the Commonwealth

9. MARSHALL, G. Parliamentary Sovereignty and the Commonwealth, (Oxford, 1957), chaps. 6-11: these deal with the history of the Statute of Westminster, and are followed by detailed discussions of the position with reference to each of the Dominions. The final chapter contains a fully documented

account of the South African crisis.

1. JENNINGS, W.I. Constitutional Laws of the Commonwealth, (3rd
   ed., Oxford, 1957), extracts from the relevant cases are
   set out, including Trethowan's case, Krause v. Commisioners
   for Inland Revenue, Moore v. Att.-Gen. for the Irish Free
   State, British Coal Corp. v. R., Ndlwana v. Hofmeyer N.O.,
   and some of the South African "crisis" cases. Pp. 124 et
   seq.: the effect of the Statute of Westminster is discussed.

2. LATHAM, R.T.E. "The Law and the Commonwealth", in W.K. HANCOCK:
   Survey of British Commonwealth Affairs, (Oxford University
   Press, 1937), pp. 522-95, (reproduced in facsimile in 1949):
   where the sovereign is any but a single person, the
   designation of the sovereign must include a statement of
   the rules for the ascertainment of its will and these are
   logically prior to it. There is a discussion of the position
   obtaining within each Commonwealth country as at 1937. Of
   especial interest is the analysis of the position in South
   Africa and the Irish Free State. Latham is probably the
   first person to suggest a "local root" for their separate
   legal systems.

3. KEITH, A.B. The Government of the British Empire, (Macmillan
   & Co., Ltd., 1935), pp. 30-48: these pages contain a
   general account of the developments leading to the Statute
   of Westminster.

4. ver LOREN van THEMAAT, H. "The Equality of Status of the
   Dominions and the Sovereignty of the British Parliament",
   (1933), 15 J.C.L., (3rd ser.), 47: the question is discussed
   what the sovereignty of the British Parliament means, and
   the conclusion is reached that it is not possible to
   maintain unlimited sovereignty as well as the equality of
   the Dominions with Great Britain.

5. DIXON, O. "The Law and the Constitution", (1935), 51 L.Q.R.
   590: this discusses the working arrangement that was
   effected between the supremacy of the Crown, of the Law
   and of Parliament, and how this has been transplanted
   overseas. The law prescribes the conditions which have to
   be fulfilled in making statutes, but on the question what
   may be accomplished by a statute Parliament is supreme over
   the law. With regard to the Statute of Westminster he
   concludes that it has restricted the power of the British
   Parliament to legislate for the Commonwealth.

6. JENNINGS, W.I. "The Statute of Westminster and Appeals to
   the Privy Council" (1936), 52 L.Q.R. 173: British Coal
   Corp. v. R., and Moore v. Att.-Gen. for the Irish Free

State are discussed in the light of the Statute of
Westminster.

1. McWHINNEY, E. "'Sovereignty' in the United Kingdom and the
    Commonwealth Countries at the Present Day", (1953), 68
    Pol.Sc.Q., 511: did the Statute of Westminster create
    Dominion status, or was it only declaratory of a fundamental
    change that had taken place? The gap between these views is
    brought out in the South African crisis.

2. OYLER, P.A., KENNEDY, W.P.M. and MacDONALD, V.C. "British
    Coal Corporation and Others v. The King: Three Comments",
    (1935), 13 Can.B.R., 615: these are three different
    commentaries on this case.

3. FRIEDMANN, W. "Trethowan's Case, Parliamentary Sovereignty,
    and the Limits of Legal Change", (1950-51), 24 Aust.L.J.,
    103: the case is examined in detail and the conclusion is
    that limitations as to manner and form apply to sovereign
    Parliaments as well as to non-sovereign Parliaments. There
    is also an inquiry into the extent to which courts will
    interfere.

4. SAWER, G. "Injunction, Parliamentary Process, and the
    Restriction of Parliamentary Competence", (1944), 60 L.Q.R.
    83: the Bilston Corporation and Trethowan cases are
    compared with reference to the manner and form rule.

5. SAWER, G. in The Commonwealth of Australia, (ed. G.W. Paton,
    Stevens & Sons, Ltd., 1952), pp. 38-45: this deals with
    the constitutional structure and of the Colonial Laws
    Validity Act and of Trethowan's case.

6. SAWER, G. "Referendum to Abolish the Upper House in New
    South Wales", [1961] P.L., 131: the doctrine that courts do
    not interfere in the legislative processes has a limited
    operation in the case of controlled constitutions.
    Trethowan's case and Clayton v. Heffron are compared.

7. GRAY, H. "The Sovereignty of Parliament Today", (1953-54),
    10 Tor.L.J. 54: the juridical basis of Parliamentary
    sovereignty is examined. "Parliament" cannot be defined
    without reference to procedure. Parliament can, therefore,
    bind itself as regards both. The Statute of Westminster
    cannot be repealed without the consent of the Dominions.

8. GRAY, H. "The Sovereignty of the Imperial Parliament", (1960),
    23 M.L.R. 647: the manner and form requirement in Section
    4 of the Statute of Westminster must be complied with
    before legislation will form part of the law of the

Dominions. There is a discussion of the Copyright Owners
Reproduction Society case and the conclusion is that
English courts should also declare that the British
Parliament is incompetent to legislate for the Dominions
without complying with Section 4.

1. BENNION, F.A.R. "Copyright and the Statute of Westminster",
   (1961), 24 M.L.R., 355: this is a reply to H. Gray's
   article (supra) to the extent of pointing out that the
   question whether Section 4 imposes a limitation on the
   British Parliament does not arise in connection with the
   Copyright Owners Reproduction Society case.

2. DIXON, O. "The Common Law as an Ultimate Constitutional
   Foundation", (1957-58), 31 A.L.J., 240: not only did the
   common law pre-exist the Australian system of government,
   but it is the source of the doctrine of supremacy of the
   British Parliament. Hence, constitutional issues involving
   Parliamentary supremacy should be resolved in the context
   of the whole law of which the common law forms a part. See
   also the discussion following the paper, at pp. 246-54.

3. HANKS, P.J. "Re-defining the Sovereign: Current Attitudes to
   Section 4 of the Statute of Westminster", (1968), 42 A.L.J.
   286: the Statute of Westminster lays down an essential
   ingredient for the validity of United Kingdom legislation
   for dominions. Unless its provision are complied with, an
   enactment is not a statute. The dispute between Sir Ivor
   Jennings and Professor H.W.R. Wade is reviewed.

4. MITCHELL, J.D.B. "Sovereignty of Parliament - Yet Again",
   (1963), 79 L.Q.R., 196: the traditional puzzles concerning
   the implications of Parliamentary Sovereignty are re-
   examined in the light of Scottish, Irish and Commonwealth
   experience. The old view of sovereignty is too simple and
   failed to allow for distinctions which are now needed.

5. KENNEDY, W.P.M. "The Imperial Conferences, 1926-30. The
   Statute of Westminster", (1932), 48 L.Q.R., 191; Essays in
   Constitutional Law, (Oxford, 1934), chaps. 6 and 7: this
   gives the background of the Statute of Westminster from a
   Canadian point of view. The interpretation of the Statute
   is also discussed, but before any case-law had arisen.

6. LLOYD, D. Introduction to Jurisprudence, (2nd ed., Stevens &
   Sons, Ltd., 1965), chap. 4: the text concerns mainly the
   Austinian theory, but there are extracts from Bentham and
   Austin and some of the Commonwealth case-law.

On the competence of Dominion and Colonial legislatures to

legislate extra-territorially even before the Statute of
Westminster, see:

1. SALMOND, J.W. "The Limits of Colonial Legislative Power",
   (1917), 33 L.Q.R., 117;

2. SMITH, H.A. "Extra-territorial Legislation", (1923), 1 Can.B.
   R., 338: and "The Legislative Competence of the Dominions",
   (1927), 43 L.Q.R., 378;

3. KEITH, A.B. "Notes on Imperial Constitutional Law", (1923),
   5 J.C.L., (3rd ser.), 274-275.

The South African Crisis

4. COWEN, D.V. Parliamentary Sovereignty and the Entrenched
   Sections of the South Africa Act, (Juta & Co., Ltd., 1951);
   the "entrenched sections" did not depend upon the Colonial
   Laws Validity Act, 1865, and their continued existence does
   not impair the sovereignty of the Union Parliament; a
   detailed discussion of the Trethowan, Moore and Ndlwana
   cases is included.

5. COWEN, D.V. "Legislature and Judiciary: I", (1952), 15 M.L.R.,
   282: this is a full discussion of the "Votes" case and the
   issues involved. The Statute of Westminster has not impaired
   the "entrenched sections". "Legislature and Judiciary: II",
   (1953), 16 M.L.R., 273: this provides a careful examination
   of the various issues and arguments that were involved in
   the conflict.

6. COWEN, D.V. "The Entrenched Sections of the South Africa Act",
   (1953), 70 S.A.L.J., 243: this explains the origin of the
   "entrenched clauses", together with a discussion of the
   cases of Ndobe and Ndlwana.

7. COWEN, D.V. The Foundations of Freedom, (Cape Town and Oxford
   University Press, 1961), chaps. 6 and 7: this gives a
   general discussion of constitutional safeguards and the role
   of the courts, and the pros and cons of the power of
   judicial review.

8. BEINART, B. "The South African Senate", (1957), 20 M.L.R.,
   549: the Senate as originally constituted in the South
   Africa Act, 1909, and its history down to the Senate Act,
   1955, are recounted in detail.

9. BEINART, B. "The South African Appeal Court and Judicial
   Review", (1958), 21 M.L.R., 587: there is a similar account
   of the Appeal Court since 1910 and of the power of review.

1. BEINART, B. "Sovereignty and the Law", (1952), 15 Tydskrif
   vir Hedensdaagse Romeins-Hollandse Reg, 101: certain rules
   are logically anterior to legislation and a legislature
   must comply with them in order to be able to legislate.

2. BEINART, B. "Parliament and the Courts", (1954), B.S.A.L.R.,
   134: it is for the courts to ensure that the legislature
   observes the rules with which it should comply in enacting
   law. Where there is a specific provision governing the
   manner and form of legislation, Parliamentary privilege
   does not exclude the courts when such a provision is
   designed to protect the interests of the outside community.
   The whole matter is examined with reference to British
   Parliamentary development.

3. COWEN, Z. "Parliamentary Sovereignty and the Limits of Legal
   Change", (1952-53), 26 Aust.L.J., 236: this is primarily a
   discussion of the "Votes" case.

4. KEETON, G.W. "The Constitutional Crisis in South Africa",
   (1953), 6 C.L.P., 22: the political background is reviewed
   historically, including a discussion of the cases of
   Ndlwana and Trethowan and Doyle v. Att.-Gen. for New South
   Wales.

5. GRISWOLD, E.N. "The 'Coloured Vote Case' in South Africa",
   (1951-52), 65 Harv.L.R., 1361: this case is discussed in
   relation to the effect of the Statute of Westminster upon
   the "entrenched sections".

6. GRISWOLD, E.N. "The Demise of the High Court of Parliament in
   South Africa", (1952-53), 66 Harv.L.R., 864: the individual
   judgments in the Appellate Division, which declared invalid
   the Act setting up the "High Court of Parliament", are
   analysed.

7. HOOD PHILLIPS, O. Constitutional and Administrative Law, (4th
   ed., Sweet & Maxwell, Ltd., 1967), Appendix, pp. 830-835:
   the "crisis" cases are discussed.

8. POLLACK, W. "The Legislative Competence of the Union
   Parliament", (1931), 48 S.A.L.J., 269: this was written
   before the Statute of Westminster and argues that the
   Colonial Laws Validity Act alone gives efficacy to the
   "entrenched" provisions and that with the repeal of that
   Act, the entrenchment disappears.

9. KEITH, A.B. The Dominions as Sovereign States, (Macmillan & Co.,
   Ltd., 1938), pp. 167-183: this is a general discussion with
   reference to all the Dominions, and stresses the point that

Legislation

the Union of South Africa was a compact between
representatives of the separate colonies.

1. McWHINNEY, E. "The Union Parliament, the Supreme Court and
the 'Entrenched Clauses' of the South Africa Act", (1952),
30 Can.B.R., 692: this gives a historical survey down to
the "Votes" case. The author criticises the purely
positivist approach of the Appellate Division and thinks
that the court should instead have approached the question
in the light of policy considerations, based on a fundamental
compact between the four original colonies. The safeguard
against any repeal of the 'entrenched" provisions could be
found as an integral part of this original agreement.

2. McWHINNEY, E. "Court versus Legislature in the Union of
South Africa: the Assertion of a Right of Judicial Review",
(1953), 31 Can.B.R. 52: the "High Court" case is examined,
as well as the basis of a judicial power of review.

3. McWHINNEY, E. Note on the "High Court Case", (1952), 30 Can.
B.R. 734.

4. McWHINNEY, E. Note on Collins v. Minister of the Interior,
(1957), 35 Can.B.R., 1203: this comments critically on the
positivist approach adopted by the judges.

5. McWHINNEY, E. Judicial Review in the English-speaking World,
(2nd ed., University of Toronto Press, 1960), chap. 6: the
author re-considers the South African crisis and criticises
the positivist approach of the judges. He repeats the thesis
that something in the nature of a fundamental law is
traceable in the country itself as a local root, namely,
the original agreement between the two rival European
peoples.

6. McWHINNEY, E. "La Crise Constitutionnelle de l'Union Sud-
Africaine", (1953), Revue Internationale de Droit Comparé,
542: a detailed treatment is provided of the historical
background to South Africa's position within the
Commonwealth and a discussion of the "crisis" cases: the
positivist approach of the judges to a political issue is
criticised.

7. WADE, H.W.R. "The Senate Act Case and the Entrenched Sections
of the Sourth Africa Act", (1957), 74 S.A.L.J., 160: the
"High Court Case" and the "Senate Case" are discussed.

8. HAHLO, H.R. and KAHN, E. The Union of South Africa. The
Development of its Laws and Constitution, (Stevens & Sons,
Ltd., 1960), pp. 146-163: this is a general review of the

sovereignty of Parliament in South Africa.

1. KAHN, E. in Annual Survey of South African Law, 1951, (Juta & Co., Ltd.), pp. 1-7: the background to the conflict is surveyed historically. Ibid., 1952, pp. 1-28: the "Votes" and "High Court" cases are summarised with a discussion of their implications. Ibid., 1953, pp. 1-4: this gives a brief account of the South Africa Act Amendment Bill, which was dropped, and the Appellate Division Bill. Ibid., 1955, pp. 1-13: this gives an account of the Appellate Division Quorum Act, 1955, and the Senate Act, 1955. Ibid., 1956, pp. 1-18: the whole of the conflict is summarised.

2. HARRIS, D.R. "The Constitutional Crisis in South Africa", (1959), 103 S.J. 995: this is a general review, recalling the attitude of the Nationalist Government in the 1930's.

3. Le MAY, G.H.L. "Parliament, the Constitution and the 'Doctrine of the Mandate'", (1957), 74 S.A.L.J., 33: the argument is that the idea of a mandate is incompatible with the sovereignty of Parliament.

4. MAY, H.J. The South African Constitution, (3rd ed., Allen & Unwin Ltd., 1955), chaps. 2 and 3: a detailed and vivid historical account is given of the events in South Africa down to 1955, especially the history of entrenchment.

5. KENNEDY, W.P.M. and SCHLOSBERG, H.J. The Law and Custom of the South African Constitution, (Oxford University Press, 1935, being the first edition of H.J. May, The South African Constitution, supra), chaps. 1-3: the background to South Africa Act and the general nature of the constitution, especially the powers of the legislature, are examined.

6. ANONYMOUS. "The State and the Judiciary", (1897), 14 Cape L.J., 94: this is an account of the constitutional crisis which was precipitated in the Transvaal by the decision in Brown v. Leyds N.O. and of the consequent attempt by the Boer government to curb the judiciary.

7. GORDON, J.W. "The Judicial Crisis in the Transvaal", (1898), 14 L.Q.R. 343: the crisis referred to above is discussed with reference to the testing power of the judiciary.

8. The following cases may be consulted on the question whether a sovereign legislature can bind intself: The Bribery Commissioner v. Ranasinghe, [1965] A.C. 172; [1964] 2 All E.R. 785; Ellen Street Estates, Ltd. v. Minister of Health, [1934] 1 K.B. 590; Pylkington's Case, Y.B. 33 Hen. VI, 17, pl. 8; Moore v. Att.-Gen. for the Irish Free State, [1935] A.C. 484;

McCawley v. R., [1920] A.C. 691; Att.-Gen. for New South Wales
v. Trethowan, [1932] A.C. 526; R. v. Ndobe, [1930] App.D. 484;
MacCormick v. Lord Advocate, 1953 S.C. 396; British Coal
Corporation v. R., [1935] A.C. 500; Ndlwana v. Hofmeyr N.O.,
[1937] App.D. 229; Copyright Owners Reproduction Society v.
E.M.I. (Australia) Pty, Ltd., (1958) 32 A.L.J.R. 306; Exp.
Bennett; Re Cunningham (1967) 86 W.N. (Pt.2) (N.S.W.) 323;
Duffy v. Ministry of Labour and National Insurance, [1962]
N.I. 6; Krause v. Commissioners for Inland Revenue, [1929]
App.D. 286; Harris v. Minister of the Interior, 1952 (2) S.A.
428 (A.D.); Minister of the Interior v. Harris, 1952 (4) S.A.
769 (A.D.); Collins v. Minister of the Interior, 1957 (1) S.A.
552 (A.D.).

The Rhodesian Crisis

1. PALLEY, C. The Constitutional History and Law of Southern
   Rhodesia 1888-1965 (Oxford: Clarendon Press, 1966): this is
   a considerable work and is valuable in providing a general
   background to the U.D.I. crisis. It gives a detailed and
   revealing analysis of the relations between the United
   Kingdom and Southern Rhodesia.

2. LEIGH, L.H. "Rhodesia after U.D.I.: Some Aspects of a Peaceful
   Rebellion" [1966] P.L. 148: this was written shortly after
   U.D.I. It reviews the constitutional development in Rhodesia
   and the legal possibilities that arise after U.D.I.

3. WELSH, R.S. "The Constitutional Case in Southern Rhodesia"
   (1967) 83 L.Q.R. 64: the judgment of the Court of first
   instance is analysed and criticised in detail. If, as the
   Court held, the 1965 Constitution is invalid and the Court
   continued to recognise the 1961 Constitution, there was no
   ground for the compromise which it adopted.

4. EEKELAAR, J.M. "Splitting the Grundnorm" (1967) 30 M.L.R. 156:
   this article outlines the Rhodesian constitutional
   development down to U.D.I. and summarises the judgment in
   the U.D.I. Case. In its concluding comment the implication
   of the judgment on the acceptance of the criterion of
   validity is dealt with.

5. DIAS, R.W.M. "The U.D.I. Case: the Grundnorm in Travail"
   [1967] C.L.J. 5: in this Note the principal points of the
   judgment are outlined, and there is particular reference to
   the weakness of Kelsen's concept of the Grundnorm and how
   the criterion of validity might be regarded.

6. LANG, A.J.G. "Madzimbamuto and Baron's Case at First Instance"
   [1965] Rhod.L.J. 65: the main grounds of the judgment are

examined. In particular, the court's rejection of the
British Secretary of State's statement, its acceptance of
the doctrine of necessity and its conclusion on the onus of
proof are criticised.

1. PALLEY, C. "The Judicial Process: U.D.I. and the Southern
Rhodesian Judiciary" (1967), 30 M.L.R., 263: judges are
influenced by their values. Biographical sketches of the
judges concerned in the U.D.I. Case are followed by a
critical analysis of the decision.

2. HEPPLE, B.A.; O'HIGGINS,P., TURPIN, C.C. "Rhodesian Crisis:
Criminal Liabilities" [1966] Crim.L.R., 5: the criminal
aspects of U.D.I., especially with regard to treason, are
discussed. See also O. HOOD PHILLIPS: "Rhodesian Crisis:
Criminal Liabilities. A Short Reply", ibid., at p. 68.

3. WHARAM, A. "Treason in Rhodesia", [1967] C.L.J., 189: this
article is of general interest. It considers U.D.I. from
the angle of the offence of treason in English Law.

4. HONORÉ, A.M. "Allegiance and the Usurper", [1967] C.L.J.,
213: the Treason Act 1495 provides that service under a de
facto sovereign is not treason against the de jure
sovereign. Various interpretations of this provision are
considered followed by the author's own interpretation.

5. HONORÉ, A.M. "Reflections on Revolutions", (1967), 2 Ir.Jur.
(N.S.) 268: when there is little chance of the old regime
being restored after a revolution, are judges authorised to
lessen that chance still further by recognising the new
regime ? Possible bases of such authority in an implied
provision in old constitution itself, in natural law, or in
a social or moral duty towards the populace are considered.

6. DIAS, R.W.M. "Legal Politics: Norms behind the Grundnorm",
(1968), 26 C.L.J., 233: the judges have contrived to assert
their independence of the Smith regime while the regime was
asserting its independence of Great Britain. The judgments
of the Appellate Division and of the Privy Council are
examined and their implications on Kelsen's doctrines
considered.

7. EEKELAAR, J.M. "Rhodesia: the Abdication of Constitutionalism"
(1969), 32 M.L.R., 19: this article explains the course of
the litigation that has arisen in connection with U.D.I.,
with particular reference to the judgments in the Appellate
Division and in the Privy Council.

8. BARRIE, G.N. "Rhodesian U.D.I. - an Unruly Horse" (1968) 1

C.I.L.S.A., 110: the judgments in the <u>Grundnorm</u> Case are reviewed so as to show the problem confronting the courts.

1. MACFARLANE, L.J. "Pronouncing on Rebellion: the Rhodesian Courts and U.D.I.", [1968] P.L., 325: all the diferent aspects of the <u>Grundnorm</u> Case are reviewed and examined. The views of the judges on each of them are criticised and the weaknesses and inconsistencies in them exposed. The judges are condemned for failing to measure up to their responsibilities.

2. MACFARLANE, L.J. "Justifying Rebellion: Black and White Nationalism in Rhodesia" [1968] 6 J.Comm.P.S., 54: this may be read for general interest. It deals with the political background to the Rhodesian crisis. Two nationalisms, white and black, were at work demanding rebellion in different ways. See also R. BROWN: "A Comment on L.J. Macfarlane's 'Justifying Rebellion: Black and White Nationalism in Rhodesia'", <u>ibid.</u> 155: Macfarlane's article is criticised on the ground that it does not do full justice to African nationalism.

3. HOPKINS, J.A. "International Law - Southern Rhodesia - United Nations - Security Council", [1967] C.L.J., 1: In this Note the author considers the various resolutions passed by the General Assembly and Security Council and questions their validity.

4. HALDERMAN, J.W. "Some Legal Aspects of Sanctions in the Rhodesian Case", (1968), 17 I.C.L.Q., 672: this is of indirect interest. It deals with the implications of the various actions taken by the United Nations.

5. McDOUGAL, M.S. and REISMAN, W.M. "Rhodesia and the U.N.: the Lawfulness of International Concern", (1968), 62 A.J.I.L., 1: the actions of the United Nations are justified. The various objections to United Nations action put forward on the Rhodesian side are considered <u>seriatim</u> and shown to be unfounded.

6. MARSHALL, H.H. "The Legal Effects of U.D.I.", (1968), 17 I.C.L.Q., 1022: this gives a brief account of the position in Rhodesia before U.D.I. and the events leading up to the <u>Grundnorm</u> Case. The holdings by the Appellate Division and the Privy Council are summarised.

7. The following cases may be consulted on the legality of a revolution: <u>The State</u> v. <u>Dosso</u> (1958), 2 Pak.S.C.R., 180; <u>Uganda</u> v. <u>Commissioner of Prisons</u>, ex p. Matovu, [1966] Eastern Africa L.R., 514; <u>Madzimbamuto</u> v. <u>Larner-Burke</u>, 1968 (2) S.A. 284; [1969] 1 A.C., 645.

S T A T U T O R Y   I N T E R P R E T A T I O N

1. WILLIS, J. "Statute Interpretation in a Nutshell", (1938), 16
   Can.B.R. 1: there are no "rules" of interpretation, but
   only approaches. This is an instructive and critical discussion of the "Literal", "Golden" and "Mischief" Rules and
   of the various presumptions classified according to
   different methods of approach.

2. CORRY, J.A. "Administrative Law and the Interpretation of
   Statutes", (1935-36), 1 Tor.L.J., 286: this contains a
   convincing demonstration of how the finding of facts and
   interpretation influence each other. Even though the
   "intention of the legislature" is a myth, there should be
   judicial co-operation with the legislature. The "Literal
   Rule" is examined in detail with reference to its history
   and its shortcomings.

3. THE LAW COMMISSION AND THE SCOTTISH LAW COMMISSION: The
   Interpretation of Statutes, (H.M. Stationery Office, 1969):
   this gives a useful, detached analysis of the nature of the
   problem, the present status of the so-called "rules" of
   interpretation and presumptions of intent and of the
   relevance, reliability and availability of information
   relating to the contexts of statutes. There is a useful
   bibliography at the end. See also THE LAW COMMISSION AND
   THE SCOTTISH LAW COMMISSION: Published Working Paper on the
   Interpretation of Statutes, (1967), on which it is based.
   For a comment on the "Working Paper", see ANONYMOUS:
   "Statutory Interpretations" (1967), S.L.T., 243.

4. MARSH, N.S. "The Interpretation of Statutes", (1967), 9 J.S.
   P.T.L. (N.S.) 416: a member of the Law Commission explains
   the Commission's approach. Inquiry into statutory interpretation is justified merely because judges approach
   statutes in what they conceive to be the values of society.
   Just as there are shades of meaning, so there are shades of
   ambiguity. The object is to provide more help in marginal
   cases.

Legislative Function

5. Science of Legal Method: Select Essays by Various Authors,
   (trans. E. Bruncken and L.B. Register, Boston Book Co.,
   1917): J.H. WIGMORE, "Preface", pp. xxvi-xxxvi: this is a
   discussion of the relationship between the judiciary and
   legislature. Since the legislative process cannot work
   perfectly some judicial legislation is necessary. There is
   also a discussion of how far legislation can control the
   judges in view of the imperfections of language, and of how

far stare decisis should apply. A. KOCOUREK, "Preface",
pp. lvii-lxvii: this discusses the defects of present
legislative methods and how these might be overcome - by
the use of statistical data as to the problem to be dealt
with as well as data as to the effectiveness of remedies,
the application of historical and comparative methods to
interpret the data and a philosophy to evaluate them.

1. BRADLEY, F.E. "Modern Legislation in the United Kingdom",
   (1894), 10 L.Q.R., 32: strict interpretation is due, not so
   much to perversity, as to ambiguity. Various suggestions
   (some no longer feasible) are offered as to how the problem
   might be eased.

2. HORACK, F.E. "The Common Law of Legislation", (1937-38), 23
   Iowa L.R., 41: legislation, like judge-made law, follows
   precedent. If there is a common law of cases, why not a
   common law of legislation ? A new legislative provision sets
   a pattern, which is copied and extended analogically. A
   predictable development might be traced.

3. COHEN, J. "On the Teaching of 'Legislation'", (1947), 47 Col.
   L.R. 1301: this comments on the failure of law schools to
   train lawyers for the role of "policy makers" and to
   partake in the legislative process and to advise on the
   achievement of legislative ends.

Intention of the Legislature

4. CURTIS, C.P. "A Better Theory of Legal Interpretation", in
   Jurisprudence in Action, (Baker Voorhis & Co., Inc., 1953),
   pp. 135-169: words have no fixed meaning, nor has the
   legislature any "intention". The author of the words has
   no control over them because others have the task of
   applying them to future events. The question is whether the
   choice made by these others out of the range of possible
   meanings is reasonable, and the criteria by which this is
   to be judged transcends the search for intention.

5. PAYNE, D.J. "The Intention of the Legislature in the
   Interpretation of Statutes", (1956), 9 C.L.P., 96: the
   search for legislative intent is a hindrance and not a help.
   A composite body has no single mind, nor can the framers of
   provisions in general words be said to have intended to
   provide for a particular event. Interpretation involves a
   delegation by the legislature of the power to deal with the
   unprovided case.

6. JONES, H.W. "Statutory Doubts and Legislative Intention",
   (1940) 40 Col.L.R., 957: the judicial process is more than

discovery and deduction. The judge is inevitably a
legislator because of the imperfections inherent in
language and the attempt to regulate the future.

1. COHEN, M.R. "The Process of Judicial Legislation", (1914),
    48 Am.L.R. 161, at pp. 178-187: it is impossible to find
    the intentions of members of the legislature. The question
    is not what they intended but what the public are expected
    to act on. The rules of interpretation are guides to the
    judges in making law out of statutes.

2. RADIN, M. "Statutory Interpretation", (1929-30), 43 Harv.L.R.,
    863: in some cases the judge makes up his mind and selects
    the interpretation which justifies it. The question whether
    the legislature envisaged the particular situation is absurd
    because the legislature has no mind. The rule excluding
    resort to extrinsic material makes reference to "intent"
    unnecessary. Even legislative history may not help to decide
    what specific events are to be included.

3. LEVI, E.H. An Introduction to Legal Reasoning, (University of
    Chicago Press, 1948), pp. 19-40: rules of interpretation
    appear to be means of finding legislative intent. A
    detailed account of a particular statute is given to show
    the ambiguity of legislative intent.

4. LLEWELLYN, K.N. Jurisprudence: Realism in Theory and Practice,
    (University of Chicago Press, 1962), pp. 227-229: few
    legislators have any "intention". Even where there is an
    intention, it may be the duty of the tribunal to apply the
    statute narrowly.

5. KELSEN, H. General Theory of Law and State, (trans. A. Wedberg,
    Harvard University Press, 1949), pp. 33-34: the "will" of
    a legislature is a fiction; an analysis of the problem
    follows.

6. HÄGERSTRÖM, A. "Inquiries into the Nature of Law and Morals",
    (ed. K. Olivecrona, trans. C.D. Broad, Almqvist & Wiksell,
    Stockholm, 1953), pp. 74-101: these contain a detailed
    examination of the difficulty of saying that the task of a
    judge is to ascertain the will of the legislature, or of
    saying that the judge's will completes the process.

7. LANDIS, J.M. "A Note on 'Statutory Interpretation'", (1929-
    30), 43 Harv.L.R., 886: this is a reply to M. Radin (supra).
    A statute is a means by which the legislature makes its
    desires known. The intention of the legislature is therefore
    important; the difficulty lies in finding it. The use of
    legislative history and extrinsic material has real

significance in this connection.

1. MacCALLUM, G.C. "Legislative Intent" in Essays in Legal
   Philosophy (ed. R.S. SUMMERS, Basil Blackwell, Oxford, 1968),
   237: the various shades of meaning of the phrase "legislative
   intent" are subjected to lengthy analysis with no clear-cut
   conclusion. The discussion centres on the debate between
   M. Radin and J.M. Landis, and on the value of different
   models of legislative intent.

2. HORACK, F.E. "In the Name of Legislative Intention", (1932),
   38 W.Vir.L.Q. 119: what is meant by legislative intent is
   considered. Although there is no such thing, it is useful
   to interpret statutes as if there were.

3. HOLMES, O.W. "The Theory of Legal Interpretation", (1898-99),
   12 Harv.L.R., 417: the question is not what the legislature
   meant, but what the statute means.

4. STONE, J. Legal Systems and Lawyers' Reasonings, (Stevens &
   Sons, Ltd., 1964), pp. 31-34, 288-292: a legislator cannot
   fix the meaning of words for all future interpreters. The
   most one can say is that he intended that his language
   should be understood according to the common interpretation
   for the time being. This explains the stress laid on the
   ordinary meaning of words and the exclusion of preparatory
   material. At pp. 288-92 an explanation is given, illustrated
   with cases, of how discretion, guided by policy, can come
   into interpretation.

5. COX, A. "Judge Learned Hand and the Interpretation of Statutes",
   (1946-47), 60 Harv.L.R., 370: reference to legislative
   intent is useful in the sense of the purpose to be
   accomplished, but it is a chimera in the sense of the
   meaning of the words used.

6. LOYD, W.H. "The Equity of a Statute", (1910), 58 U.Pa.L.R.,
   76: this used to be a phrase employed in elucidating the
   intention of the legislature. Although the courts do not
   now use it, they apply it.

(Discussions of legislative intent also appear in a good many of
the following references).

General Problems of Interpretation and Judicial Approach.

7. POUND, R. "Common Law and Legislation", (1907-8), 21 Harv.L.
   R. 383: legislation is part of the law and should be
   accepted as such. Four possible attitudes, which courts
   might adopt and their desirability, are discussed.

1. ROSS, A. On Law and Justice, (Stevens & Sons, Ltd., 1958),
    chap. 4: there is a clear demonstration of the semantic
    problems underlying interpretation, followed by a discussion
    of "syntactical", "logical" and "semantic" interpretation.
    A judge does not act automatically. He may adopt various
    attitudes, particularly important being the discussion of
    the pragmatic factors.

2. CROSS, A.R.N. Precedent in English Law, (2nd ed., Oxford,
    1968), pp. 163 et seq.: the courts have applied the analogy
    of interpreting documents. The intention of the legislature
    is a myth. There is some discussion of the chief canons of
    interpretation and some presumptions and of the role of
    stare decisis.

3. POUND, R. "Courts and Legislation", (1915), 7 Am.Pol.Sc.R.,
    361; Science of Legal Method: Select Essays by Various
    Authors, (trans. E. Bruncken and L.B. Register, Boston Book
    Co., 1917), chap. 7: this gives a detailed discussion of
    the three steps involved, (a) finding the rule, (b)
    interpreting the rule, and (c) applying the rule to the
    case. A sociological method of interpretation should be
    employed.

4. POUND, R. Jurisprudence, (West Publishing Co., 1959), III,
    pp. 654-671: there are four possible attitudes which courts
    might adopt towards legislation. The theory that courts
    should only interpret and apply, and the theory that law-
    making is doomed since law resides in the Volksgeist, are
    discussed and rejected.

5. FRIEDMANN, W. Legal Theory, (5th ed., Stevens & Sons, Ltd.,
    1967), pp. 451-462: the problem of statutory interpretation
    is to balance stability with adaptation to changing
    circumstances. For this purpose distinctions should be
    drawn between different types of statutes.

6. FRIEDMANN, W. Law in a Changing Society, (Stevens & Sons, Ltd.,
    1959), pp. 34 et seq.: this discusses the questions whether
    distinctions should be drawn between different kinds of
    statutes, and whether the application of a single set of
    rules to statutes of all kinds is satisfactory.

7. FRIEDMANN, W. "Judges, Politics and the Law", (1951), 29 Can.
    B.R., 811, at pp. 825-834: these provide a further discussion
    on the same line as above.

8. de SLOOVÈRE, F.J. "The Functions of Judge and Jury in the
    Interpretation of Statutes", (1932-33), 46 Harv.L.R., 1086:
    the questions of fact and of law that arise in interpreting

statutes and in applying them are considered.

1. BODENHEIMER, E. Jurisprudence, (Harvard University Press, 1962), pp. 272-280; 347-368: the distinction between the judicial and legislative functions is explained. If the legislative purpose is discoverable, the judges should give effect to it. But if this contemplates wholly different circumstances, restrictive interpretation should be adopted. Pp. 347-368: "historical" and "contemporaneous" interpretation of constitutions are explained.

2. GRAY, J.C. The Nature and Sources of the Law, (2nd ed., R. Gray, The Macmillan Co., New York, 1921), pp. 170-189: it is with the interpretation of the courts that statutes are imposed upon the community. Difficulties in interpretation arise when the legislature did not have any "intent" with regard to the question before the court. Here the judge has to create law by giving to the words the meaning which he would have given them.

3. PITAMIC, L. "Some Aspects of the Problem of Statutory Interpretation", (1933), 19 Am.B.A.J., 582: the problem is primarily a linguistic one since language grows and sense changes. The judges's task is to synthesise the thoughts extracted from the text.

4. AUSTIN, J. Lectures on Jurisprudence, (5th ed., R. Campbell, John Murray, 1885), II, pp. 624-630, 989 et seq.: the literal meaning is the primary index to legislative intent. This is interpretation proper. With it must be contrasted "spurious interpretation", which occurs when a judge extracts a meaning that is not the literal sense of the words and gives to a statute an extensive or restrictive effect.

5. POUND, R. "Spurious Interpretation", (1907), 7 Col.L.R., 379: the Austinian distinction is taken up. "Genuine interpretation" is where the judge attempts to ascertain the intention of the law giver; "spurious interpretation" is where he makes, unmakes or remakes the law. In an age of legislation the latter becomes an anachronism. Its good and bad elements are considered.

6. SNYDER, O.C. Preface to Jurisprudence, (The Bobbs-Merrill Co., Inc., 1954), Part III, chap. 2, pp. 354-366: statutes do not cater for all contingencies. Genuine interpretation is making an application within the framework of the statute - "interstitial" legislation. Statutes not susceptible to genuine interpretation are those conferring a wide discretion and those which are vague.

1. FREUND, E. "Interpretation of Statutes", (1917), 65 U.Pa.L.R.,
    207: there is a discussion of the strict and liberal
    construction of statutes and the use of analogy.

2. FULLER, L.L. The Morality of Law, (Yale University Press,
    1964), pp. 82-91: the idea that legislative intent is
    directed to particular situations is rejected. It is directed
    at some problem. The "mischief" rule is therefore favoured.
    It is also argued that it is better to speak of the "intent
    of the statute" rather than of the legislature or legislators.
    Judicial creativeness, as such, deserves neither praise nor
    blame; it is called into being in effecting a relation between
    the mischief aimed at and the remedy provided.

3. LLOYD, D. Introduction to Jurisprudence, (2nd ed., Stevens
    & Sons, Ltd., 1965), pp. 385-389: the attitude is that the
    common law is the basis of law and that statutes are woven
    into it. There is a brief discussion of the narrow and
    broad approaches. Pp. 435-496: extracts are given from
    Heydon's Case, Seaford Court Estates, Ltd. v. Asher, Magor
    & St. Mellons R.D.C. v. Newport Corporation, W. FRIEDMANN:
    Law and Social Change in Contemporary Britain,
    H.C. GUTTERIDGE: Comparative Law.

4. WILLIAMS, G.L. "Language and the Law", (1945), 61 L.Q.R. 71,
    at pp. 179 et seq., 302-303, 392 et seq; (1946) 62 L.Q.R.
    387, at pp. 402 et seq.: the ambiguities of words are
    discussed and explained. In marginal cases the function of
    the judge must be legislative. There is also a discussion
    of the different kinds of meaning.

5. HART, H.L.A. The Concept of Law, (Oxford, 1961), pp. 123-125:
    with verbally formulated generalisations uncertainties
    occur in particular cases. Canons of interpretation may
    lessen, but cannot remove the uncertainties. It is difficult
    to regulate unambiguously in advance fact-situation that
    are not contemplated.

6. HORACK, F.E. "The Disintegration of Statute Construction",
    in M.R. COHEN and F.S. COHEN: Readings in Jurisprudence and
    Legal Philosophy, (Prentice-Hall, Inc., New York, 1951),
    pp. 524-526: statute interpretation is simply the expression
    of judicial practice. The legislature should provide
    adequate sources of interpretation.

7. EVERSHED, F.R. "The Judicial Process in Twentieth Century
    England" (1961) 61 Co.L.R. 761: statutory interpretation is
    becoming increasingly the task of the judiciary. This
    reduces itself to battles about words rather than the
    application and evolution of principles. In the result law

tends to lose popular support and respect; it also
undermines the spirit of obedience and promotes ingenuity.
A liberal attitude towards interpretation is advocated. It
is also suggested that if parliamentary history were looked
at, this might have the effect of forcing still greater
adherence to the literal rule of interpretation.

1. DIPLOCK, K. "The Courts as Legislators", Presidential Address
    to the Holdsworth Club, 1965: courts describe what they do
    as being "interpretation", but they are legislating most of
    the time, since they have to deal with matters which the
    framers of an Act never contemplated. When statutes try to
    provide in detail for every contingency, this drives the
    courts to adopt a narrow semantic attitude. Where the
    Parliamentary design is clear, the courts should give effect
    to it. Where it is not clear, they are forced back on the
    literal rule. The danger of this is that it becomes a habit
    and the courts act on it even when the Parliamentary
    objective is clear.

2. MACMILLAN, H.P. Law and Other Things, (Cambridge University
    Press, 1938), pp. 147 et seq.: the ambiguity of language
    is discussed with reference to the interpretation of certain
    phrases in decided cases. There is also allusion to a few
    of the canons of interpretation.

3. DICKERSON, F.R. "Statutory Interpretation: Core Meaning and
    Marginal Uncertainty" (1964) 29 Miss.L.R. 1: this study is
    more important in connection with the general problem of
    meaning. Its relevance to statutory interpretation is that
    it reveals the parts played respectively by the meaning of
    words in isolation and in the light of context and purpose,
    and the indispensible relationship between them. Thus, it
    becomes wrong to treat the so-called "literal" and "purpose"
    canons as opposing and alternative approaches.

4. AMOS, M.S. "The Interpretation of Statutes", (1933-35), 5 C.
    L.J. 163: this is of general interest. It deals with the
    unsympathetic attitude of the judges and with drafting.

5. HAWKINS, F.V. "On the Principles of Interpretation with
    Reference especially to the Interpretation of Wills",
    (1858-63), 2 Trans.Jur.S. 298; J.B. THAYER, Preliminary
    Treatise on the Law of Evidence, (Sweet & Maxwell, Ltd.,
    1898), Appendix C: this is of general interest and deals
    with the problem of giving a meaning to the written word.

The "Purpose" Approach

6. DAVIES, D.J.Ll. "The Interpretation of Statutes in the Light

of their Policy by the English Courts", (1935), 35 Col.L.R.,
519: according to Heydon's Case, the judge should co-operate
with the legislature. The reasons for the present restrictive
attitude are discussed. Statutes should be accompanied by
explanatory memoranda.

1. RADIN, M. "Statutory Interpretation", (1929-30), 43 Harv.L.
   R., 863: interpretation according to purpose is not
   necessarily what the legislature intended, but the use to
   which the courts put the statute. The courts should interpret
   statutes by selecting one out of a number of likely
   consequences which the statute might have.

2. RADIN, M. "A Short Way with Statutes", (1942-43), 56 Harv.L.
   R., 388: the main task of the courts should be to implement
   the purpose of the statute. If the purpose is clear the
   implemental part should not be made more important. Both
   the purpose and means are to be found by reading the words
   of the statute; extrinsic material is relevant, but not
   controlling. Heydon's Case is re-stated in a modernised
   form.

3. LASKI, H.J. Note on the Judicial Interpretation of Statutes,
   in Annexe V to the Report of the Committee on Ministers'
   Powers, (1932, Cmd. 4060), pp. 135-137: an independent
   assessment of legislative intent is valuable, but the
   methods employed are defective. Statutes should have
   attached to them explanatory preambles and memoranda.

4. FRANKFURTER, F. "Some Reflections on the Reading of Statutes",
   (1947), 47 Col.L.R., 527: interpretation is neither an
   opportunity for the judge to make words mean what he wants,
   nor an unimaginative ritual. The judges should seek to
   effectuate the aim of the legislature as evinced in the
   wording. To exclude all extrinsic material overlooks the
   fact that enactments live in an environment; on the other
   hand, recourse to legislative history and the like should
   not outweigh the importance of the statute itself.

5. LLEWELLYN, K.N. Jurisprudence: Realism in Theory and Practice,
   (University of Chicago Press, 1962), pp. 227-229: legislation
   is meaningless without reason and purpose. A statute should
   be implemented according to its purpose so as to keep the
   law as a working whole.

6. EKELÖF, P.O. "Teleological Construction of Statutes", in
   (1958) 2 Scand.S.L. 75: if a given situation is so common
   that the authors of the statute must have contemplated it,
   the statute applies to it. If this is not clear, the judge
   should consider the cases to which the statute does apply

and consider what purpose it seeks to achieve with regard
to these. In uncertain cases the statute should be made to
apply so as to fulfil that purpose.

1. COX, A. "Judge Learned Hand and the Interpretation of Statutes",
    (1946-47) 60 Harv.L.R., 370: imprecise words should be
    construed according to the social purpose behind them.
    Legislative history might help, and so might evidence of
    specific applications contemplated by legislative committees.

2. FRANK, J.N. "Words and Music: Some Remarks on Statute
    Interpretation", (1947), 47 Col.L.R., 1259: a literal
    interpretation may sometimes be appropriate, sometimes not.
    A judge should at all times co-operate imaginatively with
    the legislature. Judicial creativeness is inevitable, but
    judges should not let their personalities run riot. The
    importance of finding the facts of each case is stressed.

3. FRANK, J.N. Courts on Trial, Myth and Reality in American
    Justice, (Princeton University Press, 1950), chap. 21: this
    repeats the point that judicial creativeness should be kept
    within proper bounds.

4. FRANK, J.N. Law and the Modern Mind, (Stevens & Sons, Ltd.,
    1949), pp. 279-284: this should be read subject to the above
    two contributions. The personality of the judge is underlined
    and also the importance of determining the facts.

5. BRUNCKEN, E. "Interpretation of the Written Law", (1915), 25
    Yale L.J. 129: in cases of doubt a statute should be
    construed to mean that which the legislator would have
    expressed had he been in possession of the facts of the
    instant case. If there are several possible interpretations
    that one should be selected which will promote maximum
    social harmony.

6. WOOD, J.C.E. "Statutory Interpretation: Tupper and the Queen"
    (1968) 6 Os.H.L.J. 92: the basis of positivism and the
    shortcomings of the "plain meaning" rule of interpretation
    are considered. Law is a purposive enterprise. Therefore,
    statutes should be construed according to the legislative
    purpose.

7. SANDS, C.D. "Statute Construction and National Development"
    (1969) 18 I.C.L.Q. 206: the judicial task with statutes is
    not to discover what the law is, but how to construe it.
    This is a matter which vitally affects the future life of
    a country.

Approach to Particular Types of Statutes

1. JENNINGS, W.I. "Courts and Administrative Law - the
   Experience of English Housing Legislation", (1935-36), 49
   Harv.L.R., 426: this is a detailed demonstration of the
   failure of the restrictive approach which, in this sphere,
   is said to stem from a bias against administrative action.

2. JENNINGS, W.I. "Judicial Process at its Worst", (1937-39), 1
   M.L.R., 111: an account is given of the failure of judicial
   interpretation of the Public Health Acts over forty-six
   years to find a solution to an urgent problem.

3. PORTER, S.L. "Case Law in the Interpretation of Statutes",
   Presidential Address to the Holdsworth Club, 1940: this
   considers the attempts of case-law to adapt the wording of
   the Workmen's Compensation Act to the facts of individual
   situations.

4. DODS, M. "A Chapter of Accidents: an Essay on the History of
   Disease in Workmen's Compensation", (1932), 39 L.Q.R. 60:
   this gives a detailed account of the chaos created by the
   application of the "plain and ordinary" meaning to the words
   "injury" and "accident".

5. de SMITH, S.A. "The Limits of Judicial Review: Statutory
   Discretions and the Doctrine of Ultra Vires", (1948), 11
   M.L.R., 306: judges are more sympathetic now than they
   used to be, but uncertainty is created by the conflicting
   canons of interpretation of statutes conferring discretion.

6. de SMITH, S.A. "Statutory Restriction of Judicial Review",
   (1955), 18 M.L.R., 575: this discusses the different
   judicial attitudes.

7. de SMITH, S.A. Judicial Review and Administrative Action,
   (Stevens & Sons, Ltd., 1959), chaps. 3, especially pp. 58-
   60, and chap. 7: statutory interpretation is discussed in
   relation to the ultra vires rule, and conflicting approaches.

8. WILLIS, J. "Three Approaches to Administrative Law: the
   Judicial, the Conceptual, and the Functional", (1935-36),
   1 Tor.L.J., 53, pp. 59-69: judicial interpretation is
   coloured by three prejudices - against statute law, against
   disregard of private rights and against discretionary powers
   in the executive.

9. WHEATCROFT, G.S.A. "A Six-finger Exercise in Statutory
   Construction" [1965] Br.T.R. 359: this is a complicated
   article on a maze of problems of the utmost technicality.

It does illustrate the special expertise that is called for in dealing with taxing statutes.

1. BEUTEL, F.K. "The Necessity of a New Technique of Interpreting the N.I.L. (Uniform Negotiable Instruments Law) - the Civil Law Analogy", (1931-32), 6 Tul.L.R., 1: this is of general interest. It shows the confusion wrought by conflicting judicial attitudes towards interpretation. The transition from precedent to written law calls for a new technique.

Continental and Common Law Methods of Interpretation

2. KOHLER, J. "Judicial Interpretation of Enacted Law" in Science of Legal Method: Select Essays by Various Authors, (trans. E. Bruncken and L.B. Register, Boston Book Co., 1917), chap. 6: interpreting a statute is not merely finding its meaning, but selecting from amongst various meanings the correct one. The criterion by which the selection should be made is that which will prove most beneficial in practice. Regard must be paid, first to the purpose, then to the consistency of the provision, and finally to the social history.

3. GÉNY, F. "Judicial Freedom of Decision: its Necessity and Method" in Science of Legal Method: Select Essays by Various Authors, (trans. E. Bruncken and L.B. Register, Boston Book Co., 1917), chap. 1: this is an account of the "free-law" method of interpretation by one of its pioneers.

4. EHRLICH, E. "Judicial Freedom of Decision: its Principles and Objects" in Science of Legal Method: Select Essays by Various Authors, (trans. E. Bruncken and L.B. Register, Boston Book Co., 1917), chap. 2: this develops further the "free-law" method of interpretation.

5. GUTTERIDGE, H.C. "A Comparative View of the Interpretation of Statute Law", (1933), 8 Tul.L.R. 1: interpretation refers not only to the ascertainment of meaning, but also to the creative activity in extending and limiting the scope of the language. Continental judges carry the investigation into legislative intent further than English judges. There is a comparison of their respective methods, as well as an evaluation of the "free-law" and "social purpose" methods.

6. GUTTERIDGE, H.C. Comparative Law, (Cambridge University Press, 1946), chap. 8: English law is rich in canons of construction, Continental law in theories. There is an account of the "free-law" and "social purpose" approaches and of the difference in approach between English and Continental judges. The difficulties of unifying systems is also discussed.

1. BONNECASE, J. "The Problem of Legal Interpretation in France", (1930), 12 J.C.L. (Ser. 3), 79: after quoting from the works of various writers the view is rejected that the legislature has infinite prevision, that the judge's task is simply to interpret the meaning of words, or that his task is simply to interpret having regard to contemporary social conditions. The judge should pay attention to the literal wording and to the social end in view at the time when the statute was made.

2. SMITH, H.A. "Interpretation in English and Continental Law", (1927), 9 J.C.L. (Ser. 3), 153: interpretation is a study of contexts. There is a needless gulf between English and Continental practice. Heydon's Case is consistent with the latter.

3. REGISTER, L.B. "Judicial Powers of Interpretation under Foreign Codes", (1917), 65 U.Pa.L.R., 39: this is of general interest. It considers the function of the judiciary under some Continental codes.

Historical Development

4. McILWAIN, C.H. The High Court of Parliament and its Supremacy, (Yale University Press, 1910), chap. 4: law-making and law-interpreting were not mutually exclusive. The legislature was a court and its enactments were not regarded as emanating from a foreign body. There is a detailed account of the development.

5. PLUCKNETT, T.F.T. A Concise History of the Common Law, (5th ed., Butterworth & Co., Ltd., 1956), pp. 328-336: in the middle ages interpretation was left to those who ordained the law. The courts used to appeal to the legislature. The historical development of the change in attitude is outlined.

6. PLUCKNETT, T.F.T. Statutes and their Interpretation in the First Half of the Fourteenth Century, (Cambridge University Press, 1922), Part I, chap. 3, Part II, chaps. 1-7, 9-10, 14 and Conclusion: not only extra-Parliamentary legislation, but interpretation also, was exercised by various bodies other than the judiciary. The evolution of a number of modern canons of interpretation is traced out in detail.

7. THORNE, S.E. A Discourse upon the Exposicion & Understandinge of Statutes with Sir T. Egerton's Additions, (Huntington Library, 1942), Introduction, pp. 1-92, and chaps. 3-11: S.E. Thorne in the Introduction suggests that interpretation in the modern sense began in the sixteenth century. He traces the early attitudes towards statutes. The chapters of

the text deal with various canons of interpretation and
reflect a most modern outlook.

1. PLUCKNETT, T.F.T. "Ellesmere on Statutes", (1944), 60 L.Q.R.
   242: a review of S.E. Thorne's edition of the Discourse.
   Plucknett suggests that the authorship of the Discourse
   should be ascribed to Sir T. Egerton himself (Lord Ellesmere).
   He answers Thorne's view that interpretation did not exist
   until the sixteenth century by saying that it did exist in
   the fourteenth century but was not apparent as at that time
   statute was regarded as an incident of normal development
   and not as an intrusion.

2. PLUCKNETT, T.F.T. Legislation of Edward I, (Oxford, 1949),
   chap. I: the nature of statute at this date and the place
   which it occupied in the process of effecting changes are
   discussed. The objection to S.E. Thorne's contention (supra)
   is repeated.

3. LANDIS, J.M. "Statutes and Sources of Law" in Harvard Legal
   Essays, (Harvard University Press, 1934), p. 213: in early
   times the courts acknowledged that behind the formal
   document lay an aim which required sympathetic consideration.
   The change came with ideas as to the separation of powers in
   the eighteenth century. The methods of interpretation today
   are outdated. A decent respect for legislation will ensure
   a better balance between legislative and judicial development
   of the law.

Canons of Interpretation

4. ALLEN, C.K. Law in the Making, (7th ed., Oxford, 1964), pp.
   482-530: this discusses generally the various canons and
   their shortcomings and suggested improvements.

5. LLEWELLYN, K.N. The Common Law Tradition. Deciding Appeals,
   (Little, Brown & Co., 1960), Appendix C, and pp. 371-382:
   parallel columns give opposing canons of interpretation on
   a wide range of points. There are twenty-eight canons of
   "Thrust and Parry", and nineteen of "Thrust and Counterthrust".

6. SALMOND, J.W. Jurisprudence, (12th ed., P.J. Fitzgerald,
   Sweet & Maxwell, Ltd., 1966), pp. 131-140: this discusses
   the literal and free methods of interpretation, the canons
   of interpretation, and their defects.

7. WILLIAMS, G.L. Learning the Law, (8th ed., Stevens & Sons,
   Ltd., 1969), chap. 7: normally the literal meaning is
   adopted, subject to the context. In cases of doubt the
   function is legislative rather than interpretative. A brief

account is given of the principal canons and presumptions.

1. HOOD PHILLIPS, O. A First Book of English Law, (5th ed.,
   Sweet & Maxwell, Ltd., 1965), chap. 10: this is a convenient
   account of the various canons and presumptions with a
   criticism of the present position.

2. KIRALFY, A.K.R. The English Legal System, (4th ed., Sweet &
   Maxwell, Ltd., 1967), pp. 121-136: this gives a general
   account of the canons and presumptions and of the internal
   and external aids to interpretation.

3. PATON, G.W. A Text-Book of Jurisprudence, (3rd ed., D.P. Derham,
   Oxford, 1964), pp. 215-221: the canons of interpretation
   are wide enough to produce divergent results. There is a
   general discussion of the present position and of the
   difficulties that it creates.

4. KEETON, G. W. The Elementary Principles of Jurisprudence,
   (2nd ed., Pitman & Sons, Ltd., 1949), pp. 89-95: this is a
   general discussion of the principal canons of interpretation.

5. VINOGRADOFF, P. Common-Sense in Law, (3rd ed., H.G. Hanbury,
   Oxford University Press, 1959), pp. 86-106: a court's first
   duty is to apply the "literal" canon of interpretation.
   There is also a discussion of the court's power to add to
   or supply gaps in the wording so as to modernise a provision.

6. DRIEDGER, E.A. "A New Approach to Statutory Interpretation",
   (1951), 29 Can.B.R., 838: this regroups the various canons
   of interpretation under four Rules:- Rule of Language, Rule
   of Inferred Intent, Rule of Declared Intent, Rule of
   Presumed Intent.

7. KOCOUREK, A. An Introduction to the Science of Law, (Little,
   Brown & Co., Boston, 1930), pp. 161-165, 191-202: a
   distinction is drawn between official and unofficial sources
   of interpretation, and an account is given of "grammatical",
   "logical", "spurious" and "historical" interpretation.

8. SILVING, H. Sources of Law (Wm.S. Hein & Co., Inc., New York,
   1968), "Statutes" p. 9: the bindingness of interpretation
   dispenses with the question whether or not it is right.
   Therefore, rules of interpretation are of more interest
   than the interpretation itself, since words mean what the
   law says they shall mean. The subjective and objective
   approaches depend upon legal fiat. Rules of interpretation
   would be useful in establishing a method of arriving at
   understanding and certainty.

1. CRAIES, W.F. Statute Law, (6th ed., S.G.G. Edgar, Sweet &
   Maxwell, Ltd., 1963): this is a standard work giving a
   detailed account of the canons and presumptions.

2. ODGERS, C.E. The Construction of Deeds and Statutes, (4th ed.,
   Sweet & Maxwell, Ltd., 1956), Part II: this, too, is a
   standard work. It is to be noted that Part I deals with
   the interpretation of other documents, which reflects the
   tendency to assimilate statutes and other documents.

3. MAXWELL, P.B. The Interpretation of Statutes, (11th ed.,
   R. Wilson and B. Galpin, Sweet & Maxwell, Ltd., 1962):
   this is perhaps the best of the standard treatises.

4. BLACKSTONE, W. Commentaries on the Laws of England, (16th ed.,
   1825), I, pp. 85 et seq.: statutes are classified as
   declaratory of the common law or remedial. As to the latter,
   the standard statement of the canons of construction are
   set out, but some of them have since been abandoned or
   modified.

5. DWARRIS, F. A General Treatise on Statutes, (2nd ed.,
   Wm. Benning & Co., 1848), chaps. 1, 8-11: this is of general
   interest only as showing the position in the first half of
   the nineteenth century. Chap. 11 is of the greatest interest,
   containing a discussion of the relation between legislation
   and judicial interpretation and between interpretation and
   judicial legislation.

Restrictive Approach: Strict Interpretation and Presumptions

6. HOPKINS, E.R. "The Literal Canon and the Golden Rule", (1937),
   15 Can.B.R. 689: the "literal" canon is discussed in relation
   to the "golden rule" with reference to a particular case.

7. E.J.C. Note in (1947), 63 L.Q.R. 156: this draws attention to
   the absurd result of refusing to fill in a gap left by a
   particular statute.

8. KAHN-FREUND, O. Note in (1949), 12 M.L.R. 97: this discusses
   the problem created by the repeal of a statutory definition
   but where the word so defined appears also in an unrepealed
   provision.

9. G.L.W. Note in (1951), 14 M.L.R. 333: the absurdity resulting
   from a literal interpretation is pointed out.

10. MITCHELL, J.D.B. Note in (1952), 15 M.L.R. 219: this deals
    with the conflict between a strict and liberal approach
    and the unfortunate results of the former.

1. A.L.G. Note in (1960), 76 L.Q.R. 215; J.L. MONTROSE, ibid.,
   at p. 359: both comment on the literal interpretation
   adopted in Hinchy's case.

2. de SMITH, S.A. Note in (1956), 19 M.L.R. 541: this comments
   on the strict interpretation of an Act by which the House
   of Lords held that it had no jurisdiction.

3. COUTTS, J.A. Note in (1937-38), 1 M.L.R. 166: examples are
   given of the restrictive interpretation of a Nothern
   Ireland statute so as not to infringe private rights. If
   Parliamentary debates had been resorted to, the result would
   have been different.

4. ABRAHAMSON, M.W. "Trade Disputes Act - Strict Interpretation
   in Ireland", (1961), 24 M.L.R. 596: this is a scathing
   comment on strict interpretation in the light of two Irish
   cases and the Parliamentary history of the Act in question.

5. STOUT, R. "Is the Privy Council a Legislative Body?" (1905),
   21 L.Q.R. 9: this considers several of the canons of
   statutory interpretation and the attitude adopted by the
   Judicial Committee of the Privy Council.

6. For a long history of criticism of strict interpretation, see
   Notes in (1890), 6 L.Q.R. 121; (1893), 9 L.Q.R. 106; 110,
   207; (1894), 10 L.Q.R. 9, 109-110, 112, 291; (1897), 13
   L.Q.R. 235-236; (1899), 15 L.Q.R. 111; (1900), 16 L.Q.R.
   222-223; (1901), 17 L.Q.R. 122; (1904), 20 L.Q.R. 114-115;
   (1921), 37 L.Q.R. 5; (1943), 59 L.Q.R. 296-297 (comment
   rather than criticism); (1960), 76 L.Q.R. 30, 211, 380.

7. WILLIAMS, G.L. "The Origin and Logical Implications of the
   Ejusdem Generis Rule", (1943), 7 The Conveyancer (N.S.),
   119: the rule may date from 1729. The maxim may thwart the
   intention of the legislature. The ways in which the maxim
   itself may be deprived of effect are considered.

8. de PINNA, L.A. "Marginal Notes and Statutes" (1964) 114 L.J.
   3: this is a short survey of the use of marginal notes,
   preambles, recitals in deeds, and schedules. L.A. de PINNA:
   "Schedules to Statutues" (1964) 114 L.J. 519: this is a
   continuation of the discussion.

9. ANONYMOUS. "Headings and Marginal Notes", (1960), 124 J.P.J.
   247: this considers briefly when these might be used and
   cases in which they have been used.

10. RADZINOWICZ, L. A History of English Criminal Law, (Stevens
    & Sons, Ltd., 1948), I, pp. 83-106: these pages contain a

detailed account of the spirit in which courts used to
interpret statutes imposing capital punishment. They tried,
on the one hand, to give effect to legislative policy, and
on the other hand to interpret doubts in favour of the
individual.

1. JACKSON, R.M. "Absolute Prohibition in Statutory Offences",
   in Modern Approach to Criminal Law, (edd. L. Radzinowicz
   and J.W.C. Turner, Macmillan & Co., Ltd., 1945), p. 262:
   this discusses the extent to which mens rea is interpreted
   as being necessary to the commission of statutory offences.

2. DEVLIN, P. Samples of Law Making, (Oxford University Press,
   1962), chap. 4: this shows how the courts are constructing
   a new body of law.

3. HALL, L. "Strict or Liberal Construction of Penal Statutes",
   (1934-35), 48 Harv.L.R. 748: the evolution of the strict
   construction of penal statutes is outlined. There is a
   careful discussion of its pros and cons and proposals for
   reform.

4. POLLOCK, F. "Abrams v. U.S.", (1920), 36 L.Q.R. 334: this is
   a critical discussion of the construction of a penal statute
   by the American Supreme Court.

5. See also Notes in (1949), 65 L.Q.R. 142; (1951), 67 L.Q.R. 13;
   C.H. de WAAL: Note in (1959) C.L.J. 173; (1960), 76 L.Q.R.
   179.

6. GOODHART, A.L. Note in (1950), 66 L.Q.R. 314: retrospective
   legislation is dealt with. A distinction should be drawn
   between civil and criminal cases. The primary purpose of
   civil law is not deterrence but the accomplishment of some
   purpose, and retrospective legislation may well accomplish
   this. The primary purpose of criminal law is deterrence,
   and retrospective legislation will not deter but will
   operate as revenge.

7. PLUCKNETT, T.F.T. Statutes and their Interpretation in the
   First Half of the Fourteenth Century, (Cambridge University
   Press, 1922), Part II, chap. 9: this discusses the
   retrospective effect of statutes.

8. WHEATCROFT, G.S.A. "The Attitude of the Legislature and the
   Courts to Tax Avoidance", (1955), 18 M.L.R. 209: a
   distinction is drawn between tax avoidance and tax evasion.
   The attitudes of the courts, the revenue department and of
   the legislature are considered. Strict interpretation should
   be abolished.

1. FLETCHER, E. "Retrospective Fiscal Legislation", (1959), Br.
   Tax R. 412: after due warning retrospective fiscal
   legislation is an effective deterrent against tax evasion.
   The history of such legislation is considered, its benefits
   and drawbacks.

2. L.C.B.G. Note on Statutes, (1950), 13 M.L.R. 482: this
   discusses the retrospective effect of s.26 of the Finance
   Act, 1950.

3. ANONYMOUS. "Acts of Prerogative: Retrospective Legislation",
   (1962), 233 L.T. 539: this discusses the propriety of the
   threat of retrospective legislation to reverse the decision
   in a case.

4. BALLARD, F.A. "Retroactive Federal Taxation", (1934-35), 48
   Harv.L.R. 592: this considers the position in America.

5. MANN, F.A. "The Interpretation of Uniform Statutes", (1946),
   62 L.Q.R. 278: when Parliament adopts international treaties,
   which aim at international uniformity, the courts should
   adopt the same aim. The attitude of English courts is
   considered and the suggestion is made that Parliament should
   here be regarded, not as law-giver, but as law-transformer.
   Its function is different.

6. LAUTERPACHT, H. "Some Observations on Preparatory Work in
   the Interpretation of Treaties", (1934-35), 48 Harv.L.R.
   549: this is of general interest and does not deal with
   interpretation of statute, but useful none the less.

7. WINDER, W.H.D. "The Interpretation of Statutes Subject to
   Case Law", (1946), 58 Jur.R. 93: the discussion is based on
   Barras v. Aberdeen Steam Trawling & Fishing Co., Ltd.
   Parliament can be presumed to intend that the judicial
   meaning given to a word should continue to be adopted.

8. GRODECKI, J.K. Note in (1957), 20 M.L.R., 636: this comments
   on a case which concerned the interpretation of a statutory
   provision which was re-enacted in another statute.

9. R.E.M. Note in (1941), 57 L.Q.R. 312: the settled judicial
   meaning given to a word under one statute should not be
   departed from when that word is adopted in another statute
   unless there is clear evidence to the contrary.

10. OWEN, A. "Judicial Interpretation of Statutes", (1955), 105
    L.J. 534: the same point is made as above.

11. FOX, H.M. "Judicial Control of the Spending Powers of Local

Authorities", (1956), 72 L.Q.R. 237: this contains an
account of the judicial interpretation of statutes
conferring powers.

1. ALLEN, C.K. Law and Orders, (2nd ed., Stevens & Sons, Ltd.,
   1956), chap. 8: some of the problems of the interpretation
   of delegated legislation are considered.

2. C.K.A. Note in (1958), 74 L.Q.R. 358: this discusses Ross-
   Clunis v. Papadopoullos and the distinction between "no
   ground" and "no reasonable ground" on which an official
   could "satisfy himself".

3. MURRAY, D.B. "When is a Repeal not a Repeal?" (1953), 16 M.
   L.R. 50: the repealing technique of draftsmen is considered
   and the attitude of the courts towards repeal provisions.

Exclusion of Legislative History

4. KILGOUR, D.G. "The Rule Against the Use of Legislative
   History: 'Canon of Construction or Counsel of Caution'?",
   (1952), 30 Can.B.R. 769: prima facie there is a case for
   the admission of legislative history. Its exclusion is not
   as absolute as might be thought. The origin of the rule is
   considered and the conclusion is that it is a counsel of
   caution and not a rule.

5. MacQUARRIE, J.T. "The Use of Legislative History", (1952),
   30 Can.B.R. 958: this is a reply to Kilgour (supra),
   arguing that it is more than a counsel of caution.

6. de SLOOVERE, F.J. "Extrinsic Aids in the Interpretation of
   Statutes", (1940), 88 U.Pa.L.R. 527: this gives careful
   consideration to the possible bases on which such aids
   might be admitted.

7. EASTWOOD, R.A. "A Plea for the Historical Interpretation of
   Statute Law", (1935), J.S.P.T.L. 1: the canons of
   interpretation give effect to an artificial "intention"
   which is the creation of the canons themselves. Extrinsic
   material should be admitted.

8. DAVIS, K.C. "Legislative History and the Wheat Board Case",
   (1953), 31 Can.B.R. 1: the refusal to consult legislative
   history violates the intention of the legislature.
   Legislative history should not be used to contradict the
   clear wording of the statute, but to elucidate doubtful
   words. The pros and cons are considered.

9. CORRY, J.A. "The Use of Legislative History in the

Interpretation of Statutes", (1954), 32 Can.B.R., 624:
careful consideration is given to what constitutes
"legislative history". Most of it is unrecorded. Resort to
it will be unhelpful in Great Britain or Canada. It is not
possible to conceal the need for judicial legislation.

1. MacDONALD, V.C. "Constitutional Interpretation and Extrinsic
   Evidence", (1939), 17 Can.B.R., 77: this is a factual
   discussion of how far the British North America Act, 1867,
   has been interpreted in the light of extrinsic aids.

2. MILNER, J.B. Correspondence on the Use of Legislative
   History, (1953), 31 Can.B.R., 228-230: the question is not
   so much the "will of Parliament" as of the government
   department concerned. Legislative history may prove to be
   as ambiguous as the wording.

3. JACKSON, R.M. Note in (1939), 55 L.Q.R., 488: this discusses
   the use of reports of Royal Commissions.

4. BENAS, B.B. "Problems for the Conveyancer. The Construction
   of Statutes", (1952), 102 L.J., 269: this comments on a
   reference to Hansard in a case so as to elucidate the
   intention of Parliament.

5. JONES, H.W. "Extrinsic Aids in the Federal Courts", (1939-40),
   25 Iowa L.R., 737: the use of such aids to discover the
   meaning and purpose of an enactment is carefully discussed.
   It includes a consideration of discussions in committees,
   debates, social background and general statistical
   information.

6. MILLER, C.A. "The Value of Legislative History of Federal
   Statutes", (1925), 73 U.Pa.L.R., 158: such history may be
   useful in the form of memoranda and briefs prepared for
   committees and may lessen judicial legislation.

7. COX, A. "Judge Learned Hand and the Interpretation of
   Statutes", (1946-47), 60 Harv.L.R., 370: this includes an
   account of how Judge Hand resorted to legislative history
   occasionally when the social purpose could not otherwise
   be discovered and when the point at issue was small.

8. JACKSON, R.H. "The Meaning of Statutes: what Congress Says or
   what the Court Says", (1948), 34 Am.B.A.J., 535: the root
   trouble is the absence of guidance from an accepted and
   consistent set of principles. Resort to legislative history
   is badly overdone. It is of dubious help and poses serious
   problems; it is not available to the lawyer when advising
   his client. (These remarks coming from a Judge of the

Supreme Court carry a great deal of weight).

1. NOTE in (1936-37), 50 Harv. L.R. on "Legislation", 813, at
   p. 822: extrinsic material is relevant in so far as it
   helps to elucidate the factual situation before the court.

2. SCHMIDT, F. "Construction of Statutes" in (1957), I Scand.
   S.L., 157: legislative material constitutes "secondary
   directives" in giving guidance to a court. It has not the
   absolute character of the "primary directives", i.e., the
   statutory text and precedents. This includes a discussion
   of what legislative material should consist of and of its
   value.

Liberal Approach.   (See also supra, The "Purpose" Approach)

3. FULLER, L.L. "Positivism and Fidelity to Law - a Reply to
   Professor Hart", (1957-58), 71 Harv. L.R., 630, at pp. 661-
   669: this is an incisive examination of Hart's distinction
   between the "core" of agreed application of words and the
   "penumbra" of unsettled applications showing where it
   breaks down. All statutory provisions can only be interpreted in the light of purpose and policy.

4. LEVI, E.H. An Introduction to Legal Reasoning, (University
   of Chicago Press 1948), pp. 19-40: the method of applying
   statute is only superficially deductive. Reference is made
   first to the kind of examples which the words do cover from
   which the court argues by analogy. Judicial interpretation
   gives a broad direction to the statute.

5. CROSS, A.R.N. Precedent in English Law, (2nd ed., Oxford,
   1968), pp. 163 et seq.: the general account includes a
   reference to the analogical method, the case in hand being
   compared with situations which were intended to be covered.

6. EKELÖF, P.O. "Teleological Construction of Statutes", (1958),
   2 Scand. S.L., 75: the analogical method of interpretation
   is referred to in another context. One should consider the
   situations to which the statute does apply in order to
   discover the purpose which it seeks to achieve with regard
   to them.

7. FRIEDMANN, W. Note in (1941-43), 6 M.L.R., 235: this
   discusses an instance of what is described as a "welcome
   and timely return to the principles of Heydon's Case".

8. GRUNFELD, C. Note in (1950), 13 M.L.R., 94: this discusses a
   decision in which the literal and mischief canons of
   interpretation were applied.

1. The following cases may be consulted as illustrating the attitude of the courts towards statutory interpretation: Magor and St. Mellons R.D.C. v. Newport Corporation, [1950] 2 All E.R., 1226; on appeal, [1952] A.C., 189; [1951] 2 All E.R., 839; Roberts v. Hopwood, [1925] A.C., 578; Liversidge v. Anderson, [1942] A.C., 206; [1941] 3 All E.R., 338; Prescott v. Birmingham Corporation, [1955] Ch. 210; [1954] 3 All E.R., 698; Ross-Clunis v. Papadopoullos, [1958] 2 All E.R., 23; [1958] 1 W.L.R., 546; Cutler v. Wandsworth City Stadium, [1949] A.C., 398; [1949] 1 All E.R., 544; Att.-Gen. v. H.R.H. Prince Ernest Augustus of Hanover, [1957] A.C., 436; [1957] 1 All E.R., 49; Inland Revenue Commissioners v. Hinchy, [1960] A.C., 748; [1960] 1 All E.R., 505; R. v. Board of Control, ex parte Winterflood, [1938] 2 K.B. 366; [1938] 2 All E.R., 463; London & North Eastern Railway Co. v. Berriman, [1946] A.C., 278; [1946] 1 All E.R., 255; Hilder v. Dexter, [1902] A.C., 474; Ellerman Lines, Ltd. v. Murray, [1931] A.C., 126; Corocraft, Ltd. v. Pan American Airways, Inc., [1969] 1 Q.B., 616; [1969] 1 All E.R., 82; Re Macmanaway, [1951] A.C., 161; Escoign Properties, Ltd. v. Inland Revenue Commissioners, [1958] A.C., 549; [1958] 1 All E.R., 406; Becke v. Smith, (1836), 2 M. & W., 191; Heydon's Case, (1584), 3 Co. Rep., 7a; Miller v. Oregon, (1907), 208 U.S., 412; Brown v. Board of Education (1954), 347 U.S., 483.

Drafting

2. BENTHAM, J. "Nomography, or the Art of Inditing Laws", in Works, (ed. J. Bowring, Wm. Tait, Edinburgh 1843), III, chaps. 3-9: "nomography" is the form to be given to the matter of which law is composed. With a view to improving draftsmanship, various kinds of imperfections are discussed and suggestions offered as to how legal language might be simplified.

3. DICKERSON, F.R. The Fundamentals of Legal Drafting, (Little, Brown & Co., 1965): this is a most readable and informative account of the problems of drafting legal documents, including statutes. It shows the process of preparing a document through various stages and how this process improves and clarifies its substance. As such it contains much that is of value to all persons engaged in legal writings of every sort.

4. Rules of Drafting, supplied by L.R. MacTAVISH, K.C., (1948), 26 Can. B.R., 1231: this is a set of detailed precepts which are "designed to ensure certainty and clarity of meaning and conciseness of expression".

1. MacDERMOTT, J.C. "Some Requirements of Justice" [1964] Jur.
   R. 103, 104-12: the difficulty is to find unequivocal
   language in which to convey the intention of Parliament.
   The "literal" school adheres to the plain meaning of words
   unless Parliament has authorised the contrary; the "realist"
   school looks at the policy of the statute and the body of
   law of which it has become a part. Four suggestions are
   offered: (a) greater use of preambles; (b) at some stage of
   the legislative process measures should be scrutinised by
   special teams of "clause-tasters"; (c) statutes might
   themselves state "This Act shall be liberally construed"
   and applied to promote its underlying purposes and policies;
   (d) courts should have discretionary power to order costs in
   cases of interpretation to be paid out of public funds.

2. CONARD, A.F. "New Ways to Write Laws", (1947), 56 Yale L.J.
   458: laws should be drafted with more emphasis on making
   the public understand what they command than on controlling
   judges. The latter are more likely to be influenced by
   clear statements of purpose. There should be titles,
   headings and sub-divisions; jargon should be avoided, there
   should be short sentences, examples and directives rather
   than propositions in the form "if X then Y".

3. GRAHAM-HARRISON, W.M. "An Examination of the Main Criticisms
   of the Statute Book and of the Possibility of Improvement",
   (1935), J.S.P.T.L.9, especially, pp. 34 et seq.: this is a
   detailed investigation into the charges levelled at statutes,
   showing that draftsmen are not always to blame. The
   conflicting approaches and canons of interpretation adopted
   by the judges also lead to confusion.

4. RAM, G. "The Improvement of the Statute Book", (1951), 1 J.S.
   P.T.L. (N.S.) 442: the process of making an Act is described
   with special reference to the task of the draftsman.
   Explanatory memoranda are not thought to be of assistance
   to the judges because of amendments during the passage
   through Parliament.

5. CARR, C. "The Mechanism of Law-making", (1951), 4 C.L.P. 122:
   this explains the origin of some modern drafting practices.

6. AMOS, M.S. "The Interpretation of Statutes", (1933-35), 5 C.
   L.J. 163: in the course of a discussion on interpretation
   the point is made that drafting a text into two languages,
   (e.g., international treaties) induces clarity. (Cf. South
   African statutes).

7. HIRANANDANI, S.K. "Legislative Drafting: an Indian View",
   (1964), 27 M.L.R.1: the problems that confront a draftsman

are stated with the utmost clarity. This short account should stand as one of the best and most convenient accounts on the topic.

1. DRIEDGER, E.A. "The Preparation of Legislation", (1953), 31 Can.B.R. 33, especially pp. 36-42: an account is given of the various matters which a draftsman has to consider.

2. DICKERSON, F.R. "Legislative Drafting in London and in Washington", (1959) C.L.J. 49: the drafting in England by a few and in America by a large group is contrasted. This includes a general discussion of draftsmen and their methods.

3. MONTGOMERIE, J. Note in (1955), 18 M.L.R. 503: this discusses briefly bad draftsmanship of the Rent Acts.

6

C U S T O M

1. ALLEN, C.K. <u>Law in the Making</u>, (7th ed., Oxford, 1964), chaps. 1 and 2 and Excursus A: this is the fullest and most convenient account for the student. The various theories about customary law are considered; and in chapter 2, which is more important for present purposes, the conditions under which local custom is accepted as law are examined in detail.

2. BRAYBROOKE, E.K. "Custom as Source of English Law", (1951), 50 Mich.L.R. 71: the distinction between custom of the people and of the courts is stressed, and the role of the latter is regarded as vital. The point is also made that customary popular action carries with it the reaction of those whose interests are invaded by such action.

3. SALMOND, J.W. <u>Jurisprudence</u>, (12th ed., P.J. Fitzgerald, Sweet & Maxwell, Ltd., 1966), chap. 6: the significance of custom and the reasons for its reception are first disscussed. After that the various types of customs are dealt with in detail.

4. SALT, H.E. "Local Ambit of a Custom" in <u>Cambridge Legal Essays</u>, (edd. P.H. Winfield and A.D. McNair, W. Heffer & Sons, Ltd., 1926), 279: this essay delimits in detail what is meant by saying that a custom is "local". The case-law on various types of claims based on custom and their classifications is considered.

5. PLUCKNETT, T.F.T. <u>A Concise History of the Common Law</u>, (5th ed., Butterworth & Co. Ltd., 1956), Part III, chap. 3: a feature of early English customary law was its flexibility and adaptability. The modern requirement of antiquity is shown to have been historically non-existent. The growth of new customs and the parts they played in various aspects of early English law are pointed out.

6. PLUCKNETT, T.F.T. <u>Legislation of Edward I</u>, (Oxford, 1949), pp. 6-10: the point is repeated that custom at this period was "an instrument for legal change rather than the fossilized remains of a remote past." The requirement of antiquity was not conceived of in the same way as now.

7. VINOGRADOFF, P. "Customary Law" in <u>The Legacy of the Middle Ages</u> (edd. C.G. Crump and E.F. Jacob, Oxford, 1926), 287: the operation of custom in the Middle Ages in various counties, principally in the spheres of family law, land law and commercial usages, is described. With regard to land law in England, the influence of the customs of the military class is to be noted.

1. BLACKSTONE, W. Commentaries on the Laws of England, (16th ed., 1825), I, pp. 67-68; 74-79: general custom, or the common law, is first discussed, then local custom. His exposition of the proof and legality of the latter might be regarded as classic. It is noteworthy that Blackstone does not sufficiently distinguish between popular custom and the custom of the courts.

2. STEPHEN, J.F. Commentaries on the Laws of England, (21st ed., L.C. Warmington, Butterworth & Co., Ltd., 1950), I, pp. 18-21; 365-366: the requirements of local custom are set out; usages of trade are also considered.

3. BENTHAM, J. A Comment on the Commentaries, (ed. C.W. Everett, Oxford, 1928), SS 18-19: this is a point by point (and occasionally captious) commentary on Blackstone's treatment of the subject. Much attention is devoted to the requisites of local custom, in particular the requirement of reasonableness.

4. BENTHAM, J. The Limits of Jurisprudence Defined, (ed. C.W. Everett, Columbia University Press, 1945), chap. 17: to speak of customary law is a fiction, since custom as a source of law is incomplete by itself.

5. AUSTIN, J. Lectures on Jurisprudence, (5th ed., R. Campbell, John Murray, 1885), I, pp. 101-103; II, pp. 523, 536-543: law is what the sovereign commands. Custom becomes law when adopted by the courts by virtue of "tacit commands" of the sovereign. Independent of this, custom is only "positive morality".

6. BROWN, W.J. The Austinian Theory of Law, (John Murray, 1906), Excursus D: sound theory should be founded on existing facts and not on a priori conceptions of law. Custom has been, and still is, a source of law. The question when custom becomes "law" is discussed at length, and the conclusion is that it does so when the judges declare it. The fact that judges say that it has previously been law is only a form of "the fiction of judicial incompetence". Judges are bound' by their own practice.

7. HART, H.L.A. The Concept of Law, (Oxford, 1961), pp. 44-47: in the course of an attack on Austin's general thesis the point is made that a coercive order, as Austin viewed it, requires a creative act. If so, custom presents a difficulty. The Austinian solution by way of "tacit command" is shown to be inadequate.

8. LOBINGIER, C.S. "Customary Law" in Encyclopaedia of the Social

Sciences, (ed. E.R.A. Seligman, Macmillan & Co., Ltd.,
1931), IV, 662: repetition may explain the origin of
customs, but it fails to indicate the point at which the
differentiation between law and non-legal custom occurs.
Custom is said to become law when it is recognised in some
way as governing a class of relations segregated as jural
(sic). Some of the factors involved in the transition are
indicated.

1. KELSEN, H. General Theory of Law and State, (trans. A.
   Wedberg, Harvard University Press, 1949), pp. 126-128:
   custom is a law-creating agency only if the "constitution"
   so permits. He disagrees with Austin on the ground that if
   custom is not "law" till the judges adopt it, the same
   should be true of statute. The difference between statute
   law and custom is that the former is a centralised agency,
   the latter is not.

2. SILVING, H. Sources of Law, (Wm. S. Hein & Co., Inc., New
   York, 1968), "Customary Law" p. 125: custom is the legal
   corollary of evolution and is a basic element in all law.
   When a legal order proclaims to be the same despite change
   even in fundamental principles, this can only be on the
   basis that it has changed by customary evolution, customary
   law being part of the legal order.

3. CARTER, J.C. Law: Its Origin, Growth and Function, (G.P.
   Putnam's Sons, 1907), especially pp. 120-136: all law is
   said to be custom, though not vice versa. Law begins as the
   product of automatic action of society. Legislation may
   reinforce custom, but is doomed if it goes against it.

4. CARTER, J.C. "The Ideal and the Actual in the Law", (1890),
   24 Am. L.R., 752, especially at p. 760: this repeats the
   above thesis, and adds that in doubtful cases the courts
   have to declare custom. The legislative function is supplementary to the judicial, namely, to catch the new and
   growing custom which is forming and to give it formal shape.

5. GRAY, J.C. "Some Definitions and Questions in Jurisprudence",
   (1892-93), 6 Harv. L.R., 21, at pp. 28-33: the idea that
   custom is law is examined and rejected. Custom as such has
   little influence. An additional factor is judicial opinions
   as to morality.

6. GRAY, J.C. The Nature and Sources of the Law, (2nd ed., R.
   Gray, The Macmillan Co., New York; 1921), chap. 12:
   according to his thesis that law is what the judges declare,
   custom is never "law" by itself, only a source of "law".
   Judicial decisions may also in some cases give rise to

custom. J.C. Carter's view (supra) is subjected to particular criticism.

1. DICKINSON, J. "The Law behind Law", (1929), 29 Col. L.R., 113, at pp. 125 et seq.: J.C. Carter's theory (supra) is criticised. The conclusion is reached that custom may inspire rules of law, but is not law ex proprio vigore.

2. HOLLAND, T.E. The Elements of Jurisprudence, (13th ed., Oxford, 1924), pp. 56-63: custom becomes law when it is enforced by political authority. When a court decides that a custom exists, it does so prospectively and retrospectively, which explains why a judge declares a custom to have been law before.

3. BUCKLAND, W.W. Some Reflections on Jurisprudence, (Cambridge University Press, 1945), pp. 52-56: the difficulties facing the Austinian view of custom are considered. Buckland's own solution is that what is law is not the custom, but the statement of the characteristics which customs should possess.

4. ROSS, A. On Law and Justice, (Stevens & Sons, Ltd., 1958), pp. 91 et seq.: a legal custom implies that legal rules, otherwise upheld, are not observed in a certain area, but are replaced by the customary rule. Outward behaviour is an indication that a feeling of obligation exists. The position in England is briefly reviewed.

5. BODENHEIMER, E. Jurisprudence, (Harvard University Press, 1962), pp. 318-324: this is a general discussion of the conditions under which custom is transformed into law. Austin's views are considered and criticised, but some of the problems involved in the alternative view are also considered.

6. PATTERSON, E.W. Jurisprudence, (The Foundation Press, Inc., 1953), pp. 223-230: a distinction is drawn between the "external" element and the "internal" element in custom, the former being the regular behaviour, the latter the conviction. The tests of local custom in English law are summarised. American applications of custom are chiefly commercial usages. No final conclusion is reached as to whether custom is "law".

7. VINOGRADOFF, P. Common-sense in Law, (3rd ed., H.G. Hanbury, Oxford University Press, 1959), chap. 6: the significance of custom as a source of law is discussed as well as the tests that it has to satisfy. The importance of custom in various parts of the Commonwealth is also touched on.

1. CROSS, A.R.N. Precedent in English Law, (2nd ed., Oxford, 1968), pp. 155-163: in the course of discussing the relation of custom to precedent, the question when custom becomes law is dealt with. W.W. Buckland's view (supra) is rejected, and the conclusion is that custom today is law before it is upheld by the courts.

2. COHEN, M.R. Reason and Law, (The Free Press, Glencoe, Illinois, 1950), pp. 65-67: a defintion of "law" which would exclude custom (e.g., Austin's) cannot be refuted by adducing a different use of the word. Law as custom and law as legislation are both said to be realities. Arbitrary definition cannot disprove the existence of one or the other. The important thing is to examine their interaction.

3. EHRLICH, E. Fundamental Principles of the Sociology of Law, (trans. W.L. Moll, Harvard University Press, 1936), chap. 19: in Roman law custom became law by passing through juristic law. At p. 455 the point is made that legal propositions do not arise fully formed, but as the creation of jurists.

4. SADLER, G.T. The Relation of Custom to Law, (Sweet & Maxwell, Ltd., 1919), chap. 4: he agrees with the view that custom is law because it will be recognised by the courts. Some customs are recognised, but not others, because the former bear certain marks. Examples of state recognition of custom are drawn from Roman, English, Welsh, Indian and Dutch law.

5. KEETON, G.W. The Elementary Principles of Jurisprudence, (2nd ed., Isaac Pitman & Sons, Ltd., 1949), chap. 6: this is an account of general and local custom and of the views of the principal writers.

6. PATON, G.W. A Text-Book of Jurisprudence, (3rd ed., D.P. Derham, Oxford, 1964), pp. 165-168: this contains a general discussion of the common law position concerning local and mercantile customs.

7. POUND, R. Jurisprudence, (West Publishing Co., 1959), III, pp. 389-409: the basis of customary law is considered with reference to the Austinian and Historical School viewpoints. Custom and law react upon each other. Custom is also considered with reference to ancient and modern Civil law, Continental law and International law.

8. POLLOCK, F. A First Book of Jurisprudence, (6th ed., Macmillan & Co., Ltd., 1929), Part II, chap. 4: local custom is an addition or exception to the common law. The various conditions of its validity are discussed, and there is also some mention of conventional custom.

1. LLOYD, D. Introduction to Jurisprudence, (2nd ed., Stevens &
    Sons, Ltd., 1965), pp. 336-339: a very broad account is
    given of the part played in English law by general, local
    and conventional custom.

2. LLOYD, D. The Idea of Law, (Penguin Books, Ltd., A688, 1964),
    chap. 10, especially pp. 228-31, 240-50: law exists on more
    than one level, and it is necessary to appreciate the under-
    lying social norms which determine much of its functioning.
    A mere habit lacks the sense of social compulsion. It is
    this socially obligatory element that is characteristic of
    custom. The development of law through custom in archaic,
    feudal and medieval European societies is traced out. The
    common law is said to be a bridge between customary and
    codified law. Local customs, constitutional customs and
    mercantile customs are explained briefly.

3. KOCOUREK, A. An Introduction to the Science of Law, (Little,
    Brown & Co., 1930), pp. 159-161: this is a summarised and
    elementary account of the different types of custom, to-
    gether with brief indications of the requirements of each.

4. CLARK, E.C. Practical Jurisprudence, (Cambridge University
    Press, 1883), pp. 316-323: the terminology and classifi-
    cations in Blackstone, Hale and Austin are considered.

5. KORKUNOV, N.M. General Theory of Law, (trans. W.G. Hastings,
    The Boston Book Co., 1909), pp. 410-419: customary law is
    built up outside all forms. Custom is said to be law
    according to the formula "what has been done ought to be
    done".

6. RATTIGAN, W.H. The Science of Jurisprudence, (3rd ed., Wildy
    & Sons, 1909), pp. 72-77: the growth of custom in early
    societies is considered with particular reference to India.
    On the question when custom becomes law, the view is taken
    that it is law ex proprio vigore.

7. VINOGRADOFF, P. Custom and Right, (Oslo, 1925), chap. 2: the
    growth of customary law in the face of the rivalry between
    custom and law is traced out in Roman law and medieval
    canon law and the laws of certain European countries. The
    idea of long usage is shown to have been developed by the
    canonists of Europe.

8. VINOGRADOFF, P. Collected Papers, (Oxford, 1928), II, chaps.
    22 and 23: the procedure for ascertaining custom in
    northern France is contrasted with that in early English
    law. In the latter chapter the attitude of the courts to-
    wards custom is traced from early times. The beginnings of

legal rules are non-litigious.

1. SCHECHTER, F.I. "Popular Law and Common Law in Medieval
    England" (1928), 28 Col.L.R. 269: the domain of the common
    law was scanty, so local law was very important and active.
    The forces by which it diminished in favour of royal justice
    are discussed.

2. CARDOZO, B.N. The Nature of the Judicial Process, (Yale
    University Press, 1921), pp. 58-64: this is of general
    interest. Custom is touched on in the context of the
    influences at work upon the judicial mind.

3. POLLOCK, F. Essays in Jurisprudence and Ethics, (Macmillan &
    Co., 1882), pp. 54-59: in the context of a general discussion
    of the nature of man-made law, the imitative force behind
    custom is emphasised. The requirement of immemorial user
    in English law is ascribed to the lesson learnt of the
    danger of relying on solitary or few instances.

4. HALL, J. Readings in Jurisprudence, (The Bobbs-Merrill Co.,
    1938), chap. 20: this might usefully be consulted for
    extracts from English and American cases as well as for
    extracts from various writers, whose works are included
    here. There are also other extracts which are more
    appropriate to other contexts.

5. The following cases may be consulted: Simpson v. Wells (1872),
    L.R. 7 Q.B. 214; Bryant v, Foot (1868), L.R. 3 Q.B. 497;
    Mercer v. Denne, [1904] 2 Ch. 534; Mills v. Colchester
    Corporation (1867), L.R. 2 C.P. 476; Broadbent v. Wilkes
    (1742), Willes 360; Wilson v. Willes (1806), 7 East, 121;
    Lawrence v. Hitch (1868), L.R. 3 Q.B. 521; The Tanistry
    Case (1608), Dav. I. R. 28; Johnson v. Clarke, [1908] 1 Ch.
    303; Blundell v. Catterall (1821), 5 B. & Ald. 268;
    Coventry (Earl) v. Wills (1863), 12 W.R. 172; Sowerby v.
    Coleman (1867), L.R. 2 Exch. 96; Goodwin v. Robarts (1875),
    L.R. 10 Exch. 337; Crouch v. Crédit Foncier of England
    (1873), L.R. 8 Q.B. 374; Iveagh v. Martin and Another,
    [1961] 1 Q.B. 232; [1960] 2 All E.R. 668.

Usage

6. DEVLIN, P. Samples of Lawmaking, (Oxford University Press,
    1962), chap. 2: this gives an account of how trade customs
    as a source of commercial law have gradually disappeared
    in the face of the written contract.

7. CHORLEY, R.S.T. "The Conflict of Law and Commerce" (1932),
    48 L.Q.R. 52: the law is in disfavour with business people

because it does not adapt itself rapidly enough to new
commercial practices.

General Custom

1. GREER, F.A. "Custom in the Common Law" (1893) 9 L.Q.R. 153:
   the part played by custom is examined. After distinguishing
   between general, local and conventional customs, the former
   is considered in detail. General custom of the realm is
   equivalent to the common law.

2. MARKBY, W. Elements of Law, (6th ed., Oxford, 1905), SS 79-91:
   there is a general account of the part played by custom in
   various countries. In England, instead of resorting to
   Roman law, the judges resorted to the custom of the realm,
   which became the common law.

Background Reading

3. JOLOWICZ, H.F. Historical Introduction to Roman Law, (2nd ed.,
   Cambridge University Press, 1952), pp. 363-365: the part
   played by custom in Roman law is explained.

4. GUTTERIDGE, H.C. Comparative Law, (Cambridge University Press,
   1946), pp. 80-81: a very brief account is given of the part
   played by custom in Continental countries.

5. ROBERTSON, L.J. "The Judicial Recognition of Custom in India"
   (1922) 4 J.C.L. (Ser. 3), 218: the attitude of Indian
   courts is shown to be different from that of English
   courts, since custom plays a more important part. The rigid
   tests applied by English courts cannot be applied.

6. ALLOTT, A.N. "The Judicial Ascertainment of Customary Law in
   British Africa" (1957) 20 M.L.R. 244: customary law here,
   as in Britain, is a derogation from the general law, but
   there are differences in finding it, while the fluid nature
   of customary law presents new problems.

7. HANNIGAN, A.St.J.J. "Native Custom, its Similarity to English
   Custom and its Mode of Proof" (1958), 2 J.A.L. 101: custom
   is not law till the courts pronounce it to be so. In Ghana
   custom is akin to English conventional custom rather than
   local custom.

8. VANDENBOSCH, A. "Customary Law in the Dutch East Indies" (1932)
   14 J.C.L. (Ser. 3), 30: the position here might usefully be
   compared with that in Britain, India and Africa.

7

VALUES

Importance of Values

1. CARDOZO, B.N. The Growth of the Law, (Yale University Press, 1924), chaps. 2-5: analysis of the judicial function should bring in the genesis, operation, growth, and ends of the law, for these give direction to legal thinking. This theme is developed by one of the most famous of American judges.

2. LLEWELLYN, K.N. The Common Law Tradition. Deciding Appeals, (Little, Brown & Co., 1960): the major contribution of this book is to show how the whole ethos, tradition and craftsmanship of the profession shapes the judge's "situation-sense" when he decides any particular case. "Situation-sense" is said to provide a basis for a reasonable measure of predictability of judicial decisions.

3. DICKINSON, J. "The Law Behind Law", (1929) 29 Col.L.R. 285: jural laws are not propositions about factual situations, but value-judgments on social relations. The article inquires into the "higher law' from which courts derive guidance.

4. COHEN, F.S. "Modern Ethics and the Law" (1934) 4 Brook. L.R. 33: logic can offer its services to desirable or undersirable ends. In deriving a rule from a given case, one has to decide that some facts in it are crucial, others not. This choice is dictated by a sense of values. The function of ethics is considered on this basis.

5. DWORKIN, R.M. "Is Law a System of Rules ?" in Essays in Legal Philosophy (ed. R.S. Summers, Basil Blackwell, Oxford, 1968), 25: law does not consist solely of rules of law; there are principles, standards and policies. They pull the application of rules one way or another. The notion of "discretion" is also examined in order to decide whether judicial use of these principles, etc. should be labelled "discretionary".

6. POUND, R. "Justice According to Law" (1913) 13 Col.L.R. 696; (1914) 14 Col.L.R. 1, 103: the administration of law involves a technical (legal) and non-technical (discretionary) element. Justice according to law requires administration of the law according to standards which may be ascertained in advance of dispute. But this is not always possible and a discretionary element has to come in. The pros and cons of various forms of adjudicating disputes are considered. See also R. POUND: Justice According to Law, (Yale University Press, 1952) and Jurisprudence, (West Publishing Co., 1959),

II, chap. 13.

1. POUND, R. Law and Morals, (The University of North Carolina Press, 1926): the theme of the book is the need for values in relation to the process of law-making and law-applying. The influence of the ideal element is traced from Greek times and the weakness of the positivist attitude is pointed out.

2. POUND, R. The Spirit of the Common Law, (Marshall Jones Co., 1921): this is of general interest, dealing with the various ideals which the common law has striven to achieve.

3. POUND, R. "A Comparison of Ideals of Law" (1933-34) 47 Harv. L.R. 1; (1933) 7 Tul.L.R. 475: ideals are part of the law. It is possible to compare the ideals of a particular age.

4. POUND, R. "Mechanical Jurisprudence" (1908) 8 Col.L.R. 605: the marks of a scientific law are conformity with reason, uniformity and certainty. But this must not be allowed to degenerate into technicality. Institutions should be founded on policy and adapted to human needs.

5. WAITE, J.B. "Judge-made Law and the Education of Lawyers" (1944) 30 Am.B.A.J. 253: the process of judicial law-making and also the training of judges for that task are considered.

6. RADCLIFFE, C.J. The Law and its Compass, (Faber & Faber, 1961): the law requires a compass by which to steer its course, i.e., values. In this connection the influence of Christianity, public policy and natural law is considered.

7. POTTER, H. The Quest of Justice, (Sweet & Maxwell, Ltd., 1951): justice, its relation to law, and the means by which it can be achieved, are discussed historically and philosophically.

8. POLLOCK, F. A First Book of Jurisprudence, (6th ed., Macmillan & Co., Ltd., 1929), chap. 2: the law presupposes ideals of justice. The relation of law to certain ideals, namely morality, certainty and equality, is outlined.

9. WRIGHT, R.A. "Causation and Responsibility in English Law" [1955] C.L.J. 163, especially pp. 164 et seq.: legal thought has an approach of its own. The "ought" of legal duty and the attribution of responsibility involves a reasoned value-judgment. This must be so since legal decisions give effect to the idea of "ought". Value-judgments are a necessary and integral part of the common law.

1. MORRIS, J.W. "Law and Public Opinion", Presidential Address
   to the Holdsworth Club (1958) the influence of public
   opinion on certain types of cases is considered.

2. HARPER, F.V. "The Forces Behind and Beyond Juristic Pragmatism
   in America" in Recueil d'Etudes sur les Sources du Droit en
   l'Honneur de F. Gény, (Librairie du Recueil, Sirey, 1934),
   II, 243: philosophy has followed science, but it leads the
   social sciences. This is because it gives direction and
   method. Juristic thought relates to the future and is
   creative, but there are limits to this.

3. FRIEDMANN, W. Law in a Changing Society, (Stevens & Sons, Ltd.,
   1959), chaps. 1-8 and 10: law reacts to social pressures.
   In these chapters this thesis is demonstrated with reference
   to different branches of the law in turn.

4. FRIEDMANN, W. Legal Theory, (5th ed., Stevens & Sons, Ltd.,
   1967), chaps. 17, 26-28, 31-33: the last three chapters
   deal with the values which the law seeks to attain. The
   earlier chapters deal with certain value philosophies.

5. FRIEDMANN, W. "Legal Theory and the Practical Lawyer" (1941)
   5 M.L.R. 103: it is impossible to avoid having to take
   values into account in the administration of law. The way
   in which they operate and the limits of their influence are
   considered.

6. FRIEDMANN, W. "Legal Philosophy and Judicial Lawmaking" (1961)
   61 Col.L.R. 821: the importance of values and of the need
   to make a creative choice between competing policies
   and ideals is illustrated from many points of view. A judge
   is not absolutely unfettered, but within limits he has
   considerable latitude.

7. JONES, J.W. "Modern Discussions of the Aims and Methods of
   Legal Science" (1931) 47 L.Q.R. 62, at pp. 78-84: the
   creative role of the judge is emphasised and some account
   is given of leading theories.

8. DENNING, A.T. The Changing Law, (Stevens & Sons, Ltd., 1953),
   especially chaps. 1-2: the spirit of the British constitution
   is said to rest on the instinct for justice, for liberty
   and for balancing right with duty, power with safeguard.
   Various aspects of the law are dealt with in this connection.

9. SCHMITTHOFF, C.M. "The Growing Ambit of the Common Law" (1951)
   29 Can.B.R. 469; (1952) 30 Can.B.R. 48: the common law has
   been able to adapt itself to the changes of the post-war
   world. The discussion concerns mainly administrative law,

but there are interesting sidelights on the working of
precedent, contract and other branches.

1. Science of Legal Method: Select Essays by Various Authors,
   (trans. E.Bruncken and L.B. Register, The Boston Book Co.,
   1917): this is a collection of writings of various
   Continental jurists, but there is one chapter contributed
   by R. Pound; and there are,in addition, Prefaces by Anglo-
   American jurists. The discretionary element in the judicial
   process is considered from several different angles, Of
   these perhaps the most interesting is that of F. Gény, who
   advocates the method of "free scientific research".

2. Recueil d'Etudes sur les Sources du Droit en l'Honneur de
   F. Gény, (Librairie du Recueil Sirey, 1934), II, M.
   FRANKLIN, p. 30: "M. Gény and Juristic Ideals and Methods
   in the United States": this deals generally with Gény's
   influence in America. A. KOCOUREK, p. 459: "Libre Recherche
   in America": the premises on which the "free law" movement
   is founded are explained and some account is given of the
   writers whose works constitute the background and foreground.
   J. DICKINSON, p. 503: "The Problem of the Unprovided Case":
   the problem is of finding grounds for reaching a decision
   where the grounds are not supplied by existing rules:
   J.G. ROGERS, p. 552: "A Scientific Approach to Free Judicial
   Decision": the norms of social conduct are not rules but
   examples. The social structure is a major element of the law
   itself.

3. WORTLEY, B.A. "Francois Gény" in Modern Theories of Law, (ed.
   W.I. Jennings, Oxford University Press, 1933), 139: marginal
   cases occur and logic alone cannot fill gaps. A legal system
   should seek to realise an ideal of justice and utility.
   Judicial discretion is vital - free scientific research
   according to justice and social utility. (See also B.A.
   Wortley, Jurisprudence, (Manchester U.P., Oceana Publications
   Inc., N.Y. 1967, chap. 12).

4. STONE, J. Legal System and Lawyers' Reasonings (Stevens & Sons,
   Ltd., 1964), pp. 212-223: a legislator cannot express his
   will on everything. It is in these spheres, according to
   Gény, that there has to be "free scientific research".
   Conceptions and deduction from them are important where the
   legislator intended given concepts to be worked out. Beyond
   this the logical method is harmful when applied to the
   changing relations in society.

5. KANTOROWICZ, H.U. and PATTERSON, E.W. "Legal Science - a
   Summary of its Methodology" (1928), 28 Col. L.R., 679, at
   pp. 698-707: the place of values in any treatment of law is

considered. The "gap" problem comes into prominence in the
application of law. Here the "free law" method is advocated.

1. CAIRNS, H. "The Valuation of Legal Science" (1940) 40 Col. L.
    R., 1: observation suggests corrections in theory;
    corrections in theory prompt refinements in observations.
    Such a procedure is open to jurisprudence. The vital
    question is whether a complete descriptive science of law
    can be constructed without introducing value elements. It
    is argued that a complete description has to include ethical
    and behaviour elements.

2. MILLER, A.S. and HOWELL, R.F. "The Myth of Neutrality in
    Constitutional Adjudication" (1959-60), 27 U.C.L.R., 661:
    neutrality is a myth and impossible in constitutional cases.
    Neutral observation is not possible even in the physical
    sciences. It is more useful to search for the values that
    can be furthered by the judicial process. What is needed is
    a purposive jurisprudence.

3. McDOUGAL, M.S. and LEIGHTON, G.C.K. "The Rights of Man in the
    World Community: Constitutional Illusions versus Rational
    Action" (1949-50), 59 Yale L.J., 60: this is of general
    interest. It concerns the interdependence of human values
    in the world community.

4. MARSH, N.S. "Civil Liberties in Europe" (1959) 75 L.Q.R., 530:
    this is a general discussion of what is implied by "civil
    liberties" especially with reference to the Convention for
    the Protection of Human Rights and Fundamental Freedoms 1950.

5. HARVEY, W.B. "A Value Analysis of Ghanaian Legal Development
    since Independence", (1964), 1 U.G.L.J., 4: "law" is said to
    be value-neutral, being merely a technique of social ordering
    available for use in support of any value-judgment that the
    manipulators of the technique entertain. The developments in
    Ghana are recounted and their significance assessed. The
    value of nationhood is said to be paramount.

6. LAMONT, W.D. The Value Judgment, (Edinburgh University Press,
    1955), chaps. 1 and 10: the nature of value judgments is
    carefully examined, and the contrast between value judgment
    and moral judgment investigated. This is recommended as one
    of the most useful non-legal discussions of the subject.

7. SHKLAR, J.N. Legalism, (Harvard University Press, 1964): this
    book is an attack on "legalism", which is the attitude of
    mind that makes a morality of rule following. Justice is an
    ideal of legalism, but need not be exclusive. Legalism is ·
    but one among many moralities in a pluralist society. The

morality of rule following is an instrument of politics and
it may succeed in some situations and not in others. The
whole book is a powerful plea for the widest accommodation
of diverse ideologies and ideals.

1. WILLIAMS, G.L. "Language and the Law" (1946) 62 L.Q.R. 387:
    the place of value-judgments is considered in the context
    of a general discussion of the function of language in law.

The Judicial Method

2. CARDOZO, B.N. The Nature of the Judicial Process, (Yale
    University Press, 1921): this is a classic exposition of
    the various factors at work in the judicial application of
    the law and the factors of which a judge takes account.

3. CARDOZO, B.N. The Paradoxes of Legal Science, (Columbia
    University Press, 1928), especially chaps. 2-3: judges have
    to balance values and should guard against substituting
    their own scale of values. Legal concepts are subordinate
    to expediency and justice.

4. HAND, L. "How Far is a Judge Free in Rendering a Decision?"
    in The Spirit of Liberty, (Hamish Hamilton, 1954), 103:
    the question is how far a judge should follow the dictates
    of his conscience or abide by the letter of the law. This
    is a simple but valuable examination of this matter by a
    well-known American judge. "The Speech of Justice", p. 13:
    judges are not passive interpreters of the law. They need
    to adopt a broader and more comprehensive outlook.

5. WASSERSTROM, R.A. The Judicial Decision, (Stanford University
    Press, 1961): this is a careful investigation into the
    nature of the judicial process. The author's own preference
    is for what he calls the "two-level justification", i.e.,
    a rule is a justification for a decision provided the rule
    itself is justifiable on utilitarian grounds.

6. GOTTLIEB, G. The Logic of Choice, (Allen & Unwin, Ltd., 1968):
    this work is an important analysis of how rules, principles
    and standards are used in reaching judicial decisions. He
    takes pains to point out that facts are not self-evident,
    but can be stated differently depending upon the context.
    Moral and policy considerations are incorporated into legal
    declarations.

7. SLESSER, H. The Art of Judgment, (Stevens & Sons, Ltd., 1962):
    the opening chapter is a demonstration of the judicial
    method by an English judge. He utters a caution against the
    tendency to exaggerate the discretionary element. See

further H. SLESSER: <u>The Judicial Office and Other Matters</u>,
(Hutchinson & Co., Ltd., 1942), chap. 3.

1. HODSON, F.L.C. "Judicial Discretion and its Exercise",
    <u>Presidential Address to the Holdsworth Club</u> (1962): too
    much discretion is bad. The scope of discretion is considered
    in relation to matrimonial disputes, criminal law, tort and
    public policy.

2. KILMUIR, The Lord (D. Maxwell-Fyffe), "The State, Citizen and
    the Law" (1957) 73 L.Q.R. 172: the problem of maintaining
    a just balance between the State and the individual is
    considered. Formerly, the State merely "held the ring"; now
    it enters into the battle. The law remains the right means
    for resolving conflicts between public and private interests.
    It should continue to change as social problems change.

3. SCRUTTON, T.E. "The Work of the Commercial Court" (1921-23)
    1 C.L.J. 6: the attributes of a good legal system are
    discussed. The portion relating to the need for impartiality
    is particularly interesting, and there are useful sidelights
    on the personal influence of particular judges.

4. HARDING, R.W. "Lord Atkin's Judicial Attitudes and their
    Illustration in Commercial Law and Contract" (1964) 27 M.L.
    R. 434: Lord Atkin's philosophy is revealed as being a
    wide, all-pervading commonsense, a firm sense of practicality
    and social responsibility and concern for principle. The
    influence of these factors is illustrated with reference
    to three famous cases.

5. POLLOCK, F. "Judicial Caution and Valour" (1929) 45 L.Q.R.
    293: the judicial function covers declaration of law and
    extension of it. In cases of first impression both caution
    and valour are required. The problem is to hold a balance
    between these two.

6. BARWICK, G. "Courts, Lawyers, and the Attainment of Justice"
    (1958) 1 Tasm.L.R. 1: in the first part of this paper it
    is pointed out that theoretically the courts neither make
    law nor do they seek to attain abstract justice. But there
    is room in applying the law to give effect to current views,
    although personal idiosyncracies also have some influence.

7. STEVENS, R. "The Role of a Final Appeal Court in a Democracy:
    the House of Lords Today" (1965) 28 M.L.R. 509: appeal
    courts are concerned with areas where the law is uncertain
    and where creative decisions are called for. Historically
    appeal courts were established for the development of the
    law. The attitude of the House of Lords is traced down to

the present time, and it is pointed out that since the
1950's there has been a departure from its former
"mechanistic" thinking.

1. DICKINSON, J.   Administrative Justice and the Supremacy of
    Law in the United States, (Harvard University Press, 1927),
    pp. 216 et seq.: to treat legal concepts as fixed and to
    apply them mechanically is harmful. The courts have been
    compelled to formulate principles of valuation.

2. DICKINSON, J.   "Legal Rules and their Function in the Process
    of Decision" (1931) 79 U.Pa.L.R. 833, at pp. 850-55: "Legal
    Rules, their Application and Elaboration", ibid. 1052: law
    is not a complete and coherent system. Discretion inevitably
    comes into its application. This depends not only on the
    nature of the case, but on the definiteness or vagueness of
    the rule. The application of a rule means the employment of
    it to decide a case; elaboration of a rule means the
    creation or extension of a rule to fill a gap. Both involve
    the use of value-judgments.

3. FRIEDMANN, W.   "Judges, Politics and the Law" (1951) 29 Can.
    B.R. 811: on one view judges should ignore political and
    social considerations; on another view, political
    legislation cannot be dealt with otherwise. The common law
    would not exist if judges had not from time to time laid
    down new principles to meet new social problems.

4. GROVE, D.L.   "The 'Sentinels' of Liberty? The Nigerian Judiciary
    and Fundamental Rights" (1963) 7 J.A.L. 152: what use has
    been made of the fundamental rights provision in the Nigerian
    Constitution? The cases fall into two groups, one concerning
    individuals alone, the other concerning the individual in
    relation to other interests. The latter involves balancing
    interests. The judicial attitude towards various freedoms
    is illustrated with the aid of cases.

5. HART, H.L.A.   "The Ascription of Responsibility and Rights"
    in Logic and Language, (ed. A.G.N. Flew, Blackwell, 1955)
    1, 145: legal concepts are not determinate and judges have
    often to decide the question of responsibility in order to
    decide what legal label to apply.

6. LLEWELLYN, K.N.   "Impressions of the Conference on Precedent"
    in Jurisprudence: Realism in Theory and Practice (University
    of Chicago Press, 1962), 116: precedents control judicial
    action even against the judges' inclinations, but sometimes
    when the urge of policy or justice is strong enough judges
    do find a way round them. Within limits precedents can be
    manipulated to favour one side or the other, but this is

not governed by arbitrary considerations.

1. FULLER, L.L. "Reason and Fiat in Case Law" (1945-46) 59 Harv.
   L.R. 376: the judge's freedom of choice is limited,
   particularly by the consideration that his decision will
   become a precedent. Hence his choice has to be shorn of
   personal predilictions and it has to conform to sentiments
   of justice.

2. NELLES, W. "Towards Legal Understanding" (1934) 34 Col.L.R.
   862, 1041: the forces that develop law are examined at
   length. It is unreal to regard the judicial process as
   mechanical. There has to be a different conception of it.

3. SEIDMAN, R.B. The Judicial Process Reconsidered in the Light
   of Role-theory" (1969) 32 M.L.R. 516: the judge's function
   is different in "clear" and "trouble" cases. In the latter
   he has a creative task to perform, and the problem is one
   of values.

4. MENDELSON, W. "The Judge's Art" (1960-61) 109 U.Pa.L.R. 524:
   this is a sympathetic examination of judicial creativeness.

5. von MEHREN, A.T. The Civil Law System: Cases and Materials,
   (Prentice-Hall, Inc., 1957), chap. 16, pp. 821-23: this is
   a brief but valuable study of the judicial process. In the
   pages mentioned its flexibility and its non-mechanical
   nature are emphasised.

6. COHEN, F.S. "The Problems of a Functional Jurisprudence"
   (1937) 1 M.L.R. 5: there is often a "plaintiff principle"
   and a "defendant principle". The choice between them depends
   upon unstated considerations.

7. MILLER, A.S. "On the Need for 'Impact Analysis' of Supreme
   Court Decision" (1964-65) 53 Georgetown L.J. 365: judicial
   decisions should be evaluated according to their social
   effects. A judge chooses between opposing premises on the
   basis of what the impact of the decision is thought to be -
   "jurisprudence of consequences". Courts now have an
   affirmative function, viz., to co-operate with other branches
   of government. Evaluation of this function requires more
   than just explanation of the bases of decision.

8. LERNER, M. "The Supreme Court and American Capitalism" (1932-
   33) 42 Yale L.J. 668, at pp. 686-701: a course of decisions
   is examined first and then the nature of the judicial
   process. The function of the Court is to partake in forming
   policy. The judge does not fashion new law according to his
   own views. The various considerations that govern his choice
   are considered.

1. McWHINNEY, E. "The Supreme Court and the Bill of Rights - the Lessons of Comparative Jurisprudence" (1959) 37 Can.B.R. 16: there is a need for a value-oriented jurisprudence. The problem is to define the limits of the new absolutes. The judicial function is considered in this light.

2. SCHWARTZ, B. "The Changing Role of the United States Supreme Court", (1950) 28 Can.B.R. 48: the sense of values of the Supreme Court is discussed in relation to national and individual interests.

3. HAND, L. The Bill of Rights. The Oliver Wendell Holmes Lectures 1958, (Harv.U.P. 1958): The Supreme Court's power to review governmental acts is not to be found in, or inferred from, the Constitution. Such power has to be assumed, but it should be used sparingly. It should not be used to question the substance of governmental acts, and in this respect the Court has been exceeding its province.

4. WECHSLER, H. "Toward Neutral Principles of Constitutional Law" (1959-60) 73 Harv.L.R. 1: the author takes issue with Judge Hand as to when courts may review legislative action. Courts do have to make value-choices, but this should be done according to principles. A principle decision is one which rests on reasons with respect to all the issues in a case and in their generality and neutrality transcend the immediate issues. Certain recent leading cases are criticised on the ground that the courts did not act on such principles.

5. POLLAK, L.H. "Racial Discrimination and Judicial Integrity: A Reply to Professor Wechsler" (1959-60) 108 U.Pa.L.R. 1: it is true that courts should act on the sort of principles advocated by Professor Wechsler, but it is argued that in the cases criticised by him the courts did in fact do so.

6. HART, H.M. "The Time Chart of the Justices" (1959-60) 73 Harv.L.R. 84: reason is the life of the law, and this means the acceptance of impersonal and durable principles. He, therefore, agrees with Professor Wechsler. The trouble is that the Supreme Court has too much work to get through.

7. HENKIN, L. "Some Relections on Current Constitutional Controversy" (1960-61) 109 U.Pa.L.R. 637: constitutional issues today are different from those of the past. In dealing with the "Controversy of the Professors" (at pp. 650 et seq.) the author agrees with Professor Wechsler, but thinks that the cases he attacked are defensible.

8. MILLER, A.S. and HOWELL, R.F. "The Myth of Neutrality in Constitutional Adjudication" (1959-60) 27 U.C.L.R. 661:

application of "neutral" principles without value-choices
is impossible. Neutrality is unattainable in social or even
in natural sciences. Choices between values are motivated
by the entire biography and heredity of the person making
the choice. Judges should be guided by a teleological
jurisprudence, which makes them participants in government.
Decisions should be made with reference to the effects of
decisions. (See also A. MUELLER and M.L. SCHWARTZ: "The
Principle of Neutral Principles" (1960) 7 U.Ca.L.A.L., 571:
this also questions the possibility of "neutral" principles".

1. GOLDING, M.P. "Principled Decision-making and the Supreme
    Court" in Essays in Legal Philosophy, (ed R.S. SUMMERS,
    Basil Blackwell, Oxford, 1968), 208: one cannot apply
    "neutral" principles in choosing between competing values.
    One may choose with reference to some other principle, which
    is more comprehensive or superior. When there is no such
    principle, a court may still formulate a principle which will
    serve in other cases of its type. Such a principle is
    "general" insofar as it transcends the instant case, but it
    is not "neutral" save as to its future application.

2. STONE, J. "'Result-orientation'and Appellate Judgment" in
    Perspectives of Law. Essays for Austin Wakeman Scott, (edd.
    R. POUND, E.N. GRISWOLD, A.E. SUTHERLAND, Little, Brown & Co.,
    1964), 347: the result of deciding with reference to "result-
    orientation" would not be different from deciding with
    reference to "neutral" principles. It is not possible to know
    what principle is applicable without reference to the facts.
    Professor Wechsler's thesis is tenable only within very
    modest limits.

3. BROWN, R.A. "Police Power - Legislation for Health and Personal
    Safety" (1928-29), 42 Harv. L.R., 866: a large number of
    decisions on certain statutes are reviewed. These show that
    the attitude of the courts is to treat the individual and
    property, not as ends in themselves, but in conjunction with
    social needs.

4. SCOTT, W.C. "Judicial Logic as Applied in Delimiting the
    Concept of Business 'Affected with a Public Interest'" (1930),
    19 Ken. L.J., 16: this examines the technique used by
    American courts in giving effect to public interests and
    public regulation. The "functional" method is contrasted
    with the "physical analogy" method.

5. NELLES, W. "The First American Labor Case" (1931-32), 41 Yale
    L.J., 165: this reviews the decision in a criminal prosecution
    for conspiracy arising out of trade combination. It shows

clearly how values played a major part.

1. BINGHAM, J.W. "Some Suggestions Concerning 'Legal Cause' at
    Common Law", (1909), 9 Col. L.R., 16, 136: one cannot know
    how a judge will decide a case, but one can grasp the
    method, considerations and influences which guide the
    courts. Judges decide as considerations of justice and
    policy dictate.

2. ROBSON, W.A. Justice and Administrative Law, (3rd ed., Stevens
    & Sons, Ltd., 1951), chap. 5, especially pp. 409-18: this is
    an inquiry into the "judicial spirit". The impartiality of
    the "good judge" is legendary. The administration of justice
    requires as much prejudice in one sense and absence of
    prejudice in another, i.e., prejudice as to what is
    socially desirable.

3. GOODHART, A.L. "The New York Court of Appeals and the House of
    Lords" in Essays in Jurisprudence and the Common Law,
    (Cambridge University Press, 1937), chap. 13: judges do not
    reach their conclusions on quite such uncertain bases as
    "hunches" and their reasons are not merely cloaks. This may
    be true in doubtful cases, but not in the majority.

4. WADE, H.W.R. "The Concept of Legal Certainty. A Preliminary
    Skirmish" (1940-41), 4 M.L.R., 183: the extent of judicial
    discretion is considered. Judges do contrive to keep
    individual preferences to a minimum.

5. FRANKFURTER, F. "John Marshall and the Judicial Function",
    (1955-56), 69 Harv. L.R., 217: the vision of a single man
    gave direction to the American Constitution, which was until
    then largely a paper scheme of government.

6. FRANKFURTER, F. "The Constitutional Opinions of Mr Justice
    Holmes", (1916), 29 Harv. L.R., 683: the influence of
    individual personalities is important. The point is
    illustrated with reference to Mr Justice Holmes's insight.

7. FRANKFURTER, F. "Twenty Years of Mr Justice Holmes's
    Constitutional Opinions" (1922-23), 36 Harv. L.R., 909:
    judges of the Supreme Court move in a field of statesmanship,
    which marks the boundaries between state and individual. The
    interpretation of the Constitution is inspired by consider-
    ations outside the law. The work of Mr Justice Holmes is
    reviewed along these lines.

8. LEVY, B.H. Cardozo and Frontiers of Legal Thinking, (New York,
    1958), chap. 2: judges do make law. The choice between
    various considerations is governed by convenience and fitness.

The judge has to be a careful student of public opinion.

1. PATTERSON, E.W. "Cardozo's Philosophy of Law", (1940), 88 U.
   Pa. L.R., 71, especially pp. 165 et seq.: Mr Justice
   Cardozo made explicit the value problems implicit in the
   judicial process.

2. HAMILTON, W.H. "Preview of a Justice", (1938-39), 48 Yale
   L.J., 819: this is an appraisal of Mr Justice Frankfurter.
   It seeks to show how heredity, culture, impulse and
   reaction that make up personality pass into legal opinions.
   Logic alone is sterile; a scheme of values makes an
   interpreter a creator.

Ideals

3. COHEN, F.S. "Field Theory and Judicial Logic", (1949-50), 59
   Yale L.J., 238: a dependable approach to the prediction of
   judicial decisions might be found by observing the judge's
   use of precedent, which will reveal his value-patterns.
   Even though individual judges may vary in their opinions,
   certain lines of precedents are discoverable.

4. DOWRICK, F.E. "Lawyers' Values for Law-reform", (1963), 79 L.
   Q.R., 556: this is an interesting approach to the question
   of values. The work of various bodies that have from time
   to time been appointed to make recommendations on law
   reform is reviewed in order to extract the values on which
   each proceeded.

5. POUND, R. "The Ideal Element in American Judicial Decision",
   (1931-32), 45 Harv. L.R., 136: judicial ideals as to
   social order are a decisive factor of legal development.
   This ideal element should receive the same thorough
   analysis as the precept element.

6. POUND, R. "Juristic Science and Law", (1917-18), 31 Harv. L.R.
   1047: this challenges the idea that law is something that
   is always given. Law is not wholly made up of rules. There
   are rules, standards and principles. The modern functional
   approach takes account of the social environment of the law.

7. POUND, R. "Do We Need a Philosophy of Law?", (1905), 5 Col. L.R.
   339; Jurisprudence in Action, (Baker, Voorhis & Co., Inc.,
   1953), 389: at the date when this was written the main
   trouble was alleged to be that the courts paid too much
   respect for the individual and too little for society. What
   was needed was philosophy of social values.

8. POUND, R. "A Survey of Social Interests", (1943-44), 57 Harv.

L.R., 1: the three major "planes" on which interests may
be considered are individual, public and social. When
weighing them, they should be considered on the same plane.
A detailed scheme of interests is given. See also R. POUND:
Jurisprudence, (West Publishing Co., 1959), IV; and for
further references, see post, Chap. 18.

1. STONE, J. Social Dimensions of Law and Justice, (Stevens &
    Sons, Ltd., 1966), Chaps. 4-8, 12, 14: Pound's scheme of
    individual and social interests is examined in detail. The
    main concern is to show how the content of substantive law
    in various branches is shaped by the interplay of
    interests. Chapter 12 discusses the way in which people
    come to hold values. The discussion is tentative since
    knowledge on the subject is still rudimentary. Chapter 14
    ties up the nature of the judicial process with social
    values.

2. O'SULLIVAN, R. "A Scale of Values in the Common Law", (1937),
    1 M.L.R. 27: freedom of the individual had become accepted
    by the time of Elizabeth. Free will is said to rank highest
    at common law. Next comes well-being and integrity, property,
    conveyance and contract.

3. DIAS, R.W.M. "The Value of a Value-study of Law", (1965), 28
    M.L.R. 397: interests are "measured" with reference to some
    yardstick, and it is these yardsticks that are of importance,
    not so much the interests themselves. There is a detectable
    hierarchy of yardsticks in the form of national and social
    safety, sanctity of the individual and sanctity of property
    in that order. Beyond that the pattern of values is a
    shifting one.

Particular Values

4. MILL, J.S. On Liberty and Considerations on Representative
    Government, (ed., R.B. McCallum, Blackwell, 1946): each
    individual should be given freedom to pursue his own
    happiness so as to contribute to the sum-total of human well-
    being, i.e., so long as he does not harm others. The enemies
    of liberty are two - the state and general opinion. Mill's
    disquisition is essentially an analysis of the values
    involved in freedom.

5. HART, H.L.A. Law, Liberty and Morality, (Oxford University
    Press, 1963): in the main Mill's thesis is adopted, namely,
    that the law should not interfere with the freedom of the
    individual except where it harms others. However, an
    important qualification is added that the law may interfere
    on grounds of paternalism to prevent people harming themselves.

1. DEVLIN, P. "Mill on Liberty in Morals" in The Enforcement of
   Morals (Oxford University Press, 1965), Chap. 6: Lord
   Devlin considers Mill's thesis particularly in relation to
   homosexuality. The fallacy in the thesis that one should
   tolerate even that which no one regards as "good" because
   it is possible that everyone may be mistaken lies in the
   failure to distinguish between freedom of thought and of
   action. When it comes to action people have to act according
   to what they believe to be good and right, even while they
   may acknowledge that they may be wrong.

2. FULLER, L.L. "Freedom - a Suggested Analysis" (1954-55) 68
   Harv.L.R. 1305: a distinction is drawn between "freedom to"
   and "freedom from". The whole question of freedom involves
   purposive action of the person whose freedom is in question,
   equal freedom of others with regard to him and a measure of
   immunity from the actions of others. Freedom and order are
   not antithetical; but a single planned order is not
   essential.

3. GOODHART, A.L. "Freedom under the Law" (1960) 1 Tasm.L.R.
   375: in the 19th century liberty and law were opposed to
   each other, but in the latter part of the 19th century
   different view began to develop. The interplay of people
   demanded more control by law, and hence legal control was
   thought of as necessary to freedom. Political, economic and
   societal liberty are reviewed in turn on this basis.

4. CARRITT, E.F. "Liberty and Equality" (1940) 56 L.Q.R. 61:
   consideration is given to the question how far the two are
   compatible with each other in social existence.

5. PARKER, H.L. "The Role of the Judge in the Preservation of
   Liberty" (1961) 35 Aust.L.J. 63: judges have played an
   important part in preserving liberty by possessing personal
   beliefs in the value of individual freedom. In protecting
   the individual against administrative action, the
   supervisory jurisdiction of courts should remain elastic.

6. SALMON, C.B. "The Bench. The Last Bulwark of Individual
   Liberty" (1967) 117 New L.J. 749: the courts have always
   been, and still are, vigilant in safeguarding the individual
   in many different ways. Some recent judicial developments
   are considered in this light. It is pointed out, though,
   that in time of war this vigilance is relaxed.

7. O'SULLIVAN, R. "The Bond of Freedom" (1943) 6 M.L.R. 177:
   justice is the binding principle of states. The great
   creation of the common law was the free individual.

1. HALE, R.L. Freedom Through Law, (Columbia University Press, 1952): this is of general interest. It deals with problems created by freedom over a wide area of law. Much of the book is also concerned with justice. (See L.L. FULLER: "Some Relections on Legal and Economic Freedoms - a Review of Robert L. Hale's 'Freedom Through Law'" (1954) 54 Col.L.R. 70).

2. LLOYD, D. The Idea of Law, (Penguin Books, Ltd., A 688, 1964), chap. 7: the "open society", i.e., one in which there is scope for the individual, is contrasted with the "closed society", i.e., one in which the community is dominent and the individual counts for nothing. Basic human rights and the principal values are set out and discussed. The chapter concludes with the international protection of human rights.

3. ARISTOTLE, Nichomachean Ethics, (trans. R. Williams, 3rd ed., Longmans, Green & Co., 1879), V: this famous discussion of justice proceeds by dividing it into distributive and corrective justice. The relation of equity to justice is also considered. (See H. KELSEN: What is Justice?, (University of California Press, 1957), 110, for a critical study of Aristotle's doctrine).

4. GINSBERG, M. On Justice in Society (Heinemann, London, 1965): Aristotle's formula of equal treatment of equals, differential treatment of unequals, is worked out in the light of modern social conditions. The main problem is to relate formal justice, which enjoins the exclusion of arbitrariness and justification for differential treatment, and substantive justice, namely the corpus of rights and duties. This is a most important and instructive work.

5. VINOGRADOFF, P. "Legal Standards and Ideals" in Collected Papers, (Oxford, 1928), II, chap, 18: the criteria discussed are equality before the law, equality of opportunity, proportion, equity and social movements.

6. VINOGRADOFF, P. Common-Sense in Law, (3rd ed., H.G. Hanbury, Oxford University Press, 1959), chap. 8: this gives consideration to the concept of equity. It deals with the part played by fairness in the interpretative process.

7. Interpretation of Modern Legal Philosophies, (ed. P. Sayre, Oxford University Press, New York, 1947): C.K. ALLEN: "Justice and Expediency", chap. 1: this considers how individual liberties are being threatened by executive action. J. HALL: "Integrative Jurisprudence", chap. 14: a philosophy of law should combine axiology, formal analysis and sociology. W.E. HOCKING: "Justice, Law, and the Cases",

chap. 15: the function of justice is dealt with. H. KELSEN: "The Metamorphosis of the Idea of Justice", chap. 18: the changes in meaning of the term "justice" since the time of the Greeks is considered. A.V. LUNDSTEDT: "Law and Justice: a Criticism of the Method of Justice", chap. 21: judgments of value differ from scientific judgments, since they depend on feelings.

1. BODENHEIMER, E. Jurisprudence, (Harvard University Press, 1962), chaps. 11-13, 17: the aim of justice is to co-ordinate the diversified efforts of members of the community in a way that will satisfy the reasonable needs and aspirations of individuals. The meaning of justice and the harmony of order and justice are discussed in a highly interesting way. In S.76 in the last-mentioned chapter value-judgments are explained.

2. BODENHEIMER, E. "Law as Order and Justice" (1957) 6 J.P.L. 194: the striving of the law towards order and justice is founded upon ideals.

3. LAMONT, W.D. The Principles of Moral Judgment, (Oxford, 1946), chap. 5: justice in the sense of distributive justice is examined. It is broken down into equality, liberty and merit.

4. OFSTAD, H. "Impartiality" in Legal Essays. A Tribute to Frede Castberg, (Universitetsforlaget, 1963), 135: impartiality is subjected to detailed investigation. It does lead to the question of justice and the distinction between "correct" and "incorrect" ethical systems.

5. ALLEN, C.K. Aspects of Justice, (Stevens & Sons, Ltd., 1958), chaps. 1-5: the first chapter is a general account of the various meanings of justice. Justice is also considered with reference to mercy, expediency and liberty.

6. HOLLAND, D.C. "Equality Before the Law" (1955) 8 C.L.P. 74: equality before the law does not exist in a number of territories for which the United Kingdom government is responsible.

7. HONORÉ, A.M. "Social Justice" in Essays in Legal Philosophy (ed. R.S. SUMMERS, Basil Blackwell, Oxford, 1968), 61: justice should be considered from the point of view of the citizen to whom just treatment is due. A more finely graded analysis than Aristotle's is given of the various manifestations of justice and of permissible departures.

8. ECKHOFF, T. "Justice and Social Utility" in Legal Essays. A Tribute to Frede Castberg, (Universitetsforlaget, 1963), 74: principles of justice and social utility are two of the

most important ideas that have had impact upon the law. The
two are compared and contrasted. Both share a place in
legal reasoning.

1. KELSEN, H. What is Justice ?, (University of California Press,
   1957), pp. 1, 209: justice is a shifting idea. It is the
   foundation of contentment and, as such, is purely subjective.
   Value-judgments are of two sorts. One sort qualifies
   conduct as legal or illegal (values of the law); the other
   qualifies the law as just or unjust (values of justice).

2. LLOYD, D. The Idea of Law, (Penguin Books, Ltd., A 688, 1964),
   chap. 6: justice is one of the aims which Man sets himself
   in order to achieve the good life. It is said that whereas
   the Greek idea embodied inequality, the modern idea is
   essentially one of equality. The manner in which the formal
   principle of equality needs to be filled out is explained at
   some length. The divergence between ethical and legal
   justice, and also the manner in which the latter can approx-
   imate to the former are discussed.

3. TAYLOR, A. "Functional Aspects of the Lawyer's Concept of
   Justice", [1966] Jur. R., 13: the relation between law and
   justice has posed problems which have been variously
   answered. The lawyer's concept of justice is one for judges.
   "Equality in the law" is a directive to law-makers; "equality
   before the law" is the specific legal contribution to the
   concept of justice.

4. LLOYD, D. Public Policy, (University of London Press, 1953),
   chaps. 1-4, 7-8: English and French law are compared. Public
   policy is considered generally and not specifically with
   reference to particular decisions. Various public and
   individual values are considered.

5. LLOYD, D. "Law and Public Policy" (1958), 8 C.L.P., 42: every
   new decision is a form of legislation, but judicial
   legislation is not openly avowed. Public policy is discussed
   in relation to civil law systems.

6. WINFIELD, P.H. "Public Policy in the English Common Law",
   (1928-29), 42 Harv. L.R., 76: the influence of public policy
   on English judges, its nature and limits are investigated
   historically. The most that judicial interpretation of
   public policy can do is to keep it abreast of prevailing
   ethical standards.

7. WRIGHT, R.A. "Public Policy" in Legal Essays and Addresses,
   (Cambridge University Press, 1939), chap. 3: the part played
   by public policy in the development of English law is

carefully considered. It does not enable the judges to give
free rein to their personal opinions.

1. RADCLIFFE, C.J. The Law and its Compass, (Faber & Faber, 1961),
    chap. 2: public policy and its influence upon the law are
    considered at some length.

2. KNIGHT, W.S.M. "Public Policy in English Law" (1922) 38 L.Q.R.
    207: this gives a general account and history of the
    doctrine.

3. RAM, J. The Science of Legal Judgment, (2nd ed., J. Townshend,
    Baker, Voorhis & Co., New York, 1871), chap. 6, S. 1:
    public policy, convenience and inconvenience are considered
    as grounds of decision in doubtful cases.

4. GOODHART, A.L. English Law and the Moral Law, (Stevens & Sons,
    Ltd., 1955): the link between law and morals is indissoluable.
    The influence of morals in various branches of the law is
    considered.

5. WINFIELD, P.H. "Ethics in English Case Law", (1931-32), 45 Harv.
    L.R., 112: morality rests in a consciousness of the difference
    between good and evil. There is a close connection between
    morals and law, but there is always an area of morals which
    is outside the law. The points of contact between morals and
    law are considered.

6. O'MEARA, J. "Natural Law and Everyday Law", (1960), 5 Nat. L.F.
    83: the judicial process leaves a great deal of discretion
    to the judge. In applying this he should be guided by
    natural law, i.e., ethical principles. There are certain
    basic things which remain good or evil everywhere always.

7. JONES, H.W. "Law and Morality in the Perspective of Legal
    Realism", (1961), 61 Col. L.R., 799: the syllogistic form
    obscures the large element of discretion that there is in
    the judicial process. The law has a moral dimension. The
    American Realists, by showing that rules do not control
    judicial decisions, have shown that this moral dimension is
    not to be found in rules either.

8. "Round Table Discussion: 'What should be the Relation of Morals
    to Law ?'" (1952), 1 J.P.L., 259: law, philosophy, theology
    and psychology are represented in this symposium. It is an
    interesting collection of views.

9. MERRILLS, J.G. "Law, Morals and the Psychological Nexus"
    (1969), 19 Tor. L.J., 46: law influences morals by providing
    a setting. It ensues security; it is itself a system of

norms to which there is a general moral duty to obey; and
it provides a standard of comparison when moral decisions
have to be made. On the other hand, morality exercises a
considerable influence on law.

1. HOCKING, W.E. "Ways of Thinking about Rights; a New Theory of
   the Relation between Law and Morals" in Law: A Century of
   Progress, (New York University Press; London: Humphrey
   Milford, 1937), II, 242: in the emergence of a right two
   factors are at work - the pressure of all the interests
   that form its content and the ethical sense of the group
   or community that give it its form.

2. COHEN, F.S. "The Ethical Basis of Legal Criticism" (1931-32)
   41 Yale L.J. 201: ethical criteria of what ought to be the
   law cannot be dismissed. The valuation of law is dependent
   upon the concept of the good life. The judge's choice is
   frequently governed by ethics, not logic.

3. BARRY, J.V. "Morality and the Coercive Process" (1962) 4 Syd.
   L.R. 28: the prohibitions of the law are one of many
   devices for influencing and controlling society. Justice
   in the law is only intelligible with reference to ethical
   standards.

4. COHEN, M.R. Reason and Law, (The Free Press, Glencoe,
   Illinois, 1950), chaps. 2-3: the moral element in criminal
   law is considered. Chapter 3 considers the standards of
   moral judgment.

5. MORRIS, H. "Punishment for Thoughts" in Essays in Legal
   Philosophy (ed. R.S. SUMMERS, Basil Blackwell, Oxford,
   1968), 95: it is not enough to say that law is concerned
   with external conduct, morals with "internal conduct".
   The statement is conceptual in that it says something about
   the nature of law. The relationship between law (mainly
   criminal law) and morals is considered from this angle.

6. KOCOUREK, A. An Introduction to the Science of Law, (Little,
   Brown & Co., 1930), pp. 121-36: law and morals may be
   compared from various points of view, the field of conduct
   that is governed, method of controlling conduct, attitude
   regarding conduct, object sought in controlling conduct.
   Law and morals mutually influence each other.

7. DEVLIN, P. "The Enforcement of Morals", Maccabaean Lecture
   in Jurisprudence of the British Academy, (Oxford University
   Press, 1959): to what extent should criminal law concern
   itself with morals and sin? A complete separation of the
   concept of crime from sin would be disastrous for the

criminal law. This theme is developed in a stimulating and
original manner.

1. DEVLIN, P. "Law and Morals" Presidential Address to the
    Holdsworth Club, (1961): the moral basis of law is
    investigated further with reference to "real" and "quasi-
    criminal" law. (See further P. DEVLIN: "Law, Democracy and
    Morals" (1962) 110 U.Pa.L.R. 635, 640).

2. DEVLIN, P. The Enforcement of Morals (Oxford University
    Press, 1965): in this series of essays Lord Devlin
    considers the part played by morality in various branches
    of law, criminal and civil. It includes the three mentioned
    above. In the last three essays he carries the discussion
    on to a different plane. Much of the criticism of the
    original lectures is answered in the course of the book.

3. GINSBERG, M. On Justice in Society, (Heinemann, London, 1965),
    chap 12: neither morality nor law are closed systems. Their
    separation cannot be defended either as an account of how
    law works or ought to work. The distinction in the Wolfenden
    Report between "public" and "private" morality is criticised.
    Lord Devlin is also criticised for not taking sufficient
    account of the part law may play in shaping the moral sense.
    There is a careful discussion of what the relation between
    law and morals should be in the general context of justice.

4. WOLHEIM, R. "Crime, Sin and Mr. Justice Devlin" (1959)
    Encounter 34: this takes issue with Mr. Justice Devlin's
    "The Enforcement of Morals".

5. HART, H.L.A. Law, Liberty and Morality, (Oxford University
    Press, 1963): the issue discussed is whether the fact that
    certain conduct is by common standards considered immoral
    constitutes a justification for making it punishable. This
    is a detailed answer to Mr. Justice Devlin. See also
    H.L.A. HART: "Immorality and Treason" (1959) The Listener
    162; H.L.A. HART: "The Use and Abuse of the Criminal Law"
    (1961) 4 Oxford Lawyer 7; G.B.J. HUGHES: "Morals and the
    Criminal Law" (1962) 71 Yale L.J. 662; R.S. SUMMERS: Review
    of H.L.A. Hart's Law, Liberty and Morality (1963) 38 N.Y.U.
    L.R. 1201.

6. ROSTOW, E.V. "The Enforcement of Morals" [1960] C.L.J. 174:
    Mr. Justice Devlin's thesis is, on the whole, defended
    against the attacks by H.L.A. Hart and R. Wolheim. A society
    does have a common morality which it is entitled to enforce.

7. WALKER, N. "Morality and the Criminal Law" (1964) How.J. 209:
    according to the "declaratory" theory, the function of

criminal law is to indicate current moral opinion and it
has been suggested that people's moral standards are
affected by what they believe to be current opinion. Hence,
according to this theory, prohibition by criminal law is
necessary to preserve moral standards, irrespective of
whether such prohibition is effective or not. The author
concludes that the evidence is against the declaratory
theory. He therefore advocates reform of the law relating
to abortion, homosexuality, etc. unless a positive
justification is proffered for using criminal law for
preserving standards in these matters.

1. WALKER, N. and ARGYLE, M. "Does the Law affect Moral Judgments?"
    (1964) 4 Br.J.C. 570: the empirical test alluded to above
    is set out in detail and its results analysed. The conclusion
    is drawn that the evidence is against the "declaratory"
    theory of the function of criminal law.

2. DWORKIN, R. "Lord Devlin and the Enforcement of Morals" (1965-
    66) 75 Yale L.J. 986: the author considers Lord Devlin's
    argument in support of the proposition that society has a
    right to protect itself, and how far the social environment
    should be protected from change. The weakness of Lord
    Devlin's position is not the assertion that a community's
    morality counts, but what counts as the community's
    morality.

3. WILLCOCK, I.D. "Crying Wolfenden too Often" [1965] S.L.T.
    113: Lord Devlin's argumentation is criticised. But the
    author concludes nonetheless that a common morality is
    desirable and that the state should seek to uphold it. The
    determination of what conduct should be punished ought to
    be left to elected and informed representatives, and that
    in a case of doubt personal liberty ought to prevail.

4. WILLIAMS, G.L. "Authoritarian Morals and the Criminal Law"
    [1966] Crim.L.R. 132: Lord Devlin's thesis is answered
    point by point. In the course of the argument certain
    aspects of the utilitarian point of view are also clarified.

5. ISON, P.G. "The Enforcement of Morals" (1967) 3 U.Br.Col.L.R.
    263: the author takes issue with Lord Devlin's thesis point
    by point. The article is purely destructive, but does not
    consider possible criticisms of Professor Hart's thesis.

6. HENKIN, L. "Morals and the Constitution: the Sin of Obscenity"
    (1963) 63 Col.L.R. 393: the basis of the article is an
    important contribution. Obscenity is forbidden, not because
    it excites people, but because it is offensive to that which
    has become part of the fabric of the society. The government

has a responsibility for maintaining communal and individual decency.

1. MITCHELL, B.G. Law, Morality, and Religion in a Secular Society (Oxford University Press, 1967): this is an acute and penetrating analysis of the positions taken up by Lord Devlin and Professor Hart. By clarifying the obscurities and ambiguities in both theses the author shows precisely where they differ. The main trend of the argument overwhelmingly supports Lord Devlin.

2. CARON, Y. "The Legal Enforcement of Morals and the So-called Hart-Devlin Controversy" (1969) 15 McGill L.J. 9: it may be necessary to enforce legally some aspects of morality, but it is better to avoid using law rather than adopt unworkable rules. The author begins by reviewing some well-known recent decisions involving morality and then turns to the Hart-Devlin controversy. His analysis is designed to show that the two sides are arguing about two different aspects of the problem.

3. GOODHART, A.L. "The Shaw Case: the Law and Public Morals" (1961) 77 L.Q.R. 560: this gives consideration to an important decision which upheld punishment for an act which was obviously wrong morally.

4. SAMUELS, A. "Obscenity and the Law" (1964) 61 L.S.Gaz. 729: the article shows the difficulty of deciding when a publication should be suppressed on grounds of obscenity. The opposing considerations of freedom to publish and protection of the public are perhaps not investigated as fully as they might have been.

5. MEWETT, A.W. "Morality and the Criminal Law" (1962) 14 Tor. L.J. 213: this discussion is mainly inspired by the Shaw case.

6. STONE, J. Social Dimensions of Law and Justice, (Stevens & Sons, Ltd., 1966), pp. 368-81: the social interest in morals is considered and the foregoing controversy is examined. It is pointed out in particular that the distinction between private and public spheres of action is not as clear-cut as might appear.

7. WILLIAMS, D.G.T. "Sex and Morals in the Criminal Law, 1954-1963" [1964] Crim.L.R. 253: this is a review of the manner in which the courts have used the criminal law to give effect to moral values. The Shaw case is criticised for infringing the maxim nulla poena sine lege.

1. ALLEN, C.K. Legal Duties, (Oxford, 1931), pp. 196-220: the
    relation between morality and legal duties is investigated,
    and their close connection pointed out.

2. LLOYD, D. The Idea of Law, (Penguin Books, Ltd., A 688, 1964),
    chap. 3: laws were originally ascribed to a divine law-giver.
    The views of the Hebrew prophets and Greek philosophers on
    the part played by morality are explained. Law and morality
    share much common ground because both seek to impose
    certain standards. The reasons why law and morality may
    diverge and the different attitudes that might be adopted
    in such cases are also discussed.

3. AMES, J.B. "Law and Morals", in Lectures on Legal History and
    Miscellaneous Legal Essays, (Harvard University Press, 1913),
    435: early law is alleged to have been unmoral since it
    attached responsibility to the act. It was the growing
    morality of the law that led to the supersession of this
    principle by the fault principle. There has been a corres-
    ponding development in contract.

4. POUND, R. Jurisprudence, (West Publishing Co., 1959), II,
    chap. 11: the relationship between law and morals is
    surveyed.

5. KANTOROWICZ, H.U. The Definition of Law, (ed. A.H. Campbell,
    Cambridge University Press, 1958), chap. 4: the relation
    between law and morals is considered with a view to a
    definition of law. The former, it is said, regulates
    external conduct, while the latter regulates internal
    conduct.

6. WHITELEY, C.H. & W.M. The Permissive Morality, (Methuen & Co.,
    Ltd., 1964): the changes that have taken place in moral
    attitudes since 1900 are vividly and brilliantly analysed.
    Though not a treatise on law, this will serve as an
    important study of the moral climate of contemporary
    society.

7. COADY, J.M. "Morality and the Law", (1961), 1 U. Br. Col. L.R.
    442: by moral precepts in law is meant that moral concepts
    are accepted as governing human conduct, and these are based
    on principles inherent in human nature itself. Christian
    moral law has its foundation in natural law. In the earliest
    days of the common law there was little, if any, conflict
    between Christian morality and the law because the judges
    were clerics. The relationship between the two should be
    preserved.

8. WESTEN, P.K. "Introduction" to "Symposium: Drugs and the Law",

(1968), 56 Calif. L.R., 1: several contrary aspects of a vast problem in the United States are outlined. The difficulty of deciding what attitude to adopt towards a changing, many-sided phenomenon and of making that attitude effective form the background to the discussions that follow. Note: there is a useful bibliography at pp. 162-166.

1. FORT, J. "Social Problems of Drug Use and Drug Policies", (1968), 56 Calif. L.R., 17: there is a good deal of looseness in the use of the words "drug", "use", "abuse", and "problem". The social and legal policies that have been adopted to deal with drugs are alleged to be the cause of the main social problems because they are irrational and ineffective.

2. GUSFIELD, J.R. "On Legislating Morals: the Symbolic Process of Designating Deviance", (1968), 56 Calif. L.R., 54: "disinterested indignation" is the feeling that impels one to condemn as immoral that which others do but which does not harm one. This differs from the feeling that condemns murder, theft, etc., as immoral, for these do harm to one. On this basis the article examines the condemnation of drink and drug addiction.

3. STEVENS, E.G. "Christianity and the Law", (1915), 49 Am. L.R. 1: this surveys the part which Christian ideas have played in shaping the law.

4. DENNING, A.T. The Changing Law, (Stevens & Sons, Ltd., 1953), chap. 4: religion has had much influence in shaping the values of the common law.

5. ST. JOHN STEVAS, N. Laws and Morals, (Burns & Oates, 1964): the attitudes of English and American law towards some controversial moral issues are considered in the light of Christian doctrine. Though written under the aegis of Catholicism, the book appraises both Catholic and Protestant views. Before a breach of moral law can be the subject of legal regulation it has to injure the common good and has to be a fit subject for legislation. The legal regulation has to be capable of enforcement and equitable in its incidence and should not cause greater evils than it eradicates.

6. BRYCE, J. Studies in History and Jurisprudence, (Oxford, 1901), II, chap. 13: this is of general interest. It deals comparatively with the interrelation between legal systems and different kinds of religion.

7. PEAR, R.H. "The United States Supreme Court and Religious

Freedom", (1949), 12 M.L.R., 167: the task of the Supreme
Court in holding the balance is explained and considered.

1. FELLMAN, D. "Religion in American Public Law", (1964), 44
   Boston L.R., 287: this is of general interest. It surveys
   at considerable length the infuence of religious attitudes
   and traces historically the separation of church and state
   and the problems to which this gives rise.

2. WULFSOHN, J.G. "Separation of Church and State in South
   African Law" (1964), 81 S.A.L.J., 90, 226: this article may
   be compared with the previous one on the position in
   America. Although there is no state religion, yet the
   Constitution declares that the people acknowledge God.

Values in Relation to Administrative Activities

3. WADE, E.C.S. "The Courts and Administrative Process" (1947),
   63 L.Q.R., 164: law is an expression of the prevailing
   balance between competing interests. The article considers
   how the courts might be used more effectively in relation
   to administrative process.

4. ALLEN, C.K. Law and Orders, (2nd ed., Stevens & Sons, Ltd.,
   1956): this is a detailed inquiry into the development of
   administrative action and a review of judicial action in
   relation to it.

5. PARKER, H.L. "Recent Developments in the Supervisory Powers
   of the Courts over Inferior Tribunals", Lionel Cohen
   Lectures V, (Magnes Press, 1959): the function of the
   courts today is to help, not merely check, governmental
   action. In the light of this policy, the methods employed
   by the courts are considered.

6. DEVLIN, P. "The Common Law, Public Policy, and the Executive"
   in Samples of Law Making, (Oxford University Press, 1962),
   chap. 6: this deals with the way in which judicial policy
   operated in the past. Today there is less inclination to
   act as watch-dogs on the executive.

7. LLOYD, D. "Ministers' Powers and the Courts", (1948), 1 C.L.
   P., 89: on the one hand, there is the view that the State
   oppresses the individual and that the function of the
   courts is to protect him; on the other, there is the view
   that the courts frustrate the best intentions of government.
   The question is how far the courts sit in judgment upon
   acts of the executive.

8. LASKI, H.J. "Judicial Review of Social Policy in England"

(1925-26) 39 Harv. L.R., 832: to apply principle to new
facts is to legislate. But a judge should be chary of
applying his own beliefs. Nothing is more dangerous than
the judicial use of authority to suppress views or experi-
ments which they dislike.

1. McWHINNEY, E. Judicial Review in the English-speaking World,
   (University of Toronto Press, 1956), pp. 46 et seq.: this
   shows how in time of emergency the courts side with the
   executive.

2. HAMSON, C.J. Executive Discretion and Judicial Control,
   (Stevens & Sons, Ltd., 1954): this is of general interest.
   It compares the English and French methods of administra-
   tive control.

3. JONES, H.W. "The Rule of Law and the Welfare State" (1958),
   58 Col. L.R., 143: the meanings of "welfare state" and
   "rule of law" are explained first. The author denies that
   the welfare state is destructive of a "rule of law". On the
   contrary, the more practical question is how it can be made
   to fulfil its task in a welfare state.

4. KALES, A.M. "'Due Process', the Inarticulate Major Premise
   and the Adamson Act", (1916-17), 26 Yale L.J., 519: a
   statute depriving a person of his liberty or property will
   be void if it violates a fundamental condition of the
   social structure. What is a fundamental condition should be
   fully argued before the court.

5. CORWIN, E.S. "Judicial Review in Action", (1926), 74 U. Pa.
   L.R., 639: this deals with the nature and development of
   the discretionary power of the courts in the United States.

6. HEWART, G. The New Despotism, (Ernest Benn, Ltd., 1929): this
   well-known book is a judicial protest against the increasing
   powers of the executive.

7. The following collection of papers published in (1960-61), 59
   Mich. L.R., are of interest: W.B. HARVEY: "The Rule of Law
   in Historical Perspective", p. 487, and "The Challenge of
   the Rule of Law", p. 603; L.K. COOPERRIDER: "The Rule of Law
   and the Judicial Process", p. 501; F.E. COOPER: "The
   Executive Departments of Government and the Rule of Law",
   p. 515; P.G. KAUPER: "The Supreme Court and the Rule of Law",
   p. 531; W.W. BISHOP: "The International Rule of Law", p.553;
   S.D. ESTEP: "The Legislative Process and the Rule of Law:
   Attempts to Legislate Taste in Moral and Political Beliefs",
   p. 575.

Values in Relation to Individual Activities

1. KEETON, R.E. "Creative Continuity in the Law of Torts" (1961-
    62), 75 Harv. L.R., 463: the expansion and refusal to
    expand responsibility are rooted in policy, and policy
    considerations are inherent in every doctrine. The part that
    should be played by doctrine is dealt with in detail.

2. LIPSTEIN, K. "Protected Interests in the Law of Torts", [1963]
    C.L.J., 85: this is a comparison of the valuation of
    interests in tort. But the general point is made that the
    protection of private interests should vary with the way in
    which they are evaluated in a changing society and changing
    economy.

3. BOHLEN, F.H. "Mixed Questions of Law and Fact", (1924) 72 U.
    Pa. L.R., 111: it is futile to try to fix minute, definite
    standards. What are needed are broad general standards, which
    give general directions for the construction of the appro-
    priate standard for each particular case. In negligence, for
    example, the "reasonable man" is a personification of the
    court's social judgment.

4. BOHLEN, F.H. "Fifty Years of Torts", (1936-37), 50 Harv. L.R.,
    725, 1225: this is of general interest. It reviews the
    development of the law of tort and the factors that have
    influenced it.

5. BOHLEN, F.H. Studies in the Law of Torts, (The Bobbs-Merrill
    Co., 1926), chap. 7: the background to the Rule in Rylands
    v. Fletcher is investigated as well as the corresponding
    situation in America.

6. MARSH, N.S. "Principle and Discretion in the Judicial Process",
    (1952), 68 L.Q.R., 226: this deals with the expansion of the
    law of torts. The determination of a duty of care is an act
    of judicial discretion.

7. ISAACS, N. "Fault and Liability", (1918), 31 Harv. L.R., 954:
    tortious responsibility develops so as to conform to a
    standard that is constantly approaching the goal of ethics.
    The views of O.W. Holmes and J.H. Wigmore are considered.

8. DIAS, R.W.M. "Remoteness of Liability and Legal Policy", [1962]
    C.L.J., 178: an attempt is made to show that the change from
    the principle of strict liability in tort to that of fault
    was prompted by a shift in fundamental policy, and that this
    is reflected in the changed attitude of the courts towards
    remoteness of damage.

144   Values

1. DENNING, A.T. "Law in a Developing Community", (1955), 33 P.
   A., 1: the operation of the law of negligence is affected
   by value-judgments. See especially the remarks on hospital
   cases at pp. 4-6.

2. MONTROSE, J.L. "Is Negligence an Ethical or a Sociological
   Concept?", (1958), 21 M.L.R., 259: the question in
   negligence cases is what ought to be done (ethical) not
   what is done by everyone else (sociological).

3. LEFLAR, R.A. "Negligence in Name Only", (1952), 27 N.Y.U.L.R.
   564: there can be answerability in negligence without
   fault. Negligence can be redefined in terms of "typicality",
   i.e., typical activities which carry with them the duty to
   compensate typical injuries.

4. PATON, G.W. "Negligence", (1949-50), 23 Aust. L.J., 158: the
   law of negligence is discussed generally and the importance
   of policy is stressed.

5. TERRY, H.T. "Negligence", (1915-16), 29 Harv. L.R., 40:
   negligence is conduct which creates an unreasonable risk.
   The various factors that are considered in determining
   reasonableness are explained.

6. CLERK, J.F. and LINDSELL, W.H.B. Torts, (13th ed., Sweet &
   Maxwell, Ltd., 1969), chap. 13, s. 891: the various considerations that have to be balanced in deciding whether any given
   piece of conduct amounts to negligence are considered in
   detail. Attention is also paid to the effects on law of the
   social policy of trying to prevent harm and of insurance.

7. MALBURN, W.P. "The Violation of Law Limiting Speed as
   Negligence", (1911), 45 Am L.R., 214: this gives consideration to the social policy behind such laws.

8. SCHULMAN, H. "The Standard of Care Required of Children",
   (1927-28), 37 Yale L.J., 618: the standard depends upon
   whether the child is plaintiff or defendant. A subjective
   standard is applied in the former case, i.e., a more
   lenient one; an objective standard is applied in the latter.

9. HORNBLOWER, W.B. "Insanity and the Law of Negligence", (1905),
   5 Col. L.R., 278: should a man be held responsible for what
   he was physically or mentally incapable of controlling?
   Ultimately the question is one of policy.

10. POWELL, R. "The Unreasonableness of the Reasonable Man", (1957),
    10 C.L.P., 104: the Reasonable Man is a doll. His power of
    reasoning may be relevant sometimes, but not always.

Therefore, "reasonable" is what he does, not what he thinks.

1. FRIEDMANN, W. "Modern Trends in the Law of Torts", (1937), 1
    M.L.R., 39: this is a general discussion showing the
    relation between the law and social conditions.

2. JAMES, F. "Accident Liability: Some Wartime Developments"
    (1945-46), 55 Yale L.J., 365: in various branches of the
    law of tort there is a tendency to modify the fault
    principle in favour of distributing the loss as equitably
    as possible. See further, "Accident Liability Reconsidered.
    The Impact of Liability Insurance", (1947-48), 57 Yale L.J.,
    549.

3. THAYER, E.R. "Public Wrongs and Private Action", (1913-14),
    27 Harv. L.R., 317: the question when breach of a statute
    grounds an action in negligence is considered. The statute
    sets an arbitrary standard, and a reasonable man is not
    supposed to violate statutes.

4. WILLIAMS, G.L. "The Effect of Penal Legislation in the Law of
    Tort", (1960), 23 M.L.R., 233: this considers the effect of
    the increasing forms of statutory responsibility.

5. LLEWELLYN, K.N. "What Price Contract? - an Essay in
    Perspective", (1930-31), 40 Yale L.J., 704: the law of
    contract is considered from a functional point of view.

6. PATTERSON, E.W. "Judicial Freedom of Implying Conditions in
    Contract" in Recueil d'Etudes sur les Sources du Droit en
    l'Honneur de F. Gény, (Librairie du Recueil Sirey, 1934),
    II, 379: the judge has latitude in deciding what words
    amount to a condition and how it should be interpreted. The
    question is, why do judges imply terms? The answer is
    considered in relation to various types of implied
    conditions.

7. EASTWOOD, R.A. "Trade Protection and Monopoly" (1950), 3 C.L.
    P., 100: this deals with the changing conception of public
    policy. The influence of policy considerations is traced
    out historically.

8. KORAH, V.L. "The Restrictive Practices Court", (1959), 12 C.
    L.P., 76: the law of conspiracy and restraint of trade were
    unequal to deal with restrictive trading agreements. The
    policy behind the establishment of the new Court is
    explained.

9. GOODHART, W.H. "The Yarn Spinners' Case and the Sherman Anti-
    Trust Act" (1959), 75 L.Q.R., 253: a useful comparison is

made of American judicial interpretation of the anti-trust
legislation and the attitude of English judges. In England
the Restrictive Practices Court has been able to make a
fresh start.

1. STEVENS, R. "Justiciability: The Restrictive Practices Court
    Re-examined", [1964] P.L., 221: the working of the Court
    over some years and its handling of policy questions is
    reviewed.

2. WHITEMAN, P.G. "The New Judical Approach to the Restrictive
    Trade Practices Act, 1956", (1967), 30 M.L.R., 398: at first
    the courts tended to interpret "agreement" in the narrow
    sense of contracts. A radical departure came in 1963 when
    they started to interpret it in the light of the underlying
    purpose.

3. WEDDERBURN, K.W. The Worker and the Law, (Penguin Books, Ltd.,
    1965): the development of labour law down to the decision in
    Rookes v. Barnard and its immediate legislative aftermath
    are reviewed. The main object of the book is to display the
    interrelation of the various parts of the law in relation to
    industrial problems and developments. Its value would be
    greater were it not written from an obviously one-sided
    point of view. Its best feature is the bibliography at the
    end.

4. THOMPSON, D. "Protection of the Right to Work", (1963), 41 Can.
    B.R., 167: this gives detailed consideration to the case-law
    on the protection of the individual workmen, especially
    against trade unions.

5. LLOYD, D. "The Right to Work", (1957), 10 C.L.P., 36: the
    courts have shown some flexibility in extending legal
    remedies to protect the right to work. (See also D. LLOYD:
    "The Disciplinary Powers of Professional Bodies", (1950) 13
    M.L.R., 281: "Judicial Review of Expulsion by a Domestic
    Tribunal", (1952), 15 M.L.R., 413: "Damages for Wrongful
    Expulsion from a Trade Union", (1956), 19 M.L.R., 121).

6. THOMAS, T.C. "Trade Unions and their Members", [1956] C.L.J.,
    67: the Bonsor case is considered.

7. WEDDERBURN, K.W. "The Right to Threaten Strikes", (1961), 24
    M.L.R., 572: (1962), 25 M.L.R., 513: (1964), 27 M.L.R., 257:
    these articles consider respectively the decisions at first
    instance, in the Court of Appeal and House of Lords in
    Rookes v. Barnard. See also K.W. WEDDERBURN: (1965), 28 M.L.
    R., 205, on Stratford & Son, Ltd., v. Lindley; C.J. HAMSON:
    [1961] C.L.J., 189; [1964] C.L.J., 159; J.A. WEIR: "Chaos

or Cosmos ? Rookes, Stratford and the Economic Torts",
[1964] C.L.J., 225; D. THOMPSON: "Protection of the Right
to Work", (1963), 41 Can. B.R., 167; W.F. FRANK: "The Right
to Strike Reconsidered", [1964] J.B.L., 199; B. GREAVES:
Rookes v. Barnard: After the General Election", (1964), 128
J.P.J., 770; G.F.L. FRIDMAN: "The 'Right' to Strike" (1964)
114 L.J. 647, 667; ANONYMOUS: "A Trade Dispute?" (1964) 235
L.T. 563; O. KAHN-FREUND: (1964) 14 Federation News, 30;
O.H. PARSONS: "The Meaning of Rookes v. Barnard" L.R.D. 1964;
I. CHRISTIE: (1964) 42 Can. B.R. 464; ANONYMOUS: "Strike
On" (1964) 98 I.L.T. 421; ANONYMOUS: "Intimidation and
Trade Unions" (1964) 98 I.L.T. 431, 437; D.W. SMITH: "Rookes
v. Barnard: an Upheaval in the Common Law Relating to
Industrial Disputes" (1966) 40 A.L.J. 81, 112.

1. HOFFMANN, L.H. "Rookes v. Barnard" (1965) 81 L.Q.R. 116: the
   various aspects of this case are fully discussed. What is
   of special interest is that, in the author's opinion, the
   decision of the House of Lords accords with the intention
   of Parliament as revealed by the Parliamentary history of
   the Trade Disputes Act, 1906.

2. HARRIS, D.R. "The Right to Strike" (1964) 108 Sol.Jo. 451,
   472, 493: the House of Lords' decision in Rooke's case is
   considered. The competing issues are set out, including
   the point that the case is a triumph of the individual
   against a union. D.R. HARRIS: "Trade Disputes and the Law"
   (1964) 108 Sol.Jo. 795: this is mainly concerned with
   Statford's case.

3. RIDEOUT, R.W. "Protection of the Right to Work" (1962) 25
   M.L.R. 137: further consideration of the same topic.

4. RIDEOUT, R.W. "Rookes v. Barnard" (1964) 3 Sol. Q. 193: the
   cases of Rookes v. Barnard and Stratford v. Lindley are
   discussed in detail and their implications considered.

5. GRUNFELD, C. Trade Unions and the Individual in English Law,
   (Institute of Personnel Management, 1964): this is a
   convenient account of the law concerning the individual in
   his relationship to his union. His discussion of Rookes's
   Case is pre-House of Lords.

6. LEWIS, N. "Trade Unions and Public Policy" (1965) 4 Sol. Q.
   12: there is a real danger in the power of trade unions.
   The question discussed is how far courts should go in
   checking oppression by unions.

7. O'HIGGINS, P. and PARTINGTON, M. "Industrial Conflict:
   Judicial Attitudes" (1969) 32 M.L.R. 53: this is a

statistical survey of fifty civil and twenty criminal cases
referred to in three leading treatises. Such conclusions as
are drawn from this limited material are necessarily
tentative.

1. KAHN-FREUND, O. "Spare-time Activities of Employees" (1946)
   9 M.L.R. 145: this considers the important decision in the
   Hivac case.

2. LEWIS, W.A. "Spare-time Activities of Employees" (1946) 9 M.
   L.R. 280: this gives further consideration to the Hivac case
   and the questions that it raises.

3. LEWIS, W.A. "Monopoly and the Law" (1943) 6 M.L.R. 97: lawyers
   have diverged in their attitude from that of economists. By
   confusing different meanings of freedom lawyers have come
   in the result to support monopoly. The shortcomings of the
   law are pointed out. (This was written before the Restrictive
   Practices Courts was established).

4. DENNING, A.T. The Road to Justice, (Stevens & Sons, Ltd.,
   1955), chap. 5: this deals, inter alia, with freedom of
   contract, freedom of association, the right to work, the
   right to strike and industrial combinations.

5. The following cases be consulted as illustrating the part
   played by value-judgments: Sommersett's Case (1772), 20
   State Tr. 1; Liversidge v. Anderson, [1942] A.C. 206;
   [1941] 3 All E.R. 338; R. v. Halliday, ex parte Zadig,
   [1917] A.C. 260; Ross-Clunis v. Papadopoullos, [1958] 2 All
   E.R. 23; [1958] 1 W.L.R. 546; Reade v. Smith, [1959] N.Z.L.
   R. 996; Horwood v. Millar's Timber & Trading Co., Ltd.,
   [1917] 1 K.B. 305; Eastham v. Newcastle United Football
   Club, Ltd., [1964] Ch. 413; [1963] 3 All E.R. 139; Best v.
   Samuel Fox & Co., Ltd., [1952] A.C. 716; [1952] 2 All E.R.
   394; R. v. Board of Control, ex parte Rutty, [1956] 2 Q.B.
   109; [1956] 1 All E.R. 769; Richardson v. L.C.C., [1957] 2
   All E.R. 330; R. v. Kemp, [1957] 1 Q.B. 399; [1956] 3 All
   E.R. 249; Bratty v. Att.-Gen. for Northern Ireland, [1963]
   A.C. 386; [1961] 3 All E.R. 523.

   Entick v. Carrington (1765), 19 State Tr. 1029; Elias v.
   Pasmore, [1934] 2 K.B. 164; Chic Fashions (West Wales),
   Ltd. v. Jones, [1968] 2 Q.B. 299; [1968] 1 All E.R. 229;
   Att.-Gen. v. De Keyser's Royal Hotel, Ltd., [1920] A.C.
   508; Burmah Oil Co. (Burma Trading), Ltd. v. Lord Advocate,
   [1965] A.C. 75; [1964] 2 All E.R. 348; Viscount SUMNER in
   Levene v. I.R.C., [1928] A.C. 217; Lord GREENE in Howard
   de Walden v. I.R.C., [1942] 1 K.B. 389; [1942] 1 All E.R.
   287; Metropolitan Asylum District v. Hill (1881), 6 App.

Cas. 193; Edgington, Bishop and Withy v. Swindon B.C.,
[1939] 1 K.B. 86; [1938] 4 All E.R. 57; Att.-Gen. of New
Zealand v. Lower Hutt City Corporation, [1964] A.C. 1469;
[1964] 3 All E.R. 179; Green (H.E.) & Sons v. Minister of
Health, [1948] 1 K.B. 34; [1947] 2 All E.R. 469; R. v.
Electricity Commissioners, [1924] 1 K.B. 171; Franklin v.
Minister of Town and Country Planning, [1948] A.C. 87;
[1947] 2 All E.R. 289.

Smith v. Baker & Sons, [1891] A.C. 325; Summers v.
Salford Corporation, [1943] A.C. 283; [1943] 1 All E.R.
68; English Hop Growers, Ltd. v. Dering, [1928] 2 K.B. 174;
Ronbar Enterprises, Ltd. v. Green, [1954] 2 All E.R. 266;
Paris v. Stepney B.C., [1951] A.C. 367; [1951] 1 All E.R.
42; Hivac, Ltd. v. Park Royal Scientific Instruments, Ltd.,
[1946] Ch. 169; [1946] 1 All E.R. 350; Cranleigh Precision
Engineering, Ltd. v. Bryant and Another, [1964] 3 All E.R.
289; Latimer v. A.E.C., Ltd., [1953] A.C. 643; [1953] 2
All E.R. 449; Davie v. New Merton Board Mills, Ltd., [1959]
A.C. 604; [1959] 1 All E.R. 346; Lister v. Romford Ice &
Cold Storage Co., Ltd., [1957] A.C. 555; [1957] 1 All E.R.
125; I.C.I., Ltd. v. Shatwell, [1965] A.C. 656; [1964] 2
All E.R. 999; Bonsor v. Musicians' Union, [1956] A.C. 104;
[1955] 3 All E.R. 518; Rookes v. Barnard, [1964] A.C. 1129;
[1964] 1 All E.R. 367; Stratford (J.T.), & Son, Ltd. v.
Lindley, [1965] A.C. 269; [1964] 3 All E.R. 102.

Donoghue v. Stevenson, [1932] A.C. 562; Rylands v. Fletcher
(1868), L.R. 3 H.L. 330; Hedley Byrne & Co., Ltd. v. Heller
& Partners, Ltd., [1964] A.C. 465; [1963] 2 All E.R. 575;
Lloyds Bank, Ltd. v. Savory, [1933] A.C. 201; Ward v.
L.C.C., [1938] 2 All E.R. 341; L.P.T.B. v. Upson, [1949]
A.C. 155; [1949] 1 All E.R. 60; Daly v. Liverpool Corporation,
[1939] 2 All E.R. 142; Daborn v. Bath Tramways Motor Co.,
Ltd., and Trevor Smithey, [1946] 2 All E.R. 333; East Suffolk
Rivers Catchment Board v. Kent, [1941] A.C. 74; [1940] 4
All E.R. 527; Haley v. London Electricity Board, [1965] A.
C. 778; [1964] 3 All E.R. 185; Cassidy v. Ministry of Health,
[1951] 2 K.B. 343; [1951] 1 All E.R. 574; Roe v. Ministry
of Health, [1954] 2 Q.B. 66; [1954] 2 All E.R. 131.

Egerton v. Earl Brownlow (1853), 4 H.L.C. 1; Beresford v.
Royal Insurance Co., Ltd., [1938] A.C. 586; [1938] 2 All
E.R. 602; Bowman v. Secular Society, [1917] A.C. 406;
Bourne v. Keen, [1919] A.C. 815; R. v. Martin Secker &
Warburg, Ltd., [1954] 2 All E.R. 683; Shaw v. D.P.P., [1962]
A.C. 220; [1961] 2 All E.R. 446.

Wilson v. Glossop, (1888), 20 Q.B.D. 354; National Bank of
Greece & Athens S.A. v. Metliss, [1958] A.C. 509; [1957]

3 All E.R. 608; <u>Short</u> v. <u>Att.-Gen. of Sierra Leone</u>, [1964]
1 All E.R. 125; <u>Roberts</u> v. <u>Hopwood</u>, [1925] A.C. 578;
<u>Prescott</u> v. <u>Birmingham Corporation</u>, [1955] Ch. 210; [1954]
3 All E.R. 698; <u>Re Walker's Decision</u>, [1944] K.B. 644;
[1944] 1 All E.R. 614.

<u>U.S., ex rel. Weinberg</u> v. <u>Schotfeldt</u> (1938), 26 Federal
Reporter Supplement, 283; <u>Schtraks</u> v. <u>Government of Israel</u>,
[1964] A.C. 556; [1962] 3 All E.R. 529; <u>Aksionairoye</u>
<u>Obschestvo A.M. Luther</u> v. <u>James Sagor & Co.</u>, [1921] 3 K.B.
532; <u>Lorentzen</u> v. <u>Lydden, & Co.</u>, [1942] 2 K.B. 202; <u>Anglo-</u>
<u>Iranian Oil Co., Ltd.</u> v. <u>Jaffrate</u>, [1953] 1 W.L.R. 246;
<u>Zoernsch</u> v. <u>Waldock</u>, [1964] 2 All E.R. 256; [1964] 1 W.L.R.
675.

Some Implications of Value-study

1. DENNING, A.T. "The Independence of the Judges" Presidential
    Address to the Holdsworth Club (1950): in the U.S.S.R.
    judges are part of the machinery for effectuating executive
    policy; in England the judges are not so dependent. In a
    country like England judicial independence is very
    important.

2. DENNING, A.T. "The Independence and Impartiality of the
    Judges" (1954) 71 S.A.L.J., 345: the position of the
    judiciary in a "free" society is further considered. See
    also A.T. DENNING: <u>The Road to Justice</u>, (Stevens & Sons,
    Ltd., 1955), chap. 2.

3. BAMFORD, B.R. "Aspects of Judicial Independence" (1956) 73
    S.A.L.J., 380: various means for securing judicial
    independence and the attributes of an independent judge are
    considered.

4. GYANDOH, S.O. "The Role of the Judiciary under the
    Constitutional Proposals for Ghana" (1968) 5 U.G.L.J., 133:
    this is an extremely useful article on the nature of
    judicial decision-making. The Constitutional proposals of
    1968 are surveyed critically with reference to judicial
    independence and the role of the judiciary in safeguarding
    the Constitution and fundamental rights. See also S.O.
    GYANDOH: "Principles of Judicial Interpretation of the
    Republican Constitution of Ghana" (1966) 3 U.G.L.R., 37.

5. COOPERRIDER, L.K. "The Rule of Law and the Judicial Process",
    (1960-61), 59 Mich. L.R., 501: how far are judges controlled
    by law? This depends on the extent of the desire on their
    part to decide as far as possible according to authority.
    The "rule of law" is not a myth.

1. DIAS, R.W.M. "The Value of a Value-study of Law" (1965) 28
    M.L.R., 397, 410-20: the implications of a value-oriented
    approach are considered, especially with reference to the
    study of law, the nature of the judicial process and the
    concept of law.

2. STEVENS, R. "Justiciability: the Restrictive Practices Court
    Re-examined" [1964] P.L., 221: although the main theme is
    the work of the Court, the point is made that judges are
    immune from criticism so long as their function is thought
    to be simply to administer law, good or bad. The wisdom of
    Parliament in entrusting this Court, which is there to make
    policy decisions, to the judiciary and thereby laying them
    open to criticism, is doubted.

3. GARLAN, E.N. Legal Realism and Justice, (Columbia University
    Press, 1941): it is pointed out in answer to the American
    Realists that ideals should be included among the elements
    of a judgment. Any attempt to determine what the law is
    involves simultaneously an attempt to determine what is
    desirable.

4. LAWSON, F.H. "The Creative Use of Legal Concepts", (1957),
    32 N.Y.U.L.R., 909: a distinction is drawn between concepts
    that come into litigation and those which are used as
    guides to action. The lawyer has to make creative use of
    concepts.

5. HOGG, J.E. "Legal Conceptions from a Practical Point of View"
    (1906), 22 L.Q.R., 172: the writer assumes that legal
    concepts are rigid and argues that they should be adapted
    to modern conditions. The assumption is questionable, but
    his thesis is acceptable.

6. MOORE, W.U. and SUSSMAN, G. "The Lawyer's Law", (1931-32), 41
    Yale L.J., 566: in advising a client a lawyer has to take
    account of many factors. One of these is the intuitional
    judgment. He should accordingly systematise more the bases
    of intuitional judgments.

7. SCHMIDHAUSER, J.R. "Stare Decisis, and the Background of the
    Justice of the Supreme Court of the United States" (1962)
    14 Tor. L.J., 194: a statistical study is provided of the
    extent to which personal background factors influence judges
    to adhere to precedent or to dissent from majority opinions.
    The general conclusion is to express a very qualified
    agreement with the proposition that personal background does
    influence judicial behaviour.

8. WEYRAUCH, W.O. The Personality of Lawyers, (Yale University

Press, 1964); interviews with a cross-section of German
lawyers are analysed and evaluated. They reveal the extent
to which personal and professional predilictions influence
their outlook and thinking.

1. GROSSMAN, J.B. "Social Backgrounds and Judicial Decision-
making", (1965-66) 79 Harv. L.R., 1551: How far is a judge
the captive or creature of personal values? Different types
of study, which have sought to answer this question, are
set out and explained.

2. PALLEY, C. "The Judicial Process: U.D.I. and the Southern
Rhodesian Judiciary" (1967) 30 M.L.R. 263: the decision in
the U.D.I. Case is approached through the personal histories
of the judges involved in it.

3. SHAPIRO, M. "The Supreme Court and Constitutional Adjudication:
of Politics and Neutral Principles" (1962-63) 31 The Geo.
Wash. L.R. 587: the role of the Supreme Court in
constitutional cases is appraised in the light of the debate
between those who view it as a political instrument and those
who see it as applying neutral and impartial principles.

8.

D U T I E S   A N D   R U L E S

1. GOODHART, A.L. English Law and the Moral Law, (Stevens &
   Sons, Ltd., 1955) especially chaps. 1 and 2: this is an
   important study of duty conceived as an "ought". The point
   is made with emphasis that command and sanction are not
   its distinctive criteria. Law is a prescription for conduct,
   not a description of it. The feeling of obligation is
   analysed, and also the distinction between the obligation
   of law and that of religion, morality, etc.

2. FULLER, L.L. The Morality of Law, (Yale University Press,
   1964), especially chaps. 1 and 2: in Chapter 1 the relation
   between duty and morality is examined. A distinction is
   drawn between the "morality of aspiration", which concerns
   ideals, and the "morality of duty", which is embodied in
   duties, and parallels are drawn with certain economic
   principles. Chapter 2 deals mainly with the "inner"
   morality, without which there can be no valid legal system
   (as to which, see post, Chapter 20); but pp. 65-70 may be
   consulted on conflicting duties, and pp. 108-10 on the
   association of law with force.

3. OLIVECRONA, K. "Law as Fact" in Interpretations of Modern
   Legal Philosophies, (ed. P. Sayre, Oxford University Press,
   New York, 1947) chap. 25: the concepts of "duty" and "rule"
   are examined. The former is said to involve the idea of
   action, imperative expression and the feeling of being
   bound. The function of rules is also dealt with.

4. HART, H.L.A. The Concept of Law, (Oxford, 1961), pp. 33-41,
   55-56; 79-88; chap. 6 passim: in the course of rejecting
   the idea of nullity as a sanction, the point is made that
   law without sanction is perfectly conceivable. The idea of
   obligation is examined and particular stress is laid on the
   use of it as a general standard of conduct, the "internal"
   and "external" aspects of rules. In Chapter 6 stress is
   laid on "rules of recognition" by which prescriptions of
   conduct are identifiable as "law".

5. ALLEN, C.K. "Legal Duties" in Legal Duties, (Oxford, 1931),
   pp. 156-220: the views of L. Duguit and A.V. Lundstedt are
   first discussed, and then from p. 196 onward the nature of
   duty itself. Duty cannot be "enforced" otherwise than by
   conscience; "legal enforcement" means the operation of a
   prescribed penalty. There is also a lengthy examination of
   the relationship between legal and moral duties.

6. CASTBERG, S.F. Problems of Legal Philosophy, (2nd ed., Oslo
   University Press; Allen & Unwin, Ltd., 1957), pp. 23, 24-33:

"law" is valid and hence duty is "legal" because of certain
accepted postulates of "validity". The idea of duty as an
"ought" is defended against the attacks of other Scandinavian
Realists.

1. HÄGERSTRÖM, A. Inquiries into the Nature of Law and Morals,
   (ed. K. Olivercrona, trans. C.D. Broad, Almqvist & Wiksell,
   Stockholm, 1953), chap. 3, especially pp. 116-256: the
   nature of command and its content are examined as a prelude
   to an investigation of the nature of duty. A feeling of
   inner compulsion is bound up with the feeling of duty. This
   feeling is said to be "external", i.e. not founded on
   valuations or a desire to avoid unpleasantness. It is an
   association of ideas with a certain form of expression.
   Various theories are considered and also the connection
   between legal and moral duty.

2. OLIVECRONA, K. Law as Fact, (Einar Munksgaard, Copenhagen;
   Humphrey Milford, 1939; reprinted by Wildy & Sons, Ltd.,
   1962), especially pp. 42-49: the feeling of being bound is
   analysed into a psychological association of ideas with the
   imperative form of expression and certain procedures.
   Chapter 2 stresses the psychological effect of constitutional
   forms of law-making; Chapter 4 considers the parts played
   by force, fear and morality.

3. OLIVECRONA, K. "The Imperative Element in Law" (1964) 18
   Rutgers L.R. 794: the imperative from in which law is
   expressed is subjected to further examination. Austin's
   Command theory, and certain other theories, which have been
   proffered in its place, are criticised. The importance of
   the imperative element is that it has suggestive influence
   over people. The Command theory neglects this suggestive
   force, but it is a mistake, while rejecting the Command
   theory, to neglect the imperative element altogether.

4. OLIVECRONA, K. "Legal Language and Reality" in Essays in
   Jurisprudence in Honor of Roscoe Pound, (ed. R.A. Newman,
   The Bobbs-Merrill Co., Inc., 1962), 151: the views of
   J. Austin, the American Realists, A. Hägerström and
   A.V. Lundstedt are touched on. "Duty", like the word "right",
   is said to be a "hollow" word, (cf. "pound" as monetary
   unit). There is no object corresponding to it.

5. von MISES, R. Positivism (Harvard University Press, 1951),
   chaps. 25 and 26, especially pp. 320-321: "ought" is
   examined, and the analysis ties up well with K. Olivecrona's
   idea of "independent imperative" by furnishing a psychological
   explanation of how it comes about. In Chapter 26 the
   importance of regulating conduct is stressed.

1. LUNDSTEDT, A.V. Legal Thinking Revised, (Almqvist & Wiksell, Stockholm, 1956), pp. 35-53; 77-122: legal duties are devoid of objectivity. Duty is a feeling which drives people to do or to abstain. The expression "legal duty" labels the effect on a person's behaviour of the maintenance of diverse rules of law.

2. AUSTIN, J. Lectures on Jurisprudence, (5th ed., R. Campbell, John Murray, 1885), chaps. 22-24: these give the "command" theory of duty in which command, duty and sanction are interrelated. Sanction is the conditional evil in the event of disobedience, which "enforces compliance" with the command. Various ways in which breaches of duty can be committed are also considered.

3. TAPPER, C.F. "Austin on Sanctions" [1965] C.L.J. 271: Austin's requirement of sanction as a test of law and in relation to obligation is subjected to penetrating analysis. His analysis is shown to be so vague as to leave numerous questions unanswered, and also inconsistent and self-contradictory.

4. BROWN, W.J. The Austinian Theory of Law, (John Murray, 1906), pp. 5-11: this is a restatement of the Austianian position.

5. HART, H.L.A. "Legal and Moral Obligation" in Essays in Moral Philosophy, (ed. A.I. Melden, University of Washington Press, 1958), 82: J. Austin's thesis of duty being sanctioned by the chance of evil is criticised. (For the purpose of the argument the necessity for sanctions is conceded though they may not be essential - see p. 99). The main argument shows how the creation of obligations leads to the foundation of a legal system.

6. HEARN, W.E. The Theory of Legal Duties and Rights, (Melbourne: John Ferres; London: Trubner & Co., 1883), chaps. 4 and 5: duty is regarded as being more important than right; command, duty and sanction are associated. A clear distinction is drawn between primary and secondary duties. Sanctions are inseparable from duty and various types of sanctions are considered.

7. TERRY, H.T. Some Leading Principles of Anglo-American Law Expounded with a View to its Arrangement and Codification, (T. & J.W. Johnson & Co., Philadelphia, 1884), pp. 84-87: duty is described from the point of view of one who is commanded or forbidden to do something. The content of duties is discussed with reference to the consequences, conduct and the state of mind. This idea is further elaborated in "Duties, Rights and Wrongs" (1924) 10 Am.B.A. J., 123.

1. JENKS, E. The New Jurisprudence, (John Murray, 1933), chaps.
   6 and 8: a consideration of whether reward can operate as a
   sanction precedes an account of penal and remedial
   sanctions. Duty is regarded as being more important than
   right. The contingent sanction is said to be essential to it.

2. HUMPHREY, J.P. "On the Definition and Nature of Laws", (1945),
   8 M.L.R., 194, at pp. 196-203: the article considers the
   specific marks of "a law", not of "law". Sanction is declared
   to be essential, but the different meanings of the term and
   duty-situations where sanctions are not present are not even
   mentioned.

3. CORBIN, A.L. "Rights and Duties", (1923-24), 33 Yale L.J., 501,
   especially at pp. 505-6, 514 et seq.: the distinction
   between legal and moral duties is said to lie in the sanction.
   The idea of enforcement and the various types of sanctions
   are considered. Breach of duty is constituted by conduct.

4. GOBLE, G.W. "The Sanction of a Duty", (1927-28), 37 Yale L.J.,
   426: the author assumes that sanction is the test of a duty
   and proceeds to consider which of all possible court reactions
   is the most useful one to regard as sanction.

5. PATTERSON, E.W. Jurisprudence, (The Foundation Press, Inc.,
   1953), pp. 159-170: this is of general interest on the
   nature of sanctions. Legal sanctions are confined to harmful
   consequences imposed by officials. The need for sanctions
   is considered, but not with specific reference to duties.

6. KELSEN, H. "Value Judgments in the Science of Law", in What
   is Justice ? (University of California Press, 1957), 209:
   duties are not dealt with directly, but the article is
   important in stressing the part played by the "ought"
   in law.

7. KELSEN, H. General Theory of Law and State, (trans. A. Wedberg,
   Harvard University Press, 1949), pp. 50-64, 71-74: sanctions
   are provided in order to bring about conformity of behaviour
   with what the legislator desires. Behaviour is wrongful only
   when a sanction is attached. To be under a duty means that
   contrary behaviour will involve a sanction. But Kelsen cannot avoid the "ought" contained in both duty and sanction
   (pp. 60-1).

8. KELSEN, H. "The Pure Theory of Law", (trans. C.H. Wilson,
   1934), 50 L.Q.R., 474, especially at pp. 494-6: this
   emphasises duty as a "normative obligation" and ties it to
   sanction.

1. KANTOROWICZ, H.U. The Definition of Law, (ed. A.H. Campbell,
   Cambridge University Press, 1958), pp. 23-25, 37-40: the
   ideas implicit in "ought" are considered, with special
   mention of a basic abd absolute rule on which the validity
   of all other rules depends.

2. VINOGRADOFF, P. Common-sense in Law, (3rd ed., H.G. Hanbury,
   Oxford University Press, 1959), chaps. 2 and 3: this
   discussion of the command theory provides a useful background to the concept of duty by pointing out that enforcement is not sufficient; recognition and purpose are just
   as important.

3. HEXNER, E. Studies in Legal Terminology, (The University of
   North Carolina Press, 1941), chap. 1: this is of general
   interest. Law as a system of rules prescribing social
   conduct is discussed.

4. DAUBE, D. Forms of Roman Legislation, (Oxford, 1956), pp.23-
   30: it is of interest to note that in Roman Law where a
   rule was well known the praetors only thought it necessary
   to specify the sanction for its contravention. When a new
   rule was laid down, the "ought" or "ought not" was first
   specified and then the sanction was prescribed.

5. DIAS, R.W.M. "The Unenforceable Duty", (1959), 33 Tul. L.R.,
   473: the importance of sanctionless duties in Roman and
   English Law is discussed.

6. SHKLAR, J.N. Legalism, (Harvard University Press, 1964);
   Part II, especially pp. 39-56: the whole book is a
   sustained attack on Positivist and Naturalist theory and
   particularly their respective attitudes towards the
   separation of law and morality. Their controversy is
   unsatisfying since both sides think in terms of "legalism",
   i.e., rule following. But this is itself a morality among
   others, and they should all be accepted as part of a social
   continuum.

7. HOLMES, O.W. "The Path of the Law', in Collected Legal Papers,
   (Constable & Co., Ltd., 1920), pp. 173-4: this is a pioneer
   expression of the view that primary rights and duties are
   meaningless terms and that, subject to allegedly negligible
   exceptions, only secondary rights and duties matter.

8. LLEWELLYN, K.N. The Bramble Bush, (New York, 1930), pp. 82-5:
   following O.W. Holmes's view, primary rights and duties are
   rejected; all that matter are secondary duties, or what the
   courts will do. The judgment of a court is regarded as a
   certain test of duty.

1. ROSS, A. On Law and Justice, (Stevens & Sons, Ltd., 1958),
    pp. 52-58, 158-64, 364: judges obey norms of decision
    voluntarily; citizens obey norms of conduct for many reasons.
    It might be desirable to abandon the notion of duty; but in
    so far as it is used, it denotes situations in which a
    person is subjected to a sanction. Nevertheless the ideas
    of "prescription" and "prohibition" are not excluded.

2. ROSS, A. Directives and Norms, (Routledge & Kegan Paul, Ltd.,
    1968), chaps. 4-5: norms are a species of directive. They
    need to be general, effective and internally accepted.

3. GOTTLIEB, G. The Logic of Choice, (Allen & Unwin, Ltd., 1968):
    the main concern of this work is with the judicial process,
    but it contains an important discussion of rules, principles
    and standards. Rules may be regulatory or constitutive.
    Following a rule differs from obeying a command in that the
    former involves more policy considerations than the latter.

4. BUCKLAND, W.W. Some Reflections on Jurisprudence, (Cambridge
    University Press, 1945), pp. 86-92, 96-106: the idea of
    sanction is dealt with, and particularly noteworthy is the
    discussion of sanction by nullity. O.W. Holmes's view that
    primary rights and duties are unnecessary is answered.
    (Compare the view on p. 106 that sanction is only a piece
    of machinery with the view on pp. 111-112 that a duty with
    no sanction is "meaningless"). See also "The Nature of the
    Contractual Obligation", (1944), 8 C.L.J., 247, which is a
    more detailed answer to Holmes.

5. LAMONT, W.D. The Principles of Moral Judgment, (Oxford, 1946),
    chap. 3: the arguments proceed on a different line from that
    adopted in the chapter. Rights are said to refer to
    interests and duties are consequent on them.

General Treatises

6. SALMOND, W. Jurisprudence, (12th ed., P.J. Fitzgerald, Sweet
    & Maxwell, Ltd., 1966), pp. 100-104, 216-217, 233-234: duty
    is "legal" because it is "legally recognised", not necessarily
    because it is legally enforced or sanctioned". The
    distinction between primary and secondary rights and duties
    is explained with reference to enforcement. The importance
    of "imperfect rights" (i.e., sanctionless duty-situations)
    is also pointed out.

7. POLLOCK, F. A First Book of Jurisprudence, (6th ed., Macmillan
    & Co., Ltd., 1929), pp. 58-61, 69-72: this is a general
    discussion in the course of which the point is made that
    while negative duties can be "enforced" by physical constraint,

positive duties are "enforceable" only indirectly. Positive
duties contemplate performance rather than breach; with
negative duties breach is more prominent.

1. GRAY, J.C. The Nature and Sources of the Law, (2nd ed.,
   R. Gray, The Macmillan Co., New York, 1921), chap. 1: this
   is another general discussion of rights and duties and
   their relation to morality, command and protection.

2. MARKBY, W. Elements of Law, (6th ed., Oxford, 1905), SS 181-
   192: this follows the Austinian association of command,
   duty and sanction. Primary and secondary duties are
   explained, and the point is made that duties regulate
   conduct.

3. HOLLAND, T.E. The Elements of Jurisprudence, (13th ed.,
   Oxford, 1924), pp. 87, 131-133: legal duties are
   distinguishable from moral duties in that the former will
   be enforced by the power of the state.

4. KOCOUREK, A. An Introduction to the Science of Law, (Little,
   Brown & Co., 1930), pp. 240-242, 247-50, 321-23: duty is
   explained in relation to claim, the latter being regarded
   as the principal concept. Law not only prescribes conduct,
   but also on occasions authorises it, and on this basis the
   relationship between duties and powers is explained. (See
   the next chapter for claims and powers).

5. KOCOUREK, A. Jural Relations, (2nd ed., The Bobbs-Merrill Co.,
   1928), pp. 9-10 note; chap. 19: the different meanings of
   "duty" are briefly indicated. In Chapter 19 sanctions,
   their origin and function, are examined. The special
   terminology which Kocourek employs is very prevalent in
   this chapter and it is, therefore, difficult to read. Its
   substance is also found in "Sanctions and Remedies" (1924)
   72 U.Pa.L.R. 91. See also "Tabulae Minores Jurisprudentiae"
   (1920-21) 30 Yale L.J., 215, at p. 222, where a distinction
   is drawn between enforceable and unenforceable jural
   relations, which are labelled respectively "nexal" and
   "simple".

6. PATON, G.W. A Text-Book of Jurisprudence, (3rd ed.,
   D.P. Derham, Oxford, 1964), pp. 74-76, 261-262: sanction
   is examined with reference to J. Austin's general theory
   of law, but not specifically with reference to duty. It
   is said that preoccupation with sanction leads to a false
   view of law. "Antecedent" and "remedial" (i.e., primary and
   secondary) rights are considered and the view of the
   American Realists is rejected.

1. KEETON, G.W. The Elementary Principles of Jurisprudence,
    (2nd ed., Isaac Pitman & Sons, Ltd., 1949), chap. 11: the
    discussion is mainly in terms of rights, but is relevant
    to duties also. The point is made that enforceability is
    not essential.

2. SNYDER, O.C. Preface to Jurisprudence, (The Bobbs-Merrill Co.,
    Inc., 1954), pp. 223-36: sanction is regarded as essential
    to the concept of law and hence of duty. It is possible
    that the writer is using the term "sanction" in a sense
    wider than in this book, for nullity is included. Laws
    without sanction are considered and it is argued that these
    have at least indirect sanctions.

3. KORKUNOV, N.M. General Theory of Law, (trans. W.G. Hastings,
    The Boston Book Co., 1909), SS 27-29: this is a general
    discussion of legal relationships, and duty is regarded as
    being of basic importance.

4. POUND, R. Jurisprudence, (West Publishing Co., 1959), I, p.
    409; IV, chap. 24: in the first volume the origin of the
    idea of duty is examined briefly. Its history and relation
    to morals is more fully examined in the fourth volume. The
    sanctionless-duty in English and Roman Law is noted.

Reasons for Obedience

5. BRYCE, J. Studies in History and Jurisprudence, (Oxford,
    1901), II, chap. 9: the reasons for obedience are listed
    in the order of indolence, deference, sympathy, fear and
    reason.

6. STJERNQUIST, P. "How are Changes in Social Behaviour
    Developed by means of Legislation?" in Legal Essays. A
    Tribute to Frede Castberg, (Universitetsforlaget, 1963),
    153: the psychological repercussions of law that go towards
    its acceptance by the community are investigated. The
    influence of legislation can only be assessed in relation
    to other social influences. Different types of laws require
    different conditions for their acceptance by the community.

7. JENNINGS, W.I. The Law and the Constitution, (5th ed.,
    University of London Press, Ltd., 1959), Appendix IV: the
    argument is directed at showing that fear of sanctions and
    the enforcement by the state, though important, are not
    the reason for obedience. Enforcement implies obedience by
    the instruments of enforcement.

8. DENNING, A.T. The Road to Justice, (Stevens & Sons, Ltd.,
    1955), pp. 2-3: people obey the law because this is a thing

which they ought to do, not because law is commanded or
because of sanctions. This sense of obligation derives from
habit and the morality of the law itself.

1. LLOYD, D. The Idea of Law, (Penguin Books, Ltd., A 688, 1964),
    chaps. 2-3: "legitimate subordination" means obedience to
    someone who is entitled to require obedience. Such
    authority may be derived from morality, personal ascendancy
    of an individual, tradition, or the ascendancy of
    institutions. Further, although Law has to depend for its
    ultimate efficacy on the degree to which it is backed by
    force, this does not mean that Law is force. But force
    cannot be dispensed with because of the basic aggressive
    drives in human nature, which have to be repressed in order
    to subject people to social discipline. In the course of
    the discussion in Chapter 3 of Law and Morality, the moral
    duty to obey the law is touched on.

2. BENTHAM, J. The Limits of Jurisprudence Defined, (ed.
    C.W. Everett, Columbia University Press, 1945), chap. 13:
    law derives its force from the motives it relies on to
    produce the desired aims. These may be alluring or coercive,
    and are contained in laws addressed to officials; these in
    turn derive their force from other laws.

3. BENTHAM, J. Works, (ed. J. Bowring, Wm. Tait, Edinburgh,
    1843), III, pp. 199-200, 230 et seq.; VIII, pp. 380-81:
    reward is considered as an inducement to conform to certain
    behaviour.

4. LLEWELLYN, K.N. Jurisprudence: Realism in Theory and Practice,
    (University of Chicago Press, 1962), chap. 18: this deals
    with law-observance vs. law-enforcement. Observance is not
    a matter of rules, but of habit and practice among various
    social groups. Law-observance requires as a prerequisite
    that folkways shall first have developed in accordance with
    the purposes behind the law.

5. FRIED, C. "Moral Causation" (1963-64) 77 Harv.L.R. 1258: how
    are people made to comply with actions which they would
    not do spontaneously? An important method of accomplishing
    this is by making the actions the right thing to do so
    that people feel a moral obligation to comply. This is
    "moral causation" and it is distinguishable from psychological
    causation and moral persuasion.

6. Law and Philosophy. A Symposium. (ed. S. Hook. New York
    University Press, 1964), Part I: the thesis of the opening
    contribution is that obedience is based on fair-play, i.e.,
    if one accepts the benefits of a just legal order, then

fair-play requires that one should obey it. The author's
limitations of the scope of this doctrine seem to deprive
it of much of its value. The other contributions indicate
its weaknesses.

1. HUGHES, G.B.J. "Civil Disobedience and the Political Question
   Doctrine", (1968), 43 N.Y.U.L.R., 1: civil disobedience takes
   two forms: that of an individual refusing to obey, and
   organised campaigns to change policy or practice. The moral
   conviction of a law-breaker may be a ground for imposing a
   light sentence, but this has its danger. Courts do not rule
   on issues involving "political question", but they should
   not shelve their responsibilities.

2. TAYLOR, R. "Law and Morality", (1968), 43 N.Y.U.L.R., 611:
   enforcement and enforceability are the key to the notion
   of a "law". Considerations of morality do not come in
   except in relation to "law" considered as an activity, in
   which case the end to be achieved becomes relevant.

3. LYNN, C. "We must Disobey!" (1968), 43 N.Y.U.L.R., 649: in a
   very few pages the point is made that individuals who
   disobey and are willing to accept the penalty are infact
   submitting to the system. If it is the system that has to
   be changed there has to be mass disobedience.

4. PUNER, N.W. "Civil Disobedience: an Analysis and Rationale"
   (1968), 43 N.Y.U.L.R., 651: the characteristics and types of
   civil disobedience and the different attitudes towards
   obedience are explained first. On the basis the American
   case-law is examined at length. The conclusion is that civil
   disobedience has a part to play in human betterment.
   Obedience is the norm, so disobedience needs to be justified
   and, within limits, it could be accommodated.

5. WASSERSTROM, R.W. "The Obligation to Obey the Law", in Essays
   in Legal Philosophy, (ed. R.S. SUMMERS, Basil Blackwell,
   Oxford, 1968), 274: disobeying law is usually wrong,
   because "illegal" is usually also "immoral" and morally
   right conduct is usually not illegal. But it does not
   follow that disobedience is always immoral. The author
   distinguishes between the claim that there is an absolute
   obligation to obey the law, and a prime facie obligation,
   which casts the onus of justifying disobedience on the
   violator. The various arguments in support of both these
   claims are considered in turn and rejected.

6. COLE, W.G. "Private Morality and Public Law", (1968), 54 Am.B.
   A.J., 158: student and other protesters do not realise the
   implications of their demands. They claim adult status but

do not accept the responsibilities that go with these.
There is also a basic lack of loyalty. Private conscience
cannot be set above law, because if this happens those who
advocate it will be among the first victims.

1. MORRIS, E.F. "American Society and the Rebirth of Civil
   Obedience", (1968), 54 AM.B.A.J., 653: dissent and protest
   are protected by the American Constitution. Disobedience is
   not quite the same. If it goes beyond a test case it is to
   be deplored, for it is self-defeating in that it destroys
   rights. The law must remain supreme.

2. The following cases may be consulted in connection with the
   nature of duty: Cattle v. Stockton Waterworks Co. (1875),
   L.R., 10 Q.B., 453; Mogul S.S. Co. v. McGregor, Gow & Co.
   (1889), 23 Q.B.D., 598; Corbett v. Burge, Warren and
   Ridgley, Ltd. (1932), 48 T.L.R., 626; Hedley Byrne & Co.,
   Ltd. v. Heller & Partners, Ltd., [1964] A.C. 465; [1963] 2
   All E.R. 575; Commissioner for Railways v. Quinlan, [1964]
   A.C. 1054; [1964] 1 All E.R. 897; Best v. Samuel Fox & Co.,
   Ltd., [1952] A.C. 716; [1952] 2 All E.R. 394; R. v. Dudley
   and Stephens (1884), 14 Q.B.D. 273; Haynes v. Harwood,
   [1935] 1 K.B. 146; Maddison v. Alderson (1883), 8 App. Cas.
   467; Curwen v. Milburn (1889), 42 Ch.D. 424; Spencer v.
   Hemmerde, [1922] 2 A.C. 507; Seymour v. Pickett, [1905] 1
   K.B. 715; Zoernsch v. Waldock, [1964] 2 All E.R. 256; [1964]
   1 W.L.R. 675; Broom v. Morgan, [1953] 1 Q.B. 597; [1953] 1
   All E.R. 849; Case of the Sheriff of Middlesex (1840), 11
   Ad & El. 273; R. v. Larsonneur (1933), 97 J.P. 206.

9

R I G H T S

1. OLIVECRONA, K. "Legal Language and Reality", in Essays in
   Jurisprudence in Honor of Roscoe Pound, (ed R.A. Newman,
   The Bobbs-Merrill Co., Inc., 1962), p. 151: the function
   of the word "right" is examined with the utmost clarity.
   Legal language shapes reality rather than reflects it. All
   talk of rights is founded on inference, and the word "right"
   serves as a sign.

2. OLIVECRONA, K. Law as Fact, (Einar Munksgaard, Copenhagen;
   Humphrey Milford, 1939; reprinted by Wildy & Sons, Ltd.,
   1962), chap. 3: the difficulties of finding a factual basis
   for rights are examined. Rights "exist" only as conceptions
   in the mind and are used to awaken patterns of conduct in
   the minds of people.

3. OLIVECRONA, K. "Law as Fact" in Interpretations of Modern
   Legal Philosophies, (ed P. Sayre, Oxford University Press,
   New York, 1947), pp. 542, 549-557: the term "right" in the
   sense of claim is examined. It is a sign that another
   person shall conform to a pattern of behaviour.

4. ARNHOLM, C.J. "Olivecrona on Legal Rights. Reflections on the
   Concept of Rights", (1962), 6 Scand. S.L., 11: K. Olivecrona's
   ideas are set out and explained. Towards the end there is a
   brief comparison of his views with those of certain
   sociologists.

5. ROSS, A. On Law and Justice, (Stevens & Sons, Ltd., 1958),
   chaps. 5 and 6: in the first of these chapters the
   ambiguities of terminology and W.N. Hohfeld's scheme are
   examined. Terms are but tools of language. In the following
   chapter "right" is considered as a technique of presentation.

6. HÄGERSTRÖM, A. Inquiries into the Nature of Law and Morals,
   (ed K. Olivecrona, trans. C.D. Broad, Almqvist & Wiksell,
   Stockholm, 1953), passim, especially, chap. 5: Hägerström's
   views are to be gathered from various portions of his work.
   "Right" is a "hollow" word, i.e., one can appreciate the
   object of it, namely, the advantage, but not a right itself.
   Psychological and historical explanations are given for
   the continued talk of rights.

7. ALLEN, C.K. "Legal Duties" in Legal Duties, (Oxford, 1931),
   pp. 156, 196-220: the relationship between morality and law
   is considered, primarily from the angle of duties, but the
   discussion is relevant also to the question of rights.

8. RATTIGAN, W.H. The Science of Jurisprudence, (3rd ed., Wildy

& Sons, 1909), pp. 26-37: moral and legal rights are
contrasted. Violation of the latter is visited by state
action. There is also a general discussion of rights and
of kinds of rights.

1. von IHERING, R. Geist des römischen Rechts, (Leipsig, 1888),
   S. 60: this is the locus classicus of the "interest" theory
   of rights.

2. SALMOND, J.W. Jurisprudence, (7th ed., Sweet & Maxwell, Ltd.,
   1924), pp. 237-240; (12th ed., P.J. Fitzgerald, Sweet &
   Maxwell, Ltd., 1966), pp. 217-221: rights are interests
   recognised and protected by law. This is a repetition of
   R. von Ihering's thesis.

3. WIGMORE, J.H. Select Cases on the Law of Torts, (Little,
   Brown & Co., 1912), II, Appendix A, SS 4-8: this gives an
   analysis of a legal relation on the basis of interest as an
   element of a legal nexus.

4. VINOGRADOFF, P. "The Foundation of a Theory of Rights", in
   Collected Papers (Oxford, 1928), II, chap. 20: in order that
   a right should exist it has to be claimed, declared as a
   right and enforceable. Historically rights have developed
   out of the recognition of claims.

5. VINOGRADOFF, P. Common-Sense in Law, (3rd ed., H.G. Hanbury,
   Oxford University Press, 1959), pp. 45-52: right is the
   range of action assigned to a particular will within the
   social order established by law. It is founded on claim.
   Different types of claims are discussed.

6. BROWN, W.J. "Re-analysis of a Theory of Rights", (1924-25),
   34 Yale L.J., 765: this is a critical comment on
   P. Vinogradoff's thesis, considering point by point the
   arguments advanced.

7. LUNDSTEDT, A.V. Superstition or Rationality in Action for
   Peace ? (Longmans, Green & Co., 1925), pp. 110-119: R. von
   Ihering's doctrine of interest is criticised. "Right" is
   purely an abstract expression for an actual situation in
   which, by virtue of certain rules maintained by force,
   certain actions have certain effects.

8. LUNDSTEDT, A.V. Legal Thinking Revised, (Almqvist & Wiksell,
   Stockholm, 1956), pp. 77-122: the absurdity of talking of
   rights is emphasised. The phrase "legal right" refers to
   actual situations. (For a comment on Lundstedt's views
   generally, see C.K. Allen, Legal Duties, supra).

1. OLIVECRONA, K. "The Legal Theories of Axel Hägerström and
    Vilhelm Lundstedt" (1959), 3 Scand. S.L., 125: the views
    of these two writers are explained more simply and clearly
    than in their originals.

2. WILLIAMS, G.L. "Language and the Law", (1946), 62 L.Q.R.,
    pp. 387, 398-399: this is a brief but illuminating analysis
    of the term "right" with comments on the views of
    P. Vinogradoff, A.V. Lundstedt, R. von Ihering and
    J.W. Salmond.

3. OLIVECRONA, K. "The Concept of a Right according to Grotius
    and Pufendorff" in Festschrift für Oscar Adolf Germann,
    (Verlag Stämpfli & Cie, Bern, 1969), 175: both Grotius and
    Pufendorff maintained that a right implied a moral power.
    After examining this thesis, it is contended that there is
    a confusion between the primary and secondary rights. The
    latter is not a facultas moralis, but implies that the use
    of force to enforce one's primary right meets with no moral
    obstacle.

4. HOLLAND, T.E. The Elements of Jurisprudence, (13th ed.,
    Oxford, 1924), chaps. 7 and 8: in the first of these
    chapters a legal right is said to be the capacity of
    controlling, with the assent and assistance of the state,
    the acts of another. The correlation between right and duty
    and various other ideas are considered. In the following
    chapter right is analysed into various "elements".

5. GRAY, J.C. The Nature and Sources of the Law, (2nd ed.,
    R. Gray, The Macmillan Co. of New York, 1921), chap. 1:
    this is a general discussion of rights and draws attention
    to the ambiguity of the term. Right consists of the ability
    to enforce the correlative duty. Absolute duties, legal and
    moral rights and rights as interests are also considered.

6. AUSTIN, J. Lectures on Jurisprudence, (5th ed., R. Campbell,
    John Murray, 1885), pp. 281-290 and Lectures 12, 16 and 17:
    the possibility of there being rights in and against the
    sovereign is considered. The discussion in Lecture 12 is of
    particular interest because of the distinction there drawn
    between "right" and "liberty", i.e., exemption from
    obligation. Lecture 16 makes the important point that duty
    is the basis of right. Lecture 17 considers absolute and
    relative duties and concludes that absolute duties are
    possible in certain cases.

7. MARKBY, W. Elements of Law, (6th ed., Oxford, 1905), chap. 4,
    SS 140-160: rights and duties are correlative, but not every
    duty need have a correlative right (absolute duty).

The sovereign has neither rights nor duties.

1. BROWN, W.J. The Austinian Theory of Law, (John Murray, 1906),
    pp. 180-181, 192-194: J. Austin's distinction between
    "right" and "liberty" is approved: He disagrees with
    Austin on the point that the sovereign may have rights and
    duties.

2. POLLOCK, F. A First Book of Jurisprudence, (6th ed.,
    Macmillan Co., Ltd., 1929), pp. 61-77: right implies a
    correlative duty. There are also other applications of
    right in the sense of freedom and power. The question of
    rights in and against the state is considered.

3. ALLEN, C.K. "Legal Duties" in Legal Duties, (Oxford, 1931),
    pp. 156, 181-193: both "power" and "interest" are combined
    in the idea that a right is a legally guaranteed power to
    realise an interest. J. Austin's thesis concerning absolute
    duties is on the whole supported.

4. CAMPBELL, A.H. "Some Footnotes to Salmond's Jurisprudence",
    (1939-40), 7 C.L.J. 206, at pp. 209-211: the question of
    rights in and against the sovereign is considered. (The
    commentary is on the 9th ed.).

5. JENKS, E. The New Jurisprudence, (John Murray, 1933), chap.
    8, pp. 174-188: the conception of absolute duties is
    rejected. There is in addition a general discussion of
    rights.

6. BUCKLAND, W.W. Some Reflections on Jurisprudence, (Cambridge
    University Press, 1945), pp. 107-110: the question of
    rights and duties in the sovereign is considered with
    reference to the views of J. Austin and others.

7. HART, H.L.A. "Definition and Theory in Jurisprudence", (1954),
    70 L.Q.R. 37, at pp. 42-49: the various characteristics of
    the proposition "A has a right" are discussed. The
    explanation of the word "right" should take the form of an
    explanation of the statement in which the word plays a
    part, the conditions under which the whole statement would
    be true and how it is used in drawing conclusions.

8. AUERBACH, C.A. "On Professor Hart's Definition and Theory in
    Jurisprudence" (1956) 9 J.L.E. 39, especially pp. 40-44:
    H.L.A. Hart's method of elucidating "right" is criticised
    on the ground that truth and falsity are inappropriate,
    and that it does not aid in solving new cases.

9. HALL, J. "Analytic Philosophy and Jurisprudence" (1966) 77

Ethics, 14, especially at pp. 24-26: Professor Hart's method of elucidation is criticised. Legal terms are not so different from non-legal terms, nor is the specification of conditions necessary to the truth of statements peculiar to legal terms. It is pointed out that Professor Hart elucidates one "anomalous" term in terms of six others; and that his demonstration is entirely hypothetical: if the specified conditions are present then it is true only to say that "X has a right".

1. SIMPSON, A.W.B. "The Analysis of Legal Concepts" (1964) 80 L.Q.R. 535: Professor Hart's elucidation of "right" is considered in the context of a general discussion of eludidation. It is pointed out (p. 557) that his demonstration is no more than a truism.

2. POUND, R. "Legal Rights", (1915-16), 26 I.J.E. 92: five senses of the term "right" are distinguished:- interest, claim, capacity, liberty and that which is just. Consideration is given to how the term "right" came to be so overworked.

3. POUND, R. Jurisprudence, (West Publishing Co., 1959), IV, chap. 21: legal concepts are discussed generally and the need for an improved terminology is stressed. The various meanings of the word "right" and the history of these usages are explained.

4. HEARN, W.E. The Theory of Legal Duties and Rights, (Melbourne: John Ferres; London: Trübner & Co., 1883), chap. 8: the origin of the term "right" is examined. Following J. Austin, a right is said to be a consequence of command for the benefit of one person and imposing a duty on another. Absolute duties are also considered.

5. BENTHAM, J. Works, (ed. J. Bowring, William Tait, Edinburgh, 1843), I, pp. 301-302: rights are advantages. Rights and duties are inseparable, the latter being restraints on liberty.

6. BEALE, J.H. A Treatise on the Conflict of Laws, (Baker, Voorhis & Co., 1935), I, pp. 58-86: rights are legalised interests in, to, or against a person or thing. Various interests and kinds of rights are considered.

7. KORKUNOV, N.M. General Theory of Law, (trans. W.G. Hastings, The Boston Book Co., 1909), SS. 22, 27, 29: the right-duty obligation is explained. A claim implies a duty. If there is no obligation, there is permission, not a right.

8. POUND, R. Readings on the History and System of the Common

Law, (2nd ed., The Chipman Law Publishing Co., Boston,
1921), chap. 8: this is a compilation of various writings.
Private interests are maintained by rights, powers and
privileges. Various spheres of interest are considered.

1. POUND, R. "The Progress of the Law", (1927-28), 41 Harv.L.R.
   175: this is of general interest. It consists of an account
   of Analytical Jurisprudence in the course of which he
   shows how various jurists have dealt with the ambiguity of
   terms that refer both to "law" and "right".

2. SMITH, G.H. "Of the Nature of Jurisprudence and of the Law",
   (1904), 38 Am.L.R. 68, at pp. 79-83: this is a shrewd
   analysis of language forms in legal speech in the course
   of which the various meanings of "right" are examined. It
   is an interesting general study.

3. The above does not include the Continental literature on
   the subject. Reference might be made to B. Windscheid,
   Lehrbuch des Pandektenrechts, I, ii, pp. 155 et seq.,
   which contains eight pages of note references to treatises
   and monographs.

The Hohfeldian Scheme

4. HOHFELD, W.N. Fundamental Legal Conceptions as Applied in
   Judicial Reasoning, (ed. W.W. Cook, Yale University Press;
   London: Humphrey Milford, 1923), chaps. 1-5: the first
   chapter contains the scheme of jural relations, some of
   the remaining chapters consist of analyses of various
   topics with its aid.

5. COOK, W.W. "Hohfeld's Contributions to the Science of Law",
   which is the "Introduction" to W.N. Hohfeld's Fundamental
   Legal Conceptions as Applied in Judicial Reasoning, (supra):
   this provides a somewhat simplified explanation of Hohfeld's
   scheme together with a sympathetic evaluation of his work.

6. STONE, J. Legal Systems and Lawyers' Reasonings, (Stevens &
   Sons, Ltd., 1964), chap. 4: Hohfeld pointed out the danger
   of chameleon-hued words, clarified confused usage and has
   revealed new aspects of the concepts involved. Various
   aspects of his contribution, in relation to those of his
   predecessors and successors, are considered. Despite certain
   criticisms which might be levelled against Hohfeld, the
   conclusion is very favourable.

7. BENTHAM, J. The Limits of Jurisprudence Defined, (ed.
   C.W. Everett, Columbia University Press, 1945), chap. 2:
   in this posthumous publication it will be seen that Bentham

had anticipated to a remarkable degree the analysis of
later jurists. The opposition between duty and liberty is
as clear as it is convincing. There is also an elaborate
examination of powers in the widest sense.

1. SALMOND, J.W. Jurisprudence, (7th ed., Sweet & Maxwell, Ltd.,
   1924, pp. 70-74; 12th ed., P.J. Fitzgerald, Sweet &
   Maxwell, Ltd., 1966), chap. 7: in the 7th edition will be
   found Salmond's own breakdown of the concept of "right",
   to which W.N. Hohfeld paid just tribute and acknowledged
   indebtedness. In the 12th edition the current editor has
   incorporated Hohfeld's scheme and eliminated Salmond's.

2. TERRY, H.T. Some Leading Principles of Anglo-American Law
   Expounded with a View to its Arrangement and Codification,
   (T. & J.W. Johnson, Philadelphia, 1884), chap. 6, SS. 113-
   127: this analysis is an important forerunner of
   W.N. Hohfeld's. Four meanings of the term "right" are
   distinguished, three of which correspond to Hohfeld's
   distinctions, namely, claim, permissive rights (privileges)
   and facultative rights, (powers).

3. HEARN, W.E. The Theory of Legal Duties and Rights, (Melbourne:
   John Ferres; London: Trübner & Co., 1883), chap. 8:
   distinctions are drawn between right (stricto sensu),
   liberty and power.

4. CORBIN, A.L. "Legal Analysis and Terminology", (1919-20), 29
   Yale L.J. 163: this contains an explanation of certain
   legal terms and is particularly important for its helpful
   and simplified exposition of Hohfeld's scheme.

5. RADIN, M. "A Restatement of Hohfeld", (1937-38), 51 Harv.L.R.
   1141: this is a critical appraisal of the Hohfeldian scheme
   which seeks to correct some of the points in the analysis.

6. GOBLE, G.W. "A Redefinition of Basic Legal Terms", (1935),
   35 Col.L.R. 535: this is an elaboration of W.N. Hohfeld's
   work and contains a fresh examination of legal relationships.

7. PATON, G.W. A Text-Book of Jurisprudence, (3rd ed. D.P. Derham,
   Oxford, 1964), chap. 12: the concept of "right" is
   considered generally and its various meanings examined.
   W.N. Hohfeld's scheme is explained in brief.

8. KEETON, G.W. The Elementary Principles of Jurisprudence,
   (2nd ed., Isaac Pitman & Sons, Ltd., 1949), chaps. 11 and
   12: the first of these chapters contains a brief account
   of W.N. Hohfeld together with a more general discussion of
   rights. The second deals with classification of rights.

1. KOCOUREK, A. "The Century of Analytic Jurisprudence since John Austin", in Law: A Century of Progress, (New York University Press; London: Humphrey Milford, 1937), II, p. 194, especially pp. 205-210: this is a historical account of the writers who have followed in the Austinian tradition. At the pages mentioned are to be found J.W. Salmond's and W.N. Hohfeld's analyses with certain critical comments on the latter.

2. KOCOUREK, A. "Plurality of Advantage and Disadvantage in Jural Relations", (1920), 19 Mich.L.R., 47: analysis on Hohfeldian lines is carried far beyond Hohfeld. Jural relations are sub-divided into 8 "nexal relations", 8 "simple" or " quasi-jural relations" and 8 "naked relations".

3. KOCOUREK, A. "The Alphabet of Legal Relations", (1923), 9 Am. B.A.J., 237: W.N. Hohfeld's terms are differently presented, the four principal terms following Hohfeld's scheme but with the addition of "common denominators" and "negative terms". (cf. Chapter 2 of Jural Relations, infra).

4. KOCOUREK, A. Jural Relations, (2nd ed., The Bobbs-Merrill Co. 1928), chaps. 1-12: jural relations are examined in minute detail. W.N. Hohfeld's scheme of eight terms is elaborated into twenty-four. The whole book is written with the aid of a technical vocabulary covering seventeen pages. This is a most advanced work. An important feature is that Kocourek dispenses with correlatives and opposites by distinguishing between Advantages (claim, immunity, privilege, power) and Disadvantages (duty, disability, inability, liability).

5. LLEWELLYN, K.N. The Bramble Bush, (New York, 1930), pp. 83-89: W.N. Hohfeld's scheme is considered from the American Realist point of view. The reaction of a court is made the determining factor.

6. SNYDER, O.C. Preface to Jurisprudence, (The Bobbs-Merrill Co., Inc., 1954), part V, chap. 1, pp. 707-716: this contains a general examination of W.N. Hohfeld's scheme.

7. WILLIAMS, G.L. "The Concept of Legal Liberty", in Essays in Legal Philosophy (ed. R.S. SUMMERS, Basil Blackwell, Oxford, 1968), 121: this is a specialised treatment of privilege or liberty. Certain modifications of W.N. Hohfeld's scheme are suggested.

8. CAMERON, J.T. "Two Jurisprudential Case Notes", [1964], Jur. R., 155-58: the first part is devoted to an examination of Musgrove v. Chung Teeong Toy with reference to W.N. Hohfeld's "liberty". It is stated that there is difficulty in ascribing

a no-right to the state correlative to an alien's common
law liberty to enter British territory. It is thought that
Musgrove's case is not a good illustration of liberty; and
further that the Hohfeldian scheme is probably not
applicable to public law.

1. FARMER, J.A. "Natural Justice and Licensing Applications:
   Hohfeld and the Writ of Certiorari" [1967], 2 N.Z.U.L.R.,
   282: the distinction between right, liberty and privilege
   has aquired significance as a result of developments in
   administrative law. There is in particular a growing
   distinction between liberty, as connoting freedom enjoyed
   by all, and privilege, as connoted a special dispensation
   from a particular law.

2. SHATTUCK, C.E. "The True Meaning of the Term 'Liberty' in
   those Clauses in the Federal and State Constitutions which
   Protect 'Life, Liberty, and Property'", (1890-91), 4 Harv.
   L.R., 365: this is earlier than W.N. Hohfeld and is of
   general interest. The conclusion is reached that liberty
   connotes absence of restraint.

3. BIGELOW, M.M. The Law of Torts, (3rd ed., Cambridge University Press, 1908), pp. 13-16: privileges in tort are
   discussed. It is pointed out that privilege is the converse
   of duty.

4. BOHLEN, F.H. "Incomplete Privilege to Inflict Intentional
   Invasions of Interests of Property and Personality",
   (1925-26), 39 Harv. L.R., 307: the occasions when the duty
   not to do certain things becomes a privilege to do them
   are discussed.

5. COHEN, L.J. Review of H.L.A. HART: The Concept of Law, (1962),
   71 Mind, 395: a good deal of space is given to a critique
   of Hart's use of the term "power". What is said here may
   usefully be considered along with Hohfeldian powers.

6. CAMPBELL, A.H. "Some Footnotes to Salmond's Jurisprudence",
   (1939-40), 7 C.L.J., 206-209: certain points connected with
   W.N. Hohfeld's scheme are amplified.

7. LLOYD, D. The Idea of Law, (Penguin Books, Ltd., A 688, 1964),
   pp. 309-18: the link between legal and moral duties is
   underlined by the use of "right", which carries a sense of
   justification. After a discussion of absolute duties and
   primary and remedial rights, W.N. Hohfeld's scheme is
   explained in broad terms with illustrative examples.

8. WORTLEY, B.A. Jurisprudence, (Manchester University Press,

Oceana Publications, Inc., New York, 1967), chap. 16: this
gives a general account of rights and duties. Contrariety
and contradiction are explained in Hohfeldian terms. There
are also illustrations of some of the Hohfeldian
distinctions.

Evaluation of W.N. Hohfeld's Contribution

1. RANDALL, H.J. "Hohfeld on Jurisprudence," (1925), 41 L.Q.R.,
   86: this is one of the first English appreciations of
   W.N. Hohfeld's work. It is a critical appraisal which
   proceeds on the basis of two main questions: whether
   Hohfeld's scheme covers the whole field of legal relations,
   and whether the scheme does more than is necessary.

2. COOK, W.W. "The Utility of Jurisprudence in the Solution of
   Legal Problems", in Lectures on Legal Topics, (The
   Macmillan Co., New York, 1928), p. 338: conceptual tools
   need to be analysed to find out whether they are adequate.
   The term "right" is examined on this basis and the different
   meanings that have been attached to it in cases. The value
   of W.N. Hohfeld's scheme for this purpose is discussed.

3. COOK, W.W. "Privileges of Labor Unions in the Struggle for
   Life", (1917-18), 27 Yale L.J., 779: the value of W.N.
   Hohfeld's analysis is demonstrated by its application to
   the decisions in two important trade union cases. The
   judicial use of the term "right" confuses different
   meanings of the term.

4. COOK, W.W. "Note on the Associated Press Case", (1918-19),
   28 Yale L.J., 387, 391: this shows that a novel rule of law
   can be said to have been created in the given case by
   examining the reasoning in it with the aid of W.N. Hohfeld's
   scheme.

5. COOK, W.W. "The Alienability of Choses in Action", (1916),
   29 Harv. L.R., 816; "The Alienability of Choses in Action:
   a Reply to Professor Williston", (1917), 30 Harv. L.R.,
   449: the value of W.N. Hohfeld's scheme when expounding
   the complex relationships involved in this branch of the
   law is demonstrated.

6. CORBIN, A.L. "Rights and Duties", (1923-24), 33 Yale L.J.,
   501: rights are analysed generally with the aid of W.N.
   Hohfeld's scheme.

7. CORBIN, A.L. "Offer and Acceptance, and Some of the Resulting
   Legal Relations", (1916-17), 26 Yale L.J., 169: the
   significance of the Hohfeldian power concept is demonstrated

by an examination of the changing relationships involved
in the formation of contracts.

1. COMMONS, J.R. Legal Foundations of Capitalism, (The Macmillan
    Co., of New York, 1932), pp. 83-134: the economic trans-
    actions of people are analysed with the aid of the Hohfeldian
    table. Criticisms of it, principally by Kocourek, are con-
    sidered and on the whole rejected. On the other hand,
    certain improvements in terminology, notably "exposure" in
    place of "no-right", are suggested. The chief interest of
    this closely reasoned section lies, not so much in its
    clarification of the Hohfeldian scheme, but in its detailed
    application of the scheme to the examination of economic
    transactions.

2. LLEWELLYN, K.N. Cases and Materials on the Law of Sales,
    (Chicago: Callaghan & Co., 1930), chap. 6: the commentaries
    interspersed between the cases on Title are written in
    Hohfeldian language and provide an example of the
    practicalities of the Hohfeldian scheme. At p. 572 attention
    is specifically drawn to the immense clarification that
    would ensue from its use in sorting out problems of Title
    in sale.

3. HAMSON, C.J. "Moot Case on Defamation", (1948), 10 C.L.J.,
    46: the opposition between W.N. Hohfeld's concepts of
    privilege and duty is utilised in deciding a hypothetical
    dispute.

4. SOLOMON, E. "Lease or License," (1959-61), 3 Syd. L.R., 136:
    the Hohfeldian analysis is applied to the distinction
    between lease and lecense. Since 1952 the grant of a
    privilege to occupy is a lease. In this light the effect
    of Addiscombe Garden Estates, Ltd. v. Crabbe, [1958] 1 Q.
    B., 513, is assessed.

5. GOBLE, G.W. "The Sanction of a Duty", (1927-28), 37 Yale L.J.,
    426: Hohfeld's scheme is utilised to examine the different
    kinds of sanction.

6. HUSIK, I. "Hohfeld's Jurisprudence," (1924), 72 U.Pa. L.R.,
    263: this is an unfavourable evaluation of W.N. Hohfeld's
    work on the basis of three questions: (1) has he shown the
    traditional usage of "right" to be inadequate ? (2) If so,
    has he succeeded in providing a more acceptable analysis ?
    (3) Is his scheme of practical value ?

7. KOCOUREK, A. "The Hohfeld System of Fundamental Legal
    Concepts", (1920), 15 Ill. L.Q., 23: this is a critique
    of W.N. Hohfeld's scheme, objecting in particular to the
    concept of jural opposite.

1. CORBIN, A.L. "Jural Relations and their Classification",
    (1920-21), 30 Yale L.J. 226: Corbin defends W.N. Hohfeld
    against A. Kocourek's criticisms, and in turn considers
    critically the utility of Kocourek's own more elaborate
    scheme: (see Jural Relations, supra).

2. POUND, R. "Fifty Years of Jurisprudence", (1936-37), 50 Harv.
    L.R. 557, especially at pp. 571-576: this is a critical
    appraisal of W.N. Hohfeld's work. Not all Pound's objections
    have proved acceptable to other writers. He points out,
    inter alia, that some of Hohfeld's opposites are "contrasts";
    that there can be more than one correlative and opposite
    to a term; that "no-right" is meaningless; that "privilege"
    might have been broken down still more; and that Hohfeld's
    scheme suffers from Hegelian weaknesses.

3. POUND, R. "Legal Rights", (1915-16), 26 I.J.E. 92: this
    article, which is a general discussion of the term "right",
    contains an incidental criticism of W.N. Hohfeld's scheme.
    Disability and Liability are said to be devoid of any
    independent jural significance: (on this see W.W. Cook in
    his "Introduction" to W.N. Hohfeld, Fundamental Legal
    Conceptions as Applied in Judicial Reasoning, pp. 9-10).

4. POUND, R. Jurisprudence, (West Publishing Co., 1959), IV,
    chaps. 21-24: in these chapters there is a full and
    critical discussion of rights generally and of W.N. Hohfeld's
    work in particular. In the main they unify and repeat Pound's
    earlier criticisms.

5. HONORÉ, A.M. "Rights of Exclusion and Immunities against
    Divesting", (1959-60) 34 Tul.L.R. 453, especially 456-458:
    W.N. Hohfeld is criticised on the ground that rights and
    duties are not always correlative; and that there is need
    of an omnibus concept of "right" in addition to specific
    terms like claims, privileges, etc.

6. COWAN, T.A. The American Jurisprudence Reader, (Oceana
    Publications, Docket Series, Vol. 8, 1956), pp. 110-124:
    this gives reprints of W.W. Cook's "Introduction" to
    W.N. Hohfeld and R. Pound's "Fifty years of jurisprudence"
    (supra).

7. BUCKLAND, W.W. Some Reflections on Jurisprudence, (Cambridge
    University Press, 1945), pp. 92-96: the distinctions
    between rights, liberties, powers and immunities are
    discussed and W.N. Hohfeld's work is criticised as being
    needlessly acute.

8. REUSCHLEIN, H.G. Jurisprudence - its American Prophets,

(The Bobbs-Merrill Co., Inc., 1951), pp. 88-91, 167-179:
Hohfeld's work is briefly summed up. It has done much to
induce clear thinking, but it has not proved to be juristic
salvation.

1. SIMPSON, A.W.B. "The Analysis of Legal Concepts" (1964) 80
   L.Q.R. 535, 549-51: W.N. Hohfeld, among others, is in error
   of trying to link an explanation of legal concepts to a
   theory of the logical functions of words or sentences. In
   this way he is forced into introducing metaphysical ideas.

2. MAHER, F.K.H. "The Kinds of Legal Rights" (1965) 5 Melb.U.L.
   R. 47: we should use legal terms in the sense in which
   lawyers use them. Hohfeld wavered between such meanings and
   those which he thought lawyers should use. Hohfeld's scheme
   is criticised as being an unnecessarily complicated way of
   solving issues. Various shades of meaning of the term
   "right" are distinguished.

3. STONE, R.L. "An Analysis of Hohfeld" (1963) 48 Minn.L.R. 313:
   the value of W.N. Hohfeld's analysis is appraised from a
   philosophical point of view. It is asserted that there are
   certain philosophically invalid assumptions underlying his
   scheme which prevents its success as a weapon of legal
   thought.

4. SMITH, J.C. "Law, Language, and Philosophy" (1968) 3 U.Br.
   Col.L.R. 59: in the course of reviewing the attitude to
   language of various legal philosophers, the work of Hohfeld
   is considered in this light. The conclusion is on the whole
   critical, but it is useful as a background to an appraisal
   of Hohfeld's contribution.

5. LLEWELLYN, K.N. Jurisprudence, Realism in Theory and Practice,
   (University of Chicago Press, 1962), chap. 26: this gives
   a pen-picture of W.N. Hohfeld as a man and as a teacher.

10

CONDUCT

Act

1. FITZGERALD, P.J. "Voluntary and Involuntary Acts" in Oxford Essays in Jurisprudence, (ed. A.G. Guest, Oxford University Press, 1961), chap. 1: the use of the term "act" is discussed with reference to criminal and civil law and evidence. Emphasis is laid on controllability as an important feature of an "act" in the law.

2. WILLIAMS, G.L. Criminal Law: The General Part, (2nd ed., Stevens & Sons, Ltd., 1961), chap. 1, especially SS. 8-13: although the substance is criminal law, there is a good deal of general discussion of the nature of "act" and its components - movement, circumstances and some, at any rate, of its consequences.

3. FLETCHER, G.P. "Prolonging Life" (1967) 42 Wash. L.R. 999: this is a stimulating discussion of the distinction between "act" and "omission" primarily from the criminal law point of view. In order to deal with the social and moral problems arising out of heart-, lung-, kidney-machines and the like, it is forcefully argued that acts ending terminal diseases should be subsumed under omission.

4. RYLE, G. The Concept of Mind, (Hutchinson's University Library, 1949), chap. 3, especially pp. 69-74: this discussion from a non-legal point of view is rewarding for a lawyer. It disposes of the need to talk of willing as a separate operation. At pp. 69-74 the distinction between voluntary and involuntary action is dealt with and the point is made that this distinction comes into prominence when the question of responsibility arises.

5. AUSTIN, J.L. "A Plea for Excuses", (1956-57), 57 P.A.S. 1: this, too, discusses action in relation to responsibility, but from a different angle. Voluntary and involuntary actions are also dealt with, though not from a legal point of view.

6. HART, H.L.A. "The Ascription of Responsibility and Rights", in Logic and Language (ed. A.G.N. Flew, Blackwell, (1955), I, 145: the language of lawyers refers to human behaviour with a view to ascribing responsibility or exemption therefrom. P. 187 et seq., deal with "action" from this angle. The statement, "He did it", is not descriptive, but an ascription of responsibility for an action. (See also H.L.A. Hart, "Negligence, Mens rea and Criminal Responsibility" in Oxford Essays in Jurisprudence, (ed.

A.G. Guest, Oxford University Press, 1961), pp. 34-38.
This essay is referred to below under "Negligence").

1. HART, H.L.A. "Varieties of Responsibility" (1967) 83 L.Q.R.
346: four different uses of the term "responsibility" are
distinguished. Of these the most important is "Liability-
responsibility". The relationship between legal and moral
responsibility is touched on.

2. KOCOUREK, A. Jural Relations, (2nd ed., The Bobbs-Merrill Co.,
1928), chap. 16: after examining the traditional views of
the nature of "act", the submission is made that "act" is
the legal concept of some result of bodily movement or some
result attributable to its absence. An act in law creates
a jural relationship. Since the latter is conceptual, so
is the former.

3. KOCOUREK, A. An Introduction to the Science of Law, (Little,
Brown & Co., 1930), pp. 266 et seq.: this is a further
discussion on the same line as above.

4. HALL, J. "Analytic Philosophy and Jurisprudence" (1966) 77
Ethics, 14; especially pp. 19-24: this criticises both
J.L. Austin and H.L.A. Hart. A statement, e.g., "He did it",
is not simply an ascription of responsibility. It is to
some extent descriptive because it presupposes competence
and normality in the actor and causation. So, too, mens
rea means not only that excuses are excluded but also that
the defendant intentionally or recklessly did whatever it
is. An excuse is itself descriptive of a mental state,
which is why it functions as an excuse.

5. HALL, J. General Principles of Criminal Law, (2nd ed., The
Bobbs-Merrill Co., Inc., 1960), chap. 6: "act" is generally
discussed with a view to elucidating what constitutes
criminal conduct. What is required is a term that will
cover voluntary actions and inactions, and the term "effort"
is suggested.

6. BRANDEN, N. "Free Will, Moral Responsibility and the Law"
(1969) 42 Southern Calif. L.R. 264: this argues for a new
concept of free will. Traditional approaches are rejected
as unsound psychologically and in law.

7. BENTHAM, J. An Introduction to the Principles of Morals and
Legislation in Works, (ed. J. Bowring, William Tait & Sons,
1843), I, chaps. 7, SS. 5 et seq., 8, 9, 10: transactions
are resolved into acts, circumstances, intention as to the
act and as to the consequences, consciousness and
consequences. In addition there are motive and general
disposition.

1. AUSTIN, J. <u>Lectures on Jurisprudence</u>, (5th ed., R. Campbell,
   John Murray, 1885), I, pp. 365-367, 410-416: acts are said
   to be movements of the body consequent upon determinations
   of the will, and forbearances are voluntary inactions. Acts
   are distinguished from their consequences.

2. SALMOND, J.W. <u>Jurisprudence</u>, (12th ed., P.J. Fitzgerald, Sweet
   & Maxwell, Ltd., 1966), pp. 352-367: an "act" has to be
   subject to the will and includes the circumstances and, as
   it has no natural boundaries, some, but not necessarily all,
   its consequences.

3. PATON, G.W. <u>A Text-Book of Jurisprudence</u>, (3rd ed., D.P.
   Derham, Oxford, 1964), chap. 13, S. 68: this gives a general
   discussion of "act" as including volition, motive, intent,
   circumstances and consequences; and of inaction as including
   intentional inaction (forbearance) and failure to comply
   with a duty (omission).

4. COOK, W.W. "Act, Intention and Motive in the Criminal Law",
   (1916-17), 26 Yale L.J., 645: "act" and "intention" are
   ambiguous terms. "Act" should be confined to willed muscular
   movement. A consequence is intended when the actor desires
   it to happen as the result of the act, or when he adverts
   to a result which will necessarily follow.

5. PERKINS, R.M. "A Rationale of <u>Mens Rea</u>", (1938-39), 52 Harv.
   L.R., 905-907; 912: "act" is discussed with reference to
   <u>actus reus</u> in criminal law. The necessity for voluntary
   conduct is discussed with reference to actions and inactions.

6. TERRY, H.T. <u>Some Leading Principles of Anglo-American Law
   Expounded with a View to its Classification, Arrangement
   and Codification.</u> (T & J.W. Johnson & Co., Philadelphia,
   1884), SS. 77-86: "act" is discussed generally with
   reference to the will, instinctive movements, omissions
   and motive. In a wide sense "act" includes some of its
   consequences.

7. MARKBY, W. <u>Elements of Law</u>, (6th ed., Oxford, 1905), SS. 213-
   216: the analysis follows that of J. Austin.

8. HOLLAND, T.E. <u>The Elements of Jurisprudence</u>, (13th ed.,
   Oxford, 1924), pp. 108-125: the account lays some stress on
   "movements of the will", which should be regarded with some
   suspicion in the light of later analyses.

9. KEETON, G.W. <u>The Elementary Principles of Jurisprudence</u>, (2nd
   ed., Isaac Pitman & Sons, Ltd., 1949), pp. 198-207: the

analysis follows that of J. Bentham with illustrations
drawn from modern case-law.

1.   HOLMES, O.W. The Common Law, (Little, Brown & Co., 1881),
     pp. 54-57: this short analysis contains Holmes's famous
     definition of "act" as a "voluntary muscular contraction".
     Circumstances, on this view, are relevant only to determine
     the wrongfulness of an act.

Automatism

2.   JENNINGS, J. "The Growth and Development of Automatism as a
     Defence in Criminal Law", (1961-62), 2 Os. H.L.J., 370:
     this contains a discussion of the English authorities and
     the relation between automatism and insanity.

3.   McDERMOTT, T.L. "The Path of Automatism", (1962), 1 Tasm. L.
     R., 695: this is another review of the law in comparison
     with insanity.

4.   HOWARD, C. "Automatism and Insanity", (1962), 4 Syd. L.R.,
     36: the conclusion is reached that automatism will only be
     accepted as a defence when the action is performed in a
     state of unconsciousness and in circumstances not amounting
     to insanity.

5.   WILLIAMS, G.L. "Automatism" in Essays in Criminal Science,
     (ed. G.O.W. Mueller, Fred. B. Rothman & Co., New York,
     Sweet & Maxwell, Ltd., London, 1961), chap. 12: this is an
     investigation of the question whether or not automatism
     should be treated as insanity.

6.   ELLIOTT, I.D. "Responsibility for Involuntary Acts: Ryan v.
     The Queen", (1967-68), 41 A.L.J., 497: it is not enough to
     speak of voluntary act as a "willed movement", for this is
     as much in need of explanation as voluntary act.
     Voluntariness is part of mens rea, not of actus reus.
     These points arose in R. v. Ryan (1967), 40 A.L.J.R., 488.

7.   TODD, E.C.E. "Insanity as a Defence in a Civil Action of
     Assault and Battery", (1952), 15 M.L.R., 486: this is a
     discussion of Morriss v. Marsden (civil case), which
     concerned the question of liability for the involuntary
     conduct of a person who had been found unfit to plead so
     far as the criminal law was concerned.

8.   PREVEZER, S. "Automatism and Involuntary Conduct", (1958),
     Crim. L.R., 361, 440: this is a discussion of involuntary
     conduct with reference principally to Hill v. Baxter, an
     important case on automatism. It tries to show to what

extent the legal treatment of the subject is inadequate.

1. EDWARDS, J.Ll.J. "Automatism and Criminal Responsibility",
   (1958), 21 M.L.R., 375: Hill v. Baxter is discussed further.

2. TURNER, J.W.C. "Towards the Deodand", (1960), Crim. L.R., 89,
   168: judicial interpretation of statute can make a person
   responsible even for involuntary conduct. One such instance,
   Kensington Borough Council v. Walters, is fully dealt with.

3. PARSONAGE, M. "Epilepsy and Driving", (1969), 133 J.P., 290:
   the law has to provide against disasters and so forbids
   epileptics from driving. After explaining the nature of
   epileptiform attacks, a doctor considers whether, subject
   to safeguards, those who have been free from attacks for a
   certain number of years should be allowed to drive.

Causation

4. GREEN, L. "Are there Dependable Rules of Causation ?", (1929),
   77 U. Pa. L.R., 601: the question is one of responsibility,
   and rules cannot be devised to take the place of decision.
   Formulae about causation are needed in order to present the
   issue that has to be decided.

5. JAMES, F. and PERRY, R.F. "Legal Cause", (1951), 60 Yale L.J.,
   761: this is a critical appraisal of the "but for" test and
   of concurrent cause, one or both of which may involve
   blameworthiness. On this latter question, the different
   opinions of various writers are discussed. The varying
   interpretations of "proximate cause" are also discussed.

6. KELSEN, H. What is Justice ? (University of California Press,
   1957), pp. 303, 325: the idea of causation is traced back to
   revenge - cause attracts effect just as wrong attracts
   punishment. Modern scientific ideas of causation separated
   themselves from revenge when the theological interpretation
   of nature was abandoned, but they continued to be based on
   the analogy of revenge - one cause, one effect. In the
   second essay the above point is developed further. With a
   normative science like law the connection between wrong and
   retribution is one of imputation - what ought to happen in
   certain circumstances.

7. PEASLEE, R.J. "Multiple Causation and Damage", (1933-34), 47
   Harv. L.R., 1127: the main point of interest is the
   discussion of the concurrence of an innocent and a blame-
   worthy cause. The view is submitted that in this event the
   party to blame should be absolved on grounds of justice and
   policy. Other variations are also considered.

1. CARPENTER, C.E. "Concurrent Causation", (1935), 83 U. Pa. L.R.
    941: this provides a clear analysis of the difficulties
    involved, especially in the application of the "but for"
    test. If of two concurrent causes one is innocent and the
    other guilty, the latter should not be absolved (C.E.
    Peaslee, supra, criticised).

2. HART, H.L.A. and HONORÉ, A.M. Causation in the Law, (Oxford,
    1959): this monograph deals exhaustively with the subject
    and also with related topics, such as voluntary and
    involuntary conduct. It incorporates articles by the authors
    under the same title in (1956), 72 L.Q.R., 58, 260, 398.

3. WILLIAMS, G.L. "Causation in the Law", (1961), C.L.J., 62:
    this discusses causation in the light of H.L.A. Hart and
    A.M. Honoré's monograph. The application of the "but for"
    test and cases of concurrent cause are considered.

4. WILLIAMS, G.L. Joint Torts and Contributory Negligence,
    (Stevens & Sons, Ltd., 1951), pp. 239 et seq.: this also
    explains the "but for" test and the way in which certain
    problems are dealt with in tort.

5. KEETON, R.E. Legal Cause in the Law of Torts, (Ohio State
    University Press, 1963): the principal thesis is that
    causation is founded on the "risk" principle, and that this
    is a rule of causation in a "cause-in-fact" sense. It is
    conceded that departures and modifications do come in.

6. COLE, R.H. "Windfall and Probability: A Study of 'Cause' in
    Negligence Law", (1964), 52 Calif. L.R., 459: the term
    "cause" is used for different purposes, at times to prevent
    an unfair pecuniary advantage being derived by the
    plaintiff, at others to decide whether the defendant was
    involved at all. This brings in policy decisions and
    prediction of probabilities. On this basis, various
    analyses, including that of H.L.A. Hart and A.M.Honoré,
    are examined.

7. MORRIS, C. "On the Teaching of Legal Cause", (1939), 39 Col.
    L.R., 1087: "factual" and "legal" cause are discussed, and
    there is a demonstration of how most tests of causation
    that are commonly used beg the question.

8. MUNKMAN, J. "Note on the Causes of an Accidental Occurrence",
    (1954), 17 M.L.R., 134: a chance happening is the result of
    the intersection of several cause sequences at a given place
    and time. The distinction is made between the "stage
    setting" and the factors that make the accident happen.

1. WRIGHT, R.A. "Causation and Responsibility in English Law",
   (1955) C.L.J. 163: causation is an experimental
   generalisation and lawyers should concentrate on how it
   operates. Decisions on causation are value-judgments.

2. BOHLEN, F.H. Studies in the Law of Torts, (The Bobbs-Merrill
   Co., 1926), chap. 9: causation is the test by which courts
   ascertain whether a particular harm is to be ascribed to a
   particular action for the purpose of responsibility.

3. BEALE, J.H. "Recovery for Consequences of an Act", (1895-96),
   9 Harv.L.R. 80: "The Proximate Consequences of an Act",
   (1920), 33 Harv. L.R. 633: the analysis contained in these
   articles has now become traditional and has come to be
   known as the "insulation" theory. Many modern discussions
   are evaluations of it.

4. SMITH, J. "Legal Cause in Actions of Tort", (1911-12), 25
   Harv.L.R. 102, 223, 303: various tests are considered and
   the "substantial factor" test is advocated.

5. TERRY, H.T. "Proximate Consequences in the Law of Torts",
   (1914-15), 28 Harv.L.R. 10: intended and foreseeable
   consequences are "proximate"; what is meant by a "violating
   cause" that may intervene is discussed.

6. EDGERTON, H.W. "Legal Cause", (1924), 72 U.Pa.L.R. 211, 343:
   no hard and fast rule can be evolved, the solution depends
   upon the balancing of conflicting interests. Legal cause
   means justly attachable cause, the legal view of causation
   being rooted in a desire to reach a just result.

7. McLAUGHLIN, J.A. "Proximate Cause", (1925-26), 39 Harv.L.R.
   149: this is a step-by-step account of the attitude that
   courts adopt towards various types of results; the "active
   force" theory is put forward.

8. GREGORY, C.O. "Proximate Cause in Negligence - a Retreat
   from 'Rationalisation'", (1938-39), 6 U.C.L.R. 36,
   especially pp. 58 et seq.: the "directness" and
   "foreseeability" tests are thought to reflect differences
   in policy concerning the desirable legal incidence of
   negligent conduct.

9. CARPENTER, C.E. "Workable Rules for Determining Proximate
   Cause", (1932), 20 Calif.L.R. 229, 396, 471: these
   represent an attempt to formulate a practical approach to
   the problems.

10. GREEN, L. Rationale of Proximate Cause, (Vernon Law Book Co.,

1927): the decisive question is whether the hazard came within the rule which the actor violated. The foreseeability test is discussed and rejected and factual cause is treated as being of minor importance.

1. ANONYMOUS. "Proximate and Remote Cause", (1870), 4 Am.L.R. 201: this provides a detailed historical account of the development of the idea of proximate cause.

2. BOGGS, A.A. "Proximate Cause in the Law of Tort", (1910), 44 Am.L.R. 88: the author provides a collection of conflicting writings and cases on causation.

3. BINGHAM, J.W. "Some Suggestions Concerning Legal Cause at Common Law", (1909), 9 Col.L.R. 16, 136: the selection of possible cause is always limited according to the point of view; for legal purposes this is responsibility. The result has to fall within the purpose of the duty that has been infringed.

4. POUND, R. "Causation", (1957-58), 67 Yale L.J. 1: this gives a general discussion of causation in the light of the social problem that is involved, including a discussion of the views of some of the writers mentioned above.

5. WIGMORE, J.H. Select Cases on the Law of Torts, (Little, Brown & Co., 1912), II, 865-875: the causation element in tortious liability is discussed, primarily in the light of the "but for" test.

6. HEYTING, W.J. "Proximate Causation in Civil Actions", (1932), 44 Jur.R. 239, especially pp. 261-285: this discusses foreseeability as a test of causation.

7. POLLOCK, F. A First Book of Jurisprudence, (6th ed., Macmillan & Co., Ltd., 1929), pp. 141-171: proximate consequences are treated as being part of the act, remote consequences as connected with intention.

8. MUELLER, G.O.W. "Causing Criminal Harm" in Essays in Criminal Science, (ed., G.O.W. Mueller, Fred B. Rothman & Co., New York, Sweet & Maxwell, Ltd., London, 1961), chap. 7: for purposes of criminal law the "but for" test should be satisfied first. It is also recognised that human conduct is purposive and it is the purpose that establishes the nexus with the outside world.

9. HALL, J. General Principles of Criminal Law, (2nd ed., The Bobbs-Merrill Co., Inc., 1960), chap. 8: causation is discussed in factual and legal perspective. Causation is a

question largely turning on policy.

1. WILLIAMS, G.L. "Causation in Homicide", (1957), Crim.L.R. 429:
   this discussion is based on a case in which it was held
   that a wound which resulted in death owing to allegedly
   improper medical treatment did not "cause" the death.

2. CAMPS, F.E. and HAVARD, J.D.J. "Causation in Homicide - a
   Medical View", (1957) Crim.L.R. 576: two medical experts
   criticise the decision, which is the basis of G.L. William's
   article (supra). The question should turn, not on whether
   the treatment was improper, but whether it was administered
   in good faith.

3. FLETCHER, G.P. "Prolonging Life" (1967) 42 Wash.L.R. 999: the
   distinction between "causing" harm and "permiting" harm to
   occur is discussed in the context of the criminal liability
   of a person who switches off a mechanical device for keeping
   someone alive, and of a person who fails to switch it on.

4. MACINTOSH, J.C. "Concurrent Negligence", (1928), 45 S.A.L.J.
   314: the question of novus actus interveniens is considered.

5. GOODHART, A.L. "The Third Man or Novus Actus Interveniens",
   (1951), 4 C.L.P. 177: the problems raised by novus actus
   interveniens are discussed with a view to subsuming them
   under the foreseeability principle.

6. BOBERG, P.Q.R. "Reflection on the Novus Actus Interveniens
   Concept", (1959), 76 S.A.L.J. 280: English and South
   African cases on the subject are reviewed.

7. "AQUARIUS". "Causation and Legal Responsibility", (1941), 58
   S.A.L.J. 232: considerations of policy and justice
   ultimately determine the result.

8. "AQUARIUS". "Causation and Legal Responsibility", (1945), 62
   S.A.L.J. 126: contributory negligence as a cause of the
   plaintiff's harm is examined in detail with reference to
   English and South African authorities to show that relative
   blameworthiness, and not causation, has been the determining
   factor.

9. Pierce v. Hau Mon (1944) Appellate Division, 175 (South Africa):
   the judgment of Watermeyer, C.J., is a judicial demonstration
   of quantitative blameworthiness as the basis of contributory
   negligence.

10. MACINTYRE, M.M. "The Rationale of Last Clear Chance", (1939-
    40), 53 Harv.L.R. 1225: this shows that the doctrine of the

"last clear chance" was only an escape through the avenue of comparative fault from the old rule of the common law.

1. BOURKE, J.P. "Damages: Culpability and Causation", (1956), 30 Aust.L.J. 283: "fault" and "responsibility" under the Law Reform (Contributory Negligence) Act, 1945, are discussed with reference to the case-law.

Omissions

2. KIRCHHEIMER, O. "Criminal Omissions", (1941-42), 55 Harv.L.R. 615: this is a careful examination of the duty to act, which is the foundation of responsibility for omissions.

3. FLETCHER, G.P. "Prolonging Life" (1967) 42 Wash.L.R. 999: liability for omissions lets in considerations of policy as to when a duty to act should be recognised. The artificiality of the traditional concepts of "act" and "omission" is mercilessly exposed.

4. HUGHES, G.B.J. "Criminal Omissions", (1957-58), 67 Yale L.J. 590: the duty to act is discussed together with a further analysis of the mens rea that is required.

Intention and Recklessness

5. WILLIAMS, G.L. Criminal Law: The General Part, (2nd ed., Stevens & Sons, Ltd., 1961), chap. 2: this is a detailed analysis of intention and recklessness. Although it deals primarily with criminal law, it is of general relevance.

6. PASSMORE, J.A. and HEATH, P.L. "Intentions", (1955), Aristotelian Society Supplementary Volume 29, 131: Passmore mainly advocates the "coherence" theory, Heath evaluates both this and the "planning" theory. Both analyses could be of legal importance.

7. TURNER, J.W.C. "Mental Element in Crimes at Common Law" in The Modern Approach to Criminal Law, (edd. L. Radzinowicz and J.W.C. Turner, Macmillan & Co., Ltd., 1945), 195, especially pp. 199-211: this analysis is now classic. The disputed question how far, if at all, negligence grounds responsibility in manslaughter does not affect the analysis of intention and recklessness.

8. ANSCOMBE, M. "Intention", (1956-57), 57 P.A.S. 321: "reason" and "cause" for acting are distinguished. An intentional action is an action the "why" of which is not a causal "why". Motive may explain actions; it does not determine, i.e. cause, them.

1. GOTLIEB, A.E. "Intention, and Knowing the Nature and Quality
   of an Act", (1956), 19 M.L.R., 270: the analysis does not
   follow the same line as in most books. Intention is also
   discussed in relation to the M'Naghten Rules of insanity.

2. STRACHEN, B. "The Mystery of a Man's Mind - his Intention",
   (1966), 130 J.P., 447: this short article concerns itself
   with proof of intention.

3. WATSON, K.T. "The Meaning of Recklessness", (1961), 111 L.J.,
   166: the meaning of this term is considered in relation to
   the Prevention of Fraud (Investments), Act, 1958, s. 13 (1).

4. KENNY, A "Intention and Purpose in Law", in Essays in Legal
   Philosophy, (ed. R.S. SUMMERS, Basil Backwell, Oxford, 1968),
   146: a philosopher examines points raised by the legal
   bracketing of liablity for foreseen consequences and
   intended consequences. The acute difficulties of defining
   "intention" are indicated.

5. For further general analyses of intention reference might be
   made to the writings of J. Bentham, J. Austin, J.W. Salmond,
   W.W. Cook, R.M. Perkins, H.T. Terry, W. Markby, T.E. Holland,
   G.W. Keeton and O.W. Holmes, which are referred to under
   "Act"; and of J.H. Wigmore and J. Hall, which are referred
   to under "Causation". For analyses of Intention in relation
   to matrimonial suits, the following might be consulted:

6. BIGGS, J.M. The Concept of Matrimonial Cruelty, (The Athlone
   Press, 1962), Part II: this provides a very clear account
   of the law prior to the cases of Gollins and Williams.
   Chapter 5 analyses the cases dealing with the mental element.

7. ALLEN, C.K. "Matrimonial Cruelty", (1957), 73 L.Q.R., 316,
   512: motive and intention are discussed in the latter part.
   The analysis of intention differs somewhat from traditional
   accounts.

8. HALL, J.C. "Matrimonial Cruelty and Mens Rea", (1963), C.L.J.
   104: this is a careful examination of intention in this branch
   of the law with especial referenc to the M'Naghten Rules.

9. GOODHART, A.L. "Cruelty, Desertion and Insanity in Matrimonial
   Law", (1963), 79 L.Q.R., 98: the nature of the presumption
   involved in the statement that "a man is presumed to intend
   the natural and probable consequences of his conduct" is
   examined. The point is made that the choice between a
   subjective and an objective view of cruelty depends upon
   policy.

1. BROWN, L.N. "The Offence of Wilful Neglect to Maintain a
   Wife", (1960), 23 M.L.R., 1: this is a discussion of what
   is meant by "wilful" in this context.

2. BROWN, L.N. "Cruelt without Culpability or Divorce without
   Fault", (1963), 26 M.L.R., 625: the cases of Gollins and
   Williams are analysed at length and their impact on the
   law of divorce considered. For other discussions of
   Gollins and Williams, see C.T. LATHAM: "Intent and Cruelty"
   (1963), 127 J.P., 126, 699; "What is Cruelty ?" (1964), 128
   J.P., 783; R. LOWE: "New Look at Cruelty", (1963), 113 L.J.,
   668, 683, 731; NOTE in (1964) 235 L.T., 339; L. ROSEN:
   "Legal Cruelty and Cruelty", (1964), 108 S.J., 887.

Inadvertence and Negligence

3. WILLIAMS, G.L. Criminal Law: The General Part, (2nd ed.,
   Stevens & Sons, Ltd., 1961), chap. 3: the "mental" and
   "conduct" theories are set out, together with a discussion
   of what is meant by "gross negligence".

4. HART, H.L.A. "Negligence, Mens Rea and Criminal Responsibility"
   in Oxford Essays in Jurisprudence, (ed. A.G.Guest, Oxford
   University Press, 1961), chap. 2: if criminal responsibility
   were to be attached to "gross negligence", this would not be
   a form of "absolute liability", since what is required is an
   ability to control actions. Negligence is a failure to
   exercise the capacities to advert, think about and control
   behaviour.

5. SALMOND, J.W. Jurisprudence, (7th ed., Sweet & Maxwell, Ltd.,
   1924), 408; and J.W. SALMOND on Torts, (15th ed., R.F.V.
   Heuston, Sweet & Maxwell, Ltd., 1969), p. 249: negligence
   is a state of mind. It is not a separate tort either. (Note
   that P.J. Fitzgerald, the editor of Jurisprudence and R.F.V.
   Heuston, the editor of Torts, adopt different views from
   that of the author).

6. BIGELOW, M.M. The Law of Torts, (3rd ed., Cambridge University
   Press, 1908), pp. 18-21, 96-98: negligence is a state of mind,
   though external standards are applied to the proof of it.

7. STREET, H. The Foundations of Legal Liability, (Thompson &
   Co., New York, 1906), I, pp. 71-123: negligence is not a
   separate tort. As to whether it is a state of mind or
   conduct, it is argued that there is truth in both views.

8. POLLOCK, F. Law of Torts, (15th ed., P.A. Landon, Stevens &
   Sons, Ltd., 1951), pp. 336-337: negligence is the contrary
   of diligence. It is therefore conduct.

1. TERRY, H.T. "Negligence", (i915-16), 29 Harv. L.R., 40:
   negligence is conduct, not a state of mind. The question
   what conduct is to be treated as negligent is investigated.

2. EDGERTON, H.W. "Negligence, Inadvertence, and Indifference;
   the Relation of Mental States to Negligence", (1925-26),
   39 Harv. L.R., 849: negligence is unreasonably dangerous
   conduct.

3. SEAVEY, W.A. "Negligence - Subjective or Objective", (1927-
   28), 41 Harv. L.R., 1: this analysis is in partial support
   of the "conduct" theory. The terms "subjective" and
   "objective" cannot be used in their literal sense. There is
   no standard "reasonable man", hence the test is only part
   objective.

4. PROSSER, W.L. Handbook of the Law of Torts, (2nd ed., West
   Publishing Co., 1955), chap. 5, pp. 119-123, 147-152:
   negligence is conduct which falls below a certain standard
   established by law.

5. WHITE, A.R. "Carelessness, Indifference and Recklessness",
   (1961), 24 M.L.R., 592; "Carelessness and Recklessness -
   a Rejoinder", (1962), 25 M.L.R., 437: carelessness connotes
   conduct (not taking care) indifference connotes a state of
   mind (not paying attention to certain risks). On this basis
   J.W. Salmond, F. Pollock and G.L. Williams are criticised.

6. FITZGERALD, P.J. and WILLIAMS, G.L. "Carelessness,
   Indifference and Recklessness: Two Replies", (1962), 25
   M.L.R., 49: these are two short replies answering the
   criticisms made by A.R. White (supra).

7. For further general analyses of Negligence reference might be
   made to the writings of J. Austin, G.W. Keeton, G.W. Paton
   and T.E. Holland, which are referred to under "Act"; and
   of J.H. Wigmore and J. Hall, which are referred to under
   "Causation". For the general nature of Negligence as a
   tort, in addition to standard works, such as J.F. Clerk &
   W.H.B. Lindsell on Torts (13th ed., Sweet & Maxwell, Ltd.,
   1969), and J. Charlesworth: Negligence (4th ed., R.A. Percy,
   Sweet & Maxwell, Ltd., 1962), reference might be made to
   the following:

8. PROSSER, W.L. Handbook of the Law of Torts, (2nd ed., West
   Publishing Co., (1955), chap. 6.

9. BOHLEN, F.H. Studies in the Law of Torts, (The Bobbs-Merrill
   Co., 1926), chap. 1.

1. GREEN, L. Judge and Jury, (Vernon Law Book Co., 1930), chaps.
   3 and 4.

2. MACHIN, E.A. "Negligence and Interest", (1954), 17 M.L.R. 405.

3. PAYNE, D.J. "The Tort of Negligence", (1953), 6 C.L.P., 236.

11

PERSONS

General

1. PATON, G.W. A Text-Book of Jurisprudence, (3rd ed., D.P.
   Derham, Oxford, 1964), chap. 16: this is a convenient
   general account of "person" as a right and duty bearing
   unit. Human beings and corporate persons are dealt with as
   well as practical problems concerning the liability of
   unincorporated associations.

2. SALMOND, J.W. Jurisprudence, (12th ed., P.J. Fitzgerald,
   Sweet & Maxwell, Ltd., 1966), chap. 10: this is also a
   general discussion of various aspects of the topic,
   including the legal position of animals, the dead, unborn
   children and dual capacity. Legal persons, sole and
   aggregate, are explained, and the purpose of incorporation.

3. KEETON, G.W. The Elementary Principles of Jurisprudence,
   (2nd ed., Pitman & Sons, Ltd., 1949), chap. 13, especially
   pp. 162 et seq.: this is a fairly good general account of
   the subject.

4. POUND, R. Jurisprudence, (West Publishing Co., 1959), IV,
   pp. 191-261; 384-405: this is a full and detailed account
   of natural and legal persons and of the various theories
   concerning the latter.

5. GRAY, J.C. The Nature and Sources of the Law, (2nd ed.,
   R.Gray, The Macmillan Co., New York, 1921), chap. 2: this
   is another general account of "normal" and "abnormal"
   persons. The account of juristic persons includes
   descriptions of Roman and Continental legal institutions.

6. HOLLAND, T.E. The Elements of Jurisprudence, (13th ed.,
   Oxford, 1924), pp. 93-100; 339-357: these pages contain
   another general account of "natural" and "artificial"
   persons.

7. POLLOCK, F. A First Book of Jurisprudence, (6th ed.,
   Macmillan & Co., Ltd., 1929), Part I, chap. 5: natural
   and artificial persons are considered. Pollock thinks the
   realist view to be the soundest view, although he points
   out that the common law has not formally committed itself
   to any view. Corporate liability for wrongdoing is also
   touched on.

8. MARKBY, W. Elements of Law, (6th ed., Oxford, 1905), ss.
   131-145: this is a very general account of natural and
   juristic persons.

1. JENKS, E. The New Jurisprudence, (John Murray, 1933), chap.
   7: legal persons are considered with reference to will.
   Jenks inclines towards the realist theory.

Human Beings

2. BARRY, J.V. "The Child en ventre sa mere", (1940-41), 14
   Aust.L.J. 351: the attitude of the law towards the unborn
   child is generally discussed.

3. WINFIELD, P.H. "The Unborn Child", (1942), 8 C.L.J. 76: the
   extent to which the unborn child is recognised in the law
   of property, criminal law, contract and tort is dealt with.

4. ATKINSON, S.B. "Life, Birth, and Live-birth", (1904) 20 L.Q.
   R. 134: this article discusses in detail the question when
   a child is deemed to be born alive, (based on the state of
   medical knowledge at that date).

5. WILLIAMS, G.L. The Sanctity of Life and the Criminal Law
   (Faber & Faber, Ltd., 1958), chaps. 1, 5-6, 8: the author
   deals challengingly with the social, moral, religious,
   medical, legal and other aspects of abortion and euthanasia.
   The boundaries of the law are luminously expounded (although
   some developments since publication call for modification
   in detail).

6. AUSTIN, J. Lectures on Jurisprudence, (5th ed., R. Campbell,
   John Murray, 1885), I, pp. 347-355: Austin deals with
   physical or natural persons and legal or fictitious persons.
   But his treatment of the former is more valuable than the
   latter, since he was writing before the Companies Act.

7. WHITFELD, L.A. "The Rule as to Posthumous Children - the
   Decision in Elliott v. Joicey", (1935-36), 9 Aust.L.J.
   294: this is principally a note on the case, which is a
   decision of the House of Lords as to when a child en ventre
   sa mere is to be regarded as living.

8. WRIGHT, C.A. Note in (1935), 13 Can.B.R. 594: another note on
   the case of Elliott v. Joicey.

9. SEABORNE-DAVIS, D. "Child-killing in English Law" in Modern
   Approach to Criminal Law, (edd. L. Radzinowicz and
   J.W.C. Turner, Macmillan & Co., Ltd., 1945), chap. 17: the
   question when a child becomes a person in the eyes of the
   law relating to homicide is dealt with in the course of a
   general discussion.

10. CANNON, R.W. "Born Alive" [1964] Crim.L.R. 748: an accused

stabbed a pregnant woman, who was very near to giving
birth. The child was surgically extracted alive, but died
three days later of a stab wound that had damaged it in
utero. The particular discussion of when a child is "born
alive" is on p. 754.

1. ANONYMOUS. "Injury to an Unborn Child", (1939) 83 Sol.Jo. 185:
   the matter is considered with reference to the law of tort,
   crime and property.

2. WILLIAMS, G.L. "The Legal Unity of Husband and Wife", (1947)
   10 M.L.R. 16: the origin of the idea and the significance
   of it in various branches of the law are discussed in
   detail. (The position dealt with is prior to the Law
   Reform (Husband and Wife) Act, 1962).

3. KAHN-FREUND, O. "Inconsistencies and Injustices in the Law
   of Husband and Wife", (1952) 15 M.L.R. 133: (1953) 16 M.L.
   R. 34, 148: these articles are of general interest and a
   useful discussion of the position prior to the Law Reform
   (Husband and Wife) Act, 1962.

4. MOSSE, R.L. "Can a Person Sue Himself ?" (1944), 94 L.J. 262:
   dual capacity is dealt with in connection with a case in
   which a widow, as administratrix of the estate of her
   infant son, who had been killed in a collision, sued
   herself as administratrix of her deceased husband's estate,
   he having been killed in the same collision.

5. SIMPSON, K. "The Moment of Death: a New Medico-legal Problem"
   (1968) 112 Sol.Jo. 435: new techniques of keeping people
   alive poses medical, moral and legal problems. A leading
   pathologist draws attention to some of these.

Miscellaneous

6. DUFF, P.W. "The Personality of an Idol", (1927), 3 C.L.J. 42:
   the interesting decision of the Judicial Committee of the
   Privy Council recognising the personality of an idol is
   discussed.

7. VESEY FITZGERALD, S.G. "Idolon Fori", (1925), 41 L.Q.R. 419:
   this article, too, deals with the personification of a
   Hindu idol.

Corporation sole

8. MAITLAND, F.W. "The Corporation Sole" and "The Crown as a
   Corporation" in Selected Essays (edd. H.D. Hazeltine,
   G. Lapsley, P.H. Winfield, Cambridge University Press, 1936),

chaps. 1 and 2; Collected Papers (ed. H.A.L. Fisher,
Cambridge University Press, 1911), pp. 210, 244: in these
two classic essays the origin of the corporation sole is
investigated and the attribution of the idea to the Crown.

1. KEETON, G.W. The Elementary Principles of Jurisprudence,
    (2nd ed., Pitman & Sons, Ltd., 1949), pp. 152-162: this is
    one of the best short discussions of the topic.

2. BLACKSTONE, W. Commentaries on the Laws of England, (16th ed.,
    1825), I, pp. 239-250, 467: the prerogative and its
    attributes are discussed. In the latter place corporations
    aggregate and sole are dealt with.

3. CARR, C.T. The General Principles of the Law of Corporations,
    (Cambridge University Press, 1905), chap. 4: this contains
    a general account of the corporation sole and its early
    history.

The Crown

4. POLLOCK, F. and MAITLAND, F.W. The History of English Law
    before the Time of Edward I, (2nd ed., with Introduction by
    S.F.C. Milsom, Cambridge University Press, 1968), I, pp. 511-
    526: the early history of the position of the Crown is
    examined in detail. Many features were incompatible with
    the idea of a corporation sole.

5. HOLDSWORTH, W.S. A History of English Law, (5th ed., Methuen
    & Co., Ltd.), III, pp. 480-482; IV, pp. 202-203; IX, pp.
    4-7: these pages give brief historical accounts of the
    Crown as a corporation sole.

6. PATON, G.W. A Text-Book of Jurisprudence, (3rd ed.,
    D.P. Derham, Oxford, 1964), pp. 311-315: in the course of
    a discussion of the state as a legal person it is pointed
    out that the idea of the Crown as a corporation sole is
    used instead in English law. The anomalies are also
    considered, especially in the sphere of commonwealth
    relations.

7. MOORE, W.H. "The Crown as Corporation", (1904), 20 L.Q.R.
    351: the position of the Crown in relation to the British
    Empire and some of the difficulties that arise are
    considered. This is of general interest as throwing a light
    on the position before the Dominions attained their present
    position.

8. HAGGEN, G.L. "The Function of the Crown" (1925) 41 L.Q.R. 182:
    this deals with the various aspects in which the Crown

becomes the means of expressing the corporate capacity of
the nation. There is also an account of the growth of the
idea.

1. BORCHARD, E.M. "Governmental Responsibility in Tort" (1926-
   27) 36 Yale L.J. at pp. 774-780: the state as a person is
   dealt with, and English and Continental thought on the
   matter are contrasted.

2. G.A.H. "The Crown as Protector of Infants", (1961) 105 Sol.
   Jo. 673: this is a brief discussion of a judicial decision
   on the matter.

3. ANONYMOUS. "Local Authorities and Parental Rights", (1961),
   231 L.T. 342: this deals with the same point as above.

4. JEWELL, R.E.C. "Education and Deprived Children: Statute and
   Prerogative", (1962) 125 J.P.J. 320, 356: this is a further
   discussion of the Crown's powers as parens patriae.

Corporation aggregate

5. GOWER, L.C.B. The Principles of Modern Company Law, (3rd ed.,
   K.W. Wedderburn, O. Weaver, A.E.W. Park, Stevens & Sons,
   Ltd., 1969), chap. 4: this contains a full discussion of
   the extent to which a company is distinct from its members
   and generally the advantages and disadvantages of
   incorporation.

6. BERLE, A.A. and MEANS, G.C. The Modern Corporation and
   Private Property, (The Macmillan Co., New York, 1933):
   this contains an important study of the separation of
   ownership from the power to control, and the consequences
   of this development. The whole book is a synthesis of a
   legal and economic approach.

7. BURNHAM, J. The Managerial Revolution, (Putnam & Co., Ltd.,
   1944): the managers will gain control over the instruments
   of production and gain preference in the distribution of
   products indirectly through their control of the state.
   This theme is developed with reference to various countries.

8. CARR, C.T. The General Principles of the Law of Corporations,
   (Cambridge University Press, 1905): this volume contains
   a general discussion of corporate personality, the
   attitude of the courts, creation, extinction and some of
   the theories on the subject.

9. POLLOCK, F. and MAITLAND, F.W. The History of English Law
   before the time of Edward I, (2nd ed., with Introduction

by S.F.C. Milsom, Cambridge University Press, 1968), I,
pp. 660-667: this contains an account of the early corporate
idea in the form of boroughs and guilds.

1. KE CHIN WANG, H. "The Corporate Entity Concept (or Fiction
    Theory) in the Year Book Period" (1942) 58 L.Q.R. 498;
    (1943) 59 L.Q.R. 72: the separateness of the corporate
    entity had not become established at this date, but there
    were developments in that direction. If any theory is
    applicable, it would be the Realist theory; but the point
    is made that the matter is simply one of convenience.

2. LUBASZ, H. "The Corporate Borough in the Common Law of the
    Late Year-Book Period" (1964) 80 L.Q.R. 228: this paper
    is partly in answer to that of Ke Chin Wang. The question
    is not whether the fiction theory had been received into
    the common law, but what the common law theory was. Since
    ecclesiastical groups require license for their
    establishment, the fiction theory is appropriate for them.
    A township is not so found and often goes back to time
    immemorial. The question is not how it was created, but
    what it meant to be a borough.

3. HOLDSWORTH, W.S. A History of English Law, (5th ed., Methuen
    & Co., Ltd.), III, pp. 469-490: a historical account is
    given of the many groups which existed in English law and
    of their nature. At pp. 482-487 an account is given of the
    development of the separation of the corporation from its
    members.

4. ULLMANN, W. "The Medieval Theory of Legal and Illegal
    Organisations", (1944) 60 L.Q.R. 285: the medieval
    commentators on Roman law were the first to attempt to
    establish a criterion for distinguishing between legal and
    illegal organisations.

5. RAYMOND, R.L. "The Genesis of the Corporation", (1905-6) 19
    Harv.L.R. 350: this considers the origin of the idea, who
    invented it, the principle on which it rests and what the
    idea is. The idea originates, it is said, in a mode of
    thought, and the extent to which a group is treated as one
    depends on practical convenience.

6. LASKI, H.J. "The Personality of Associations" (1915-16) 29
    Harv.L.R. 404: no lawyer dares to neglect the phenomenon
    of group life. Some of the ways in which this phenomenon
    shows itself are set out.

7. FIFOOT, C.H.S. Judge and Jurist in the Reign of Queen
    Victoria, (Stevens & Sons, Ltd., 1959), chap. 3: this gives

an account of how the judges in successive cases and step
by step accepted the idea of corporate liability into the
common law.

1. ARNOLD, T.W. The Folklore of Capitalism, (Yale University
   Press; London: Oxford University Press, 1937), chaps. 8-10:
   human needs are met by institutions which are initially
   founded on some ideaíogy. The business corporation evolved
   out of the small trader with whom was associated the
   ideology of freedom of the individual to acquire wealth.
   This ideaíogy, when carried over to large corporations,
   results in monopolies.

2. DOUGLAS, W.O. and SHANKS, C.M. "Insulation from Liability
   through Subsidiary Corporations", (1929-30), 39 Yale L.J.,
   193: this shows, mainly with reference to tort and contract,
   how corporate responsibility has developed within business
   units using corporate form.

3. CATALDO, B.F. "Limited Liability with One-man Companies and
   Subsidiary Corporations", (1953), 18 L.C.P., 473: the
   doctrine of limited liability need not rest on the separateness of the corporate entity. The point is considered with
   reference to the one-man company and subsidiary companies.

4. FULLER, W. "The Incorporated Individual: a Study of the One-
   man Company", (1937-38), 51 Harv. L.R., 1373: this is
   devoted to a discussion of the various problems that arise
   with reference to their special judicial results and
   implications.

5. MANSON, E. "One Man Companies", (1895), 11 L.Q.R., 185: this
   article is an interesting early comment on actual control
   being vested in a ruling spirit in most companies and on
   shareholders being but dividend drawers.

6. MANSON, E. "The Evolution of the Private Company", (1910), 26
   L.Q.R., 11: this is a general defence of one-man companies.

7. MASTEN, C.A. "One Man Companies and their Controlling Shareholders", (1936), 14 Can. B.R., 663: this examines the
   various situations in which respectively the company is
   treated as being distinct from its members and when it is
   not.

8. SILK, J. "One Man Corporations - Scope and Limitations",
   (1952), 100 U. Pa. L.R., 853: the elucidation of these has
   been mainly a judial task. Various questions concerning the
   capacity of the sole shareholder to bind his company, use
   its property for his personal benefit and his own personal
   liability are dealt with.

1. KIRALFY, A.K.R. "Some Unforeseen Consequences of Private
   Incorporation", (1949), 65 L.Q.R., 231: this draws
   attention to certain important matters, such as fire
   insurance, special bank account, identification of the
   dominant shareholder and so on.

2. WALKER, E.S. "Corporate Personality (or the Metaphysics of
   a Local Authority)", (1959), 123 J.P.J., 89: this is a
   short note on some early definitions.

3. H.N.B. "Proving a Company's Intention", (1956), 100 Sol. Jo.
   695, 851: a single individual usually controls the details
   of a company's property interests, subject to the general
   direction by the Board. This article deals with the
   question how this might best be proved in court.

4. FRIDMAN, G.F.L. "A Company's Mind", (1957), 24 Solicitor 149:
   this is a discussion, with reference to the principal cases,
   of how a mental state can be imputed to a corporation
   through an individual who is sufficiently high up in the
   managerial hierarchy.

5. EDITORIAL: "The Mind of a Company", (1957), 1 J.B.L., 14:
   this is a short comment on imputing the mind of managers
   to a company.

6. ARNOLD, J.C. "The Control of a Company", (1959), 26 Solicitor
   167; (1960), 27 Solicitor 13: in these two short discussions what is meant by "control" for specialised purposes
   is discussed. The principal question is whether, for
   purposes of the valuation of shares for estate duty, a
   court is bound by the register of members or may look
   beyond it.

7. PENNINGTON, R.R. "Control of a Company", (1960), 104 Sol. Jo.
   1088: this article is of limited interest: it is concerned
   with a point that arose in a particular dispute.

8. FRANKS, M. "'Control' and 'Controlling Interest'" (1957),
   107 L.J., 467: the question what is meant by these terms
   for special purposes is dealt with.

9. WORMSER, I.M. Frankenstein Incorporated, (McGraw-Hill Book
   Co., Inc., 1931), this is a general account, with a brief
   historical introduction, of the evils of big business
   corporations unless those in control heed the public good.
   Attention is also drawn to the shortcomings of the law.

10. MERVYN JONES, J. "Claims on Behalf of Nationals who are
    Shareholders in Foreign Companies", (1949), 26 B.Y.I.L.,225:

this is concerned with corporations at international law. Diplomatic intervention is permissible on behalf of nationals, which include corporations. The problem of intervention on behalf of nationals, who are shareholders in foreign corporations, is also considered.

1. ANONYMOUS: "Residence of Companies", (1959), 26 Solicitor 299, 305: this is a discussion of what "residence" means for tax purposes.

2. D.R.S.: Note on "Residence of a Company", (1960), Br. Tax R., 58: a particular decision on the point is discussed.

Lifting the mask of personality

3. GOWER, L.C.B. The Principles of Modern Company Law, (3rd ed., K.W. Wedderburn, 0. Weaver, A.E.W. Park, Stevens & Sons, Ltd., 1969), chap. 10: a detailed discussion of the attitude of the courts in penetrating the corporate mask.

4. WORMSER, I.M. The Disregard of the Corporate Fiction and Allied Corporate Problems, (Baker, Voorhis & Co., 1927), chaps. 1-2: this is a further detailed investigation of the judicial attitude, English and American, to penetrating the corporate mask. See also I.M. WORMSER, "Piercing the Veil of Corporate Personality", (1912), 12 Col. L.R., 496.

5. NOTE: "'Corporate Entity' - its Limitations as a Useful Legal Conception", (1926-27), 36 Yale L.J., 254: this is a discussion of two cases in which the corporate entity was ignored in order to reach a just result. But the "entity idea" is sometimes convenient; no rules can be laid down as to when it will be used and when not.

6. HOGG, J.E. "The Personal Character of a Corporation", (1915), 31 L.Q.R., 170; (1917), 33 L.Q.R., 76: the Daimler case is discussed as decided by the Court of Appeal and House of Lords respectively.

7. VAUGHAN WILLIAMS, R.E.L. and CHRUSSACHI, M. "The Nationality of Corporations", (1933), 49 L.Q.R., 334: a detailed examination of the Daimler case and of its implications is included in this discussion.

8. McNAIR, A.D. "The National Character and Status of Corporations", (1923-24), 4 B.Y.I.L., 44: this article is principally a discussion of the Daimler case.

9. NOREM, R.A. "Determination of Enemy Character of Corporations" (1930), 24 A.J.I.L., 310: this is a further critique of the

Daimler case in the light of the law as it stood up to that date.

1. DOMKE, M. "The Control of Corporations", (1950), 3 I.L.Q., 52: an account is given of the American law as to the enemy character of corporations.

2. SAMUELS, A. "Lifting the Veil", [1964] J.B.L., 107: the separate persona will be recognised and acted upon prima facie unless public interest and public policy require otherwise. The circumstances in which the mask will be lifted are briefly reviewed.

3. LLOYD, D. The Idea of Law, (Penguin Books, Ltd., A 688, 1964), pp. 300-9: there is a brief discussion of human beings and group persons. The realist theory, in particular, is criticised. The methods of incorporation and consequences are explained with special reference to the separateness of the corporate person.

4. LEWIS, J.R. "Using the Veil for Improper Purposes", (1966), 4 Legal Exec. 72: this is a short summary of the ways in which courts strive to prevent fraud and injustice being peretrated behind the corporate facade.

5. RUTHVEN, E.K.B. "Lifting the Veil of Incorporation in Scotland" [1969] Jur. R. 1: Scots law has not really faced this question, so the lead has come from England. Parallels are drawn for Scotland from the examination of English cases. These are grouped under the headings of statutory cases, trade with the enemy and common law instances.

6. KAHN-FREUND, O. "Some Reflections on Company Law Reform", (1944), 7 M.L.R., 54-59: this article was written before the Companies Act, 1948, but it contains a useful discussion of the abuse of the separateness of the corporate entity.

7. COHN, E.J. and SIMITIS, C. "'Lifting the Veil' in the Company Law of the European Continent", (1963), 12 I.C.L.Q., 189: the positions in West Germany, Switzerland, France and Italy are reviewed in the light of the Anglo-American attitude.

The ultra vires rule

8. GOWER, L.C.B. The Principles of Modern Company Law, (3rd ed., K.W. Wedderburn, O. Weaver, A.E.W. Park, Stevens & Sons, Ltd., 1969), chap. 5: this is probably the best and most easily accessible discussion of the problem in the light of modern case-law.

1. STONE, F.F. "Ultra Vires and Original Sin", (1939-40), 14
   Tul L.R., 190: an amusing an instructive discussion. Just
   as Man was created by God and fell from grace as the result
   of original sin, so he in turn created corporations, whose
   sins assume many forms. The wages of corporate sin and the
   means of punishing and of redressing its evils are also
   dealt with.

2. HARNO, A.J. "Privileges and Powers of a Corporation and the
   Doctrine of Ultra Vires", (1925-26), 35 Yale L.J., 13: the
   Hohfeldian analysis is applied to the problem, which is
   made to appear in a new light. While privileges and
   immunities can be accorded to individual members, their
   powers of wrongdoing need not be similarly treated.

3. STREET, J.H.A. A Treatise on the Doctrine of Ultra Vires,
   (Sweet & Maxwell, Ltd., 1930): this a very detailed,
   technical treatment of the topic and useful for reference.

4. CARDEN, P.T. "Limitations on the Powers of Common Law
   Corporations", (1910), 26 L.Q.R., 320: the question whether
   the doctrine of ultra vires applies to common law corporations is considered with reference to possible changes
   in the attitude of the law.

5. HUDSON, A.H. "Common Law Corporations and Ultra Vires",
   (1961), 28 Solicitor 7: it is argued that the ultra vires
   doctrine has no application to these.

6. FURMSTON, M.P. "Common Law Corporations and Ultra Vires"
   (1961), 24 M.L.R., 518: a further considerations of the
   question.

7. WARREN, E.H. "Executed Ultra Vires Transactions", (1909-10),
   23 Harv. L.R., 496; "Executory Ultra Vires Transactions"
   (1910-11), 24 Harv. L.R., 534: the discussion of both these
   topics is conducted in the light of the question how far
   the personality of a corporation extends.

8. HARRIMAN, E.A. "Ultra Vires Corporation Leases", (1900-1),
   14 Harv. L.R., 332: various objections to the validity of
   such leases are considered.

9. CARPENTER, C.E. "Should the Doctrine of Ultra Vires be
   Discarded ? " (1923-24), 33 Yale L.J., 49: after an examination of the present Anglo-American law the conclusion
   is reached that the doctrine should be abolished.

10. STEVENS, R.S. "A Proposal as to the Codification and Restate-
    ment of the Ultra Vires Doctrine" (1926-27), 36 Yale L.J.,

297: this is of general interest and reveals some of the
difficulties.

1. ULLMANN, W. "The Delictual Responsibility of Medieval
   Corporations" (1948), 64 L.Q.R. 77: the evolution of the
   medieval doctrine is examined in detail, showing that it
   cannot be fitted into any modern theory. This article is
   particularly interesting for the light it sheds on the
   functional attitude of the medieval lawyers.

2. WELSH, R.S. "The Criminal Liability of Corporations" (1946),
   62 L.Q.R. 345: this is perhaps the best discussion of this
   question.

3. EDGERTON, H.W. "Corporate Criminal Responsibility" (1926-27),
   36 Yale L.J. 827: the American point of view is presented,
   but there is also reference to English cases.

4. CANFIELD, G.F. "Corporate Responsibility for Crime" (1914),
   14 Col.L.R. 469: the corporate entity is not a fiction in
   the sense of a supposition contrary to fact. It is analogous
   to implied conditions. The entity theory is then considered
   with reference to criminal responsibility.

5. LEE, F.P. "Corporate Criminal Liability" (1928), 28 Col.L.R.
   1, 181: this is a detailed discussion of the Anglo-American
   law as to the criminal responsibility of shareholders,
   directors, officers, and employees, concluding with a
   discussion of the relevance of the "entity" theory.

6. WARREN, E.H. "Torts by Corporations in Ultra Vires
   Undertakings" (1925), 2 C.L.J. 180: the position in English
   law is considered by an American lawyer.

7. GOODHART, A.L. "Corporate Liability in Tort and the Doctrine
   of Ultra Vires" in Essays in Jurisprudence and the Common
   Law, (Cambridge University Press, 1937), chap. 5:
   E.H. Warren's views (supra) are considered. The logical
   conclusion is reached that corporations cannot be
   responsible for ultra vires torts.

8. CLERK, J.F. and LINDSELL, W.H.B. Torts, (13th ed., Sweet &
   Maxwell, Ltd., 1969), SS. 167-73: this sets out the
   position in the English law of tort.

9. WINFIELD, P.H. A Textbook of the Law of Tort, (8th ed.,
   J.A. Jolowicz and T. Ellis Lewis, Sweet & Maxwell, Ltd.,
   1967), pp. 728-31: it is pointed out, in opposition to
   A.L. Goodhart (supra), that there is no reason to suppose
   that the law is logical in its approach to these questions.

1. SALMOND, J.W. The Law of Torts, (15th ed., R.F.V. Heuston,
   Sweet & Maxwell, Ltd., 1969), pp. 571-576: the position in
   the English law of torts is set out and the views summarised.

2. STREET, H. The Law of Torts, (4th ed., Butterworth & Co.,
   Ltd., 1968), pp. 470-72: the tortious responsibility of
   corporations and of unincorporated bodies is dealt with.

3. ASHTON-CROSS, D.I.C. "Suggestion Regarding the Liability of
   Corporations for the Torts of their Servants" (1950), 10
   C.L.J. 419: some illuminating Scottish decisions are
   referred to in the discussion of the problem generally.

Public Corporations

4. ROBSON, W.A. "The Public Corporation in Britain Today" in
   Problems of Nationalised Industry, (ed. W.A. Robson, George
   Allen & Unwin, Ltd., 1952), chap. 1: this is an examination
   of the public corporations set up by the nationalisation
   legislation and of their structure and control, both
   Parliamentary and ministerial. (The other chapters are
   also useful on more detailed aspects. For the pre-
   nationalisation position, see Public Enterprise, (ed.
   W.A. Robson, Allen & Unwin, Ltd., 1937).

5. GRIFFITH, J.A.G. and STREET, H. Principles of Administrative
   Law, (4th ed., Isaac Pitman & Sons, Ltd., 1967), chap. 7:
   this is another discussion of public corporations and
   of their control, Parliamentary, ministerial and judicial.

6. The Public Corporation: A Comparative Symposium, (ed.
   W. Friedmann, Stevens & Sons, Ltd., 1954): various authors
   respectively discuss the working of public corporations in
   various countries. The editor discusses the position in
   Britain (pp. 162-189), and sums up at pp. 541-594.

7. WADE, E.C.S. "The Constitutional Aspect of the Public
   Corporation" (1949), 2 C.L.P. 172: this is a careful
   examination of the public corporation, both before and
   after nationalisation, with reference to the factors that
   influenced its form and structure. Particular attention is
   devoted to the problem of control.

8. FRIEDMANN, W. "The New Public Corporations and the Law" (1947),
   10 M.L.R. 233, 377: this is an early appraisal of what was
   at that date still experimental.

9. FRIEDMANN, W. Law and Social Change in Contemporary Britain,
   (Stevens & Sons, Ltd., 1951), chap. 9: this contains a
   further analysis of some of the juristic questions that

arise.

1. WADE, E.C.S. and PHILLIPS, G.G. Constitutional Law, (7th ed.,
   E.C.S. Wade and A.W. Bradley, Longmans, 1967), chap. 21:
   this is a general account and of their position in the
   framework of the constitution.

2. WADE, H.W.R. Administrative Law, (2nd ed., Oxford, 1967),
   pp. 33-41: a short and general account.

3. GORDON, L. The Public Corporation in Great Britain, (Oxford
   University Press, 1938): this is a pre-war study, which is
   of interest in that the problems of control that might be
   adopted for the semi-independent bodies that then existed
   are considered and assessed.

4. CHESTER, D.N. "Public Corporations and the Classification of
   Administrative Bodies", (1953), I Pol.S. 34: this
   investigates the origin and use of the term "public
   corporation" and inquires into their nature with a view to
   classifying them.

Unincorporated associations

5. MAITLAND, F.W. "The Unincorporate Body" in Selected Essays,
   (edd. H.D. Hazeltine, G. Lapsley, P.H. Winfield, Cambridge
   University Press, 1936), chap. 3; Collected Papers, (ed.
   H.A.L. Fisher, Cambridge University Press, 1911), III,
   p. 271: the connection between trusts and corporations is
   considered. The trust is shown to have been "a most
   powerful instrument of social experimentation"; an
   important result being that it was a substitute for
   personified institutions.

6. MAITLAND, F.W. "Trust and Corporation" in Selected Essays,
   (supra), chap. 4; Collected Papers, (supra), p. 321: this
   comparison of trust and corporate bodies shows how greatly
   the trust concept fulfilled the function of incorporation
   from early times. There is also a valuable discussion of
   unincorporated bodies.

7. FORD, H.A.J. Unincorporated Non-profit Associations, (Oxford,
   Clarendon Press, 1959): this is one of the best and most
   convenient accounts of unincorporated associations. Is
   there a theory on which these may be held liable for harm
   suffered by persons as a result of group activity? This
   kind of activity has attracted to itself special rules and
   a legal order cannot remain neutral with regard to them.

8. LLOYD, D. The Law Relating to Unincorporated Associations,

(Sweet & Maxwell, Ltd., 1938), especially the Introduction
and Conclusion: the thesis is that there should be varying
degrees of personality which can be accorded to each
particular class of association according to the exigencies
of the particular case.

1. LASKI, H.J. "The Personality of Associations" (1915-16), 29
   Harv.L.R. 404: associations do have a reality of their own
   that manifests itself as much in law as in ordinary speech.

2. WARREN, E.H. Corporate Advantages Without Incorporation,
   (Baker, Voorhis & Co., New York, 1929), especially pp. 1-15,
   841-846: philosophy has nothing to contribute; it is what
   the courts do that matters. A legal unit is "whatever has
   capacity to acquire a legal right and/or incur a legal
   obligation".

3. FRIEDMANN, W. Law and Social Change in Contemporary Britain,
   (Stevens & Sons, Ltd., 1951), chaps. 7, 9: the trust and
   corporation are considered. Developments since
   F.W. Maitland's day have narrowed the distinction between
   unincorporate and incorporated bodies.

4. FRIEDMANN, W. Law in a Changing Society, (Stevens & Sons
   Ltd., 1959), chap. 9: this is a general discussion of the
   role played by corporations in the national and
   international scene.

5. GOWER, L.C.B. The Principles of Modern Company Law, (3rd ed.,
   K.W. Wedderburn, O. Weaver, A.E.W. Park, Stevens & Sons,
   Ltd., 1969), chap. 11: companies are distinguished from
   other types of association (including public corporations).

6. WARREN, E.H. "Collateral Attack on Incorporation. A. De Facto
   Corporations" (1906-7), 20 Harv.L.R. 456; (1907-8), 21 Harv.
   L.R. 305: these two articles are also relevant on the
   ultra vires rule and how far the matter depends on the
   extent of corporate personality. The first article is less
   relevant than the second, but both should be read together.
   Where the legislature has not incorporated an association
   the rights and duties are of individuals.

7. CARPENTER, C.E. "De Facto Corporations" (1911-12), 25 Harv.L.
   R. 623: this considers the varying degrees to which
   American courts recognise the corporate nature of
   unincorporate associations. It is an answer to E.H. Warren's
   contention (supra).

8. DODD, E.M. "Dogma and Practice in the Law of Associations"
   (1928-29), 42 Harv.L.R. 977: a concept should be examined

with a view to finding out what it means and whether that
meaning is in accord with social policy. On this basis the
author controverts E.H. Warren's thesis (supra) with
reference to history and trend of modern decisions.

1. BURDICK, F.M. "Are Defectively Incorporated Associations
    Partnerships?" (1906), 6 Col.L.R. 1: after an examination
    of the authorities the conclusion is in the affirmative.

2. CHAFEE, Z. "Internal Affairs of Associations Not for Profit"
    (1929-30), 43 Harv.L.R. 993: the attitude of Anglo-American
    courts to such bodies is examined as well as the
    relationship between them and their members and the nature
    of the remedies available.

3. WEDDERBURN, K.W. "Corporate Personality and Social Policy:
    the Problem of the Quasi-corporation" (1965), 28 M.L.R. 62:
    the modern tendency on the part of the courts is to
    interpret statutes concerning group activities as granting
    impliedly either corporate status or at least the ability
    to sue and defend in the group name. The changed attitude
    of the courts in this sphere has been governed by
    considerations of policy.

4. WILLIAMSON, R.M. "The Free Church Case" (1904), 20 L.Q.R. 415:
    this is of general interest. The background of the case is
    set out and the implications of the decision are briefly
    considered.

5. LLOYD, D. "Actions Instituted by or Against Unincorporated
    Bodies" (1949), 12 M.L.R. 409: this deals in detail with the
    problems created by various sorts of unincorporated bodies
    in the procedural field.

6. LLOYD, D. "The Disciplinary Powers of Professional Bodies"
    (1950), 13 M.L.R. 281: in this is considered the exercise
    of powers by unincorporated bodies and the attitude of the
    courts.

7. ANONYMOUS. "Expulsion of Member of Club" (1926), 70 Sol.Jo.
    828: in the light of an unreported decision the relationship
    between members and a club is considered.

8. STURGES, W.A. "Unincorporated Associations as Parties to
    Actions" (1923-24), 33 Yale L.J. 383: this article should be
    read as suggesting a reason why such associations used not
    to be able to sue in their own name.

9. LLOYD, D. Note in (1953), 16 M.L.R. 359: the law is
    unsatisfactory with regard to the tortious responsibility of

unincorporated associations and the use of a representative
action.

1. NOTE: "Unions as Juridical Persons", (1956-57), 66 Yale L.J.,
   712: this is an inquiry in some detail into the Anglo-
   American law. The conclusion is reached that unions are
   juridical persons.

2. NOTE: "Responsibility of Labor Unions for Acts of Members",
   (1938), 38 Col. L.R., 454: various aspects of the matter
   are dealt with.

3. WITMER, T.R. "Trade Union Liability: the Problem of the
   Unincorporated Corporation", (1941-42), 51 Yale L.J., 40:
   the British Taff Vale case and the American Coronado case
   are discussed. Attention is drawn to the tendency to
   assimilate these bodies to corporations.

4. DICEY, A.V. "The Combination Laws as Illustrating the
   Relation Between Law and Opinion in England During the
   19th. Century", (1903-4), 17 Harv L.R., 511: this is a
   consideration of the body of rules which regulate the
   freedom of workmen to combine for the purpose of determining
   by agreement the terms on which they will sell their labour,
   and the corresponding freedom of employers to combine for
   determining by agreement the terms on which they will
   engage labour. (See also Law and Public Opinion in England
   during the 19th. Century, (2nd ed., Macmillan & Co., Ltd.,
   1932), pp. 154, 169).

5. GELDART, W.M. "The Status of Trade Unions In England", (1912)
   25 Harv. L.R., 579: a trade union is shown to constitute an
   aggregate of phenomena which bears a resemblance to a
   corporation.

6. KAHN-FREUND, O. "The Illegality of a Trade Union", (1944),7
   M.L.R., 192: the influence of the old common law attitude
   towards trade unions in the interpretation of legislation
   is discussed.

7. SHIRBANIUK, D.J. "Actions By and Against Trade Unions in
   Contract and Tort", (1957-58), 12 Tor. L.J., 151: the
   English and Canadian law is considered at length. In view
   of the acceptance in practice of unions as entities distinct
   from their members, the formal recognition of them as
   "persons" would not be a radical one.

8. GRAVESON, R.H. "The Status of Trade Unions", (1963), 7 J.S.P.
   T.L.(N.S.) 121: this is a very general account of their
   legal position and touching indirectly on the problem of
   their persona.

1. LLOYD, D. "Damages for Wrongful Expulsion From a Trade Union",
   (1956), 19 M.L.R., 121: a full discussion of the Bonsor
   case with particular attention to how far a registered
   trade union is a legal entity.

2. THOMAS, T.C. "Trade Unions and Their Members", (1956), C.L.J.,
   67: the implications of the Bonsor decision are considered.

3. SYKES, E.I. "The Legal Status of Trade Unions", (1957), 2 Syd.
   L.R., 271: this is a discussion of the position of
   registered and unregistered trade unions, mainly with
   reference to the Bonsor case.

4. CAMPBELL, E. "Legal Personality, Trade Unions, and Damages
   for Unlawful Expulsion", (1954-56), 3 U. Wes. Aus. A.L.R.,
   393: although the article is concerned with Bonsor's case
   and the position of trade unions in the light of a detailed
   survey of English and Australian law, it also discusses the
   various theories as to legal personality. It is, on the
   whole, a very good discussion.

5. WEDDERBURN, K.W. "The Bonsor Affair: a Post-script", (1957),
   20 M.L.R., 105: a further investigation into the Bonsor
   case with particular reference to the extent to which a
   trade union is a "legal entity".

6. WEDDERBURN, K.W. "The Right to Threaten Strikes", (1961), 24
   M.L.R., 572; (1962), 25 M.L.R., 513: these two articles are
   based respectively on the decision at first instance and
   on appeal of Rookes v. Barnard, a conspiracy case. They
   are of indirect relevance to the question of the nature of
   trade unions at law. (See further (1964), 27 M.L.R., 257).

7. WEDDERBURN, K.W. "Corporate Personality and Social Policy:
   the Problem of the Quasi-corporation", (1965), 28 M.L.R.,
   62: the orthodox view that "persons" in law are either
   human beings or corporations failed to provide solutions
   for an increasing number of situations which developing
   society threw up. The courts are now more ready to treat
   a body or institution as a "legal entity".

8. ANONYMOUS: "Legal Entities" (1964), 235 L.T., 578: this is a
   note on "entities" that are neither human beings nor
   corporations. Such entities are creatures of statute, and
   which can sue and be sued.

Theories

9. HALLIS, F. Corporate Personality, (Oxford University Press,
   1930); this is a detailed study of most of the better

known theories on the subject. In the Introduction there are some questionable assertions, especially that English lawyers have adopted the Fiction Theory.

1. DUFF, P.W. Personality in Roman Private Law, (Cambridge University Press, 1938), chaps. 1, 9: in the first chapter words such as "persona", "caput" and "universitas" are examined. The last chapter is a clear, critical account of various modern theories.

2. WOLFF, M. "On the Nature of Legal Persons", (1938), 54 L.Q.R. 494: an incisive and often amusing discussion of four of the principal theories, with the Fiction Theory preferred.

3. MICHOUD, L. La Théorie de la Personnalité Morale, (2nd ed., Librarie Générale de Droit et de Jurisprudence, Paris, 1924), I and II: this work, in French, is one of the outstanding surveys of this subject. Volume I, which deals with the concept of person, is especially relevant.

4. MACHEN, A.W. "Corporate Personality", (1910-11), 24 Harv. L. R., 253, 347: some of the leading Continental theories are reviewed. The nature of corporate personality is examined in an interesting way. The law recognises the unity of a group as a fact. Hence the important question is not why it does so, but why it refuses to recognise, e.g., partnership unity. A corporation is no fiction, but its personality is, and this is said to be why the distinction between incorporated and unincorporated bodies is so vague.

5. SMITH, B. "Legal Personality", (1927-28), 37 Yale L.J., 283: the fact that courts decide on grounds of utility is emphasised. Much confusion has arisen because of the tendency to read into legal persons the attributes of human beings.

6. COHEN, F.S. "Transcendental Nonsense and the Functional Approach" (1935), 35 Col. L.R., 809, especially pp. 809-817: the dangers of "thought without roots in reality" are pointed out with reference to corporations. The whole article is a powerful plea for a functional approach to legal problems.

7. VINOGRADOFF, P. "Juridical Persons" in Collected Papers, (Oxford, 1928), chap. 17: the life of a group has two sides, the social which is real, and the legal which is artificial. The relative importance of these two varies with the individualist or collectivist values of the system.

8. DEWEY, J. "The Historical Background of Corporate Personality"

(1925-26), 35 Yale L.J., 655: the concept of "person" is a
purely legal one, but some popular notions have crept in
because of the belief that before anything is entitled to
be called "person" it should possess certain properties.
The article also examines the historical background of
some of the theories.

1. DEWEY, J. Philosophy and Civilisation, (G.P. Putnam's Sons,
   1931), 141: in this essay a modern philospher examines the
   conception of "legal person". Many needless difficulties
   are said to have been caused by the use of the wrong
   logical method. On this basis the approaches of the various
   theories are examined.

2. HART, H.L.A. "Definition and Theory in Jurisprudence", (1954),
   70 L.Q.R., 37, at pp. 49-59: the theoretical difficulty
   arises when the question is asked what "it" is that owes
   money whenever it is said that "Smith & Co. owe White £10".
   The answer is to be found by elucidating the whole statement and how it is used in drawing conclusions.

3. NÉKAM, A. The Personality Conception of the Legal Entity,
   (Harvard Studies in the Conflict of Laws, Harvard University
   Press, 1938), III: the premise of the argument is that legal
   ideas are the product of emotion clothed with reason. The
   tendency in modern times is to regard the individual as the
   unit, and from this has stemmed the idea that "legal
   entities" should resemble individuals.

4. POLLOCK, F. "Has the Common Law Received the Fiction Theory
   of Corporation ?" in Essays in the Law, (Macmillan & Co.,
   Ltd., 1922), chap. 6: the answer, according to Pollock, is
   that English law has not committed itself to any theory. On
   the whole, he favours the realist theory.

5. DUGUIT, L. The Progress of Continental Law in the 19th.
   Century, (John Murray, London, 1918), 87-100: personality
   exists only where there is will. If a group has a will
   apart from the wills of its members, it is a "person". But
   Duguit's main concern is whether the group is pursuing a
   purpose which conforms with social solidarity. If it is,
   all actions within that purpose should be recognised and
   protected. A collective will is unprovable; but there is
   such a thing as collective purpose.

6. BRODERICK, A. "Hauriou's Institutional Theory: an Invitation
   to Common Law Jurisprudence", (1965), 4 Sol. Q. 281: the
   state may grant legal "personality" to a group which is not
   organised or rationised. When this happens there is talk of
   the fiction theory. But when an institution is organised,

it has a "moral personality", and the state ought then to
accord legal personality to it.

1. BERLE, A.A. "The Theory of Enterprise Entity" (1947), 47 Col.
   L.R. 343: this article is concerned mainly with the
   development of the corporation in modern business and the
   divergence between corporate theory and economic facts.
   The corporate entity takes its being from the reality of
   the underlying enterprise. This theory might be said to
   systematise the law of corporations and is a functional
   theory. See also W.O. DOUGLAS and C.M. SHANKS, "Insulation
   from Liability Through Subsidiary Corporations" (1929), 39
   Yale L.J. 193; G.D. HORNSTEIN, "Legal Controls for Intra-
   corporate Abuse" (1941), 41 Col.L.R. 405; C.L. ISRAELS,
   "Implications and Limitations of the 'Deep Rock Doctrine'"
   (1942), 42 Col.L.R. 376.

2. MOORE, W.U. "Rational Basis of Legal Institutions" (1923), 23
   Col.L.R. 609: to ask what is the rational basis of an
   institution is to pose a non-existent problem. The question
   should concern the purpose of institutions. This depends on
   the end, and the end is chosen before the rational process
   is directed towards achieving it. But ends are but means
   to other ends. So the real question is: what are the means
   to legal institutions, and to what proximate ends are
   legal institutions means?

3. STONE, J. Social Dimensions of Law and Justice, (Stevens &
   Sons, Ltd., 1966), pp. 367-432: these pages deal with the
   development of the corporation and the severance of control
   from ownership. The problems of social responsibility,
   which this has created, is alluded to.

4. WORTLEY, B.A. Jurisprudence (Manchester University Press;
   Oceana Publications, Inc., New York. 1967), chap. 18: this
   chapter on "Personality" gives a very general account. It
   is chiefly important in stressing that the tendency of
   legal development has been towards the concept of enterprise
   unity.

5. KORKUNOV, N.M. General Theory of Law, (trans. W.G. Hastings,
   The Boston Book Co., 1909), S. 28: law presupposes
   conflicting interests and relations between individuals.
   Corporations are said to be "moral" persons. The Fiction,
   Realist and Purpose theories are mentioned. Legal
   personality is likened to parantheses in algebra.

6. HOHFELD, W.N. Fundamental Legal Conceptions as Applied in
   Judicial Reasoning, (ed. W.W. Cook, Yale University Press,
   London: Humphrey Milford, 1923), chaps. 6-7: this theory

dissolves a company into a multitude of jural relations
between individuals. "Corporate personality" is a procedural
device of convenience.

1. KOCOUREK, A. <u>Jural Relations</u>, (2nd ed., The Bobbs-Merrill Co.,
   1928), chap. 17: a distinction is drawn between the idea
   of "legal person" and "legal personality". The former is a
   concept to which is attributed a capacity for being in
   legal relationship; the latter is the sum total of legal
   relationships.

2. RADIN, M. "The Endless Problem of Corporate Personality"
   (1932), 32 Col.L.R. 643: it contains a critical review of
   the controversies as well as of corporate existence and
   responsibility. So far as a "person" means that a group
   constitutes a new item, there is no support in the facts;
   as facilitating reference to a complex group of facts, the
   idea of "person" is useful. (See also M. RADIN, "A
   Restatement of Hohfeld" (1937-38), 51 Harv.L.R. 1141, at
   pp. 1160-1162).

3. TIMBERG, S. "Corporate Fictions" (1946), 46 Col.L.R. 533,
   especially pp. 540 et seq.: corporate autonomy is discussed
   in various contexts, national and international. The
   nominalist view, M. Radin's in particular (<u>supra</u>), is
   criticised. The question is when and how far should the
   state dispel the corporate fiction. There is not just one
   fiction, there are many.

4. CANFIELD, G.F. "The Scope and Limits of the Corporate Entity
   Theory" (1917), 17 Col.L.R. 128: personality is a legal
   conception, but it is not a fiction because it involves no
   false deduction or pretence. Canfield opposes the Hohfeldian
   nominalism and holds to the entity theory.

5. BATY, T. "The Rights of Ideas - and of Corporations" (1919-20),
   33 Harv.L.R. 358: the "real existence" of corporations is
   a shorthand phrase. But there is something; "person" is an
   idea, the idea of groupness.

6. PICKERING, M.A. "The Company as a Separate Legal Entity"
   (1968), 31 M.L.R. 481: the view that a company is a separate
   entity is supported. The exceptions are classified as
   exceptions to the principles delimiting the scope of a
   company's legal capacity, exceptions to the principle of
   separate property and contractual rights, and exceptions
   to the company's independent procedural capacity.

7. SNYDER, O.C. <u>Preface to Jurisprudence</u>, (The Bobbs-Merrill Co.,
   Inc., 1954), Part V, chap. 2, pp. 778-786: this is a general

discussion of the nature of natural and juristic persons.
The Hohfeldian view is supported.

1. KELSEN, H. General Theory of Law and State, (trans. A. Wedberg,
   Harvard University Press, 1949), pp. 93-109: even a physical
   person is the unification of a complex of legal norms.
   Therefore, the contrast between physical and juristic
   persons is mistaken. See also H. KELSEN, Pure Theory of
   Law (trans. M. Knight, University of California Press,
   1967), pp. 168-192.

2. KELSEN, H. "The Pure Theory of Law" (trans. C.H. Wilson),
   (1934) 50 L.Q.R. 474, at pp. 496-498: this is a simplified
   version of the same thesis as above.

3. von SAVIGNY, F.C. "Jural Relations" (trans. W.H. Rattigan,
   Savigny's System of Modern Roman Law, Bk. II, Wildy & Sons,
   1884), pp. 175 et seq.: Savigny is the principal supporter
   of the Fiction Theory. This gives the original version of
   his thesis.

4. SALMOND, J.W. Jurisprudence, (7th ed., Sweet & Maxwell, Ltd.,
   1924), chap. 15, pp. 339-342: Salmond was the principal
   exponent of the Fiction Theory among English writers. The
   7th edition is the last by Salmond himself: (but see now
   12th edition, P.J. Fitzgerald, pp. 328-330).

5. JONES, J.W. Historical Introduction to the Theory of Law,
   (Oxford, 1940), chap. 6: the Fiction Theory is indirectly
   discussed in the course of a general account of the use of
   fictions.

6. SOHM, R. The Institutes. A Text-Book of the History and
   System of Roman Private Law, (trans. J.C. Ledlie, Oxford,
   1901), pp. 195-205: the Realist Theory is rejected.
   Juristic personality is said to be created by law, but is
   not fictitious.

7. GIERKE, O. Natural Law and the Theory of Society 1500-1800
   (trans. E. Barker, Cambridge University Press, 1934),
   Introduction, pp. lvii-lxxxvii: in the Introduction Barker
   examines the principal theories, especially the Fiction,
   Bracket and Realist Theories. He propounds his own view of
   the "personality of purpose". In the main text the Realist
   Theory of Gierke, its chief supporter, is to be found in
   detail.

8. GIERKE, O. Political Theories of the Middle Age, (trans.
   F.W. Maitland, Cambridge University Press, 1900),
   Introduction, pp. xviii-xliiii: in this classic Introduction

214   Persons

Maitland made Gierke's work familiar to the English public.
He elaborates Gierke's ideas, but considers also the Fiction,
Concession and Bracket Theories. Although Maitland is
thought to have been a convert to the Realist Theory, he
does not commit himself and leaves the question unanswered.
Chapters 3, 4 and 8 of the main text contain Gierke's views
on the idea of unity in Church and State, organism and
personality.

1. MAITLAND, F.W. "Moral Personality and Legal Personality" in
    Selected Essays (edd. H.D. Hazeltine, G. Lapsley,
    P.H. Winfield, Cambridge University Press, 1936), chap. 5;
    Collected Papers, (ed. H.A.L. Fisher, Cambridge University
    Press, 1911), III, p. 304: the nature of natural persons
    and corporations is discussed. He stresses the fact that
    a united body differs from its component members by no
    fiction of law but in the very nature of things.

2. GELDART, W.M. "Legal Personality" (1911), 27 L.Q.R. 90: there
    is a discussion of the Fiction and Realist Theories and
    the latter is preferred. Groups other than corporations
    are recognised in law because they are real and not a
    pretence.

3. BROWN, W.J. "The Personality of the Corporation and the State"
    (1905), 21 L.Q.R. 365: corporate personality is not a mere
    metaphor or fiction. A corporation is real, but in a sense
    different from human beings. They are psychical realities,
    having unity of spirit, purpose, interests and organisation.

4. BROWN, W.J. The Austinian Theory of Law, (John Murray, 1906),
    pp. 254-270: in this Excursus the state and corporations
    are examined. He repeats his view as to the nature of
    corporations and argues that on this basis the state is a
    legal person.

5. VINOGRADOFF, P. Common-sense in Law, (3rd ed., H.G. Hanbury,
    Oxford University Press, 1959), pp. 52-61: legal persons
    are considered in the context of rights and duties. The
    Realist Theory is favoured.

6. DEISER, G.F. "The Juristic Person", (1919), 57 U.Pa.L.R. 131,
    216, 300: "persona ficta" is said to be an inheritance
    from Roman law. The idea of a corporation rests on the
    conception of rights and of concerted action. Various ways
    of looking at the problem are considered, the Realist view
    being ultimately favoured.

7. McDOUGAL, W. The Group Mind, (Cambridge University Press,
    1920): this is of general interest. It analyses the group

mind from a psychological point of view. The author would
support the Realist Theory as against the Fiction Theory.

1. FOLEY, H.E. "Incorporation, Multiple Incorporation, and the
   Conflict of Laws", (1928-29), 42 Harv.L.R. 516: the
   principal theories are discussed. Legal personality is the
   law-created capacity to enter into relationships at law.
   An incorporated association is a real entity. When several
   states incorporate the same association, that body has
   several personalities.

2. YOUNG, E.H. "The Legal Personality of a Foreign Corporation"
   (1906), 22 L.Q.R. 178: the practice of courts normally
   proceeds on something like a Fiction Theory. But the
   solution of problems involving a corporation which is
   subject to rights and duties of another system of law
   proceeds on a Realist conception.

3. YOUNG, E.H. "The Status of a Foreign Corporation and the
   Legislature", (1907), 23 L.Q.R. 151, 290: the nature of
   corporate personality is discussed passim.

4. FRIEDMANN, W. Legal Theory, (5th ed., Stevens & Sons, Ltd.,
   1967), chap. 34: he points out that the various theories
   have not sought to solve any problems, but to explain the
   nature of personality. The principal theories are briefly
   reviewed.

12

POSSESSION

1. SHARTEL, B. "Meanings of Possession", (1932), 16 Minn. L.R., 611: the traditional attempts to define possession have failed because they attempt the impossible. There are many meanings of the term and these can only be understood with reference to the purpose in hand. The elaboration of this theme is one of the best contribution to the subject.

2. BINGHAM, J.W, "The Nature and Importance of Legal Possession" (1915), 13 Mich. L.R., 534, especially pp. 549-565; 623 et seq.: after a survey of related terms, the situations of "being in possession" are considered. What is meant when it is said that legal possession exists is that a person has certain rights called "possessory" rights. The vesting of these rights is determined by practical juridical considerations of justice and policy.

Roman Law

The following is a very brief selection. The Continental literature is enormous.

3. von SAVIGNY, F.C. Rechts des Besitzes, (6th ed., trans. as Possession, by E. Perry; S. Sweet, 1848): this is the classic exposition of the animus and corpus theory.

4. von IHERING, R. Der Besitwille, (Jena, 1889; trans. by O. de Meulenaere in the Supplement to L'Esprit du Droit Romain, A. Maresque, 1891): Grund des Besitzesschutzes, (Jena, 1868; trans. as above in the Supplement, A. Maresque, 1882): these deal with possession and with the interdicts. They contain a painstaking demolition of Savigny's theory, as well as his own theory.

5. LIGHTWOOD, J.M. "Possession in Roman Law", (1887), 3 L.Q.R., 32: the author was one of the earliest advocates of Ihering's theory, which is here examined and the reasons why possession was protected considered.

6. BOND, H. "Possession in the Roman Law", (1890), 6 L.Q.R., 259: this draws attention to the failure to distinguish between the questions, Why was possession protected ? and, Why should possession be protected ? Ihering's theory is considered with approval.

7. BUCKLAND, W.W. A Text-book of Roman Law from Augustus to Justinian, (3rd ed., P. Stein, Cambridge University Press, 1963), pp. 196-199: this contains a brief summary of the theories of Savigny and Ihering with some comment on each.

1. RADIN, M. Handbook of Roman Law, (West Publishing Co., 1927),
   pp. 384-392: he shows that the corpus and animus theory
   does not fit many cases. Ihering's critique of Savigny is
   approved, but even with his theory there are difficulties.
   There is a different group of claims in different situations
   called possession. There is no essential characteristic.

2. DIAS, R.W.M. "A Reconsideration of Possessio", (1956), C.L.J.
   235: possessio was a device of legal policy and convenience.
   This can be illustrated by an examination of the texts.

English Law

   In addition to the articles by B. Shartel and J.W. Bingham
   (supra), the following are relevant to the thesis that
   possession is a device of convenience.

3. KOCOUREK, A. Jural Relations, (2nd ed., Bobbs-Merrill Co.,
   1928), chap. 20: the law is concerned only with jural
   relations between parties, which in the case of possession
   are the right to possess and the right of possessing. The
   investitive facts are exhausted as soon as the jural
   relation is created. There is no further need for an
   additional enduring fact called possession. In ultimate
   analysis the matter is one of policy.

4. PATON, G.W. "Possession", (1935), 1 Res Judicata, 187: the
   law of possession represents a clash between logic and
   convenience. Not only does the terminology vary, but many
   complicating factors enter into the decision in particular
   circumstances.

5. PATON, G.W. A Text-book of Jurisprudence, (3rd ed., D.P.
   Derham, Oxford, 1964), chap. 22: possession is a fact to
   which the law attaches certain consequences. For reasons of
   convenience and policy each system builds differently round
   the fact of physical control. There is an outline of the
   theories of Savigny and Ihering and of the clash between
   convenience and theory.

6. LIGHTWOOD, J.M. A Treatise on Possession of Land, (Stevens &
   Sons, Ltd., 1894), chaps. 1, 2 and 4: there is a comparison
   of Roman and English law, as well as a critical discussion
   of Savigny, Holmes and Pollock and Wright. In chapter 4
   attention is drawn to some of the artificial doctrines
   connected with possession.

7. THAYER, A.S. "Possession", (1904-5), 18 Harv. L.R., 196:
   attempts to define possession are necessarily futile. The
   conditions under which legal possession exist are technical

and subject to no limit of variation. Holmes's explanation of physical power is criticised.

1. THAYER, A.S. "Possession and Ownership", (1907), 23 L.Q.R., 175, especially pp. 175-187; 314: if possession follows from taking, this implies a rule that taking gives the right of possession. This rule developed from the habitual submission of others. Possession as the continuous dealing with a thing to the exclusion of others is a fiction.

2. HARRIS, D.R. "The Concept of Possession in English Law", in Oxford Essays in Jurisprudence, (ed. A.G. Guest, Oxford University Press, 1961), chap. 4: possession is used as a functional and relative concept. In doubtful cases the judges' views as to the merits and policy come in. The factors relevant to possession are considered.

3. BENTHAM, J. The Limits of Jurisprudence Defined, (ed. C.W. Everett, Columbia University Press, 1945), pp. 78-85: what is meant by possessing a thing is examined. Physical and legal possession are contrasted. The latter carries title to the thing.

4. BENTHAM, J. Works, (ed. J. Bowring, Wm. Tait, 1843), i, pp. 221-222; 326-327; III, pp. 188-189: the advantages of possession and reasons for protecting it are considered. He points out that the idea of possession differs according to the nature of the subject-matter and the circumstances.

5. WILLIAMS, G.L. "Language and the Law", (1945), 61 L.Q.R., 384, at pp. 390-391: this exposes the fallacy in Salmond's theory and indicates that there is a complex legal idea which is governed by the purpose of the particular rule.

Adaptations of Savigny's theory to English Law

6. SALMOND, J.W. Jurisprudence, (7th ed., 1924, chaps. 13 and 14; 11th ed., G.L. Williams, 1957, chaps. 13 and 14; 12th ed., P.J. Fitzgerald, Sweet & Maxwell, Ltd., 1966), chap. 9: this is a detailed account based on the corpus and animus theory. The author's own views have been modified considerably by the successive editors.

7. HOLMES, O.W. The Common Law, (Little, Brown & Co., Boston, 1881), chap. 6: the author adopts the Savignian thesis of corpus and animus, laying stress on the latter.

8. HOLMES, O.W. "Possession", (1877-78), 12 Am. L.R., 688: this is an earlier version of what later appeared in The Common Law, but it includes certain matters not discussed therein.

1. POLLOCK, F. and WRIGHT, R.S. An Essay on Possession in the
    Common Law, (Oxford, 1888), Part I: the emphasis is on
    corpus rather than on animus.

2. POLLOCK, F. A First Book of Jurisprudence, (6th ed., Macmillan
    & Co., Ltd., 1929), pp. 181-193: a very general discussion
    of possession and of its legal effects, but proceeding on
    the "classic" line.

3. POUND, R. Jurisprudence, (West Publishing Co., 1959), V,
    chap. 29: possession is defined as physical control with
    the will to exercise such control for oneself. There is a
    discussion of the reasons why possession is protected and
    of the physical and mental elements.

4. TAY, A.E.S. "The Concept of Possession in the Common Law:
    Foundations for a New Approach"(1964), 4 Melb. U.L.R., 476:
    possession "is present control of a thing, on one's own
    behalf and to the exclusion of all others". This is sub-
    mitted as the "standard case" in comparison with which
    divergent uses of the term "possession" can be understood.

5. HARRIS, D.R. "Comment", (1964), 4 Melb. U.L.R., 498: the
    author takes issue with Miss Tay's contention (supra),
    pointing out not only certain weaknesses in her position
    but also that basically it is not very dissimilar to his
    own.

6. TERRY, H.T. Some Leading Principles of Anglo-American Law
    Expounded with a View to its Arrangement and Codification,
    (Philadelphia, 1884), chap. 10: this begins by accepting
    Savigny's theory without question. Although English law is
    admitted to be different from Roman law, the corpus and
    animus theory is applied none the less and various aspects
    of English law discussed in the light of it.

7. MARKBY, W. Elements of Law, (6th ed., Oxford, 1905), chap. 9:
    this, too, begins with an acceptance of Savigny's theory
    and an explanation of the physical and mental elements. Of
    25 pages in the chapter, only four and a half (pp. 197-203)
    are in fact devoted to English law.

8. AUSTIN, J. Lectures on Jurisprudence, (5th ed., R. Campbell,
    John Murray, 1885), I, pp. 51-53: Austin's lectures
    finished prematurely and he never discussed possession. In
    these introductory pages he foreshadows a future discussion
    and draws certain distinctions. It is, perhaps, noteworthy
    that he alludes to Savigny's treatise as "consummate and
    masterly; and of all books which I pretend to know accur-
    ately, the least alloyed with error and imperfections" (p.53).

1. HOLLAND, T.E. The Elements of Jurisprudence, (13th ed.,
    Oxford, 1924), pp. 194-208: he refers to Savigny's theory
    as "the accepted view', but Ihering has an honourable
    mention. The treatment is based largely on Holmes.

2. KEETON, G.W. The Elementary Principles of Jurisprudence,
    (2nd ed., Pitman & Sons, Ltd., 1949), chap. 15: possession
    depends on the degree of control and anything short of the
    requisite degree is "custody". Possession is the continuing
    exercise of a claim to the exclusive control of a thing.
    This leads to a discussion of corpus and animus.

3. STEWART, R.D. "The Difference Between Possession of Land and
    Chattels", (1933), 11 Can.B.R. 651: "actual" possession is
    a matter of fact, "legal" possession is established by law.
    The former requires animus and corpus. The degree of control
    differs in the case of land and chattels.

4. GOODEVE, L.A. Modern Law of Personal Property, (9th ed.,
    R.H. Kersley, Sweet & Maxwell, Ltd., 1949), pp. 32-41:
    possession requires control, which varies with the nature
    of the chattel, and the intention to control. Cases which
    do not fit into these requirements are "exceptions".

5. CROSSLEY VAINES, J. Personal Property, (4th ed., Butterworth
    & Co., Ltd., 1967), pp. 47-55: this account chiefly follows
    Pollock and Wright, and distinguishes between control or
    de facto possession, legal possession without control and
    the right to possess.

6. MATTHEWS, A.S. "Mental Element in Possession", (1962), 79
    S.A.L.J. 179: this argues that convenience and policy are
    only explanations of the prevailing confusion; the courts
    do not use them as determinants. The article is limited to
    interdict possession (mandament van spolie of Roman-Dutch
    law), the treatment of which largely follows Holmes.

7. HALL, J.S. "Possession, Custody, and Ownership: a
    Philosophical Approach" (1960), 27 The Solicitor, 85: this,
    too, is influenced by Holmes. The law must be subordinated
    to instinct and must uphold the desire to retain what is
    possessed. Possession implies a degree of control, which
    varies. There is an account of seisin in early land law
    and of the philosophisings of Kant and Locke.

8. GOODHART, A.L. "Three Cases on Possession", in Essays in
    Jurisprudence and the Common Law, (Cambridge University
    Press, 1937), chap. 4: a demonstration of the unfortunate
    results of applying preconceived theories about possession
    to Bridges v. Hawkesworth, South Staffordshire Water Co. v.

Sharman and Elwes v. Brigg Gas Co.

1. FIFOOT, C.H.S. Judge and Jurist in the Reign of Queen
   Victoria, (Stevens & Sons, Ltd., 1959), chap. 4: this tries
   to explain the persistence of Savigny's influence
   notwithstanding Ihering's demolition of his theory. After
   a discussion of some situations in civil and criminal law
   the conclusion is reached that possession is a word which
   has a changing content.

Special aspects of possession

For the history of the subject, especially the connection between
possession and seisin, the following might be consulted.

2. POLLOCK, F. and MAITLAND, F.W. The History of English Law
   before the time of Edward I, (2nd ed., with Introduction
   by S.F.C. Milsom, Cambridge University Press, 1968), pp.
   29-46.

3. MAITLAND, F.W. Collected Papers, (ed. H.A.L. Fisher,
   Cambridge University Press, 1911), I, "Seisin of Chattels",
   p. 344; "Mystery of Seisin", p. 358; "The Beatitude of
   Seisin", pp. 406, 432.

4. AMES, J.B. "The Disseisin of Chattels", in Select Essays in
   Anglo-American Legal History, (Cambridge University Press,
   1909), III, p. 541.

5. HOLDSWORTH, W.S. A History of English Law, (5th ed., Methuen
   & Co., Ltd.), iii, pp. 88-101; vii, pp. 23-31; 447-478.

6. BARLOW, A.C.H. "Gift Inter Vivos of a Chose in Possession by
   Delivery of a Key", (1956), 19 M.L.R. 394: this considers
   some of the cases on the delivery of a key.

7. CLERK, J.F. "Title to Chattels by Possession", (1871), 7
   L.Q.R. 224: this considers the extent to which a bailee
   can recover damages against a wrongdoer by virtue of his
   possession.

8. DICEY, A.V. A Treatise on the Rules for the Selection of the
   Parties to an Action, (Wm. Maxwell & Son, 1870), pp. 333-
   366: trespass to land can be brought by a possessor. The
   distinction between occupation and possession is discussed
   as well as the right to possess as the basis for suing in
   trespass to goods.

9. RIESMAN, D. "Possession and the Law of Finders", (1939), 52
   Harv.L.R. 1105: this is an elaborate discussion of finder

cases. It argues that possession is largely irrelevant and
shows the contradictions that result by arguing on the
basis of possession. The word possession may have an inner
core of fairly settled meaning, but for the lawyer the
periphery is more important. Here, certainly in finder
cases, varieties of complex social interests come in. The
article also contains a comment on Shartel's view.

1. MARSHALL, O.R. "The Problem of Finding", (1949), 2 C.L.P. 68:
   this begins with an examination of legal policy and proceeds
   on that basis to consider the position of the finder in
   relation to various other persons. Possession is necessarily
   a very flexible concept.

2. TAY, A.E.S. "'Bridges v. Hawkesworth' and the Early History of
   Finding" (1964), 8 Am.J.L.H. 224: the early history of the
   law relating to finding is set out. This leads the author
   to the conclusion that Bridges v. Hawkesworth is not wrongly
   decided, but is the last representative of an earlier line
   of decisions based on the forms of action.

3. TAY, A.E.S. "Possession and the Modern Law of Finding" (1964),
   4 Syd.L.R. 383: A piece-meal approach to possession will
   only hinder the predictable application of the law. The
   finding cases are reviewed in order to demonstrate that
   they bring out the fundamental criteria of possession.
   Each situation should be considered in the light of control
   as the basis of possession.

4. TAY, A.E.S. "Problems in the Law of Finding: the U.S.
   Approach" (1964), 37 Aust.L.J. 350: the American case-law,
   it is submitted, has developed the distinction between
   property that has been misplaced (i.e., put down and left)
   and property that has been lost.

5. TAY, A.E.S. "The Essence of Bailment: Contract, Agreement or
   Possession?" (1966), 5 Syd.L.R. 239: bailment is analysed
   as a relation between a person and a thing, requiring
   neither agreement with, nor knowledge of, a particular
   bailor.

6. TAY, A.E.S. "Bailment and the Deposit for Safe-keeping"
   (1964), 6 Malaya L.R. 229: this continues the previous
   theme with an examination of a number of authorities.

7. TAY, A.E.S. "Possession, Larceny, and Servants: Towards
   Tidying up a Historical Muddle" (1965-66), 16 Tor.L.J.
   145: possession is not manual detention; it is control.
   A servant qua servant is only a master's instrument, i.e.,
   so long as the servant's actions are part of the master's

use or enjoyment.

1. RUSSELL, W.O. on Crime, (12th ed., J.W.C. Turner, Stevens &
    Sons, Ltd., 1964), II, pp. 1027-1156: this is a full
    historical account of the part played by possession in the
    law of larceny.

2. TURNER, J.W.C. "Two Cases on Larceny", in Modern Approach to
    Criminal Law, (edd. L. Radzinowicz and J.W.C. Turner,
    Macmillan & Co., Ltd., 1948), chap. 19: this deals with
    the artificial reasoning in R. v. Middleton and R. v. Riley.

3. EDWARDS, J.Ll.J. "Possession and Larceny", (1950), 3 C.L.P.
    127: the dichotomy between "physical" and "legal"
    possession is discussed, followed by a demonstration of the
    difficulties that have arisen and the distinctions that
    have been drawn in larceny cases.

4. CROSS, A.R.N. "Larceny and the Formation of a Felonious
    Intent after Taking Possession", (1949), 12 M.L.R. 228:
    this is a note on Ruse v. Read.

5. CARTER, P.B. "Taking and the Acquisition of Possession in
    Larceny", (1957), 14 M.L.R. 27: this draws an interesting
    distinction between obtaining possession and "taking" in
    the sense of knowing that one has obtained the possession.

6. LOWE, J.T. "Larceny by a Trick and Contract", (1957), Crim.
    L.R. 28, 96: this shows that the effect of the decisions
    would seem to be that in criminal law a person may be
    said to have taken and carried away goods without consent
    when, on the same facts, in civil law he may be said to be
    in possession with consent.

7. NOTE in (1930), 46 L.Q.R. 135: a critique of R. v. Harding.

8. WYLIE, J.C.W. "Adverse Possession: an Ailing Concept?" (1965),
    16 N.I.L.Q. 467: this article may be consulted for a
    general review of the manner in which possession has been
    used by courts in connection with this branch of the law.

13

O W N E R S H I P

1. HONORÉ, A.M. "Ownership" in Oxford Essays in Jurisprudence,
    (ed. A.G. Guest, Oxford University Press, 1961), chap. 5:
    ownership of a standard type is considered, its incidents,
    the nature of the thing owned, title and split ownership.

2. TURNER, J.W.C. "Some Reflections on Ownership in English Law"
    (1941), 19 Can. B.R., 342: this article begins with a brief
    examination of the way in which different writers have used
    the word "ownership" and of its history. The conclusion is
    that the characteristic feature of ownership is its
    enduring quality.

3. SALMOND, J.W. Jurisprudence, (7th ed., Sweet & Maxwell, Ltd.,
    1924), chap. 12: this edition contains the classic dis-
    cussion by Salmond himself. For versions modified by sub-
    sequent editors, see 11th. edition, G.L. Williams, chap. 12,
    especially p. 303, note (c), in which the main criticism of
    Salmond's analysis are considered. For G.L. Williams's own
    criticism see also "Language and the Law" (1945), 61 L.Q.R.,
    at p. 386, where the point is made that the ownership is
    used in different senses. 12th edition, P.J. Fitzgerald,
    (1966), chap. 8, in which Salmond's original treatment is
    considerably modified.

4. COOK, W.W. "Hohfeld's Contribution to the Science of Law" in
    W.N. Hohfeld, Fundamental Legal Conceptions as Applied in
    Judicial Reasoning, (ed. W.W. Cook, Yale University Press,
    1923), pp. 11-15: Salmond's analysis is criticised for its
    failure to distinguish between claims, etc.

5. COOK, W.W. "The Utility of Jurisprudence in the Solution of
    Legal Topics" in Lectures on Legal Topics, (The Macmillan
    Co., New York, 1928), pp. 338-358: this is an analysis of
    ownership with the aid of the Hohfeldian table into a
    multitude of claims, etc.

6. KOCOUREK, A. Jural Relations, (2nd ed., The Bobbs-Merrill
    Co., 1928), chap. 18: the concept of "thing" is analysed in
    detail. "Ownership" is examined both as a jural relation
    and as an infra-jural relation. The conclusion is that it
    is an infra-jural relation between a person and a thing-
    element.

7. ROSS, A. "Tu-Tu" (1956-57), 70 Harv. L.R., 812: the lessons
    to be drawn from the analysis of a taboo word are applied
    to terms like "ownership". This word, it is said, has no
    semantic reference and is only a technique of
    presentation.

1. SIMPSON, A.W.B. "The Analysis of Legal Concepts", (1964), 80
   L.Q.R., 535, 551: Ross's thesis is criticised. Concepts
   are useful. The fact that a word has no semantic reference,
   i.e., that the "thing" does not exist, does not imply that
   the word has no meaning.

2. HARGREAVES, A.D. An Introduction to the Principles of Land
   Law, (4th ed., G.A. Grove and J.F. Garner, Sweet & Maxwell,
   Ltd., 1963), chap. 6: this is probably the clearest and
   most convenient historical account. There is a comparison
   of the English and Roman Law as to the concept of absolute
   ownership. Emphasis is placed on the historical need to
   conceive of interests in land as "things".

3. POLLOCK, F. and MAITLAND, F.W. The History of English Law
   before the Time of Edward I, (2nd ed., with an Introduction
   by S.F.C. Milsom, Cambridge University Press, 1968), II,
   chap. 4, SS. 2, 6-7: this is an incomparable survey of the
   development of the idea of ownership in land and chattels
   through the remedies that were available.

4. HOLDSWORTH, W.S. A History of English Law, (Methuen & Co.,
   Ltd.), III, chap. 1, SS. 5-7; VII, chaps. 1, SS. 1-2;
   2, SS. 1-2: this is a detailed historical account of the
   shaping of the idea of ownership in land and chattels.

5. LIGHTWOOD, J.M. A Treatise on Possession of Land, (Stevens &
   Sons, Ltd., 1894), chaps. 5 and 6: this remains as one of
   the best accounts of the development in land law. It is
   enriched by fruitful comparisons with Roman law.

6. HARGREAVES, A.D. "Terminology and Title in Ejectment" (1940),
   56 L.Q.R., 376: a careful argument is presented to the
   effect that English law still knows no absolute ownership,
   but only relatively of title. (See also A.D. Hargreaves,
   "Modern Real Property" (1956), 19 M.L.R., 14, especially,
   pp. 16 et seq.).

7. HOLDSWORTH, W.S. "Terminology and Title in Ejectment - a
   Reply" (1940), 56 L.Q.R., 479: in reply to A.D. Hargreaves
   it is argued that English law does recognise an absolute
   ownership.

8. CHESHIRE, G.C. The Modern Law of Real Property, (10th ed.,
   Butterworths, 1967), pp. 27-39: this explains the nature
   of the title in land with reference to the doctrine of
   estates and the remedies.

9. MEGARRY, R.E. and WADE, H.W.R. The Law of Real Property,
   (3rd ed., Stevens & Sons, Ltd., 1966), pp. 996-1002:

this also is an explanation of the nature of title in land
with reference to the effect of limitation.

1. DENMAN, D.R. Origins of Ownership, (Allen & Unwin, Ltd.,
    1958): in this study the evolution of ownership in land
    is traced in detail. It might be consulted for the
    background.

2. THAYER, A.S. "Possession and Ownership", (1907), 23 L.Q.R.,
    175, 314: possession and ownership are investigated with
    with reference to Roman and English law. In the latter
    part he discusses the relativity of ownership in English
    law.

3. KIRALFY, A.K.R. "The Problem of a Law of Property in Goods",
    (1949), 12 M.L.R., 424: the evolution of ownership in
    chattels is dealt with. There are signs now of the recog-
    nition of an absolute ownership in them.

4. NOYES, C.R. The Institution of Property, (Humphrey Milford,
    1936): this work may be used for reference. It examines the
    nature of property and ownership in Roman law and its evol-
    ution in English feudal law. The modern structure is
    analysed.

5. BENTHAM, J. Works, (ed. J. Bowring, William Tait, 1843), I,
    pp. 308-9: property is the creation of law; it is the
    foundation of the expectation of deriving certain advant-
    ages from the thing said to be possessed.

6. AUSTIN, J. Lectures on Jurisprudence, (5th ed., R. Campbell,
    John Murray, 1885), II, pp. 774-783, 789-802: things and
    ownership are considered in a general way. He also con-
    siders what he calls "modes of property", which include
    life interests.

7. TERRY, H.T. Some Leading Principles of Anglo-American Law
    Expounded with a View to its Arrangement and Codification,
    (T & J.W. Johnson & Co., Philadelphia, 1884), SS. 45-47:
    this is chiefly an examination of "thing", drawing atten-
    tion to some of the analytical difficulties.

8. CROSSLEY VAINES, J. Personal Property, (4th ed., Butterworths,
    1967), chap. 4: attention is drawn to the distinction
    between ownership of real and personal property.

9. KEETON, G.W. The Elementary Principles of Jurisprudence, (2nd
    ed., Sir Isaac Pitman & Sons, Ltd., 1949), chap. 14: this
    contains a general discussion of co-ownership and of legal
    and equitable ownership.

1. PATON, G.W. A Text-Book of Jurisprudence, (3rd ed.,
   D.P. Derham, Oxford, 1964), chap. 21: there is a useful
   discussion of the concept of thing and of ownership.

2. POUND, R. Jurisprudence, (West Publishing Co., 1959), V,
   chap. 30: ownership is dealt with in detail. The limitations
   imposed upon its component liberties and powers have always
   existed; it is the emphasis that has varied.

3. HOLLAND, T.E. The Elements of Jurisprudence, (13th ed.,
   Oxford, 1924), pp. 101-107, 208-216: in the earlier part
   things are discussed and classified; the latter part is a
   general discussion of ownership.

4. MARKBY, W. Elements of Law, (6th ed., Oxford, 1905), chap. 8:
   he appears to subscribe to the "residuary right" view of
   ownership. He does not define ownership, but owner. A
   discussion of the peculiar English doctrine of estates is
   included.

5. HEARN, W.E. The Theory of Legal Duties and Rights, (John
   Ferres, Melbourne; Trubner & Co., London, 1883), chap. 10,
   S. 1: ownership is a collective term for an aggregate of
   "rights". These are generally described.

6. POLLOCK, F. A First Book of Jurisprudence, (6th ed.,
   Macmillan & Co., Ltd.), Part I, chaps. 6-7: the first
   chapter is concerned with "thing", (see also "What is a
   'Thing'?" (1894), 10 L.Q.R. 318); the latter part of the
   second chapter deals with ownership. This described it in
   terms of the residue of the privileges of use and powers of
   disposal allowed by law.

7. VINDING KRUSE, L.F. The Right of Property, (Oxford University
   Press, I (trans. P.T. Federspiel, 1939), II (trans.
   D. Philip, 1953): this is of general interest. The first
   volume, which deals with types and objects of property is
   of greater relevance than the second, which is a detailed
   account of the transfer of property. Of particular interest
   are the analysis of thing (p. 121), real and personal
   rights (p. 124) and the limitations of property (p. 165).

8. WILSON, G.P. "Jurisprudence and the Discussion of Ownership"
   (1957), C.L.J. 216: it is suggested that ownership should be
   considered in the context of the use of things.

9. For some of the difficulties and doubts concerning the concept
   of thing, the following might be consulted: H.W. ELPHINSTONE:
   "What is a Chose in Action?" (1893), 9 L.Q.R. 311; C. SWEET:
   "Choses in Action" (1894), 10 L.Q.R. 303, (on the whole

agreeing with Elphinstone); S. BROADHURST: "Is Copyright a
Chose in Action?" (1895), 11 L.Q.R. 64; T.C. WILLIAMS:
"Property, Things in Action and Copyright", ibid, 223
(replying to Broadhurst); C. SWEET: "Choses in Action,"
ibid, 238. (See also F. Pollock, supra).

1. CAMPBELL, A.H. "Some Footnotes to Salmond's Jurisprudence"
   (1940), 7 C.L.J. 206, at pp. 217-220: there are observations
   on trust and beneficial ownership and legal and equitable
   ownership, and also critical comments on Salmond's thesis
   as to ownership.

2. SCOTT, A.W. The Law of Trusts, (3rd ed., Little, Brown & Co.,
   1967), SS. 1, 130: it is argued that under the guise of
   enforcing personal rights the Chancellors evolved a new
   property interest, a form of equitable ownership. The
   beneficiary's interest is treated as an equitable estate in
   land.

3. SCOTT, A.W. "The Nature of the Rights of the Cestui Que Trust",
   (1917), 17 Col.L.R., 269: the nature of the beneficiary's
   interest in the trust property is discussed and the views
   of various writers are considered. The conclusion is that
   it is an interest in the property, a kind of ownership.

4. WILLIAMS, G.L. "Interests and Clogs" (1952), 30 Can.B.R. 1004:
   what is meant by an "interest in property" is considered.
   This does not deal directly with the benficiary's interest
   in trust property but the discussion is useful for the
   light it throws on this matter.

5. LATHAM, V. "The Right of the Beneficiary to Specific Items
   of the Trust Funds" (1954), 32 Can.B.R. 520: this is an
   important discussion as to how far the benficiary "owns"
   the subject-matter of the trust. Attention is drawn to
   the demands of justice and convenience in resolving this
   question in different situations.

6. STONE, H.F. "The Nature of the Rights of the Cestui Que
   Trust" (1917), 17 Col.L.R. 467: this is in reply to
   A.W. Scott (supra). The beneficiary has only personal
   rights against the trustee and no proprietary rights in
   the res.

7. HART, W.G. "What is a Trust?" (1899), 15 L.Q.R. 294: towards
   the end of this article useful observations are made on
   the nature of "trust ownership".

8. HART, W.G. "The Place of Trust in Jurisprudence" (1912), 28
   L.Q.R. 290: after a discussion of the various views as to

whether trusts create real or personal right, the conclusion
is drawn that they are personal.

1. MAITLAND, F.W. <u>Equity</u>, (ed. J.W. Brunyate, Cambridge
   University Press, 1936), pp. 17, 29-32, 106-152: he denied
   that law and equity were in conflict and that the
   beneficiary was not the owner of the trust property because
   the trustee was. Equitable rights are <u>in personam</u> with a
   resemblance to rights <u>in rem</u>.

2. LANGDELL, C.C. <u>A Brief Survey of Equity Jurisdiction</u>, (2nd
   ed., The Harvard Law Review Association, 1908), chap. 1:
   equitable rights are <u>in personam</u>.

3. WINFIELD, P.H. <u>The Province of the Law of Tort</u>, (Cambridge
   University Press, 1931), pp. 109-112: the beneficiary's
   right is considered and the views of the chief protagonists
   are mentioned. He thinks the right is <u>in rem</u>.

4. HANBURY, H.G. "The Field of Modern Equity" (1929), 45 L.Q.R.
   196, 197-199: equitable rights and interests are hybrids
   standing mid-way between rights <u>in rem</u> and <u>in peronam</u>.
   See also <u>Modern Equity</u>, (8th ed., Stevens & Sons, Ltd.,
   1962), pp. <u>446 et seq</u>.

5. SWAN, K.R. "Patent Rights in an Employee's Invention" (1959),
   75 L.Q.R. 77: this is of general interest. It deals with the
   ownership of inventions and considers the position as
   between employer and employee.

6. WIREN, S.A. "The Plea of the <u>Jus Tertii</u> in Ejectment" (1925),
   41 L.Q.R. 139: this contains a full examination of the
   authorities as at that date.

7. ATIYAH, P.S. "A Re-examination of the <u>Jus Tertii</u> in
   Conversion" (1955), 18 M.L.R. 97: this is a critical account
   of the general accepted view. The article is indirectly
   relevant on the question whether absolute ownership in
   chattels is recognised or not.

8. JOLLY, A. "The <u>Jus Tertii</u> and the Third Man" (1955), 18 M.L.R.
   371: a reply to P.S. Atiyah and throws light on the right
   to obtain possession as constituting ownership.

9. BUCKLAND, W.W. <u>A Text-Book of Roman Law from Augustus to
   Justinian</u>, (3rd ed., P. Stein, Cambridge University Press,
   1963), pp. 186-189: this is a brief description of <u>dominium</u>
   in Roman Law, which might be contrasted with the idea of
   ownership in English law.

1. ALLOTT, A.N. "Towards a Definition of 'Absolute Ownership'"
   (1961), J.A.L. 99: this is of general interest, especially
   the suggested final definition. The problem is considered
   mainly with reference to African land law. See also
   S.R. SIMPSON: "Towards a Definition of 'Absolute Ownership'
   II", ibid, p. 145: this criticises the need for a definition
   and the definition itself; A.N. Allott's reply, ibid, p.
   148.

2. VINOGRADOFF, P. Outlines of Historical Jurisprudence, (Oxford
   University Press, 1922), II, chap. 10; this considers the
   extent to which and the basis on which things are
   attributed to persons. It varies in different systems
   according to the social order. This thesis is developed
   mainly with reference to Greek law.

3. MALINOWSKI, B. Crime and Custom in Savage Society, (Kegan
   Paul, Trench, Trubner & Co., Ltd., 1926), chap. 2: this is
   of general interest. It deals with ownership among the
   Tobriand islanders. Ownership carried distinct obligations.

4. LOWIE, R.H. "Incorporeal Property in Primitive Society"
   (1927-28), 37 Yale L.J. 551: this is also of general
   interest. It deals with the extent to which ownership was
   recognised in primitive societies. There is a form of
   communism up to a point (ownership of necessaries), but
   private ownership of incorporeal property (spells and
   incantations).

5. LLOYD, D. The Idea of Law, (Penguin Books, Ltd., A 688, 1964),
   pp. 319-25: the difficulties of comprehending the nature
   of ownership are indicated with reference to the ownership
   of "property", of "rights" and of "things".

Ownership in relation to society

6. COHEN, M.R. "Property and Sovereignty" in Law and the Social
   Order, (Harcourt, Brace & Co., New York, 1933), 41:
   property and sovereignty are now distinguished, but early
   law makes no such distinction. This is because ownership
   of land meant political power. Property as power, the
   justifications of property and limitations on property
   rights are dealt with.

7. PHILBRICK, F.S. "Changing Conceptions of Property in Law"
   (1938), 86 U.Pa.L.R. 691: the distinction is drawn between
   property for use, which is held for consumption, and
   property for power, which is available for alienation.
   These two ideas are developed in some detail.

1. ELY, R.T. <u>Property and Contract in their Relation to the</u>
   <u>Distribution of Wealth,</u> (The Macmillan Co., New York, 1914)
   I, Book I, chap. 3, 5: property, private property, public
   property are defined and discussed with reference to their
   individual and social aspects.

2. HALLOWELL, A.I. "The Nature and Function of Property as a
   Social Institution", (1943), 1 J.L. Pol. S., 115: property
   implies not only rights and duties but also specific social
   sanctions. The core of property as a social institution
   lies in a complex system of recognised rights and duties
   with reference to the control of valuable objects.

3. HARDING, R.W. "The Evolution of Roman Catholic Views of
   Private Property as a Natural Right" (1963), 2 Sol. Q. 124:
   it is alleged that Thomas Aquinas did not regard private
   property as a natural right, but as a right which natural
   law permitted and condoned. It derives its strength from
   convenience, not principle. Common ownership, however, was
   the natural right. The change in doctrine to the effect
   that private ownership is a natural right is a subsequent
   development ascribed to Papal interpretation.

4. BRODERICK, A. "The Radical Middle: The Natural Right of
   Property in Aquinas and the Popes", (1964), 3 Sol. Q. 127:
   R.W. Harding's thesis is refuted. For Aquinas private
   property is a natural right. When human reason, reflecting
   upon experience, perceives that general benefit would not
   best be achieved by common property, then private property
   comes into being. Hence, in so far as private property
   rests on a judgment of the consequences by human reason,
   it is a natural right. On this basis later Papal
   Encyclicals are examined so as to show that they did not
   discard Aquinas's doctrine of common property and substitute an absolutist doctrine.

5. BERLE, A.A. and MEANS, G.C. <u>The Modern Corporation and</u>
   <u>Private Property,</u> (The Macmillan Co., New York, 1939),
   Books I and II: this discusses corporate ownership and how
   this has brought about the divorce between ownership and
   control.

6. JONES, J.W. "Forms of Ownership", (1947-48), 22 Tul. L.R.,
   82: the most important part of this article for present
   purposes is the discussion of the "control" theory of ownership and "value" theory which seeks to protect as many
   interests as possible from expropriation.

7. FRIEDMANN, W. <u>Law in a Changing Society,</u> (Stevens & Sons,
   Ltd., 1959), chap. 3: this discusses the part played by

property in society, with mention of the concept of the trust and estates and shows how a functional and elastic concept has developed. The changes brought about by corporate enterprise are also touched on. (This is a revised version of Law and Social Change in Contemporary Britain, (Stevens & Sons, Ltd., 1951, chap. 2).

1. COHEN, M.R. and COHEN, F.S. Readings in Jurisprudence and Legal Philosophy, (Prentice-Hall Inc., New York, 1951), chap. 1: extracts from a number of writers, ancient and modern, are given, including a number already referred to above. This is a most useful compilation.

2. STONE, J. Social Dimensions of Law and Justice, (Stevens & Sons, Ltd., 1966), pp. 243-254: ownership is considered with reference to the prevailing social and economic order according to which the law protects interests in property. The sociological implications of philosophic theories of property are also dealt with.

3. RENNER, K. The Institution of Private Law and their Social Functions, (trans. A. Schwarzschild, ed. O. Kahn-Freund, Routledge & Kegan Paul, Ltd., 1949): this classic analysis is mainly concerned with showing how the owner-producer has been replaced by the capitalist employer and labouring employee. The editor's Introduction should also be read in which attention is drawn to certain developments which have taken place since Renner wrote. (See W. FRIEDMANN: Legal Theory, 5th ed., Stevens & Sons, Ltd., 1967, pp.368-373, for a summary of Renner's thesis).

4. HAZARD, J.N. Law and Social Change in the U.S.S.R., (Stevens & Sons, Ltd., 1953), chap. 1: property is the key to power, and ownership is an instrument of social change. An account of nationisation in Russia is given.

5. GSOVSKI, V. Soviet Civil Law, (Ann Arbor, University of Michigan Law School, 1948), I, chap. 16: the nature of ownership in Russia is explained. Within the limits of the law, the owner has the right to possess, liberty to use and power to dispose. An account is also given of "personal ownership", which is said to differ from private ownership in capitalist countries.

6. The Law of the Soviet State, (ed. A.Y. Vyshinski, trans. H.W. Babb, The Macmillan Co., New York, 1948), chap. 3, S. 5: this considers the economic basis of the Soviet order. It explains in an entirely partial manner the progress of the U.S.S.R. towards nationalising means of production and the two forms of socialist property, state property and property

of the co-operative societies, on the one hand, and private property on the other.

1. SCAMMELL, E.H. "Nationalisation in Legal Perspective", (1952), 5 C.L.P., 30: the question of national ownership is considered with reference to commercial undertakings and services, the common features of difficult cases and their implications.

2. JEWKES, J. "The Nationalisation of Industry", (1953), 20 U.C. L.R., 615: this discusses the pros and cons of nationalisation in Britain with reference to its efficiency in raising the standard of living. The conclusion is that nationalisation has proved barren.

3. HANSON, A.H. Parliament and Public Ownership, (Cassell & Co., Ltd., 1961): the question of the nature and extent of Parliamentary control over nationalised industries is considered. It provides useful general reading.

4. Nationalisation. A Book of Readings, (ed A.H. Hanson, Allen & Unwin, Ltd., 1963): the editor's "Introduction" gives a brief, general idea of the why and the how of nationalisation. The extracts give detailed analyses of particular aspects.

14

P O S I T I V I S M.

T H E   A U S T I N I A N   T H E O R Y   O F   L A W

Positivism

1. AGO, R. "Positive Law and International Law", (trans. J.A. Hammond, 1957), 51 A.J.I.L., 691: the development of the idea of positive law from medieval times is traced. Originally it denoted law resulting from some creative act as opposed to natural law; then such law was treated as the only "valid" law; more recently there have been further changes. The value of positivism and its weakness are indicated.

2. HART, H.L.A. "Analytical Jurisprudence in Mid-twentieth Century: a Reply to Professor Bodenheimer" (1956-57), 105 U. Pa. L.R., 953: certain misunderstandings about positivism are corrected. A distinction is drawn between law and legal concepts, on the one hand, and between theories of law and definitions of concepts. It is incorrect to say that analytical jurisprudence needs no assistance from other disciplines.

3. HART, H.L.A. "Positivism and the Separation of Law and Morals" (1957-58), 71 Harv. L.R., 593: this is a modernistic defence of the separation of the "is" and the "ought". It is also important in clarifying what it is that positivists maintain as distinct from what they have been supposed to maintain. See also L.L. FULLER, "Positivism and Fidelity to Law - A Reply to Professor Hart", ibid., p. 630: which challenges Hart's thesis.

4. DICKERSON, F.R. "Statutory Interpretation: Core Meaning and Marginal Uncertainty", (1964), 29 Miss. L.R., 1: Hart seeks to find the "is" of law in the inner core of meaning which most words possess. Fuller rejects this, arguing that context purpose (i.e., considerations of "ought") determine meaning in each given instance. In this study the author reconciles this apparent conflict by showing the importance of both and how they are interrelated.

5. MORISON, W.L. "Some Myths about Positivism", (1959-60), 68 Yale L.J., 212: this also dispels some of the misconceptions that have gathered round Austin's contribution to jurisprudence, and presents his work afresh.

6. KOCOUREK, A. "The Century of Analytical Jurisprudence since John Austin" in Law: A Century of Progress, (New York University Press, 1937), II, 194: the meaning of "analytical

jurisprudence" is first considered; then the work of Austin
and others in the analytical field; and finally the
contribution as a whole is appraised.

1. KESSLER, F. "Theoretic Bases of Law" (1941-42), 9 U.C.L.R. 98,
   at pp. 105-8: positivism is regarded as being the necessary
   opponent of natural law. It would be wrong to assume that
   considerations of justice have no part in it, for justice
   lies in security and the ending of disorder. The
   contribution and defects of positivism are briefly reviewed.

2. KESSLER, F. "Natural Law, Justice and Democracy - Some
   Reflections on Three types of Thinking about Law and
   Justice" (1944-45), 19 Tul.L.R. 32, at pp. 39-54: positivism
   is reviewed and explained. The element of justice in it,
   namely, the care of security, is further developed. Its
   weaknesses are also pointed out.

3. FULLER, L.L. Law in Quest of Itself, (The Foundation Press,
   Inc., 1940): the controversy between the naturalists and
   positivists is critically considered. The separation of
   the "is" and the "ought" is subjected to especial
   condemnation as narrow and misleading. In no legal activity
   can "ought" be avoided.

4. STUMPF, S.E. "Austin's Theory of the Separation of Law and
   Morals" (1960-61), 14 Vand.L.R. 117: an explanation is
   given of the evolution of the separation of law from morals
   and of Austin's distinction between what the law is and
   whether it is good or bad. It is said that the very concept
   of law is meaningless until the nature of Man is brought
   into consideration; and it is alleged that Austin himself
   contemplated implicitly the moral characteristics of law
   and sovereignty.

5. COHEN, M.R. "Positivism and the Limits of Idealism in the
   Law" (1927), 27 Col.L.R. 236: positivism is itself an ideal.
   The notion that law is a complete and closed system is
   false. But, on the other hand, it is necessary to distinguish
   distinguish between the law that is and the law that ought
   to be. The two are inseparable, but never completely
   identified.

6. LASERSON, M.M. "'Positive' and 'Natural Law' and their
   Correlation" in Interpretation of Modern Legal Philosophies,
   (ed. P. Sayre, Oxford University Press, New York, 1947),
   chap. 20: this is a complicated statement of a simple
   theme, viz., the lag between positive law and natural law.

7. HALL, J. "Concerning the Nature of Positive Law" (1948-49),

58 Yale L.J. 545: a full understanding of positive law
depends upon a sound understanding of history. Modern
positivism seems to be largely a restatement of ancient
viewpoints, including the exclusion of morality as
''ideology''. But a sharp separation between law and ethics
is untrue, inadequate and misleading.

1. BRECHT, A. "The Myth of Is and Ought" (1940-41), 54 Harv.L.R.
    811: the history and the logic behind the separation of the
    ''is'' and ''ought'' is examined. The gulf between them is not
    unbridgable, for it is said that the feeling that something
    ought to be is a part of human equipment.

2. SHKLAR, J.N. Legalism, (Harvard University Press, 1964):
    ''legalism'' is the attitude of mind that makes a morality
    out of rule following. Both Positivist and Naturalist legal
    theorists are of this way of thinking. But rule morality
    is only one among many in a pluralist society. To make it
    exclusive is to constrict one's outlook. The Positivist
    insistence on a separation between the ''is'' and t!.e ''ought''
    is an ideology. The book is a sharp attack on Positivism
    Naturalism.

3. POUND, R. "The Scope and Purpose of Sociological Jurisprudence"
    (1910-11), 24 Harv.L.R. 591, at pp. 594-98: the principal
    features of analytical jurisprudence are set out as well
    as the objections to it from a sociological point of view.

4. POUND, R. "The Progress of the Law" (1927-28), 41 Harv.L.R.
    174: analytical jurisprudence on the Continent is reviewed
    during the years 1914-1927. It includes a certain amount of
    restatement of the original Austinian position.

5. POUND, R. "Fifty Years of Jurisprudence" (1936-37), 50 Harv.
    L.R. 557, at pp. 564-82: the revival of analytical
    jurisprudence in the 19th century and the work of
    Continental and of Anglo-American analytists is reviewed.

6. POUND, R. "Classification of Law" (1923-24), 37 Harv.L.R.
    933, at pp. 945-51: the part played by analytical and
    historical theories in the matter of classification is
    considered.

7. BRYCE, J. "Studies in History and Jurisprudence", (Oxford,
    1901), II, pp. 178-84: this is a critical appraisal of the
    Bentham-Austin approach.

8. AMOS, M.S. "Some Reflection on the Philosophy of Law" (1927),
    3 C.L.J. 31: On Austin's work it is maintained that the
    path of advancement is to be found in his tradition. It is

useful to be able to regard law as a logical edifice of axioms.

1. BODENHEIMER, E. Jurisprudence, (Harvard University Press, 1962), pp. 89-93: the origins of positivism and what it contends are explained. Attention is drawn to the emphasis that was placed on tested or verifiable data.

2. FRIEDMAN, W. Legal Theory, (5th ed., Stevens & Sons, Ltd., 1967), chap. 21: this contains a brief explanation of the evolution and chief contentions of positivism.

3. LLOYD, D. The Idea of Law, (Penguin Books, Ltd., A. 688, 1964), chap. 5: the impetus for positivism came with the Renaissance. The distinction between the "is" and the "ought", and Bentham's separation of law as it is from law as it ought to be are explained. Austin was concerned with the scientific exposition of the fundamental notions which provide the framework of a system. This gave rise to conceptual analysis, the limitations of which are indicated.

4. LOCKE, J. An Essay on Human Understanding, (33rd ed., William Tegg, 1862): this is of general interest; it constitutes one of the principal challenges of the a priorism of natural law theories and, as such, might be regarded as providing a foundation for positivism.

5. HUME, D. A Treatise on Human Nature in The Philosophical Works of David Hume, (edd. T.H. Green and T.H. Grose, Longmans, Green & Co., 1874), I: this is also of general interest; it constitutes the most formidable attack on the prevailing ideas and inspired the positivist attitude of mind. A cardinal tenet is that an "ought" cannot be derived from an "is". (His Inquiry concerning Human Understanding is essentially an abridgement of the present work).

6. STERN, K. "Either-Or or Neither-Nor" in Law and Philosophy. A Symposium. (ed. S. Hook. New York University Press, 1964), p. 247: on Hume's thesis that an "ought' cannot be derived from an "is" the author suggests that there may be some types of statements which are neither normative nor descriptive. In these cases it might be possible to derive a normative conclusion from non-normative premises.

7. COMTE, A. The Positive Philosophy, (trans. H. Martineau, Bell & Sons, 1896), I, chap. 1: the nature and methods of a positive philosophy are explained. Comte regarded positivism as the third stage in the development of thinking, representing the turning away from the resort to ultimate principles.

The Imperative theory of law

1. BENTHAM, J. The Limits of Jurisprudence Defined, (ed.
   C.W. Everett, Columbia University Press, 1945): this is a
   pioneer and powerful exposition of analytical jurisprudence,
   but all the time law is made to serve certain ends.
   Particularly noteworthy are Bentham's ideas as to
   sovereignty and command and the hitherto unsuspected extent
   of his influence on Austin.

2. AUSTIN, J. Lectures on Jurisprudence, (5th ed., R. Campbell,
   John Murray, 1885), I, chaps. 1-6: the nature of law and
   sovereignty need to be clarified before embarking upon a
   study of the leading notions of law, which to Austin was
   jurisprudence. The idea of law, strictly so called, as the
   command of a sovereign supported by sanction is developed
   in detail.

3. AUSTIN, J. The Province of Jurisprudence Determined and the
   Uses of the Study of Jurisprudence, (ed. H.L.A. Hart,
   Weidenfeld and Nicholson, 1954): this contains the first
   six lectures on law and sovereignty. In the Introduction
   Hart summarises Austin's thesis and the criticisms of Bryce
   and Maine. He also alludes to Austin's failure to take
   account of the notion of a rule (see further H.L.A. Hart,
   The Concept of Law, infra).

4. HOBBES, T. A Dialogue between a Philosopher and a Student of
   the Common Laws of England in The English Works of Thomas
   Hobbes, (ed. W. Molesworth, John Bohn, 1840), vol. 6:
   Hobbes refutes Coke's thesis that law is "artificial
   reason" and says it is simple "natural reason", and that it
   is constituted as "law" by the command of the sovereign. A
   judgment is "law" only between the parties, so he would
   reject the law-constitutive force of precedent. Custom is
   not "law" of its own.

5. HALE, M. "Sir Matthew Hale on Hobbes: an Unpublished
   Manuscript", first published by F. Pollock and
   W.S. Holdsworth in (1921), 37 L.Q.R. 274; also in
   W.S. Holdsworth, History of English Law, (Methuen & Co.,
   Ltd., 1945), V, Appendix III: Hale challenges Hobbes's
   thesis that the basis of laws is sovereign authority, as
   well as Coke's thesis that it is "artificial reason". Law,
   says Hale, is a socio-historical product. Also, sovereign
   powers accrue to the sovereign by certain laws of the
   kingdom and, as such, there are certain inherent qualifi-
   cations of these powers.

6. MILL, J.S. "Austin on Jurisprudence" in Dissertations and

Discussions, (Longmans, Green, Reader and Dyer, 1868), III,
p. 206: this is a lengthy review of Austin's theory of law
and his analysis of legal concepts. It is particularly
interesting as being the comments of one of Austin's most
famous pupils.

1. STEPHEN, L. The English Utilitarians, (Duckworth & Co., 1900),
    III, pp. 317-36: the work of Austin as the inheritor of the
    utilitarian tradition is assessed.

2. SCHWARZ, A.B. "John Austin and the German Jurisprudence of
    his Time", (1934-35), 1 Politica, 178: the nature and
    extent of the German influence on Austin is assessed in
    detail. There is also a brief review of his influence on
    Continental writers.

3. HOLDSWORTH, W.S. Some Makers of English Law, (Cambridge
    University Press, 1938), pp. 248-64: a useful account is
    given of Bentham and Austin, which might be read as a
    general background to their work.

4. DILLON, J.F. The Laws and Jurisprudence of England and
    America, (Macmillan & Co., 1894), chaps. 11 and 12: the
    work of Bentham is appraised (but this was before the
    discovery and publication in 1945 of The Limits of
    Jurisprudence Defined). Reference might also be made to
    chapter 1 where there is a brief consideration of the
    Austinian definition of law.

5. EASTWOOD, R.A. and KEETON, G.W. The Austinian Theories of
    Law and Sovereignty, (Methuen & Co., Ltd., 1929): this
    short book is one of the best simplified restatements of
    the Austinian position. The doctrine of sovereignty, in
    particular, is dealt with in some detail and is traced out
    historically.

6. BROWN, W.J. The Austinian Theory of Law, (John Murray, 1906),
    chaps. 1, 2, 3, 5, Excursus B, E: the chapters reproduce
    the Austinian text in an abridged form with occasional
    notes. Excursus B deals with sovereignty. The distinction
    between "legal" and "political" sovereignty is examined.
    In Excursus E various objections to the conception of
    positive law as the command of the state are considered.

7. HEARNSHAW, F.J.C. The Social and Political Ideas of some
    Representative Thinkers of the Age of Reaction and
    Reconstruction, (ed., F.J.C. Hearnshaw, Harrap & Co., Ltd.,
    1932), chap. 9: the life and work of Austin is portrayed
    against the background of social conditions and ideas. His
    theories of law and sovereignty are outlined with

particularly critical comments on the latter.

1. MANNING, C.A.W. "Austin Today: or 'The Province of
    Jurisprudence' Re-examined" in Modern Theories of Law,
    (ed. W.I. Jennings, Oxford University Press, 1933), chap.
    10: this is a re-interpretation of the Austinian theory
    so as to make it adaptable to modern society. What it says
    is therefore not necessarily what Austin himself said.

2. OLIVECRONA, K. Law as Fact, (Einar Munksgaard, Copenhagen;
    Humphrey Milford, 1939; reprinted by Wildy & Sons, 1962),
    chap. 1: the nature of a rule of law is considered. There
    is a convincing demolition of the command theory and an
    explanation of the imperative form in which rules are
    expressed.

3. HART, H.L.A. The Concept of Law, (Oxford, 1961), chaps. 2-4
    and 10: Austin's concept of law is reconstructed afresh to
    demonstrate its weaknesses, which are developed at length.
    In chapter 10 the similarities and differences between
    municipal and international law are considered.

4. KELSEN, H. General Theory of Law and State, (trans. A. Wedberg,
    Harvard University Press, 1949), pp. 30-37: in the general
    context of developing a "pure" theory of law, the command
    theory is rejected as introducing an "impure" (psychological)
    element. The "will" of a legislator breaks down on analysis.

5. CLARK, E.C. Practical Jurisprudence, (Cambridge University
    Press, 1883), Part I: this is an interesting and wide-
    ranging discussion of the notion of law centred on Austin.
    The derivation of the word and its synonyms in other
    languages are considered and is shown to connote that which
    is fitting or proper, not what is commanded.

6. WILLIAMS, G.L. "International Law and the Controversy
    Concerning the Word 'Law'" in Philosophy, Politics and
    Society, (ed. P. Laslett, Blackwell, Oxford, 1956), chap.
    9: much of the dispute between the Austinians and the
    International lawyers as to whether International Law is
    "properly" called "law" is exposed as verbal.

7. HARRISON, F. On Jurisprudence and the Conflict of Law,
    (Oxford, 1919), chap. 2 and Annotations by A.H.F. Lefroy,
    II-III: Austin's view is said to be appropriate only to
    lawyers. It concentrates on force, not on regularity which
    is also implied in the word "law". The nature of enabling
    laws and laws relating to construction and procedure as
    well as rules are considered.

1. CROSS, A, R.N. Precedent in English Law, (2nd ed., Oxford,
    1968), pp. 199-201: Austin's theory is considered with
    reference to judicial precedent. His idea of "tacit command"
    is examined and rejected.

2. GRAY, J.C. The Nature and Sources of the Law, (2nd ed.,
    R. Gray, The Macmillan Co., New York, 1921), pp. 85-89: the
    command theory is critically reviewed. In particular, the
    weakness is indicated of saying that one commands things
    to be done when one has power (which is not exercised) of
    forbidding them to be done.

3. GRAY, J.C. "Some Definitions and Questions in Jurisprudence"
    (1892-93), 6 Harv.L.R. 21, at pp. 25-27: the law does not
    comprise all the sovereign's commands, for there are
    commands, which are not law. On the other hand, law
    includes much that are not sovereign commands.

4. VINOGRADOFF, P. Common-sense in Law, (3rd ed., H.G. Hanbury,
    Oxford University Press, 1959), chap. 2: the command theory
    is rejected as being inadequate from a historical point of
    view. Law depends, not on enforcement, but ultimately on
    recognition.

5. VINOGRADOFF, P. Outlines of Historical Jurisprudence, (Oxford
    University Press, 1920), I, pp. 115-23: Austin's
    contribution is critically examined. The separation between
    law and positive morality is condemned, and the emphasis
    on sanction is regarded as misleading. The difficulties of
    Austin's theory of sovereignty with reference to the United
    States of America are pointed out.

6. POUND, R. Jurisprudence, (West Publishing Co., 1959), II,
    pp. 68-79, 132-163: in the first section the progress of
    the analytical movement in England is recounted. In the
    second section the doctrines are considered, beginning with
    the views of Austin and then of his successors.

7. STONE, J. Legal System and Lawyers' Reasonings (Stevens &
    Sons, Ltd., 1964), chap. 2: Austin's system is not a
    literal representation of any particular legal order; it
    gives a hypothetical order. It is an apparatus for seeing
    the degree of logical consistency within a given order and
    not a representation of the law itself. There is, therefore,
    a gap between his hypothetical system and an actual system.
    Austin underestimated this gap. Consistently with this, it
    is said that Austin's use of "sovereignty", "command" etc.
    is not descriptive, as with Hobbes and Bodin. Logical
    coherence is best seen if a legal order is arranged as if
    its propositions were commands of a sovereign.

1. JONES, J.W. Historical Introduction to the Theory of Law, (Oxford, 1940), chap. 3: the notion of sovereignty and its relation to law is traced historically from Bodin to Austin.

2. BODENHEIMER, E. Jurisprudence, (Harvard University Press, 1962), pp. 93-98: this contains a brief review of the work of Austin and of the Austinians.

3. FRIEDMANN, W. Legal Theory, (5th ed., Stevens & Sons, Ltd., 1967), chaps. 22-23: in the first of these chapters the work of Austin and the modifications of his successors are dealt with. There is mention also of the conterparts of the imperative theory in Germany and France. The second chapter appraises analytical study.

4. LIGHTWOOD, J.M. The Nature of Positive Law, (Macmillan & Co., 1883), chap. 13: Austin's views are set out and explained at length.

5. MARKBY, W. Elements of Law, (6th ed., Oxford, 1905), chap. 1: Markby was one of Austin's earliest followers. His views are adopted as the basis of the book. Austin's position is definded against certain criticisms of it.

6. HOLLAND, T.E. The Elements of Jurisprudence, (13th ed., Oxford, 1924), chap. 4: Austin's theory is modified to the extent of saying that positive law is enforced by sovereign political authority, not so much commanded.

7. HEARN, W.E. The Theory of Legal Duties and Rights, (Melbourne: John Ferres; London: Trubner & Co., 1883), chap. 1: the command theory is adopted and explained and certain objections to it are considered.

8. SALMOND, J.W. Jurisprudence, (7th ed., Sweet & Maxwell, Ltd., 1924), chap. 2: the author states that law consists of rules that are recognised and acted on by courts. This chapter gives his famous analysis of "civil law", including a discussion of the imperative theory. In the 11th ed. (G.L. Williams, 1957), pp. 53-58, the command theory is considered in general terms, and some objections to it are contained in Note (b) on p. 55. In Appendix I sovereignty is treated, and, although Austin is not specifically mentioned, some implications of his theory come into it. In the 12th ed. (P.J. Fitzgerald, 1966), pp. 25-35, the editor deals more fully with the command theory and outlines the principal objections that various writers have made.

9. KEETON, G.W. The Elementary Principles of Jurisprudence, (2nd ed., Isaac Pitman & Sons, Ltd., 1949), chaps. 3 and 4:

after a brief historical introduction Austin's theory of
sovereignty is explained. The discussion of the nature of
law is substantially concerned with the imperative theory.

1. PATON, G.W. A Text-Book of Jurisprudence, (3rd ed.,
   D.P. Derham, Oxford, 1964), pp. 4-14, 70-83, 302-306: these
   pages contain brief accounts of Bentham and Austin, and the
   latter's theory is outlined, both as to the nature of law,
   sovereignty, and international law.

2. PATTERSON, E.W. Jurisprudence, (The Foundation Press, Inc.,
   1953), pp. 82-91: the requirements of the imperative theory
   of law are considered. The separation of the law that is
   from what ought to be law as well as an excessive reliance
   on logic are condemned. There are further allusions at pp.
   107-8, 123-24 and 127.

3. JENKS, E. The New Jurisprudence, (John Murray, 1933), pp. 36-
   41: the idea of law as a command is considered and rejected.
   The need for generality in law is also dealt with.

4. LLOYD, D. Introduction to Jurisprudence, (2nd ed., Stevens &
   Sons, Ltd., 1965), chap. 4: sovereignty, the imperative
   theory and the principal objections to them are set out.
   The extracts form various writers include those from Bodin,
   Hobbes, Rousseau, Bentham, Austin, Bryce, de Jouvenal and
   Rees. The case-law is taken from cases mentioned in Chapter
   3 of this book.

5. JOLOWICZ, H.F. Lectures on Jurisprudence, (ed. J.A. Jolowicz,
   The Athlone Press, 1963), chap. 1 and pp. 106-18: the first
   chapter gives an easy introduction to Austin's theory of
   law and sovereignty. Pp. 106-18 contain criticisms of
   Austin's idea of sovereignty and of law as command.

6. BUCKLAND, W.W. Some Reflections on Jurisprudence, (Cambridge
   University Press, 1945), chaps. 1, 5, 9 and pp. 107-10:
   Austin's views as to law and sovereignty are presuppositions
   in his study of jurisprudence. In the main, Austin is
   defended against some of his critics but his confusion of
   the legal and political sovereign is pointed out. The
   question of rights and duties in the sovereign is considered
   at the end.

7. TAYLOR, R. "Law and Morality" (1968) 43 N.Y.U.L.R. 611: laws
   are described as particular commands addressed by
   particular men to others. Their authority is the power of
   the commander to secure obedience. On this basis the
   separation of law and morals, enforceability, enforcement
   and the "perfect law" are explained.

1. FULLER, L.L. "Americal Legal Philosophy at Mid-century"
   (1953-54), 6 J.L.E. 457, at pp. 459-67: in the course of
   a review of E.W. Patterson's Jurisprudence (supra), the
   Austinian theory is considered as well as the implications
   of a concept of law supported by force.

2. CAMPBELL, A.H. "Some Footnotes to Salmond's Jurisprudence"
   (1940) 7 C.L.J. 206, at pp. 209-11: the problems connected
   with rights and duties in the sovereign are considered.
   These do not arise if law is not conceived of as emanating
   from the will of the sovereign.

3. HASTIE, W. "Introduction" to G.F. Puchta and Others: Outlines
   of the Science of Jurisprudence, (trans. W. Hastie, T. & T.
   Clark, Edinburgh, 1887): this is a general appraisal of the
   contribution of the Analytical School and pointing out its
   limitations. A more historical approach is advocated.

4. TAPPER, C.F. "Austin on Sanctions [1965] C.L.J. 271: the view
   that Austin, though he may have been wrong, was at least
   clear and consistent is challenged. By examining his views
   on sanctions it is shown that he was muddled, inconsistent
   and ambiguous. But it is also pointed out that it is in
   these very inconsistencies that one finds the real value
   of Austin, namely, the germs of so many subsequent theses.

5. SMITH, J.C. "Law, Language, and Philosophy" (1968) 3 U.Br.
   Col.L.R. 59: in the course of reviewing the attitude to
   language of various legal philosophers, Austin's technique
   is explained and considered.

6. RADBRUCH, G. "Anglo-American Jurisprudence through Continental
   Eyes", (1936), 52 L.Q.R. 530: the greater part of this
   article is devoted to an appraisal of the work of Austin
   and his successors, which is compared with contemporary
   developments in Continental juristic thought.

H.L.A. HART and positivism

7. HART, H.L.A. The Concept of Law, (Oxford, 1961): after
   demolishing Austin in the first four chapters, he proceeds
   to formulate his own concept of law as the union of primary
   rules (creating duties) and secondary rules (creating
   powers and the "rule of recognition"). On this basis he
   considers various well-known questions concerning law, and
   in chap. 10 deals with the similarities and differences
   between municipal and international law.

8. HART, H.L.A. "Positivism and the Separation of Law and Morals"
   (1957-58) 71 Harv.L.R. 593: positivism has many meanings,

but the bone of contention between positivists and naturalists lies in the insistence of the former on separating the "is" and the "ought".

1. SMITH, J.C. "Law, Language, and Philosophy" (1968) 3 U.Br. Col.L.R. 59: in the course of reviewing the attitude to language of various legal philosophers, Professor Hart's technique is explained and considered.

2. FULLER, L.L. "Positivism and Fidelity to Law - a Reply to Professor Hart" (1957-58) 71 Harv.L.R. 630: is the positivist separation of the "is" and the "ought" a distinction that is, or ought to be? For the distinction just cannot be preserved in practice. Professor Hart's contentions are considered point by point.

3. FULLER, L.L. The Morality of Law, (Yale University Press, 1964), pp. 133-145, 153-157, 184-186: Hart's basic distinction between rules conferring powers and rules imposing duties is criticised as being too unsure. Hart's contention that power conferred by his "rule of recognition" is inextinguishable is also controverted as being unfounded; and his distinction between "pre-legal" and "legal" societies is rejected as bearing no correlation to anthropological data: pp. 133-45. Hart's views as to the relation between law and morality are criticised at pp. 153-157 and 184-186.

4. COHEN, L.J. Review of H.L.A. Hart, The Concept of Law (1962) 71 Mind, 395: Hart's key distinction between "primary" and "secondary" rules is examined, and the idea that the clue to law lies in their union is rejected as being unhelpful. In particular, the different sorts of powers contained in the "secondary rules" category are critically examined and it is alleged that Hart tends to overload the power concept.

5. SUMMERS, R.S. "Professor H.L.A. Hart's Concept of Law" (1963) D.L.J. 629: this analysis is recommended as being one of the best critiques of Hart's book. The article begins by explaining the theory and then points out certain objections to it. The concluding section is especially valuable for it sets out Hart's analytical methods.

6. DWORKIN, R.M. "Is Law a System of Rules?" in Essays in Legal Philosophy (ed. R.S. SUMMERS, Basil Blackwell, Oxford, 1968), 25: the author points to the part played by doctrines (principles, standards and policies) as distinct from rules of law, and these originate independently of a "rule of recognition". Resort to them is more than just a matter of

discretion, but if they are part of "law", then Hart's
positivist concept ceases to be adequate.

Sovereignty

1. REES, W.J. "The Theory of Sovereignty Restated" in Philosophy,
   Politics and Society, (ed. P. Laslett, Blackwell, Oxford,
   1956), chap. 4: the different senses in which the word
   "sovereignty" can be used are distinguished and analysed in
   order to discover what would be a useful approach today. The
   Austinian conception figures prominently in the discussion,
   as well as the traditional objections to it.

2. MAINE, H.J.S. Lectures on the Early History of Institutions,
   (John Murray, 1875), chaps. 12 and 13: here Maine
   formulates his famous historical criticism of the Austinian
   theory of sovereignty, especially in the second of the two
   chapters.

3. BRYCE, J. Studies in History and Jurisprudence, (Oxford, 1901),
   II, chap. 10: a distinction is drawn between the de jure
   and de facto sovereign. Austin's commander is the former,
   but he is shown to have attributed to it features
   appropriate to the latter. The views of Bentham and Austin
   are subjected to detailed criticism.

4. DEWEY, J. "Austin's Theory of Sovereignty" (1894), 9 Pol.Sc.
   Q. 31: it is alleged that some, Main in particular,
   misconceived Austin's theory, which is re-examined chiefly
   with reference to the United States. When ascribing
   sovereignty to part of the body politic, important questions
   and difficulties arise.

5. MATTERN, J. Concepts of State, Sovereignty and International
   Law, (John Hopkins Press, Baltimore; Humphrey Milford, 1928),
   chap. 5: the Austinian theory of sovereignty and its
   modifications by Dicey and Brown are set out. The whole
   book is of general interest as providing an account of
   theories of sovereignty since Bodin.

6. SIDGWICK, H. Elements of Politics, (2nd ed., Macmillan
   & Co., 1897), pp. 23-29, chap. 31 and Appendix A: some of
   the limitations on sovereign power are considered as well
   as the difficulties which Austin's view encounters with
   reference to the American Constitution. In chapter 31 the
   whereabouts of sovereignty is shown to be a more complex
   matter than was assumed by Austin. Appendix A is a critique
   of Austin's doctrine. The ideas of the illimitability of
   sovereignty and "tacit command", in particular, are
   rejected.

1. DICEY, A.V. The Law of the Constitution, (10th ed.,
    E.C.S. Wade, Macmillan & Co., Ltd., 1961), pp.
    71-85: in the course of his classic exposition of the doctrine of the
    sovereignty of Parliament, Dicey considers the difficulties
    of Austin's concept of sovereignty and the limitations that
    do exist on Parliamentary sovereignty.

2. MERRIAM, C.E. History of the Theory of Sovereignty since
    Rousseau, (The Columbia University Press, 1900), chap. 8:
    the origins of the Austinian theory and the views of Bentham
    are explained. There is also an account of the theory itself
    and of the principal criticisms of it.

3. LASKI, H.J. A Grammar of Politics, (4th ed., Allen & Unwin,
    Ltd., 1938), chap. 2: sovereignty is considered historically
    as a theory of law and as a theory of political organisation.
    In the historical context, the views of Bodin and Hobbes,
    inter alia, are mentioned. As a theory of law, the
    Austinian view is examined (pp. 50-55). The assumptions
    that underlie it make it useless as an explanation of the
    modern state for political purposes.

4. LINDSAY, A.D. The Modern Democratic State, (Oxford University
    Press, 1947), chap. 9: the origins of the doctrine of
    sovereignty are traced out and the Austinian version of it,
    its merits and weaknesses are examined. Sovereignty is
    claimed for the constitution, and the argument follows
    H. Kelsen's analysis, though Kelsen is not mentioned (as
    to Kelsen, see next chapter).

5. HARRISON, F. On Jurisprudence and the Conflict of Laws,
    (Oxford, 1919), chap. 1 and Annotation by A.H.F. Lefroy,
    I: Austin's view on sovereignty is, within limits,
    appropriate only to a lawyer. From a historical point of
    view it is open to objection, and in this connection
    Maine's criticisms are considered.

6. HEARN, W.E. The Theory of Legal Duties and Rights, (Melbourne:
    John Ferres; London: Trubner & Co., 1883), chap. 2: the
    Austinian theory of sovereignty is adopted and explained.

7. JENKS, E. The New Jurisprudence, (John Murray, 1933), pp.
    73-84: the main criticism is directed at Austin's idea of
    "political society" and the requirement that there has to
    be a sovereign in every such society. The attributes which
    Austin claimed for his sovereign are also considered and
    rejected.

8. McILWAIN, C.H. Constitutionalism and the Changing World,
    (Cambridge University Press, 1939), chap. 4: sovereign

power is a purely juristic term and has no application outside law. The discussion is in general terms, but the
theories of Bodin, Hobbes and Austin are alluded to in the
course of it, especially the influences on Austin.

1. DICKINSON, J. "A Working Theory of Sovereignty" (1927), Pol.
   Sc. Q., 524: three types of sovereignty are distinguished,
   legal sovereignty, sovereignty in international law and
   popular (political) sovereignty. Although this is not based
   on Austinian premises, it could usefully be read alongside
   that theory.

2. MITCHELL, J.D.B. "A General Theory of Public Contracts" (1951)
   63 Jur. R., 60: the conflict between the sanctity of contracts and sovereignty is considered. In the course of it
   there is a critical appraisal of the conceptions of sovereignty of Bodin, Hobbes and Austin.

3. POUND, R. "Law and State - Jurisprudence and Politics" (1943-
   44) 57 Harv. L.R., 1193, at pp. 1211-21: sovereignty rose
   into prominence with the rise of centralised governments
   after the Middle Ages. It is a juristic conception and the
   part which it plays is considered.

4. van KLEFFENS, E.N. "Sovereignty in International Law", (1953)
   I Hague Receuil, 1: this is of general interest only. It is
   a long and detailed account of the origins of the word
   "sovereignty" and of the development of the idea from
   antiquity, Greek, Roman and medieval times down to the
   present. It deals entirely with the part played by the
   doctrine in international law.

5. FRIEDRICH, C.J. The Philosophy of Law in Historical
   Perspective, (University of Chicago Press, 1958), chaps. 8
   and 11: in the first of these chapters the work and
   influence of Bodin is dealt with. In the latter that of
   Hobbes, Bentham and Austin is considered in relation to
   each other.

6. SNYDER, O.C. Preface to Jurisprudence, (The Bobbs-Merrill Co.
   Inc., 1954), Part II, chaps. 2 and 3: this is of general
   interest. Some of the traditional questions that have
   arisen in connection with sovereignty, both nationally and
   internationally, are posed. The discussion proceeds from an
   American point of view.

7. SCHWARZENBERGER, G. "The Forms of Sovereignty", (1957), 10
   C.L.P., 264: this article might usefully be referred to on
   Austin's requirement that the sovereign should not be
   dependent upon some other sovereign.

1. LLOYD, D. The Idea of Law, (Penguin Books, Ltd., A 688, 1964),
    chap. 8: the origins of the modern idea of sovereignty and
    Austin's idea of law as the command of a Sovereign are out-
    lined. (In this connection reference might also be made to
    Chapter 2 on Law and Force). It is said that a legal theory
    is required to accomodate limitations on a sovereign legis-
    lature and judicial review, while a power theory is
    required in revolutionary situations. The chapter also
    deals with state sovereignty in relation to international
    law.

2. Reference might also be made to the following:- O. GIERKE,
    Political Theories of the Middle Age, (trans. F.W. Maitland,
    Cambridge University Press, 1900), chaps. 5, 6 and pp. 92-
    93; H.E. COHEN, Recent Theories of Sovereignty, (University
    of Chicago Press, 1937); F. POLLOCK, An Introduction to
    the History of the Science of Politics, (Macmillan & Co.,
    1895), chap. 4. See also the bibliography at the end of
    Chapter 4, section entitled, Development and Nature of
    Sovereignty,

15

THE PURE THEORY

1. KELSEN, H. Pure Theory of Law, (trans. M Knight, University of California Press, 1967): this is an English translation of the second German edition of Reine Rechtslehre, (1960). It makes accessible to English readers the principal exposition of Kelsen's theory. Modifications in his thought are indicated in notes.

2. KELSEN, H. General Theory of Law and State, (trans. A. Wedberg, Harvard University Press, 1949): in this austerely reasoned book the Pure Theory is set out in full. Of all Kelsen's many works this also is easily accessible and might be regarded as representing his mature views, modified in some respects so as to meet earlier criticisms.

3. KELSEN, H. What is Justice ? (University of California Press, 1957): of this collection of essays the following are the most relevant:- "Value Judgments in the Science of Law" (p. 209): this contains an outline of the Pure Theory and shows his views on the relation between values and the law. "The Law as a Specific Social Technique" (p. 231): in which law as a coercive order monopolising the use of force is developed, as well as the relation between wrongdoing and sanction. "Why Should the Law be Obeyed ?" (p. 257): this considers various possibilities and rejects them all in favour of the position occupied by the Grundnorm. "The Pure Theory of Law and Analytical Jurisprudence" (p. 266): which considers the relationship of justice to the maintenance of a positive legal order and of sociological to normative jurisprudence. "Law, State and Justice in the Pure Theory of Law" (p. 288): which stresses the need to free the science of law from animism and how and why considerations of justice should be kept apart.

4. KELSEN, H. "The Pure Theory of Law" (trans. C.H. Wilson), (1934), 50 L.Q.R., 474; (1935), 51 L.Q.R., 517: the aims and contentions of the Pure Theory are set out. Some of the forms of expression used in these articles has been altered in the General Theory of Law and State (supra).

5. KELSEN, H. "The Function of the Pure Theory of Law", in Law: A Century of Progress, (New York University Press, 1937), 231: the Pure Theory is general jurisprudence. The distinction between the science of law and sociology, morals and politics needs to be maintained.

6. KELSEN, H. "On the Basic Norm" (1959), 47 Calif. L.R., 107: a norm means that something ought to be done. The "existence" of a norm is its validity, which derives ultimately

from the Basic Norm. Kelsen is at pains to refute the
suspicion that the Pure Theory is "a kind of natural law
doctrine".

1. KELSEN, H. "What is the Pure Theory of Law ?" (1959-60), 34
    Tul. L.R., 269: law is not a fact; one cannot infer an
    "ought" from an "is". As a prescription, a norm is neither
    true nor false; it is valid or invalid. Effectiveness is a
    condition of validity, but not identical with it. There is
    an explanation of "purity" and of the basic norm.

2. POLLOCK, F. "Laws of Nature and Laws of Man" in Essays in
    Jurisprudence and Ethics, (Macmillan & Co., 1882),42: this
    was not written with reference to Kelsen, but the substance
    is relevant. Natural laws do not involve disobedience and
    punishment. On the other hand, human laws are not just
    statements of what will happen on disobedience, for they
    are needed to guide people who do not wish to disobey and,
    moreover, the "happening" of the penalty is dependent on
    many factors.

3. KELSEN, H. "Centralisation and Decentralisation" in Authority
    and the Individual, (Harvard Tercentenary Publications,
    Harvard University Press, 1937), p. 210: the Pure Theory is
    given practical application to a modern problem. Since,
    according to the theory, "state" and "legal order" are
    identical, centralisation and decentralisation are partic-
    ular forms of the legal order; they are shown to be
    problems concerning validity relating to jurisdiction and
    the creation of legal norms.

4. KELSEN, H. "Derogation" in Essays in Jurisprudence in Honor
    of Roscoe Pound, (ed. R.A. Newman, The Bobbs-Merrill Co.,
    Inc., 1962), 339: a norm may lose its validity in various
    ways. Derogation means repeal. Repeal relates to the norm
    repealed, therefore it is a dependent norm and it cannot
    be violated.

Commentaries and Critiques

5. EBENSTEIN, W. The Pure Theory of Law, (University of
    Wisconsin Press, 1945): this sets out in a somewhat
    uncritical fashion the general Kelsen doctrine. It also
    endeavours to show that the doctrine is not without
    practical importance (chap. 5).

6. LAUTERPACHT, H. "Kelsen's Pure Science of Law" in Modern
    Theories of Law, (ed. W.I. Jennings, Oxford University
    Press, 1933), chap. 7: a general account is given of
    Kelsen's doctrine. The criticism is made of the wholesale

rejection of natural law and also that there might be an
element of natural law in the doctrine.

1. LATHAM, R.T.E. "The Law and the Commonwealth" in W.K. HANCOCK:
    Survey of British Commonwealth Affairs, (Oxford University
    Press, 1937), pp. 522-95, (reproduced in facsimile in 1949):
    the structure of the Commonwealth is examined in the light
    of what is meant by formal unity, based on Kelsen's
    analysis. The nature of the Grundnorm is considered in
    detail with reference to constitutional law; it can be
    indeterminate and shifting. The discoverability of a
    Grundnorm in the Commonwealth is even more difficult.

2. VOEGELIN, E. "Kelsen's Pure Theory of Law" (1927), 42 Pol.
    Sc.Q. 268: this is a review of Kelsen's Allgemeine
    Staatslehre, 1925. Explanation is given of the separation
    of the "ought" from the "is" and the centre of gravity of
    Kelsen's doctrine as resting on enforcement. A demonstration
    is given of how Hohfeld's distinctions of "right" might be
    deduced from enforcement is given (quaere whether this
    would correspond with practice in view of sanctioness
    duty-situations).

3. PARKER, R. "The Pure Theory of Law" (1960-61) 14 Vand.L.R.
    211: this is a simplified re-statement of Kelsen's
    doctrine. Its weakness in relation to international law is
    pointed out.

4. de BUSTAMANTE y MONTORO, A.S. "Kelsenism" in Interpretations
    of Modern Legal Philosophies, (ed. P. Sayre, Oxford
    University Press, New York, 1947), chap. 3: certain
    developments and re-interpretations of Kelsen's doctrines,
    neo-Kelsenism, so as to meet the needs of the day are
    explained. Value-judgments, it is argued, should be placed
    above the law.

5. PATTERSON, E.W. "Hans Kelsen and his Pure Theory of Law"
    (1952-53) 40 Calif.L.R. 5: a short biography of Kelsen is
    followed by an account of his chief contributions to
    legal theory.

6. WILK, K. "Law and the State as Pure Ideas: Critical Notes on
    the Basic Concepts of Kelsen's Legal Philosophy" (1940-41)
    51 Ethics 158: this contains an acute analysis of the
    correspondence between the normative world of law and
    social reality. Kelsen, it is alleged, fails to draw an
    adequate distinction between normative and other types of
    hypothetical judgments. The further criticisms are both
    penetrating and shrewd.

1. HÄGERSTRÖM, A. Inquiries into the Nature of Law and Morals, (ed. K. Olivecrona, trans. C.D. Broad, Almqvist & Wiksell, Stockholm, 1953), pp. 51-55, 257-98: the earlier passage is a criticism of an early and misleading statement by Kelsen as to the nature of the "ought". The latter chapter is a detailed review of Kelsen's thesis. The practical emptiness of his theory is pointed out and there are some damaging criticisms of his views on international law. (Note that these comments were made on Kelsen's publications in 1911 and 1925).

2. ROSS, A. Review of Kelsen's What is Justice? (1957) 45 Calif. L.R. 564: this is a short but penetrating commentary on the essays contained in the book. The observations on Kelsen's basic conceptions should be particularly noted.

3. ROSS, A. On Law and Justice, (Stevens & Sons, Ltd., 1958), pp. 66-67, 80-84: the treatment of "validity" might usefully be contrasted with Kelsen's treatment of it. This, to Ross, is the basis of a prediction that a judge will act in a certain way.

4. CHRISTIE, G.C. "The Notion of Validity in Modern Jurisprudence" (1963-64) 48 Minn.L.R. 1049: legal norms, as prescriptions of conduct, cannot be true or false; but assertions of validity can be true or false with reference to their validity. The views of validity of Kelsen and Ross are considered and compared with reference to concrete situations. Kelsen's analysis is preferred.

5. LUNDSTEDT, A.V. Legal Thinking Revised, (Almqvist & Wiksell, Stockholm, 1956), pp. 402-6: Kelsen's doctrine is sharply criticised. The attempt to free a theory of law from the world of fact is rejected as absurd. The whole doctrine is criticised for failing to take account of actual activities and the influence of the maintenance of law on the feelings of people.

6. STONE, J. Legal System and Lawyers' Reasonings (Stevens & Sons, Ltd., 1964), chap. 3: Kelsen's theory of law is critically reviewed and its limitations pointed out. The assertion that what is cannot justify what ought to be is criticised on the ground that, on Kelsen's own showing, the validity of every norm does depend in part at least on the efficacy of the system. Further, the difficulties and ambiguities inherent in the "basic norm" concept are exposed, and various other aspects of his doctrine, especially with regard to international law, are also dealt with.

1. STONE, J. "Mystery and Mystique of the Basic Norm", (1963),
   26 M.L.R. 34: this is an acute inquiry into the obscurity
   that still surrounds Kelsen's idea of the Grundnorm. His
   various statements about it are collated from different
   writings to show that Kelsen may not be clear in his own
   mind. Its range of possible meanings and their implications
   are considered.

2. WILSON, C.H. "The Basis of Kelsen's Pure Theory of Law"
   (1934-35) 1 Politica 54: there is first an explanation of
   the main ideas in Kelsen's doctrine. Criticisms are then
   levelled at the necessity for a fundamental norm, the
   distinction between a theory of law and ethics, the notion
   of validity, and finally the whole theory is alleged to
   suffer from contradictions.

3. PATTERSON, E.W. Jurisprudence, (The Foundation Press, Inc.,
   1953), pp. 259-65: Kelsen's doctrine is outlined with
   illustrative references to America. Certain general
   criticisms are made of it.

4. LLOYD, D. Introduction to Jurisprudence, (2nd ed., Stevens &
   Sons, Ltd., 1965), chap. 5: the influence of Kant and Hume
   on Kelsen is mentioned and the differences between Austin
   and Kelsen are summarised. Allusion is made to the
   ambiguities of the Grundnorm and to the difficulties of
   trying to unify municipal and international law.

5. FRIEDMANN, W. Legal Theory, (5th ed., Stevens & Sons, Ltd.,
   1967), chap. 24: a summary of Kelsen's doctrine is followed
   by a careful evaluation of it.

6. JONES, J.W. Historical Introduction to the Theory of Law,
   (Oxford, 1940), chap. 9: while Austin has been criticised
   as being too abstract, Kelsen would say that a theory of
   law cannot be too abstract. The essence of a rule is found
   in the possibility of disobedience, not obedience. An
   account of the theory then follows.

7. ALLEN, C.K. Law in the Making (7th ed., Oxford, 1964), pp.
   52-64: a general account of the theory is followed by a
   criticism of its sterility. The Grundnorm is likened to
   Austin's sovereign in a new guise. The considerable
   difficulties of ascertaining it in international law are
   pointed out.

8. BODENHEIMER, E. Jurisprudence, (Harvard University Press,
   1962), pp. 98-102: this gives a brief general account of
   the doctrine and of the "theory of concretization".

1. BODENHEIMER, E. "Power and Law: a Study of the Concept of
   Law" (1939-40) 50 Ethics, 127, at pp. 130-33: this, too,
   gives a brief account of the doctrine.

2. JOLOWICZ, H.F. Lectures on Jurisprudence, (ed., J.A. Jolowicz,
   The Athlone Press, 1963), chap. 11: the principal points in
   Kelsen's theory are simply and attractively stated.

3. CASTBERG, F. Problems of Legal Philosophy, (2nd ed., Oslo
   University Press; London: Allen & Unwin, Ltd., 1957), pp.
   44-47: Kelsen's doctrine is outlined in the course of a
   general discussion of validity. The question which
   postulate of validity should be adopted has to be answered
   with reference to social reality. The validity of
   customary law is said to pose some difficulty.

4. BUCKLAND, W.W. Some Reflections on Jurisprudence, (Cambridge
   University Press, 1945), pp. 18-24: Kelsen's views as to
   the identity of state and law and the nature of law are
   considered critically. The difficulties surrounding the
   notion of the Grundnorm, especially in international law,
   are pointed out.

5. CROSS, A.R.N. Precedent in English Law, (2nd ed., Oxford,
   1968), pp. 204-207: comment is made on the Grundnorm being
   "presupposed" and that a change in it amounts to a
   "revolution". It is said that the abandonment of the
   doctrine of stare decisis would be a "revolution" only in
   a strained sense of the term.

6. PATON, G.W. A Text-Book of Jurisprudence, (3rd ed.,
   D.P. Derham, Oxford, 1964), pp. 14-18, 81-83, 309-311:
   these three passages deal respectively with a simplified
   general account of the theory, the position of international
   law and the identity of state and law.

7. GINSBERG, M. Reason and Unreason in Society, (Longmans,
   Green & Co., Ltd., 1947), pp. 234-39: the sense in which
   Kelsen is to be described as a positivist is examined. The
   Grundnorm may be grounded in "impure" factors, but if it
   is based on morals the separation between law and morality
   cannot be maintained. The question is raised whether such
   a separation is itself moral.

8. DIAS, R.W.M. "Legal Politics: Norms behind the Grundnorm"
   (1968) 26 C.L.J. 233: the Rhodesian U.D.I. Case shows the
   working in practice of a revolutionary situation. Kelsen's
   doctrines do not apply here and some of its limitations
   are exposed.

1. SILVING, H. "Analytical Limits of the Pure Theory of Law",
    (1942-43), 28 Iowa L.R., 1: the claims of a "pure science"
    of law and attacks against it are considered with reference
    to what such a science purports to do and how far it can be
    "pure". The relation between jurisprudence and natural
    sciences and ethics is critically reviewed.

2. SILVING, H. "Law and Fact in the Light of the Pure Theory of
    Law" in Interpretation of Modern Legal Philosphies, (ed.
    P. Sayre, Oxford University Press, New York, 1947, chap. 31:
    the relationships between law and fact, substantive law and
    procedure, law and justice are explained. The finding of
    fact in a case is part of the concretizing process.

3. JONES, J.W. "Modern Discussions of the Aims and Methods of
    Legal Science", (1931), 47 L.Q.R., 62, at pp. 78-84:
    Kelsen's Pure Theory is outlined, and its principal weak-
    nesses and implications are indicated.

4. FRIEDRICH, C.J. The Philosophy of Law in Historical
    Perspective, (university of Chicago Press, 1958), pp. 171-
    77: the place of Kelsen's theory in the evolution of legal
    theory is examined. The Grundnorm should be considered in
    relation to historical, political and other realities.

5. GOLUNSKII, S.A. and STROGOVICH, M.S. "The Theory of the State
    and Law" in Soviet Legal Philosophy, (trans. H.W. Babb,
    Harvard University Press, 1951), pp. 419-22: Kelsen's
    doctrine is criticised from a Marxist point of view. The
    abstract nature of his thought is said to mark the decline
    of bourgeois legal thought.

6. HART, H.L.A. The Concept of Law, (Oxford, 1961), chap. 6: the
    criterion of validity depends upon the acceptance of a
    "rule of recognition" with which to identify rules of law.
    This must in turn rest on extra-legal considerations. It
    should be noted that this is not a restatement of Kelsen's
    Grundnorm, but something similar to it.

7. STONE, J. Legal System and Lawyers' Reasonings, (Stevens &
    Sons, Ltd., 1964), pp. 131-34: Professor Hart's "rule of
    recognition" is considered in the context of a discussion
    of Kelsen's doctrine. Certain objections are made as to
    what is implied by "recognition".

The Pure Theory and international law

8. JONES, J.W. "The 'Pure' Theory of International Law" (1935),
    16 B.Y.I.L., 5: the main points in a dualist conception of
    the relationship betweeen municipal and international law

and its implications are first considered. This leads on to
a consideration of the advantages of a monist conception.
But there are difficulties here too, of which the chief is
the selection of a Grundnorm. It is alleged that Kelsen has
given his hypothesis a "political core".

1. KUNZ, J.L.   "On the Theoretical Basis of the Law of Nations",
    (1925), 10 Tran. Gro. S., 115: an avowed Kelsenite puts
    forward the case for the primacy of international law. The
    fact that Kelsen could see no theoretical reason for pre-
    ferring the primacy of international law is alleged to be
    the weak point in his theory. See further J.L. KUNZ, "The
    Vienna School of Law and International Law" (1936), 11 N.Y.
    U.L.Q., 370.

2. COHEN, H.E.   Recent Theories of Sovereignty, (University of
    Chicago Press, 1937), chap. 5: this considers Kelsen's
    attitude towards the question of sovereignty in inter-
    national law. There has to be a choice between the primacy
    of municipal law and of international law. In choosing the
    latter Kelsen abandons juristic purity and makes an ethical
    choice.

3. MATTERN, J.   Concepts of State, Sovereignty and International
    Law, (John Hopkins Press, Baltimore: Humphrey Milford, 1928)
    chap. 10: this gives an account of the view of Kelsen and
    Verdross of the state and international law.

4. STERN, W.B.   Note on "Kelsen's Theory of International Law",
    (1936), 30 Am. Pol. Sc. R., 736: the basis of customary
    international law is said to be pacta sunt servanda, but the
    international legal order is analogous to primitive law.
    This state of affairs is gradually being overcome.

5. JANZEN, H.   "Kelsen's Pure Science of Law", (1937), 31 Am. Pol.
    Sc. R., 205: there is a general explanation of the Pure
    Theory, both as to its municipal and international aspects.
    The doctrine of the unity and primacy of the latter is
    developed in some detail and in the course of it the criti-
    cisms of J.W. Jones and W.B. Stern (supra) are considered.

6. LLOYD, D.   The Idea of Law, (Penguin Books, Ltd., A 688, 1964),
    pp. 193-98: these pages provide a brief explanation of
    Kelsen's hierachy of norms. The Grundnorm is considered
    with reference to municipal and international law.

7. Law and Politics in the World Community, (ed. G.A. Lipsky,
    University of California Press, 1953): this collection of
    essays deals severally with specific problems and they
    all bear some relation to Kelsen's teachings. The volume is

of general interest only, but the editor's Introduction is
useful as an assessment of Kelsen's work in the international
sphere.

16

T H E   H I S T O R I C A L

A N D   A N T H R O P O L O G I C A L   A P P R O A C H E S

The Historical School

1. von SAVIGNY, F.C. On the Vocation of Our Age for Legislation
   and Jurisprudence, (2nd ed., trans. A. Hayward, Littlewood
   & Co., 1831): Savigny constantly likens the national
   character of law to that of language. Law, like language,
   grows, strengthens and dies with the development of the
   nation. This theme and the function of jurists are outlined.

2. von SAVIGNY, F.C. System of the Modern Roman Law, (trans.
   W. Holloway, J. Higginbotham, Madras, 1867), SS. 7-16: the
   positive law lives in the general consciousness of the
   people. The idea of what constitutes a "people" is
   elaborated so as to allow for local variations. The role of
   jurists and of legislation is explained.

3. PUCHTA, G.F. in Outlines of the Science of Jurisprudence,
   (trans. W. Hastie, T. & T. Clark, Edinburgh, 1887),
   especially pp. 37-63: peoples have different individualities,
   natures and tendencies. These constitute the national
   character, which is reflected in the particular system. The
   common consciousness constitutes the national mind and
   spirit.

4. KANTOROWICZ, H.U. "Savigny and the Historical School of Law",
   (1937) 53 L.Q.R. 326: details of Savigny's academic career
   are given and also an explanation of the rise in prestige
   of the academic profession. There is an important difference
   between Austin and Savigny, the former's work being
   rationalisation and the latter's sociological description.
   Savigny's advocacy of Roman Law as the "national" law of
   Germany is closely examined.

5. BRYCE, J. "The Interpretation of National Character and
   Historical Environment on the Development of the Common
   Law" (1908) 24 L.Q.R. 9: this is a most interesting
   inquiry into the causes of the differences between the
   legal ideas and methods of the Common Law and other
   systems.

6. DICKINSON, J. "Social Order and Political Authority" (1929)
   23 Am.Pol.Sc.R. 293, at pp. 301-12, 593: custom is said to
   be an agency of social control. The interests of individuals
   are largely produced by it. Custom also helps to adjust
   competing interests.

1. EHRLICH, E. Fundamental Principles of the Sociology of Law, (trans. W.L. Moll, Harvard University Press, 1936), chap. 19, especially pp. 443-61: there is a damaging criticism of the views of Savigny and Puchta. These are said to refer to two different things, namely, customary law which is a norm of conduct, and juristic law which is a norm for decision. Legal propositions do not emerge ready made; they are always the creation of jurists.

2. WEYRAUCH, W.O. The Personality of Lawyers, (Yale University Press, 1964): though not devoted to Savigny's doctrines, the whole of the investigation analysed in this book discredits Savigny's idea that lawyers reflect a specialised manifestation of the Volksgeist. On the contrary, it reveals the peculiar and unrepresentative character of the prejudices and predilictions of the legal profession.

3. STAMMLER, R. "Fundamental Tendencies in Modern Jurisprudence" (1923) 21 Mich.L.R. 623: the events of 1814 which led to the publication of Savigny's On the Vocation are reviewed in detail. The three main contentions of the Historical School are considered and it is concluded that the contribution of the School has been to show that legal development is dependent upon historical limitations to some extent.

4. POPPER, K.R. The Open Society and Its Enemies, (5th ed., Routledge & Kegan Paul, Ltd., 1966): this edition combines both volumes. They constitute a closely reasoned argument against the inevitability of historical development. There is an important distinction between scientific prediction and historical prophecy, which has been overlooked all too often. Volume II begins with a critical examination of Hegel's doctrine. See also K.R. POPPER: Poverty of Historicism, (Routledge & Kegan Paul, Ltd., 1957).

5. AUSTIN, J. Lectures on Jurisprudence, (5th ed., R. Campbell, John Murray, 1885), II, pp. 675-81: Savigny's views are considered in the general context of the desirability of codification. Savigny's objections to codification are considered and rejected. It is noteworthy that J. Bentham is said to belong to the Historical School (p. 679).

6. KORKUNOV, N.M. General Theory of Law, (trans. W.G. Hastings, The Boston Book Co. 1909), pp. 116-22: the Historical School opposed the hypotheses of Natural law with that of evolution, but it does not explain how the spirit of the people is formed. The theory was thus incomplete and this enabled Natural law to reappear in the ideas of Hegel.

1. LEONHARD, R. "Methods Followed in Germany by the Historical
   School of Law" (1907) 7 Col.L.R. 573: although one cannot
   judge a law without knowledge of its special history, yet
   uncongenial laws do exist. The principal objections to the
   Historical School are formulated.

2. SUMNER, W.G. Folkways. A Study of the Sociological Importance
   of Usages, Manners, Customs, Mores and Morals (Ginn & Co.,
   Publishers, The Athenaeum Press, Boston, U.S.A., 1907),
   especially chaps. 1 and 2: the theme of this work is
   closely akin to that of Savigny and is essentially a
   parallel development. Folkways is a societal force and
   grows unconsciously. Folkways give rise to laws; they are
   not themselves law.

3. SAWER, G. Law in Society (Oxford, 1965), pp. 171-4: this is
   a brief commentary on the work of W.G. Sumner and a
   comparison of his work with that of Savigny.

4. POUND, R. Interpretations of Legal History, (Cambridge
   University Press, 1923), chap. 6: while refraining from
   evolving a theory of law from the work of great lawyers,
   attention is forcefully drawn to the significant
   contributions made by such people to the development of
   law.

5. ROSS, A. On Law and Justice, (Stevens & Sons, Ltd., 1958),
   pp. 344-47: the Historical School is criticised as being
   a Natural Law philosophy which conceals a political
   attitude.

6. CARTER, J.C. Law: Its Origin, Growth and Function,
   (G.P. Putnam's Sons, New York, 1907): he begins by arguing
   for a philosophy of law in interpreting the progress of
   law. After considering and rejecting competing philosophies,
   he finds the explanation in custom, of which law is a
   specialised agency. Judges are the mouthpiece of custom;
   legislation has a part to play, but its role is secondary.

7. CARTER, J.C. "The Ideal and the Actual in the Law" (1890) 24
   Am.L.R. 752: justice is the aim of all law. Legislation
   does not always achieve it. This is because the just rule
   has to be found, not made. Law is the unconscious product
   of the society.

8. ARONSON, M.J. "The Juridical Evolutionism of James Coolidge
   Carter", (1953-54) 10 Tor.L.J. 1: this gives a detailed
   account of Carter's evolutionary interpretation of law.

9. FIELD, D.D. "Codification" (1886) 20 Am.L.R. 1: the author

represented the American counterpart of Thibaut in
advocating codification. Judges should not make law and the
public are entitled to know the law in advance. No country
has gone back on a code.

1. CARTER, J.C. "The Province of the Written and the Unwritten
   Law" (1890) 24 Am.L.R. 1: this opposes Field's project.
   See also D.D. FIELD: "Codification - Mr. Field's Answer to
   Mr. Carter", ibid., p. 255; S. WILLISTON: "Written and
   Unwritten Law" (1931) 17 Am.B.A. 39: this reviews the Field-
   Carter controversy on the issue of codification.

2. GRAY, J.C. The Nature and Sources of the Law, (2nd ed.,
   R. Gray, The Macmillan Co., New York, 1921), pp. 89-93;
   233-39; 283-91: Savigny's views are outlined and the
   principal difficulties considered. In the latter passage
   Mr. Carter's views are explained and subjected to careful
   criticism.

3. BRYCE, J. Studies in History and Jurisprudence, (Oxford,
   1901), II, pp. 184-86: this is of general interest. The
   advantages and weaknesses of the historical method are
   dealt with.

4. WALTON, F.P. "The Historical School of Jurisprudence and
   Transplantation of Law" (1927) 9 J.C.L. (3rd ser.) 183:
   Savigny's theory and the way in which he sought to justify
   his advocacy of Roman law are explained. The criticism is
   developed that his theory fails to account for the
   successful exportation of legal systems to other countries.

5. LIPSTEIN, K. "The Reception of Western Law in Turkey" (1956)
   6 Annales de la Faculte de Droit d'Instanbul, 10, 225: the
   reception of Swiss law in Turkey in 1926 is examined in
   various aspects. There is a difference between the
   reception of Roman law in Europe and receptions of modern
   law, the latter being determined by codification and
   colonial policies. This and the next article contain
   important and interesting demonstrations that the
   Volksgeist is strongest, or even only extant in family law.

6. LIPSTEIN, K. "The Reception of Western Law in a Country of a
   Different Social and Economic Background: India" (1957-58),
   8-9 Revista del Instituto de Derecho Comparado, 69, 213:
   the reception of English law in India is examined on lines
   similar to the above.

7. HARDY, M.J.L. Blood Feuds and the Payment of Blood Money in
   the Middle East, (Beirut, 1963): this little book is of
   interest as showing the resiliance of ancient custom in the

face of the introduction of Western ideas. It also shows
the difficulties with which one legal system adjusts
itself to procedures taken from some other cultural
background.

1. POUND, R. "Comparative Law and History as Bases for Chinese
   Law" (1947-48) 61 Harv.L.R. 749: the problem in China at
   that date was whether to adopt the latest legal
   institutions of Western societies or to adapt traditional
   Chinese institutions. The practicability of each is
   illuminatingly considered.

2. CLARK, E.C. Practical Jurisprudence, (Cambridge University
   Press, 1883), Part I, chaps. 7, 11-16: this is a historical
   and philological investigation into the meanings of the
   word "law". Law used to connote that which was considered
   to be fitting, the sanction being general displeasure. See
   also E.C. CLARK: History of Roman Private Law. Part II.
   Jurisprudence, (Cambridge University Press, 1914), I, S.5.

3. BARKER, E. Introduction to O. GIERKE: Natural Law and the
   Theory of Society, 1500-1800, (trans. E. Barker, Cambridge
   University Press, 1950), S. 4: the factors against which
   the Historical School reacted are set out and there is an
   attempt to enter into what it is that is signified by
   Volksgeist. The part played by Gierke on the side of the
   "Germanists" as against the "Romanists", such as Savigny,
   is also explained. See also E. TROELTSCH, Appendix I, in
   which he traces the divergence between Germanic and West
   European thought. The former embraced the ideal of a
   historically-creative group-mind.

4. GIERKE, O. Natural Law and the Theory of Society, 1500-1800,
   (supra): in this is set out the group-theory of legal
   evolution.

5. HEGEL, G.W.F. Philosophy of Right, (trans. T.M. Knox, Oxford,
   1967): this most difficult work might be used for reference.

6. STACE, W.T. The Philosophy of Hegel, (Dover Publications Inc.,
   1955), Part IV, pp. 374-438: this is one of the best and
   most readable accounts of Hegel's philosophy. In the
   section referred to his views of law are set out and
   explained.

7. FRIEDRICH, C.J. The Philosophy of Law in Historical
   Perspective, (University of Chicago Press, 1958), chap. 15:
   this, too, is one of the clearest short expositions of
   Hegel's views on law and government. Its main interest lies
   in the way it shows how the use of his philosophy to

support a totalitarian regime is a perversion of what he
said. There is a briefer account of the Historical School.

1. CAIRNS, H. Legal Philosophy from Plato to Hegel, (The John
Hopkins Press, 1949), chap. 14: this contains an account
of Hegel's philosophy, with particular reference to his
theory of law. It is not as easy reading as the rest of the
Cairn's book.

2. SABINE, G.H. A History of Political Theory, (3rd ed., Harrap
& Co., Ltd., 1963), chaps. 30, 32 and 35: the first of
these chapters contains a most readable exposition of
Hegel's dialectic method and theory of society and
concludes with a critical appraisal of it. The latter part
of chapter 32 gives an account of the Spencerian philosophy.
Chapter 35 concerns Fascism and National Socialism.

3. MAINE, H.J.S. Ancient Law, (ed. F. Pollock, John Murray,
1930), chap. 1: Maine's view is relevent here in so far as
he made the famous generalisation about the movement of
progressive societies hitherto being one from status of
contract.

4. DICEY, A.V. Law and Public Opinion in England during the
19th Century, (2nd ed., Macmillan & Co., Ltd., 1932),
chaps. 7-8: Dicey draws attention in detail to tendencies
since Maine wrote towards a return to status.

5. Law and Opinion in England in the 20th Century, (ed.
M. Ginsberg, Stevens & Sons, Ltd., 1959), chap. 1: the
hints thrown out by Dicey are pursued and the changes in
society and social conditions in the 20th century are
examined.

6. GRAVESON, R.H. Status in the Common Law, (The Athlone Press,
1953), chap. 3: it is pointed out that English law never
did quite fit Maine's statement, for the movement away
from status was not necessarily towards contract. The
effects of state interference today and standard form
contracts are considered.

7. On the Nazi and Fascist conceptions of law, see J.W. JONES:
The Nazi Conception of Law, (Oxford Pamphlets on World
Affairs, No. 21, 1939); J.W. JONES: Historical Introduction
to the Theory Of Law, (Oxford, 1940), pp. 278-300;
G. DEL VECCHIO: "The Crisis in the State" (1935) 51 L.Q.R.
615; J. STONE: "Theories of Law and Justice of Fascist
Italy" (1937) 1 M.L.R. 177; H.A. STEINER: "The Fascist
Conception of Law" (1936) 62 L.Q.R. 1267; A.H. CAMPBELL:
"Fascism and Legality" (1946) 62 L.Q.R. 141; N.S. MARSH:

"Some Aspects of the German Legal System under National
Socialism" (1946) 62 L.Q.R. 366.

General accounts of the historical approach

1. POUND, R. Interpretations of Legal History, (Cambridge
   University Press, 1923), chaps. 1 and 4: the first
   chapter reviews the historical approach. The points are
   made that Savigny's view was idealistic, that he based law
   on social pressure and that he assumed evolution as a
   datum. Chapter 4 deals with the ethnological and biological
   interpretations. (For a critical review, see F. POLLOCK:
   "Plea for Historical Interpretation" (1923) 39 L.Q.R. 163).

2. ALLEN, C.K. Law in the Making, (7th ed., Oxford ,1964), pp.
   87-129: the origins and general nature of the historical
   and biological approaches are first described. Later the
   views of the Savigny's school are considered and criticised
   in detail.

3. LIGHTWOOD, J.M. The Nature of Positive Law, (Macmillan & Co.,
   1883), chap. 12: Savigny's theory of law is approached
   through a comparison of English and German views as to the
   relationship between law and morality. There is a very full
   account of Savigny's doctrine and the criticisms of it by
   Ihering.

4. PATTERSON, E.W. Jurisprudence, (The Foundation Press, Inc.,
   1953), pp. 403-35: this begins with an explanation of five
   uses that have been made of history. Savigny's views are
   explained and considered, followed by accounts of Maine,
   the American historical movement (including the Field-
   Carter controversy), Spencer and Hegel. The account of
   Hegel is particularly recommended.

5. STONE, J. Social Dimensions of Law and Justice, (Stevens &
   Sons., Ltd., 1966), Chap. 2: the work of Savigny is set
   against the cultural background of his time, and due
   acknowledgment is made to the pioneer contribution he made
   to sociological jurisprudence. His main problem was
   reconciling his thesis of the Volksgeist with the reception
   of Roman Law into Germany. His later works, the History
   and System, are shown to represent the unfolding of the
   broad plan outline in his original essay. The major
   objections to the Volksgeist theory are developed. For
   further objections, see pp. 160-3.

6. FRIEDMANN, W. Legal Theory, (5th ed., Stevens & Sons, Ltd.,
   1967), chaps. 16, pp. 174-78; and 18: Savigny and his
   followers are dealt with in outline, but Maine is given

prominence and attention is drawn to some of the
developments since his day. In chapter 18 the Nazi and
Fascist theories are considered.

1. BODENHEIMER, E. Jurisprudence, (Harvard University Press,
   1962), pp, 65-69; 70-79: the roots of the Historical School
   are briefly explored and an account is given of the work of
   Savigny, Puchta, and their English and American followers.
   The Biological School is also considered.

2. JONES, J.W. Historical Introduction to the Theory of Law,
   (Oxford, 1940), chap. 2: a good deal of information is
   provided as to the background to the debate between the
   German codifiers and their opponents. The teaching of
   Savigny is considered critically and the work of Beseler
   and Gierke is also set out.

3. VINOGRADOFF, P. Outlines of Historical Jurisprudence,
   (Oxford University Press, 1920), I, chaps. 6 and 7: in the
   first of these chapters is explained how reaction to reason
   and conquest produced the age of Romanticism. An account
   is also given of the struggle between the "Germanists" and
   "Romanists". In the latter chapter evolutionary theories
   are dealt with, especially those of Maine and the
   biologists.

4. HOLDSWORTH, W.S. Some Makers of English Law, (Cambridge
   University Press, 1938), chap. 12: the chapter begins with
   an account of the Historical School and the movement in
   England. This is followed by sketches of Maine, Maitland
   and Pollock.

5. JOLOWICZ, H.F. Lectures on Jurisprudence, (ed. J.A. Jolowicz,
   The Athlone Press, 1963), chap. 8: this gives a brief and
   simplified account of the Historical School.

6. PATON, G.W. A Text-Book of Jurisprudence, (3rd ed.,
   D.P. Derham, Oxford, 1964), pp. 18-21: this gives a very
   brief, general account and some of the principal criticisms.

7. POUND, R. Jurisprudence, (West Publishing Co., 1959), I, pp.
   81-87; II, pp. 169-83, 217 et seq.: in these pages will be
   found a general account of the teachings of the Historical
   School. Much the same was previously said by Pound in "The
   Scope and Purpose of Sociological Jurisprudence" (1910-11)
   24 Harv.L.R. 591, at pp. 598-604, where he also points out
   that the Historical School proceeded too much on an a
   priori basis.

8. POUND, R. "The End of Law as Developed in Juristic Thought"

(1916-17) 30 Harv.L.R. 201, at pp. 209 et seq.: the
historical jurists were more concerned with the content of
law than with its purpose. Maine's teaching is alleged to
have been derived rather more form Roman law than from other
systems.

1. RATTIGAN, W.H. The Science of Jurisprudence, (3rd ed., Wildy
   & Sons, 1909), SS. 10-11: as an answer to the Austinian
   conception of law as a command, a summary is given of the
   importance of customary and historical development of the
   law.

2. GOLUNSKII, S.A. and STROGOVICH, M.S. "The Theory of the State
   and Law" in Soviet Legal Philosophy, (trans. H.W. Babb,
   Harvard University Press, 1951), pp. 408-413: the doctrines
   of the Historical School and of Hegel are considered and
   criticised from a Marxist point of view.

3. De MONTMORENCY, J.E.G. "Savigny" in Great Jurists of the
   World, (edd. J. Macdonell and E. Manson, John Murray, 1913),
   561: this gives an account of Savigny's life and work.

4. HALL, J. Readings in Jurisprudence, (The Bobbs-Merrill Co.,
   1938), chap. 2: extracts are given from the writings of
   Savigny, Puchta, Barker, Stammler, Pound, Korkunov, Maine,
   Campbell and Carter.

5. COHEN, M.R. and COHEN, F.S. Readings in Jurisprudence and
   Legal Philosophy, (Prentice-Hall, Inc., 1951), pp. 73-76,
   110-13; 124-25; 386-94: these pages contain extracts from
   the writings of Hegal (on Property and Contract), Maine,
   Savigny and Carter.

6. MORRIS, C. The Great Legal Philosophers, (University of
   Pennsylvania Press, 1959), chaps. 12 and 13: the first of
   these chapters contains extracts from Savigny's On the
   Vocation; the second contains extracts from Hegel's
   Philosophy of Right.

7. LLOYD, D. Introduction to Jurisprudence, (2nd ed., Stevens &
   Sons, Ltd., 1965), chap. 9: the essentials of Savigny's
   doctrine are set out and there are also extracts from
   Savigny and Maine.

8. LLOYD, D. The Idea of Law, (Penguin Books, Ltd., A 688, 1964),
   pp. 251-55: these pages provide an outline of the views of
   Savigny and touch on the English representatives of the
   Historical School. At pp. 202-4 Hegel's approach is touched
   on.

1. HARRISON, F. On Jurisprudence and the Conflict of Laws, (Oxford, 1919), chap. 3: Annotations by A.H.F. LeFroy, pp. 173-79: the value of the historical method is considered with reference to the work of Savigny, Maine and others.

2. AMOS, M.S. "Some Reflections on the Philosophy of Law" (1927) 3 C.L.J. 31, at pp. 32-33: this is interesting for the critical remarks that are made on the limited value and the dangers of too close an adherence to the Historical School.

3. POSNETT, H.M. The Historical Method in Ethics, Jurisprudence, and Political Economy, (Longmans, Green & Co., 1882): in this little work the place of the historical method in evolving a theory out of social experience is considered. The methods of Spencer, Austin, Bentham, and Maine, inter alia, are dealt with.

Law and Anthropology

4. MAINE, H.J.S. Ancient Law, (ed. F. Pollock, John Murray, 1930), chap. 1 and Note B: this is the classic exposition of how custom originated in judgments, and then became codified, the codified law being thereafter developed by "progressive" societies.

5. STONE, J. Social Dimensions of Law and Justice, (Stevens & Sons, Ltd., 1966), Chap. 3: the general theme of finding correlations between social and legal development is introduced with an account of the work and contribution of Maine, and a less full account of the work of Vinogradoff. The latter part of the chapter pursues that theme into modern society and shows the increasing difficulties of finding simple correlations.

6. BURROW, J.W. Evolution and Society. A Study in Victorian Social Theory, (Cambridge University Press, 1966), chap. 5: Maine's sociological contribution is assessed in the light of what is known of his career and the influences on his thought.

7. HOCART, A.M. Kings and Councillors, (Cairo Printing Office, 1936): the social organisation for ritual and the evolution of this into government is traced out in detail and is supported by an abundance of evidence. This most important book is unfortunately difficult to obtain.

8. MALINOWSKI, B. Crime and Custom in Savage Society, (Kegan Paul, 1932), pp. 1-68: the idea of the savage who blindly follows custom is dispelled as a myth. Rules of law with a

definite obligation to obey stand out from mere rules of custom. Law consists in the mutuality of service involved in complex social arrangements.

1. MALINOWSKI, B. "A New Instrument for the Interpretation of Law - especially Primitive" (1941-42) 51 Yale L.J. 1237: four meanings of "law" are distinguished, and which of them are applicable to primitive society is considered. The chief source of social constraint lies in the organisation of the group for the achievement of certain ends.

2. HOGBIN, H.I.P. Law and Order in Polynesia, (Christophers, 1934): note also Malinowski's Introduction. The latter repeats his thesis that reciprocity is one of the elements in the dynamic mechanism of legal enforcement. Law needs to be defined with reference to function, not form. Hogbin, too, develops the reciprocal nature of legal obligations.

3. SCHAPERA, I. "Malinowski's Theories of Law" in Man and Culture, (ed. R.W. Firth, Routledge & Kegan Paul, Ltd., 1957), 139: Malinowski's views are critically discussed. His concept of primitive law is alleged to have changed in his writings.

4. HOBHOUSE, L.T., WHEELER, G.C., GINSBERG, M. The Material Culture and Social Institutions of the Simpler Peoples, (Chapman & Hall, 1930), especially chap. 2: a warning is given in the opening pages of how easy it is to form theories on the basis of preconceived ideas and to see only corroborative evidence. The authors are accordingly extremely modest in drawing conclusions. The main point is that the stage of economic culture is determined by the ways in which people obtain their food. On this basis a classification of primitive peoples is given. In chapter 2 there is an attempt to correlate social institutions with the stage of economic development. The tables on pp. 86-119 are well worth studying.

5. VINOGRADOFF, P. "The Teaching of Sir Henry Maine" in Collected Papers, (Oxford, 1928), chap. 8: in this appraisal of Maine's work the dividing line between his contribution and that of the Savigny school is indicated. The historical method as followed by the German school is said to have been inadequate.

6. ROBSON, W.A. "Sir Henry Maine Today" in Modern Theories of Law, (ed. W.I. Jennings, Oxford University Press, 1933), chap. 9: Maine's work is appraised in detail. His contributions to legal theory are evaluated and their shortcomings indicated in the light of more modern research.

1. ALLEN, C.K. "Maine's 'Ancient Law'" in Legal Duties, (Oxford, 1931), 139: this is a study of Ancient Law, which is described as a manifesto of Maine's work. The principal criticisms of his conclusions are recounted and considered.

2. LYALL, A.C., GLASSON, E., von HOLTZENDORFF, F., COGLIOLO, P.: "Sir Henry Maine" (1884) 4 L.Q.R. 129: these are appreciations of Maine written by an Englishman, Frenchman, German and an Italian, and their respective estimates of his work.

3. DIAMOND, A.S. Primitive Law, (Longmans, Green & Co., 1935): Maine is severely criticised. Primitive societies are shown to have been more complex than Maine supposed. Also, primitive law is said to have had little connection with religion. He takes issue with Maine on several other points as well.

4. DIAMOND, A.S. The Evolution of Law and Order, (Watts & Co., 1951): the point is repeated that the association of law with religion is a comparatively late development. This work expands the theme of Primitive Law (supra).

5. HARDY, M.J.L. Blood Feuds and the Payment of Blood Money in the Middle East, (Beirut, 1963): this short account of the pre- and post-Mohammed methods of settling disputes about injuries shows that there was a close connection between religious and secular institutions.

6. GLUCKMAN, M. The Judicial Process among the Barotse of Northern Rhodesia, (Manchester University Press, 1955): this contains a record of the settlement of actual disputes that arose among the Lozi tribe. Their judicial process is basically similar to that of western countries. The functions and nature of law is considered and compared with the law of developed societies.

7. MARCH, J.G. "Sociological Jurisprudence Revisited, A Review (more or less) of Max Gluckman" (1955-56) 8 Stan.L.R. 499: a long critical review of Gluckman's The Judicial Process among the Barotse and the task which he tries to accomplish.

8. GLUCKMAN, M. Politics, Law and Ritual in Tribal Society (Blackwell, Oxford, 1965): this is a work of general interest on the growth and evolution of societies. Chaps. 3-5 are the most relevant to the development of law and administration, and presents a view developed from the author's earlier works.

9. GULLIVER, P.H. Social Control in an African Society. A Study

of the Arusha: Agricultural Masai of Northern Tanganyika
(Routledge & Kegan Paul, 1963): in societies which lack
centrally organised courts and centrally appointed judges,
disputes are settled by means of networks of relationships
that exist within the society, or by a process of bargaining.
Resort to supernatural settlement operates in the last
resort. The illustrative cases are of particular interest.

1. HOCART, A.M. Kingship, (Oxford University Press, 1927): the
    significance of various ceremonial rites and doctrines
    relating to monarchy are traced back to their original
    sources.

2. DRIBERG, J.H. "The African Conception of Law" (1934) 16 J.C.
    L., (3rd Ser.), 230: the nature of African tribal law is
    considered. Its overall object is to maintain social
    equilibrium.

3. HOEBEL, E.A. The Law of Primitive Man, (Harvard University
    Press, 1954): the "law-ways" of the Eskimos, Ifuago
    (Phillipines), Comanche, Kiowa and Cheyenne Indians,
    Tobriand Islanders and the Ashanti (West African) are
    investigated. Maine is criticised for having introduced
    the myth of the rigid nature of law, but is defended
    against Diamond's criticism of his association of primitive
    law and religion. The general conclusion is that all
    primitive societies have rules enforced by controlled
    sanctions.

4. CAIRNS, H. Law and the Social Sciences, (Routledge & Kegan
    Paul, Ltd., 1935), chap. 2: the functional approach has
    yielded fruit. The contributions of anthropology are
    enumerated and explained.

5. LOWIE, R.H. "Incorporeal Rights in Primitive Society" (1927-
    28) 37 Yale L.J. 551: the idea of primitive communism is
    inconsistent with the prevalence of individually owned
    forms of incorporeal property, such as spells and
    enchantments.

6. LLEWELLYN, K.N. and HOEBEL, E.A. The Cheyenne Way, (University
    of Oklahoma Press, 1941): three possible methods of
    approach are considered, namely a search for norms of
    conduct, a description of practice and an examination of
    trouble cases. The third is adopted since this tests the
    norms and combines with it the behaviour of society. A case
    study of the law of the Cheyenne Indians is conducted on
    this basis.

7. TWINING, W. "Two works of Karl Llewellyn - II" (1968) 31 M.L.

R. 165: this paper, which is the second of two, is devoted
mainly to Llewellyn's anthropological contribution in
conjunction with Hoebel. Its significance lies in case-
analysis as a tool of field-work supplementing other field
techniques.

1. FULLER, L.L. "Irrigation and Tyranny" (1965) 17 Stan.L.R.
    1021: this paper is a critical commentary of K.A. Wittfogel's
    thesis that communities depending upon large-scale
    irrigation systems usually tend towards tyranny. Professor
    Fuller is inclined to support the thesis, but for wholly
    different reasons. In the course of his analysis he
    considers the various sociological and other considerations
    that this kind of investigation is bound to bring in.

2. MAINE, H.J.S. Dissertations on Early Law and Custom, (John
    Murray, 1901); Village Communities in the East and West,
    (John Murray, 1895); Lectures on the Early History of
    Institutions, (John Murray, 1905): these three works are
    of general interest and might be consulted for Maine's own
    views.

3. PATON, G.W. A Text-Book of Jurisprudence, (3rd ed.,
    D.P. Derham, Oxford, 1964), chap. 2, pp. 42 et seq.: no
    single factor should be regarded as being characteristic
    or predominant. This is a convenient account of the
    development of law in the light of modern research.

4. SIMPSON, S.P. and STONE, J. Cases and Readings on Law and
    Society, (West Publishing Co., 1948), Part I: a large
    number of extracts are given from various legal historians
    and anthropologists on primitive law and social control.

5. LLOYD, D. Introduction to Jurisprudence, (2nd ed., Stevens &
    Sons, Ltd., 1965), pp. 332-335: primitive people do possess
    "law", distinguishable as such, and which is flexible and
    capable of developing. Extracts are given from Hoebel and
    Gluckman.

6. LLOYD, D. The Idea of Law, (Penguin Books, Ltd., A 688, 1964),
    pp. 231-39: it is untrue to say that in primitive societies
    religious and secular rules cannot be distinguished, nor
    that primitive law is rigid, nor that sanctions are absent.
    The vital contrast between primitive law and modern law is
    that in the former there is no centralised agency for
    developing law. Development does, however, take place in
    other ways. Primitive law is also contrasted with modern
    International law.

7. SAWER, G. Law in Society (Oxford, 1965), chaps. 3-4: the

question whether primitive societies have "law" reflects a difference as to sociological theory and is not merely a dispute about the use of words. Primitive societies may, however, serve as models for social study. In chap. 4 the works of some of the leading authorities are commented on.

1. HALL, J. Readings in Jurisprudence, (The Bobbs-Merrill Co., 1938), chap. 19: extracts from Malinowski and Timasheff are given.

2. COHEN, M.R. and COHEN, F.S. Readings in Jurisprudence and Legal Philosophy, (Prentice Hall, Inc., 1951), chap. 12: extracts from various authors are given, including Malinowski and Hoebel.

3. For further general reading the following might be consulted: R.H. LOWIE: Primitive Society, (Routledge & Kegan Paul, Ltd., 1921), chaps. 14 and 15; W.I. THOMAS: Primitive Behaviour, (McGraw Hill Book Co., Inc., 1937), chap. 15: D. DAUBE: Biblical Law, (Cambridge University Press, 1941); H.F. JOLOWICZ: Historical Introduction to Roman Law, (2nd ed., Cambridge University Press, 1952); G.R. DRIVER and J.C. MILES: The Assyrian Law, (Oxford, 1935); G.R. DRIVER and J.C. MILES: The Babylonian Laws, (Oxford, 1952-55, 2 vols.; E.A. WESTERMARCK: The Origin and Development of the Moral Ideas, (Macmillan & Co., Ltd., 1906), 2 vols.

17

THE ECONOMIC APPROACH

1. MARX, K. and ENGELS, F. Manifesto of the Communist Party, (Foreign Languages Publishing House, Moscow, 1955): the essentials of the development of the class struggle, the establishment of the proletariat dictatorship and the allegedly inevitable triumph of communism are set out here.

2. SCHLESINGER, R.B. Soviet Legal Theory, (2nd ed., Routledge and Kegan Paul, Ltd., 1951): the legal theory underlying the Marxist approach to law and society is explained from its theoretical beginnings down to modern times.

3. DAVID, R. and BRIERLEY, J.E.C. Major Legal Systems in the World Today (Stevens & Sons, Ltd., 1968) Part II: this gives a penetrating and highly readable account of the theoretical Marxist basis of socialist law and its principal practical manifestations. The Section includes also accounts of the positions in other Communist countries. Since the book is a work on comparative law, the treatment of each legal system proceeds on the basis of policy and function.

4. BOBER, M.M. Karl Marx's Interpretation of History, (2nd ed., Harvard University Press, 1948): this work provides a careful and detailed study of the factors underlying Marxist ideas. Its various aspects are critically examined and the weaknesses indicated.

5. GSOVSKI, V. Soviet Civil Law, (Ann Arbor, 1948), I and II, especially Part I, chap. 5: the first volume is an extended account of Soviet law, its theory and various branches of it; the second volume gives the texts of various codes. Part I of Volume I deals generally with the nature and sources of Soviet law. In chapter 5 the concept of law is examined. Present-day developments and the attempts to reconcile these with Marx's teachings are also dealt with.

6. GRZYBOWSKI, K. Soviet Legal Institutions, (Ann Arbor, 1962): this is a fairly recent analysis of Soviet law. It is a comparative study. Of particular interest are chapters 4 and 5, the former showing how law is to aid in the training of the population, the latter showing the acceptance of law as a necessary institution.

7. HAZARD, J.N. Law and Social Change in the U.S.S.R., (Stevens & Sons, Ltd., 1953): this is an important collection of studies of various aspects of Soviet law and of the ways in which traditional legal conceptions are moulded to serve governmental policy.

1. ENGELS, F. The Origin of the Family, Private Property and the
State, (Foreign Languages Publishing House, Moscow, 1954):
the historical evolution of society from its primitive to
its modern stage in terms of the class struggle is
explained. Law is linked with the state. The anthropology
is suspect.

2. ENGELS, F. Anti-Duhring, (Foreign Languages Publishing House,
Moscow, 1954): in this polemic against the contentions of
Duhring a good many of the theoretical points of the
Marx-Engels theory of social evolution can be found.

3. MARX, K. Capital, (Foreign Languages Publishing House, Moscow,
1954) I and II: the work was left unfinished, and it is not
easy reading. In it the labour theory of value and the
relation of capital to labour is examined minutely.

4. OAKESHOTT, M.J. The Social and Political Doctrines of
Contemporary Europe, (2nd ed., Cambridge University Press,
1941), chap. 3: fairly extensive quotations are given from
the writings of Marx, Engels and Lenin.

5. Soviet Legal Philosophy, (20th Century Legal Philosophy Series),
Vol. V, (trans. H.W. Babb, Harvard University Press, 1951):
works and sections of works are given in such an order as
to depict the successive stages of development in Soviet
"interpretations" of Marx. The writers are V.I. Lenin,
P.I. Stuchka, M.A. Reisner, E.B. Pashukanis, J.V. Stalin,
A.Y. Vyshinsky, P. Yudin, S.A. Golunskii, M.S. Strogovitch
and I.P. Trainin. The Introduction by J.N. Hazard should
be read as an essential preliminary.

6. For general reference see also K. MARX and F. ENGELS: Selected
Correspondence (Foreign Languages Publishing House, Moscow,
1956): K. MARX and F. ENGELS: Selected Works, (Foreign
Languages Publishing House, 1951), I and II.

7. SALTER, F.R. Karl Marx and Modern Socialism, (Macmillan &
Co., Ltd., 1921): this is an early work bringing Marx as a
man to life and discussing his principal contentions. It
is of considerable interest as showing the extent to which
his prophecies had already materialised as well as failed
to do so even at that date.

8. LASKI, H.J. Karl Marx, (Allen & Unwin, Ltd., 1922): this is
a short account of Marx's background, his life and career
and an appreciation of his philosophy.

9. BUKHARINE, N.I. Le Theorie du Materialisme Historique,
(Editions Sociales Internationales, 1925): this is of

general interest. It gives an early picture of the application of Marxist theories in Russia, written shortly after the revolution but before many of the major problems arose. Bukharine's views were later officially repudiated.

1. Marxism and Modern Thought, (trans. R. Fox, Routledge & Sons, Ltd., 1935): lengthy extracts are given of the writings of Bukharine and six others. These are of general interest, especially Bukharine's contribution, as showing the attitude of early Soviet writers.

2. VYSHINSKY, A.Y. The Law of the Soviet State, (trans. H.W. Babb, The Macmillan Co., New York, 1954), especially chap. 1: this is in a sense an official exposition of Soviet law and the Soviet view of law. It is marred by its derisive and violent language. An account is given of the organisation and structure of Soviet government, but its content of legal theory is evasive and self-contradictory.

3. FULLER, L.L. "Pashukanis and Vyshinky: a Study in the Development of Marxian Legal Thinking" (1948-49) 47 Mich. L.R. 1157: Vyshinsky's book (supra) is critically reviewed and both his and Pashukanis's doctrines are compared, the latter being explained in some detail. Vyshinsky's book shows by implication that the Soviet conception of Marxism can alter in the face of facts.

4. DENISOV, A. and KIRICHENKO, M. Soviet State Law, (Foreign Languages Publishing House, Moscow, 1960): the nature and character of law are explained with reference to the social structure of the U.S.S.R. Particular attention is devoted to the rights of citizens. The Appendix gives the text of the Constitution (Fundamental Law) of the U.S.S.R.

5. Government, Law and Courts in the Soviet Union and Eastern Europe, (edd. V. Gsovski and K. Grzybowski, Stevens & Sons, Ltd., 1959), I and II: these volumes cover the law and governmental institutions of eleven countries (including Russia) in eastern Europe (East Germany is omitted). The object is to inquire into the extent to which individual rights are protected. The result is an extremely critical and somewhat one-sided account. In the Introductory chapter Gsovski deals with the doctrine of Marxism as they apply to law.

6. RENNER, K. The Institutions of Private Law and their Social Functions, (trans. A. Schwarzschild, ed. O. Kahn-Freund, Routledge & Kegan Paul, Ltd., 1949): Renner's thesis has previously been considered in the chapter on Ownership. It might usefully be considered here as a demonstration of the

function of law from a Marxist point of view.

1. SAWER, G. Law in Society (Oxford, 1965), pp. 177-82: this is
    a brief critique, primarily of K. Renner's work, but
    designed to bring out the interrelation between law and
    social behaviour.

2. SCHLESINGER, R.B. Marx, His Time and Ours, (Routledge & Kegan
    Paul, Ltd., 1950): this is a detailed study of the basis of
    Marx's thought and his analysis of society, together with
    its national and international implications. This calm and
    impersonal assessment of merits and demerits of Marxism is
    well worth study.

3. POPPER, K.R. The Open Society and Its Enemies, (5th ed.,
    Routledge & Kegan Paul, Ltd., 1966): both volumes argue
    against the inevitability of evolution. Volume II begins
    with a critique of Hegel and proceeds to a detailed
    investigation of Marxism on this basis.

4. SABINE, G.H. A History of Political Theory, (3rd ed., Harrap
    & Co., Ltd., 1963), chaps. 33 and 34: the first of these
    chapters deals with the dialectic interpretation of Marx
    and Engels; the second with post-Marxist communism. The
    relation between Hegel and Marx is particularly stressed.

5. HAZARD, J.N. "Soviet Law: an Introduction", (1936) 36 Col.L.
    R. 1236: the origin of the capitalist state according to
    Marxist interpretation is explained. This is a most helpful
    simplification of Marx's own laboriously detailed
    exposition. The principles of law which derive from this
    view of history are also explained.

6. DOBRIN, S. "Soviet Jurisprudence and Socialism" (1936) 52 L.
    Q.R. 402: this was written before the doctrines of
    Pashukanis were finally discredited. The difficulties in
    the way of evolving a theory of law in Russia are explained.
    With reference to Pashukanis's doctrine, the theories of
    such pre-1914 German writers, which accorded with Marxist
    dogma and which influenced Pashukanis, are examined.

7. BERMAN, H.J. Justice in the U.S.S.R. An Interpretation of
    Soviet Law, (Harvard University Press, 1963): in Part I the
    author demonstrates the mental feats performed by Soviet
    jurists to move away from Marxist doctrines but at the same
    time to preserve him as the official prophet. In Part II
    the roots of Soviet legal thinking are traced back over
    1000 years. In Part III the "parental" nature of Soviet law
    is examined. This is the tutoring of the masses for
    membership in the communist society.

1. SCHLESINGER, R.B. "Recent Developments in Soviet Legal Theory" (1942), 6 M.L.R. 21: Soviet jurists now realise the need for a theory of law. The various theories that have been proffered since the abandonment of Pashukanis's theory are considered, as well as the Soviet attitude towards international law.

2. GSOVSKI, V. "The Soviet Concept of Law" (1938) 7 F.L.R. 1: after examining the stages through which the attitude towards law has passed the conclusion is reached that traditional concepts have been reinstated.

3. BODENHEIMER, E. "The Impasse of Soviet Legal Philosophy" (1952-53) 38 Corn.L.Q. 51: based on the collection entitled Soviet Legal Philosophy (supra), this is an independent demonstration of the development of Soviet views about law and the difficulties into which they have been led. It is a very useful article.

4. LAPENNA, I. State and Law: Soviet and Yugoslav Theory, (The Athlone Press, 1964): the development of Soviet and Yugoslav interpretations of Marxist doctrines relating to state and law are set out. This is a demonstration, with many quotations, of the inconsistencies, evasions and distortions that have been resorted to by Russian writers.

5. KIRALFY, A.K.R. "Characteristics of Soviet Law" (1952) 2 Os. H.L.J. 279: attention is drawn to the influential position of the Communist Party, though this has no standing in law. Various other aspects of Soviet public and private law and procedure are also considered.

6. NOVE, A. "Some Aspects of Soviet Constitutional Theory" (1949) 12 M.L.R. 12: this article constitutes a summary of the main contentions of the Marxist attitude to law. The basic premise is that the Party represents the wishes of the people. Therefore, the law and the constitutional forms of government should express Party policy. The dangers in all this of the abuse of power are pointed out.

7. BERMAN, H.J. "Soviet Law and Government" (1958) 21 M.L.R. 19: the Russian revolution, it is observed, is still unfolding. The central feature of their system is the identity of politics and social control. A planned economy cannot function without a highly developed legal system, but the law does not bind the highest authority.

8. CONQUEST, R. Justice and the Legal System in the U.S.S.R. (The Bodley Head, 1968): this booklet provides brief accounts of the development and present state of Soviet

jurisprudence and outlines of some of its main branches.
Each chapter has a valuable bibliography.

1. MORGAN, G.G. Soviet Administrative Legality, (Stanford
   University Press, 1962): the central figure in this book is
   the Public Prosecutor. The picture which emerges is that
   there is little in the way of protection for the rights of
   the individual against administrative acts. Even the Public
   Prosecutor cannot question the acts of higher officials.

2. HAZARD, J.N. "Socialism, Abuse of Power and Soviet Law" (1950)
   50 Col.L.R. 448: nationalisation brings the citizen into
   direct contact with officialdom. Where there is no
   competition between those who provide public services there
   tends to be slackness and abuse. The various measures that
   have been adopted in Russia to deal with this problem are
   considered. Such measures cannot curb policy, but they do
   restrain officials.

3. KIRALFY, A.K.R. "The Campaign for Legality in the U.S.S.R."
   (1957) 6 I.C.L.Q. 625: the problem of balancing security
   for the individual and unquestioning obedience to the
   government is considered with reference to various aspects
   of Soviet administration.

4. KIRALFY, A.K.R. "The Rule of Law in Communist Europe" (1959)
   8 I.C.L.Q. 465: this article sets out the extent to which
   the government is free from control and the extent to
   which individuals and bodies can find remedies.

5. NIKIFOROV, B.S. "Fundamental Principles of Soviet Criminal
   Law" (1960) 23 M.L.R. 31: this is of general interest. A
   Russian writer explains the enactment of 1958.

6. HAZARD, J.N. "Soviet Codifiers Release the the First Drafts"
   (1959) 8 A.J.C.L. 72: this is another comment on the new
   criminal code and criminal procedure.

7. HAZARD, J.N. "Cleansing Soviet International Law of anti-
   Marxist Theories" (1938) 32 A.J.I.L. 244: the denunciation
   of Pashukanis called for a revision of international law
   theories. The theoretical aspects of Korovin's and
   Pashukanis's theories of international law are explained.

8. KOROVIN, E.A. "The Second World War and International Law"
   (1946) 40 A.J.I.L. 742: this represents a Russian and
   typically monocular view of the role of the U.S.S.R. in
   international affairs since the end of the Second World
   War. It contains a plea for a new view of sovereignty.

1. SETON-WATSON, H. "Soviet Foreign Policy in 1961" (1961) 2
   International Relations, 197: the trend of events and the
   policy of th U.S.S.R. determines their attitude towards
   international law. In the light of these factors the
   position in 1961 is reviewed.

2. TAMMELO, I. "Coexistence and Communication: Theory and
   Reality in Soviet Approaches to International Law" (1965)
   5 Syd.L.R. 29: this is an important demonstration of the
   immense language communication problems that divide the
   Soviets and the West. Their attitude to international law
   is explained in the light of this problem.

3. HAZARD, J.N. and WEISBERG, M.L. Cases and Materials on Soviet
   Law, (Columbia University Press, 1950): the cases presented
   in this volume are most valuable in conveying an idea of
   the conditions of life and the contexts in which legal
   problems arise in Russia. It also reveals the extent to
   which the Soviet Supreme Court intervenes on behalf of the
   individual.

4. SCHLESINGER, R.B. "A Glance at Soviet Law" (1949) 65 L.Q.R.
   504: this is a comment on the collection of materials,
   which at the time of writing was in circulation in advance
   of publication (supra). Certain decisions of the Soviet
   courts are discussed in so far as these shed light on their
   general attitude.

5. FEIFER, G. Justice in Moscow, (The Bodley Head, Ltd., 1964):
   a journalist writes in detail of the working and spirit of
   ordinary tribunals in Moscow. It is noteworthy that
   development has been moving nearer to West European ideas
   and that it has come to be realised that legality is more
   effective in cultivating a loyal citizenry that arbitrariness.
   The chief feature of Soviet trials is that they try, not the
   crime, so much as the man; the emphasis is on safeguarding
   and improving society.

6. SIMPSON, S.P. and STONE, J. Cases and Readings on Law and
   Society, (West Publishing Co., 1948), I, Part IV, chap. 1:
   III, Part VI, chaps. 1 S. 3 and 3: in Book I the economic
   background of law is given with extracts from Marx and the
   American writer Brooks Adams (inter alia). In Book III,
   chap. 1 extracts from Marx and Engels, Lenin, Stalin and
   other publications are given. Chapter 3 contains extracts
   from various Russian and non-Russian writers on the nature
   of law.

7. STRACHEY, E.J.St.L. The Theory and Practice of Socialism,
   (Victor Gollancz, 1936): this book might be consulted as a

matter of general interest. It contains an analysis along
socialist lines and indicates the differences between
socialism and communism.

1. LASKI, H.J. The State in Theory and Practice, (Allen & Unwin
   Ltd., 1935): the ways in which owners of property and
   producers of goods used social institutions to accomplish
   their own ends are traced. A change is not possible
   without revolution. Capitalism and war are said to be
   related and armaments tend to increase under pressure from
   industrialists.

2. LASKI, H.J. Law and Justice in Soviet Russia, (Hogarth Press,
   1935): this is a panegyric of Soviet administration of law,
   especially criminal law, and of its superiority over the
   common law. The idea of social service has led to emphasis
   on the rehabilitation of offenders. (See also H.J. LASKI:
   Studies in Law and Politics, Allen & Unwin, Ltd., (1932),
   especially pp. 276 et seq.).

3. LASKI, H.J. "The Crisis in the Theory of the State" in Law:
   A Century of Progress, (New York University Press, 1937;
   reprinted in A Grammar of Politics, 4th ed., Allen &
   Unwin, Ltd., 1938): the Marxist conception of the state and
   law is defended and the doctrine of the withering away of
   law is foreshadowed even as late as 1937.

4. HOOK, S. From Hegel to Marx, (Victor Gollancz, Ltd., 1936):
   the development of Marx's views is traced in detail, as
   well as his reactions to the theories of various other
   writers since Hegel.

5. WEBB, S. and B. Soviet Communism: A New Civilisation ?
   (Longmans Green & Co. Ltd. 1935), I and II: these volumes
   may be used for reference purposes. They contain a detailed
   estimate of developments in Russia, and although legal
   theory is not dealt with specifically they provide a
   useful background to most aspects of Soviet law.

6. DJILAS, M. The New Class, (Thames & Hudson, 1957): this is a
   frank appraisal of communism by a disillusioned communist.
   It provides a good deal of information about the origins
   of Marx's ideas and about the result of their implementation
   in practice.

7. RUSSELL, B. Freedom and Organisation, 1814-1914, (Allen &
   Unwin, Ltd., 1934), chaps. 15-20: the progress of socialism
   is traced from the first British socialist, Robert Owen,
   and the British trade union movement. There is an account
   of the life and work of Marx, the application of dialectic

materialism in his political view is explained and its
weaknesses indicated.

1. KELSEN, H. The Communist Theory of Law, (Stevens & Sons, Ltd.,
   1955): the views on law of the various writers whose works
   are included in Soviet Legal Philosophy (supra) are
   critically considered. Some of the contradictions in their
   theories are exposed. The book is on the whole nihilistic
   in its attitude.

2. KELSEN, H. The Political Theory of Bolshevism, (University
   of California Press, 1948): this is a short critique of
   the communist theory, and in particular the dangers of
   relying on Hegel's dialects are pointed out. The various
   contradictions into which the Soviet theorists have been
   forced are also indicated.

3. OLIVECRONA, K. Law as Fact, (Einar Munksgaard, Copenhagen;
   Humphrey Milford, 1939; reprinted Wildy & Sons, 1962), pp.
   181-92: it is pointed out that the Marxists emphasise the
   use of force in capitalist societies but try to conceal it
   in their own. Force is an instrument without which society
   cannot function. There can be, therefore, no foundation
   for the prediction that law and state will wither away.
   Moral standards, too, are dependent on the regular
   application of force.

4. BERMAN, H.J. "Principles of Soviet Criminal Law" (1946-47)
   56 Yale L.J. 803: the early Revolutionary period introduced
   "crime by analogy" i.e. socially dangerous acts. After 1936
   criminal law was viewed as necessary even under socialism.

5. KIRALFY, A.K.R. "The Juvenile Law-breaker in the U.S.S.R."
   (1952) 15 M.L.R. 472: when confronted with a familiar
   problem the Soviet authorities have had to resort to
   familiar methods of dealing with it. The need to put young
   offenders to useful work and to stress family responsibility
   is pointed out.

6. HAZARD, J.N. "Soviet Government Corporation", (1942-43) 41
   Mich.L.R. 850: after a brief historical introduction to the
   topic, the creation and nature of these corporations are
   examined. They are independent legal persons which manage
   state-owned property.

7. BERMAN, H.J. "Commercial Contracts in Soviet Law" (1947) 35
   Calif.L.R. 191: Soviet state business enterprises are
   described very fully from the highest directing authorities
   downwards. Of particular interest are the extension of the
   concept of legal person and the tasks of the special

tribunals which deal with commercial contracts. The
contracts are examined in detail, and some specimen
decisions are included at the end.

1. COLLARD, D. "State Arbitration in the U.S.S.R." (1955) 18 M.
   L.R. 474: there has to be some speedy and efficient method
   of dealing with disputes between commercial concerns. This
   is accomplished by state arbitration. The nature and
   function of this institution are examined.

2. BERMAN, H.J. "Soviet Family Law in the Light of Russian
   History and Marxist Theory" (1946-47) 56 Yale L.J. 26: the
   pre-Revolutionary position in Russia and the Marxist theory
   of family relations are set out first. In the immediate
   post-Revolutionary period there was a tendency to preach
   the withering away of the family as well as law. Now,
   however, it is said that the task of law is to strengthen
   the socialist family. The various ways in which this end is
   sought are explained.

3. SVERDLOV, G.M. "Modern Soviet Divorce Practice" (trans.
   D. Collard, 1948), 11 M.L.R. 163: this article is of
   interest as showing the increasingly strict attitude taken
   by the Soviet government towards the sanctity of marriage.

4. WOLFF, M.M. "Some Aspects of Marriage and Divorce Laws in
   Soviet Russia" (1949) 12 M.L.R. 290: the position today is
   contrasted with the pre- and immediate post-Revolution
   positions. The steps towards increased respect for the
   family tie are traced out.

5. COHEN, J.A. "The Chinese Communist Party and Judicial
   Independence: 1949-1959" (1969) 82 Harv.L.R. 967: the 1954
   Chinese Constitution guaranteed judicial independence, but
   this appears to have been regretted soon after and courts
   were increasingly subordinated to Party control. The author
   examines in detail what "independence" means in this
   context and how the provision came to be included in the
   Constitution, and traces the subsequent relations between
   judges and the Party step by step. (See also S. LUBMAN:
   "Form and Function in the Chinese Criminal Process" (1969)
   69 Col.L.R. 535).

6. FRIEDMANN, W. Legal Theory, (5th ed., Stevens & Sons, Ltd.,
   1967), chap. 29: Renner's doctrine is first summarised and
   is followed by an account of legal developments in the
   U.S.S.R. and in Britain.

7. JONES, J.W. Historical Introduction to the Theory of Law,
   (Oxford, 1940), pp. 270-78: the teachings of Marx about the

progress of the class struggle and the evolution of
communism are explained with reference to developments in
the U.S.S.R.

1. LLOYD, D. Introduction to Jurisprudence, (1st ed., Stevens &
   Sons, Ltd., 1959), chap. 8: Hegel's doctrine is first
   explained and then Marx's adaptation of it. There is also
   a general outline of the position in Russia from the
   Revolution onwards.

2. LLOYD, D. The Idea of Law, (Penguin Books, Ltd., A 688, 1964),
   pp. 204-7, 220-22: the origin of Marx's doctrines in
   Hegelianism is explained briefly. In the latter pages the
   position in the Soviet Union and the principal contrasts
   between this and Western countries are set out.

3. PATTERSON, E.W. Jurisprudence, (The Foundation Press, Inc.,
   1953), pp. 435-38: the account of Marx follows that of
   Hegel. The main weaknesses of the Marxist theory are
   pointed out.

4. STONE, J. Social Dimensions of Law and Justice, (Stevens &
   Sons, Ltd., 1966), Chapter 10, and pp. 579-88: the
   severity of law in the Stalin period is not a "deviation"
   from "pure Marxism", since the Marxist doctrine is
   ambivalent. The state, differing from the bourgeoise state,
   can and should survive in socialism, which is but a
   transitional condition. At pp. 579-88 there is further
   discussion of the persistence of the economic determinist
   thesis.

5. BODENHEIMER, E. Jurisprudence, (Harvard University Press,
   1962), pp. 79-81, 239-40: the first section contains a
   very brief account of three main principles underlying the
   Marxist theory; the second mentions the theory of
   Pashukanis in outline.

6. ROSS, A. On Law and Justice, (Stevens & Sons, Ltd., 1958),
   pp. 347-57: Marx is said to have confused determinism with
   predestination. Certain parallels between the approaches
   of the Historical School and Marxism are indicated, and
   the general attitudes of both are criticised.

7. TIMASHEFF, N.S. "The Crisis in the Marxian Theory of Law"
   (1939) 10 N.Y.U.L.Q. 519: the manner in which Soviet
   jurists, led by Vyshinsky, revised their original ideas
   about law so as to accommodate its indispensability in the
   socialist scene is demonstrated.

8. TIMASHEFF, N.S. An Introduction to the Sociology of Law,

(Harvard University Committee on Research in the Social Sciences, 1939), pp. 371-74: there is a brief discussion of Marxist doctrine in the general context of theories which amount to a negation of law.

1. SOROKIN, P. Contemporary Sociological Theories, (Harper & Bros., New York, 1928), chap. 10: the economic interpretation of law goes much further back then Marx and Engels. The objections to the Marxist doctrines are set out in detail. The chapter also deals with relation between economic and other social phenomena.

2. CARLSTON, K.S. Law and Structure of Social Action, (Stevens & Sons, Ltd., 1956), pp. 74-84: the main difference in the position of the individual in the western world from that in the Communist world is said to be that in the former his choice of the roles that he plays in daily life is relatively free from governmental interference. The sphere of policy determination is more free from legal control in the communist world than in the west.

3. CAIRNS, H. Law and the Social Sciences, (Kegan Paul, Trench, Trubner & Co., Ltd., 1935), chap. 4: the inter-relation between law and economics is discussed. Various institutions of law are considered from this point of view and the weakness of an exclusively economic interpretation is pointed out.

4. JENKS, E. "Recent Theories of the State" (1927) 43 L.Q.R. 186, at pp. 196-203: this article was written at an early stage in the history of the Revolution and is mainly based on the views of Bukharine, which have since been discredited in Russia. It points out the main objections to Marxism, but also notes that there is some connection between economic conditions and legal doctrines.

5. FRIEDRICH, C.J. The Philosophy of Law in Historical Perspective, (University of Chicago Press, 1958), chap. 16: the theory of Marx and Engels is explained with reference to its Hegelian basis. The point is made that the Marxist exposure of ideologies has revealed its own ideology of social justice.

6. GINSBERG, M. On Justice in Society, (Heinemann, London, 1965), chap. 5: the ethical basis of economic justice is considered, chiefly in relation to property rights. The law fixes certain minima, but above that property differences need to be justified on a principle of proportionate equality, i.e., that differential treatment requires justification. What the relevant differences are is

considered in detail. In the course of the chapter the
shortcomings of the Marxist analysis are set out.

1. BRUNNER, E. Justice and the Social Order, (trans.
    M. Hottinger, Lutterworth Press, 1945), chap. 18,
    especially pp. 156-60: the question of social and economic
    justice is considered primarily from a Christian point of
    view. At pp. 156-60 justice in a capitalist and in a
    communist order are contrasted.

2. KANTOROWICZ, H.U. "Has Capitalism Failed in Law?" in Law: A
    Century of Progress, (New York University Press, 1937), II,
    p. 320: the author denies that capitalism has failed. The
    criticisms of capitalism are considered. Its failure has
    lain in not adapting law to changing conditions, but this
    has nothing to do with capitalism as such.

3. WILBERFORCE, R.O. "Law and Economics", Presidential Address
    to the Holdsworth Club, 1966: this is of general interest.
    Lord Wilberforce argues that lawyers have approached great
    changes in economic life with the aid of out-of-date or
    traditional concepts. These do not yield results which
    accord with the realities of the comtemporary world. There
    is now a need for lawyer-economists and economist-lawyers.

4. ROBINSON, H.W. "Law and Economics" (1939) 2 M.L.R. 257: this
    is of general interest. It constitutes a plea for a
    greater correlation of law and economics and criticises
    economists for not having faced the problems revealed by
    Marxism.

5. REUSCHLEIN, H.G. Jurisprudence - its American Prophets, (The
    Bobbs-Merrill Co., Inc., 1951), pp. 91-94, 265-71: Brooks
    Adams, writing at the beginning of the century, was an
    exponent of the idea that the common law was determined by
    economic factors. In the later passage the views of Laski
    are considered.

6. BEARD, C.A. An Economic Interpretation of the Constitution
    of the United States, (The Macmillan Co., New York, 1935):
    the thesis is that the Constitution was drafted by a small
    group who stood to benefit financially and who were
    especially concerned with the protection of acquired
    property. He endorses the theme that economic factors do
    play some part in moulding the law, but emphasises the
    fact that they are not exclusive.

7. BURDICK, F.M. "Is Law the Expression of Class Selfishness?"
    (1911-12) 25 Harv.L.R. 349: after an examination of

English and American decisions the author concludes that
law is not the expression of class interests, but
represents an honest attempt to do justice impartially.

1. COMMONS, J.R. "Value in Law and Economics" in Law: A Century
   of Progress, (New York University Press, 1937), II, 332:
   the varying criteria of value since Adam Smith are
   considered. Whereas the economists tended to base themselves
   on Bentham and the lawyers on Blackstone, it is said that
   neither side went to extremes.

2. PARRY, D.H. "Economic Theories in English Case-law" (1931)
   47 L.Q.R. 183: the various ways in which economic theories
   can influence law and the influence of particular economic
   theories are examined.

3. BOHLEN, F.H. Studies in the Law of Torts, (The Bobbs-Merrill
   Co., 1926), pp. 368-77: in the course of discussing the
   Rule in Rylands v. Fletcher, the effect of the different
   social and economic conditions in England and America are
   considered.

4. POUND, R. Interpretations of Legal History, (Cambridge
   University Press, 1923), chap. 5: the origins of the
   economic interpretation of law are set out. The attempt to
   discover an exclusively economic interpretation is viewed
   critically, especially in relation to the Rule in Rylands
   v. Fletcher and the doctrine of common employment (now
   obsolete). It is pointed out that those who attacked the
   injustice of the doctrine of common employment assumed the
   justice of the doctrine of vicarious responsibility. (See
   also R. POUND: "The Scope and Purpose of Sociological
   Jurisprudence" (1911-12) 25 Harv.L.R. pp. 162-68).

5. POUND, R. "The Economic Interpretation and the Law of Torts"
   (1939-40), 53 Harv.L.R. 365: this is a detailed examination
   of whether the economic factor is the sole or decisive
   factor. It is pointed out that many rules of tort are not
   and never were in accordance with the interests of the
   English landed gentry. The attack on the doctrine of common
   employment is further considered.

6. POUND, R. "Fifty Years of Jurisprudence" (1937-38) 51 Harv.L.
   R. pp. 777-85: the various tenets of the economic theory of
   law are reviewed with reference to developments in Russia.

7. POUND, R. The Ideal Element in Law, (University of Calcutta,
   1958), chap. 9: the economic interpretation can furnish
   only a partial explanation. Three of the main deficiencies
   are discussed.

1. POUND, R. Jurisprudence, (West Publishing Co., 1959), I, pp.
   227-64: three types of economic interpretations are
   distinguished. At pp. 254-64 the Marxist doctrine of
   economic determinism is dealt with.

2. GOLD, J. "Common Employment" (1937) 1 M.L.R. at pp. 225-30:
   the doctrine of common employment is ascribed to class bias
   and contentions to the contrary by Bohlen, Burdick and
   Pound are criticised.

3. HALL, J. Theft, Law and Society, (2nd ed., The Bobbs-Merrill
   Co., Inc., 1952), chap. 3: in this chapter the economic
   factors that have shaped the law of larceny are traced.

18

THE SOCIOLOGICAL APPROACH

Sociology of law and sociological jurisprudence

1. POUND, R. "Sociology of Law and Sociological Jurisprudence"
(1943-44), 5 Tor.L.J., 1: the sociology of law is said to
proceed from sociology towards law, sociological
jusrisprudence from history and philosophy to the
utilisation of the social sciences. The work of some
sociologists and anthropologists is considered.

2. LEPAULLE, P. "The Function of Comparative Law with a Critique
of Sociological Jurisprudence" (1921-22), 35 Harv.L.R.,
838: in the earlier part of the article the difference
between sociological jurisprudence and sociology is
discussed. The difference relates to the method and
objective.

3. GURVITCH, G. Sociology of Law, (Routledge & Kegan Paul, Ltd.,
1947): whenever men come together in society there is a
common feeling out of which emerges rules of behaviour. The
task of sociology is to enumerate and classify the main
types of social life. The task of sociological jurisprudence
is to study the types of law which these produce. The first
part of the book concerns the work of others. In the latter
part the thesis is that there are several layers of social
organisation. At the eighth layer there is said to be the
"collective mind", which interacts with spiritual values
and sets standards. The function of law is to regulate
behaviour so as to harmonise with the values of the
collective mind.

4. TIMASHEFF, N.S. "What is 'Sociology of Law'?" (1937), 43 A.J.
S., 225: human behaviour in society in its relation to law
is the object of the sociology of law. It is a casual
investigation whose chief methods are introspective
observations of one's own consciousness in relation to law,
the study of behaviour in relation to law and experimental
tests.

5. TIMASHEFF, N.S. An Introduction to the Sociology of Law,
(Harvard University Committee on Research in the Social
Sciences, 1939): law is a combination of power and ethics.
Ethics is the realisation of patterns of conduct by means
of group conviction; power is the imposition of patterns
of conduct by force. The two are independent, but they
overlap, "ethical imperative co-ordination". "Law" covers
rules emanating from the state, "upper state level of law",
and rules emanating from social groups, e.g., clubs, "lower
social level".

1. SAWER, G. Law in Society (Oxford, 1965): the book does not
    develop any specific theory, but deals generally with such
    matters as the distinction between the sociology of law
    and sociological jurisprudence, aspects of primitive and
    archaic systems, courts, judges, lawyers and the development
    of an accepted social order (which becomes identified with
    "lawyers' Law") and social administration which introduces
    modifications. In time these, too, become absorbed into the
    accepted social order. In the course of all this there are
    many superficial accounts of well-known theories.

2. CAIRNS, H. The Theory of Legal Science, (University of North
    Carolina Press, 1941): a pure science of law should study
    human behaviour as a function of disorder. Law consists of
    one set of patterns of conduct concretised in rules.
    Jurisprudence is not as yet in a position to formulate
    sociological principles; so its function is merely to
    describe. The field of study comprises six elements that
    are said to be present in all systems.

3. STONE, J. Social Dimensions of Law and Justice, (Stevens &
    Sons, Ltd.), Chap. 1: the need for both overall theory and
    guidance in dealing with ad hoc problems is considered in
    detail. Attention is also paid to the best way in which
    lawyers might study the "external relations" of law, and
    there are reviews of the development of sociological study.
    The question whether there is a meaningful distinction
    between sociology of law and sociological jurisprudence is
    discussed. The views of Timasheff and Cairns are criticised.

4. SOROKIN, P. Contemporary Sociological Theories, (Harper &
    Bros., 1928): the various forms which sociological
    theorising has assumed are examined in detail. The
    important feature of the book is its presentation of the
    factual material by which theories are to be evaluated.

5. GINSBERG, M. Reason and Unreason in Society, (Longman, Green
    & Co., 1947), Part I: this is of general interest only. The
    problems and methods of sociology, the development of the
    subject and the work of some leading figures in the field
    are dealt with.

6. SEAGLE, W. The Quest for Law, (Alfred A. Knopf, 1941): this
    is a historical study. The phenomena of social life are
    investigated in order to discover the regularities and
    connections between certain social phenomena as such, or
    between certain natural and social phenomena. As applied to
    law, the study involves a consideration of laws of all times
    and places.

1. CASTBERG, F. Problems of Legal Philosophy, (2nd ed., Oslo Universtiy Press; Allen & Unwin, Ltd., 1957), pp. 10-15: sociology aims at discovering the social rules which govern the legal relations of human beings. It is a causal science dealing with law as a psycho-physical phenomenon.

2. SALMOND, J.W. Jurisprudence, (11th ed., G.L. Williams, Sweet & Maxwell, Ltd., 1957), pp. 14-17: the nature of legal sociology is considered very generally. Works on the sociology of law are approved as being useful, but those on sociological jurisprudence are treated as being of little value.

3. KOCOUREK, A. An Introduction to the Science of Law, (Little, Brown & Co., 1930), pp. 226-28: the aims and objects of the sociological school are briefly summarised.

4. SHKLAR, J.N. Legalism, (Harvard University Press, 1964): The entire plea in this book is that legal theorists should abandon "legalism" and pay heed to the social situation around them. "Legalism" is the attitude of mind that makes a morality of rule following; but this is only one morality in a pluralist society. Law, it is argued, is an instrument of politics and, as such, may appropriately be applied in certain situations, but not in others. The book is a criticism of Positivism and Natural Law theorising, but no constructive suggestion is offered to further its plea.

5. EHRLICH, E. "Montesquieu and Sociological Jurisprudence" (1915-16), 29 Harv.L.R., 582: Montesquieu's work is regarded as the pioneer attempt to found a sociology of law, and is considered from this angle.

6. ILBERT, C. "Montesquieu" in Great Jurists of the World, (edd. J. MacDonell and E. Manson, John Murray, 1913), 417: an account is given of the life and work of Montesquieu. His sociological approach is touched on in the course of the discussion of The Spirit of Laws.

7. HAZO, R.G. "Montesquieu and the Separation of Powers" (1968) 54 Am.B.A.J. 665: an account is given of his life and contributions. These were a new classification of governments, a pioneer insistence on the influence of climate and environment and the doctrine of the separation of powers.

8. HOLMES, O.W. "Montesquieu" in Collected Legal Papers, (Constable & Co. Ltd., 1920), 250: in this charmingly written account of Montesquieu's life an attempt is made to show how threads drawn from various aspects of his career and character united to produce his The Spirit of Law.

1. EMMET, D. Rules, Roles and Relations, (Macmillan, 1966):
    neither sociology nor ethics can be insulated from each
    other. Patterns of social behaviour are not just
    regularities of how people act, but are the result of ideas
    as to what is the right, useful or proper thing to do.
    People rely on expectations of mutual behaviour, derived
    from social roles. The nature of sociological explanation
    and moral judgment, and the influence of roles, are
    considered along these lines.

R. von Ihering

2. von IHERING, R. Law as a Means to an End, (trans. I. Husik,
    The Boston Book Co., 1913): this is Ihering's classic
    exposition of his view that law is designed to fulfil some
    purpose.

3. von IHERING, R. Geist des romischen Rechts, (Leipzig, 1898),
    II, pp. 309-89: this is a prior revelation of Ihering's
    conviction that law serves purpose. He perceived in his
    study of Roman law that it was based on interests and that
    the task of the law was the reconciliation of conflicting
    interests.

4. STONE, J. Legal System and Lawyers' Reasonings, (Stevens &
    Sons, Ltd., 1964), pp. 224-229: the Pandectists tried to
    bridge the gap between the Roman Law and the needs of the
    countries that had received it centuries later. But
    deduction from the Corpus Juris provided answers unsuited
    to contemporary needs. It is in this context that the work
    of Ihering is touched on.

5. STONE, J. Human Law and Human Justice, (Stevens & Sons, Ltd.,
    1965), pp. 147-159: the work of Ihering is discussed in
    relation to contemporary thought. He reacted against the
    individualist attitude of mind, including that of Bentham
    and Mill, however much he admired their work. It is pointed
    out that as a theory of justice his concept of social
    utility is unhelpful, since this is not something given or
    known, but what is sought to be discovered.

6. PATTERSON, E.W. Jurisprudence, (The Foundation Press, Inc.,
    1953), pp. 459-64: this contains a short account of the
    work of Ihering.

7. JENKINS, I. "Rudolph von Ihering" (1960-61), 14 Vand.L.R.,
    169: Ihering's work is appraised in an interesting way.
    The author contends that Ihering sought to inquire into
    the foundations of legal order and to relate law to the
    whole of man's cultural and spiritual setting. His followers,

on the other hand, have limited themselves to tracing the relation between law and political and economic forces.

1. MORRIS, C. The Great Legal Philosophers, (University of Pennsylvania Press, 1959), chap. 16: extracts from Ihering's works are included and might be regarded as fairly representative of his main thesis.

2. FRIEDRICH, C.J. The Philosophy of Law in Historical Perspective, (University of Chicago Press, 1958), chap. 17: the earlier part of this chapter is devoted to an account and estimation of Ihering's contribution.

3. MACDONELL, J. "Rudolph von Ihering" in Great Jurists of the World, (edd. J. MacDonell and E. Manson, John Murray, 1913), 590: an account is given of the life, character and various works of Ihering. There are also short appraisals of the latter.

4. GOLUNSKII, S.A. and STROGOVICH, M.S. "The Theory of the State and Law" in Soviet Legal Philosophy, (trans. H.W. Babb, Harvard University Press, 1951), pp. 413-15: the views of Ihering are considered from a Marxist point of view and rejected. He is praised for having attempted to be more "realistic" than his predecessors, but is alleged to have failed to perceive the class character of the institutions with which he dealt.

5. The Jurisprudence of Interests, (trans. M.M. Schoch, Harvard University Press, 1948): it is convenient to append some reference to the Tübingen School here (although in the text it is dealt with immediately before the work of Pound). This School more or less took up the task where Ihering left it and considers purpose in the practical interpretation of the law.

E. Ehrlich

6. ERHLICH, E. Fundamental Principles of the Sociology of Law, (trans. W.L. Moll, Harvard University Press, 1936), especially pp. 489-506: in this series of essays the author develops his central thesis that the development of law lies in society. There are also discussions of the methods of legal sociology, justice, custom and codification.

7. ERHLICH, E. "Sociology of Law" (trans. N. Isaacs, 1921-22), 36 Harv.L.R., 129: laws may differ from country to country, but in so far as there is a social order among civilised societies, there are elements in common. Society is older than law and must have had some kind of order before legal provisions came into being.

1. MORRIS, C. The Great Legal Philosophers, (University of Pennsylvania Press, 1959), chap. 18: extracts from the works of E. Erhlich are given.

2. VINOGRADOFF, P. Collected Papers, (Oxford, 1928), II, chap. 11: the trend towards sociological jurisprudence is considered, principally with reference to the work of Ehrlich.

3. SAWER, G. Law in Society, (Oxford, 1965), pp. 174-7: this is a brief critique of Ehrlich's doctrine, pointing out its inconsistencies.

J. Bentham

4. BENTHAM, J. Works, (ed. J. Bowring, William Tait, 1843), I: two of Bentham's most important works are included in this volume, namely, An Introduction to the Principles of Morals and Legislation and A Fragment on Government. The principle of utility is explained at the outset and runs through most of Bentham's work.

5. BENTHAM, J. The Theory of Legislation, (5th ed., trans. R. Hildreth, Trubner & Co., Ltd., 1887): this is another of Bentham's important contributions. The editor's Introduction is especially deserving of study, for he makes out a reasoned case for supposing that Bentham will prove to have been one of the greatest Europeans.

6. HOLDSWORTH, W.S. A History of English Law, XIII, (ed. A.L. Goodhart and H.G. Hanbury, Methuen & Co., Ltd., 1952), pp. 41-155: in this posthumously published volume of Holdsworth's History is to be found a full account of the background and the life and work of Bentham, and shorter accounts of James and J.S. Mill. At pp. 68-81 the principle of utility is discussed.

7. Jeremy Bentham and the Law. A symposium, (edd. G.W. Keeton and G. Schwarzenberger, Stevens & Sons, Ltd., 1948), especially chaps. 12 and 13: Bentham's contribution to law is discussed from various angles. In chapter 8, G. Schwarzenberger considers Bentham's contribution to international law, including his invention of the name, while in chapter 12, W. Friedmann draws attention to the inter-related nature of Bentham's thought and considers his many contributions as a lawyer and social reformer. In chapter 13, A.J. Ayer examines the principle of utility in detail. It might also be noted that H.F. Jolowicz followed up his contribution about Bentham in this volume with a further article, entitled "Jeremy Bentham and the Law", (1948) 1 C.L.P. 1.

1. AUSTIN, J. Lectures on Jurisprudence, (5th ed., R. Campbell, John Murray, 1885), I, chaps. 2-4: Austin, as befits Bentham's pupil, endeavours to work the utility principle into his discussion of the nature of law. Utility is the test by which the tendency of action is evaluated. The principle is considered in relation to the laws of God, and is defended against certain objections.

2. HART, H.L.A. "Bentham and Sovereignty" (1967) 2 Ir.Jur. (N.S.) 327: Bentham was a greater thinker than Austin. Austin's concept of sovereignty excluded legal limitations on sovereign power, any division of it and a plurality of sovereigns each with full power. Bentham did not commit himself to such extremes although his treatment of sovereignty is hesitant and sometimes obscure.

3. PATTERSON, E.W. Jurisprudence, (The Foundation Press, Inc., 1953), pp. 439-59: this is a short but very good account of Bentham. A brief account of his life is given and is followed by a discussion of his principle of utility with reference to ethics and legislation in turn.

4. ROSS, A. On Law and Justice, (Stevens & Sons, Ltd., 1958), chap. 13: Bentham's utilitarianism is subjected to acute criticism. "Social Welfare" is a mythical idea, since the community is not an independent unit.

5. DOWRICK, F.E. Justice According to the English Common Lawyers, (Butterworths, 1961), chap. 6: the idea of utility as a principle of justice is examined, primarily with reference to the work of Bentham. Mention is also made of his predecessors, and of his successors, who gave it much of its impetus.

6. STONE, J. Human Law and Human Justice, (Stevens & Sons, Ltd., 1965), chap. 4: the utilitarian philosophy of Bentham is developed at length. Its origins, background and influence are gone into in detail. The major criticisms of his pleasure-pain calculus are also discussed.

7. JOLOWICZ, H.F. Lectures on Jurisprudence, (ed. J.A. Jolowicz, The Athlone Press, 1963), pp. 101-6: this contains a brief account of Bentham's work and influence.

8. BAUMGARDT, D. Bentham and the Ethics of Today, (Princeton University Press, 1952), especially pp. 165-320: in this important book the author considers Bentham's ethical theory and the evolution of his thought with reference to his writings. At pp. 165-320 the principle of utility is considered with reference to An Introduction to the

Principles of Morals and Legislation.

1. COING, H. "Bentham's Influence on the Development of
   Interessenjurisprudenz and General Jurisprudence" (1967) 2
   Ir.Jur. (N.S.) 336: the author begins by outlining Bentham's
   influence on Germanic thought through Beneke and Ihering.
   He then shows that German interessenjurisprudenz did not
   get quite as far as Bentham's principle of the greatest
   happiness of the greatest number.

2. HOLDSWORTH, W.S. Some Makers of English Law, (Cambridge
   University Press, 1938), pp. 248-56: a somewhat short
   account is given of Bentham and his work and the reasons
   for its influence.

3. ATKINSON, C.M. Jeremy Bentham. His Life and Work, (Methuen &
   Co., 1903): a readable and detailed account is given of
   Bentham's life and work. The book is of general interest.

4. EVERETT, C.W. The Education of Jeremy Bentham, (Columbia
   University Press, 1931): Bentham's early career is
   recounted. Chapter 9 is of direct relevance in that it
   deals with the origins of his An Introduction to the
   Principles of Morals and Legislation.

5. ALLEN, C.K. Legal Duties, (Oxford, 1931), 119: in this paper,
   entitled "The Young Bentham", an account is given of his
   early career as providing a background to his later work.

6. HOLLOND, H.A. "Jeremy Bentham, 1748-1832" (1948), 10 C.L.J.,
   3: this gives a most readable and convenient account of
   Bentham's life and work in historical perspective.

7. OGDEN, C.K. Jeremy Bentham, 1832-2032, (Kegan Paul, Trench,
   Trubner & Co., Ltd., 1932): this short booklet contains a
   lecture which assesses Bentham's work with reference to
   the past, present and future. A list of the reforms
   effected by him is given at pp. 19-20.

8. SMITH, J.C. "Law, Language, and Philosophy" (1968) 3 U.Br.Col.
   L.R. 59: Bentham was in his way an acute semanticist. In
   the course of reviewing the attitude to language of various
   legal philosophers, that of Bentham is explained and
   considered.

9. HERON, D.C. An Introduction to the History of Jurisprudence,
   (J.W. Parker & Son, 1860), Part VI, chap. 3: an account is
   given of Bentham's work and influence.

10. RANDALL, H.J. "Jeremy Bentham" (1906), 22 L.Q.R., 311: this

contains a general appreciation of Bentham's contribution.
See also J.L. STOCKS: Jeremy Bentham, 1748-1832, (Manchester
University Press, 1933).

1. NYS, E. "Notes Inedites de Bentham sur le Droit International"
   (1885), I L.Q.R., 225: this is a short account (in French)
   of certain notes left by Bentham on the formation of an
   international order. The Notes themselves are reproduced
   verbatim.

2. ZANE, J.M. "Bentham" in Great Jurists of the World, (edd.
   J. MacDonell and E. Manson, John Murray, 1913), 532: this
   is, on the whole, an uncomplimentary appraisal of Bentham's
   work. It is stated that his lack of historical sense, his
   contempt for case-law and his ignorance of Roamn law
   disqualify him from the title to being a jurist. It is
   also alleged that he was out of touch with the times.

3. JENNINGS, W.I. "A Plea for Utilitarianism" (1938), 2 M.L.R.,
   22: the subject of "jurisprudence" begins with Bentham.
   Generality in it is not to be found in legal concepts so
   much as in social phenomena.

4. COHEN, F.S. Ethical Systems and Legal Ideals, (Falcon Press,
   1933), chaps. 2 and 3: it is unquestionable that criticism
   and improvement of law has to stem from an ethical basis.
   The most appropriate basis is utilitarian. The law should
   be criticised according as it tends to produce happiness.

5. ECKHOFF, T. "Justice and Social Utility" in Legal Essays. A
   Tribute to Frede Castberg, (Universitetsforlaget, 1963),
   74: the principles of justice and social utility are
   explained and compared and the parts they respectively play
   are demonstrated.

6. LUMB, R.D. "Natural Law and Legal Positivism" (1958-59) 11
   J.L.E., pp. 503-8: the Utilitarian doctrine, as expounded
   by Bentham and Austin, is compared with natural law and
   criticised on various grounds.

7. MORRIS, C. The Great Legal Philosophers, (University of
   Pennsylvania Press, 1959), chapter 11: at pp. 262-76 there
   are extracts from An Introduction to the Principles of
   Morals and Legislation. The rest of the chapter contains
   passages from The Limits of Jurisprudence Defined. Chapter
   15, which contains extracts from the writings of J.S. Mill
   might also be consulted.

8. RUSSELL, B. Freedom and Organisation: 1814-1914, (Allen &
   Unwin, Ltd., 1934), chaps. 9-12: chapter 9 deals with

Bentham, and chapter 12 with the Benthamite doctrine. The two intervening chapters deal with Mill and Ricardo.

1. FRIEDRICH, C.J. The Philosophy of Law in Historical Perspective, (The University of Chicago Press, 1958), chap. 11: the influence of Hobbes is traced through Hume to the Utilitarians. Among the latter, the contributions of Bentham and of Austin are discussed.

2. MURRAY, R.H. The History of Political Science from Plato to the Present, (Heffer & Sons, Ltd., 1926), chap. 10: the utilitarian outlook is examined in detail from the time of Hume onwards. There are good accounts of the work of Bentham and of the two Mills.

3. SABINE, G.H. A History of Political Theory, (3rd ed., Harrap & Co. Ltd., 1963), chaps. 31 and 32: these two chapters are concerned with liberalism, in the course of which the greatest happiness principle of Bentham is considered at length as well as his views on law. In the first part of the second chapter Mill's contribution is dealt with.

R. Pound

4. POUND, R. "The Scope and Purpose of Sociological Jurisprudence" (1910-11), 24 Harv.L.R., 591, at pp, 611-19; (1911-12), 25 Harv.L.R., pp. 140-47, 489: the origins of the sociological movement are first traced out in the course of a general survey of jurisprudential schools. The work of Ihering is touched on and his insistence on interests. Sociological jurisprudence tries to ensure that law-making, interpretation and application take more account of social facts.

5. POUND, R. "A Survey of Social Interests" (1943-44), 57 Harv. L.R., 1, (being a rewriting of "A Study of Social Interests" (1921), 15 Papers and Proceedings of the American Sociological Society, 16): interests are divided into individual, public and social. For some purposes it is convenient to regard a given claim from the point of view of one category, for other purposes from another. When weighing interests they should be considered on the same plane. Generally, it is expedient to consider interests on a social plane. The scheme of interests is set out in detail.

6. POUND, R. "Interests of Personality" (1914-15), 28 Harv.L.R., 343, 445: after a general explanation of what "interests" are, individual interests are considered in detail. It is pointed out that the securing of individual interests is also a social interest: hence they should be considered on

this plane. The ways in which individual interests might
be classified are then considered.

1. POUND, R. "Individual Interests of Substance - Promised
   Advantages" (1945-46), 59 Harv.L.R., 1: the task of a
   legal order is to secure reasonable individual expectations
   so far as they may be harmonised with the least friction
   and waste. The history of the law shows a progressive
   recognition of the interest, both social and individual,
   in the fulfilment of promises.

2. POUND, R. "Mechanical Jurisprudence" (1908), 8 Col.L.R., 605:
   law is a means towards the administration of justice. It
   should be judged by its results. It should neither become
   too scientific for people to appreciate its working, nor
   petrified by technicality (mechanical). The institutions of
   law should be founded on policy and adapted to human needs.

3. POUND, R. "Law in Books and Law in Action" (1910), 44 Am.L.
   R., 12: attention is drawn to the growing divergence
   between legal principle and how it actually operates.
   Jurisprudence should proceed by taking account of social
   facts.

4. POUND, R. "The Administration of Justice in the Modern City"
   (1912-13), 26 Harv.L.R., 302: the problem that confronted
   administrators immediately after the American Revolution is
   contrasted with those confronting modern administrators.
   On this basis the need for a sociological approach is
   stressed.

5. POUND, R. "The End of Law as Developed in Legal Rules and
   Doctrines" (1913-14), 27 Harv.L.R., 195: this is a lengthy
   inquiry into the policies underlying successive periods of
   legal development, starting with archaic law and ending
   with modern law.

6. POUND, R. "The End of Law as Developed in Juristic Thought"
   (1913-14), 27 Harv.L.R., 605; (1916-17), 30 Harv.L.R., 201:
   this is an inquiry parallel to the last one, but viewed
   from the angle of legal theory.

7. POUND, R. "The Theory of Judicial Decision" (1922-23), 36
   Harv.L.R., 640, 802, 940: judges are guided by the
   prevalent legal theory. In the 17th and 18th centuries this
   was the theory of Natural Law. A theory of judicial
   decision for today has to take account of two factors, to
   decide the particular dispute justly and to declare the law
   for the future. All this brings in the idea of social
   engineering.

1. POUND, R. "Fifty Years of Jurisprudence" (1936-37), 50 Harv.
    557; (1937-38), 51 Harv.L.R., 444, 777: in the last decade
    of the 19th century the Historical and Analytical Schools
    were dominant. The 20th century has witnessed the rise of
    the Social-philosophical school. The various movements of
    the century are reviewed.

2. POUND, R. in My Philosophy of Law, (Boston Law Book Co.,
    1941), p. 249: law is a form of social control and the end
    of law is, therefore, social control, which is to adjust
    relations and order behaviour so as to satisfy as many
    demands as possible with the least friction and waste.

3. POUND, R. "Natural Natural Law and Positive Natural Law"
    (1952), 68 L.Q.R., 330; (1960), 5 Nat.L.F. 70: the
    distinction is drawn and amplified in the second article.
    The function of natural law ideology is said to be both
    creative and critical.

4. POUND, R. "The Lawyer as a Social Engineer" (1954), 3 J.P.L.,
    292: a social engineer is one who makes a social process
    achieve its purpose with the minimum waste or friction.
    The lawyer's task is to satisfy as many demands as possible
    in this way. The ways in which this has to be accomplished
    are explained, and there is a plea for a Department of
    Justice.

5. POUND, R. The Spirit of the Common Law, (Marshall Jones Co.,
    Boston, 1921), chap. 8: the preceding chapters deal with
    different stages of legal development. The present stage is
    that of the socialisation of law, which requires social
    engineering. The differences in the results that would be
    obtained by a social approach to law from those obtained by
    other approaches are illustrated.

6. POUND, R. An Introduction to the Philosophy of Law, (Yale
    University Press, 1922), chap. 2, especially pp. 89-99: the
    question, "What is the end of law?" has had various answers
    given to it throughout the ages. At the present time the
    wants of man are prominent, and there is a need to balance
    the wants and desires of men. There is some discussion as
    to how interests are to be valued and balanced.

7. POUND, R. Interpretations of Legal History, (Cambridge
    University Press, 1923), chap. 7: in this chapter the
    "engineering interpretation" is explained and advocated.
    It is introduced by way of an explanation of Kohler's views.

8. POUND, R. Contemporary Juristic Theory, (Ward Ritchie Press,
    1940), chap. 3: this contains a discussion of social

engineering and the adjustment of interests so as to
produce the minimum of waste and friction.

1. POUND, R. Social Control Through Law, (Yale University Press,
    1942): law is a means of social control by controlling
    internal (i.e., human) nature. The function of law is social
    engineering, but in this task morals, religion and education
    also have a part to play.

2. POUND, R. Jurisprudence, (West Publishing Co., 1959), I, chap.
    6; II, pp. 79 et seq., 186 et seq., 272 et seq.: in chapter
    6 of the first volume there is a full historical survey of
    the different types of sociological jurisprudence. It puts
    Anglo-American and Continental thought in perspective. In
    the second volume theories of law from social-philosophical
    and sociological points of view are considered, including
    the views of Comte, Ehrlich and others. The sociological
    view of the relationship between law and morals is also
    explained.

3. PATTERSON, E.W. "Roscoe Pound on Jurisprudence", (1960), 60
    Col.L.R., 1124, especially at pp. 1128-29: this is a review
    of Pound's Jurisprudence (supra). Sociology is specifically
    touched on at p. 1128.

4. PATTERSON, E.W. "Pound's Theory of Social Interests" in
    Interpretations of Modern Legal Philosophies, (ed. P. Sayre,
    Oxford University Press, New York, 1947), chap. 26: the
    characteristics of a social interest are discussed, foremost
    among which is the fact that it should serve as a measuring
    device for individual interests. For legislative purposes,
    social interests are guides to what ought to become law;
    for judicial purposes, they are analogous to rules of law.
    "Weighing" interests means "making a choice".

5. PATTERSON, E.W. Jurisprudence, (The Foundation Press, Inc.,
    1953), pp. 509-27: an explanatory account is given of
    Pound's philosophy. This is a useful summary of his many
    writings.

6. PATON, G.W. "Pound and Contemporary Juristic Theory" (1944),
    22 Can.B.R., 479: the relation of Pound's work to
    administrative law, modern Realism, sociology and
    sociological jurisprudence and legal philosophy is discussed
    in turn. According to the analysis, Pound is regarded as a
    sociological jurist rather than as a sociologist. Pound's
    "social engineering" is said to be a relativist philosophy
    (i.e., relative to time and place) despite Pound's own
    criticism of relativist philosophies as "give it up
    philosophies".

1. STONE, J. "A Critique of Pound's Theory of Justice" (1934-35),
   20 Iowa L.R., 531: Pound's theory is examined with reference
   to its origins and the claims which Pound makes. The
   difficulties which it encounters are also indicated.

2. STONE, J. "The Golden Age of Pound" (1962), 4 Syd.L.R. 1:
   this is primarily a review of Pound's Jurisprudence. Its
   importance lies in the criticisms that are made of the
   theory of interests. Stone also questions Patterson's
   interpretation of Pound's meaning of "social interest"
   (supra).

3. STONE, J. "Roscoe Pound and Sociological Jurisprudence"
   (1964-65) 78 Harv.L.R. 1578: this tribute, written as a
   memorial to Roscoe Pound, estimates the present state of
   sociological jurisprudence in relation to Pound's work.
   (For other appreciations in the same volume, see T.C. CLARK:
   "Tribute to Roscoe Pound", p. 1; E.N. GRISWOLD: "Roscoe
   Pound - 1870-1964", p. 4; A.E. SUTHERLAND: "One Man in his
   Time, p. 7; A.L. GOODHART: "Roscoe Pound, p. 23;
   A.W. SCOTT, "Pound's Influence on Civil Procedure", p.1568;
   A.T. von MEHREN: "Roscoe Pound and Comparative Law", p.
   1585).

4. STONE, J. Human Law and Human Justice (Stevens & Sons, Ltd.,
   1965), chap. 9: in this chapter the author collates all
   his previous accounts, critiques and defences of Pound's
   work. The ambiguities in Pound's position and the
   difficulties which his theory of interests encounters are
   set out in detail.

5. STONE, J. Social Dimensions of Law and Justice, (Stevens &
   Sons, Ltd., 1966), chap. 4: Pound's scheme of listing de
   facto interests, though criticised, is adopted as being
   the best model. Of particular interest is the author's
   rejection of Pound's category of "public interests". The
   nature of interests and public policy are explained at
   length.

6. HARDING, A.L. "Professor Pound makes History" in Southern
   Methodist University Studies in Jurisprudence, (ed.
   A.L. Harding, SMU Press, 1957), IV, p. 3: this is a
   discussion of Pound's address in 1906 and the impact which
   his thought, as expounded in it, has since made.

7. BOWKER, W.F. "Basic Rights and Freedoms: What are they?"
   (1959), 37 Can.B.R., 43: this may be read as a contrast to
   Pound's scheme. Individual interests are listed on a
   different plan altogether. (The other contributions to this
   volume are also useful).

1. LEPAULLE, P. "The Function of Comparative Law with a Critique
   of Sociological Jurisprudence" (1921-22), 35 Harv.L.R., 838:
   after explaining the difference between sociological
   jurisprudence and sociology (<u>supra</u>), Pound's theory is
   criticised on the ground that there are basic weaknesses in
   his idea of "interest" and "balancing".

2. FRIED, C. "Two Concepts of Interests: Some Reflections on the
   Supreme Court's Balancing Test" (1962-63), 76 Harv.L.R.,
   755: a distinction is drawn between "wants" and "interests".
   The balancing test is ambiguous, for it can be stated in
   different ways. In order to decide in which way the issue
   should be stated, the court has to decide upon its own role.
   The issue should be stated in a way that does not pre-judge
   it.

3. ROSS, A. <u>On Law and Justice</u>, (Stevens & Sons, Ltd., 1958),
   chaps. 12 and 17: in the first of these chapters the point
   is made in the course of a general discussion of justice
   that one meaning of this word is the equal balancing of the
   interests to be affected by a decision. But the question
   remains as to how interests are to be "weighed". Chapter 17
   is a powerful criticism of the whole idea of "interests".
   Interests are attitudes based on needs as distinct from
   those based on morals. All interests are experienced by
   individuals, but they may coincide, be connected or be
   shared. The division of them into individual and social
   categories is regarded as futile.

4. DICKINSON, J. "Social Order and Political Authority" (1929),
   23 Am.Pol.Sc.R., 293, at pp. 294-301: the author points out
   the futility of trying to catalogue interests and gives
   reasons why any such attempt is bound to fail.

5. LLEWELLYN, K.N. <u>Jurisprudence. Realism in Theory and Practice</u>,
   (University of Chicago Press, 1962), chap. 1: the doctrine
   of balancing of interests gives no indication of how to
   identify interests and how to balance them. In this paper
   the "realist" criticism of Pound's doctrine is formulated.

6. WILSON, B. "A Choice of Values" (1961), 4 Can.B.J., 448:
   Pound's idea of social engineering is said to be
   particularly appropriate to modern social legislation. The
   balancing of interests is considered with reference to the
   law of nuisance.

7. PROSSER, W.L. <u>Handbook of the Law of Torts</u>, (2nd ed., West
   Publishing Co., 1955), chap. 1, pp. 12-20: social engineering
   is considered with reference to the law of torts, which is
   concerned with the adjustment of conflicting interests of

individuals so as to achieve a desirable social result. The various factors that have to be taken into account are listed and explained.

1. GROSSMAN, W.L. "The Legal Philosophy of Roscoe Pound" (1934-35), 44 Yale L.J., 605: Pound's doctrine is explained with reference to the work of three of his predecessors, namely, Ihering, Kohler and James. The engineering theory itself is critically examined and its shortcomings indicated.

2. AMOS, M.S. "Roscoe Pound" in Modern Theories of Law, (ed. W.I. Jennings, Oxford University Press, 1933), 86: what people think about law affects the kind of law that they make. It is not possible for judges simply to apply the law. They need to think as legislators, i.e., to take account of the purpose of law.

3. DOWRICK, F.E. Justice According to the English Common Lawyers, (Butterworths, 1961), chap. 7: Pound's contribution towards the achievement of social justice is explained and is then compared with similar, though isolated, utterances and decisions that have been made by English judges.

4. SAWER, G. Law in Society (Oxford, 1965), chap. 9: the main concern of this chapter is with Pound's interest theory. Attention is drawn to the inadequate treatment of the interests of institutions as such.

5. MORRIS, C. The Great Legal Philosophers, (University of Pennsylvania Press, 1959), chap. 22: this reproduces Pound's contribution to My Philosophy of Law (supra).

6. KOCOUREK, A. "Roscoe Pound as a Former Colleague Knew Him" in Interpretations of Modern Legal Philosophies, (ed. P. Sayre, Oxford University Press, New York, 1947), chap. 19: this provides an amusing and lively sketch of Pound as a man.

7. CLARK, T.C., GRISWOLD, E.N., SUTHERLAND, A.E., GOODHART, A.L.: "Roscoe Pound" (1964-65) 78 Harv.L.R. 1, 4, 7, 23: these four tributes to Pound's life and work provide assessments of his contribution.

L. Duguit

8. DUGUIT, L. Law in the Modern State, (trans. F. and H.J. Laski, Allen & Unwin, Ltd., 1921): the meaning of sovereignty and the collapse of traditional ideas about sovereignty and the state are set out in detail. The Introduction, pp. xvi-xxxiv outlines the main points of Duguit's doctrine and the objections to it.

1. DUGUIT, L. in <u>Modern French Legal Philosophy</u>, (trans.
   F.W. Scott and J.P. Chamberlain, The Macmillan Co., New
   York, 1921), Part II, chaps. 8-11: Duguit sets out his
   theory in some detail and compares the theories of some
   other writers. Chapter 9 is the most important, as it
   contains the core of this theory. Also of interest is Part
   I, chap. 11, in which Charmont critically summarises Duguit's
   doctrine.

2. DUGUIT, L. "The Law and the State" (trans. F.J. de Sloovere,
   1917), 31 Harv.L.R., 1: the state is not a person apart
   from the individuals in it; nor is there any will of the
   state apart from those of individuals. The whole idea of
   natural rights of man is unsupported, since Man has always
   lived in society, <u>i.e.</u>, has always been dependent.

3. DUGUIT, L. "Objective Law" (trans. M. Grandgent and
   R.W. Gifford, 1920), 20 Col.L.R., 817; (1921), 21 Col.L.R.,
   17, 126, 242: the distinction between "objective" and
   "subjective" law is explained. An inquiry into the latter
   is useless. Men are united in society; they have common as
   well as diverse needs. This produces a division of labour,
   <u>i.e.</u>, organic solidarity. An economic or moral rule becomes
   a legal rule when it is penetrated by the consciousness of
   the mass of individuals composing a given group. (This
   serial article should only be used by way of comparison
   with Duguit's other writings).

4. LASKI, H.J. "M. Duguit's Conception of the State" in <u>Modern
   Theories of Law</u>, (ed. W.I. Jennings, Oxford University
   Press, 1933), chap. 4: Duguit's work is regarded as an
   outstanding contribution to legal and social philosophy.
   Nevertheless, certain radical criticisms are levelled at
   his conception of social solidarity and the inferences
   which he purported to draw from it.

5. ALLEN, C.K. <u>Legal Duties</u>, (Oxford, 1931), pp. 158-167: Duguit's
   idea that there are no rights, only duties, is considered
   in detail. In the course of the discussion his general
   doctrine is outlined.

6. ALLEN, C.K. <u>Law in the Making</u>, (6th ed., Oxford, 1958), pp.
   574-90: Duguit's thesis is explained in order to show how
   he arrived at his idea of decentralisation. Criticism is
   directed at this idea from the angle of administrative law.
   (This section has been omitted from the 7th ed., 1964).

7. BROWN, W.J. "The Jurisprudence of M. Duguit" (1916), 32 L.Q.
   R., 168: the main points of Duguit's thesis are outlined
   and their implications are considered. Brown's criticism is

that law and the social sciences should be kept separate,
for otherwise it would not be possible to construct a
science of law.

1. GUPTA, A.C. "The Method of Jurisprudence", (1917), 33 L.Q.R.,
   154: W.J. Brown's criticism of Duguit on the ground that
   the latter confuses law and the social sciences is objected
   to. No one has succeeded in delimiting either subject and
   there is, therefore, no reason why a science of law from a
   sociological point of view should not be attempted.

2. ELLIOTT, W.Y. "The Metaphysics of Duguit's Pragmatic
   Conception of Law", (1922), 37 Pol. Sc. Q., 639: criticism
   is directed at Duguit's central idea of social solidarity
   and his views on the function of the state. The article also
   exposes the idealism that underlies Duguit's theory.

3. BUCKLAND, W.W. Some Reflections on Jurisprudence, (Cambridge
   University Press, 1945), pp. 6-11: this is a short but
   incisive critique of Duguit's contentions concerning
   sovereignty and the validity of law.

4. JOLOWICZ, H.F. Lectures on Jurisprudence, (ed. J.A. Jolowicz,
   The Athlone Press, 1963), chap. 10: this is a simplified
   and short account of Duguit's doctrine.

5. GOLUNSKII, S.A. and STROGOVICH, M.S. "The Theory of the State
   and Law" in Soviet Legal Philosophy, (trans. H.W. Babb,
   Harvard University Press, 1951), pp. 422-25: this brief
   critique is interesting in that it comes from Soviet writers
   who are viewing law from a Marxist point of view.

6. JENNINGS, W.I. "The Institutional Theory" in Modern Theories
   of Law, (ed. W.I. Jennings, Oxford University Press, 1933),
   chap. 5: the author points out that the "institutional
   theory", which originated in the work of Hauriou and Renard,
   is a sociological theory. It seeks to explain why society
   is organised in a particular way.

7. STONE, J. "Two Theories of 'The Institution'" in Essays in
   Jurisprudence in Honor of Roscoe Pound, (ed. R.A. Newman,
   The Bobbs-Merrill Co., Inc., 1962), 296: this is a long and
   difficult article. Two different interpretations are
   contrasted and each is examined in detail.

General

8. BRODERICK, A. "Hauriou's Institutional Theory: an Invitation
   to Common Law Jurisprudence" (1965), 4 Sol. Q., 281: the
   evolution of Hauriou's thought is traced through various

stages. An institution is a social, not a juridical,
phenomenon. In order to have juridical significance it is
necessary to see whether an institution produces certain
effects.

1. STONE, J. Social Dimensions of Law and Justice, (Stevens &
    Sons, Ltd., 1966), Chap. 11 et seq.: these chapters stress
    the importance of institutions in the social functioning of
    law and the formation of socio-ethical convictions. Social
    control is exercised through adjustment of the inter-
    relation of institutions. The views of Hariou, Renard and
    Romano are given prominence. Their relation to Duguit's
    work is considered, especially its misrepresentation at the
    hands of Hauriou.

2. STONE, J. Social Dimensions of Law and Justice, (Stevens &
    Sons, Ltd., 1966): this volume pursues in massive detail
    the combination of judicial technique, ideals of justice
    and social interests in the task of social control through
    law. In the first chapter the waste of labour resulting
    from the lack of co-ordination of the work of social
    scientists and lawyers is deplored. In the course of the
    book the author does attempt to throw bridges across the
    morass of knowledge between the various islands of
    systematised sciences.

3. BODENHEIMER, E. Jurisprudence, (Harvard University Press,
    1962), chaps. 6 and 8: the first of these chapters deals
    with the utilitarianism of Bentham and Mill, whose doctrines
    are compared and contrasted; and also with the views of
    Ihering. The second chapter is concerned with sociological
    jurisprudence. The views of various jurists are considered,
    including Ehrlich and Pound. It is to be noted that the
    Realist approach is also subsumed under this chapter.

4. FRIEDMANN, W. Legal Theory, (5th ed., Stevens & Sons, Ltd.,
    1967), chaps. 26 and 27: in the first chapter, the utilitar-
    ianism of Bentham and Mill is dealt with. Ihering saw that
    the wisdom of Roman law lay, not in refining concepts, but
    in moulding them to serve practical ends. In the second
    chapter, the views of modern sociologists and the need for
    balancing interests are considered.

5. DICEY, A.V. Law and Public Opinion in England during the 19th
    Century, (2nd ed., Macmillan & Co., Ltd., 1932), chaps. 1,
    2, 6, 7 and 8: this classic work depicts the background to
    law extremely well. It demonstrates the influence of public
    opinion on law and the nature of law-making opinion. Chapter
    6 deals with Benthamite utilitarianism; chapters 7 and 8
    deal with the growth of collectivism.

1. Law and Opinion in England in the 20th Century, (ed. M.
   Ginsberg, Stevens & Sons, Ltd., 1959), especially pp. 99-
   225: Ginsberg's introductory contribution is most useful in
   explaining the developments in the present century since
   Dicey's day. The pages referred to are concerned specifically with particular aspects of the law.

2. FRIEDMANN, W. Law in a Changing Society, (Stevens & Sons,
   Ltd., 1959): the first two chapters deal generally with the
   reaction of law to social pressure and with the use of law
   as an instrument of social engineering. Most of the remaining chapters deal with specific aspects of the law. (See
   also Law and Social Change in Contemporary Britain, Stevens
   & Sons, Ltd., 1951, which has been superseded to some extent
   by the other book).

3. An Introduction to the History of Sociology, (ed. H.E. Barnes,
   University of Chicago Press, 1948): this is a collection of
   essays on the individual personalities of various countries,
   starting with Comte. It is useful for reference.

4. HALL, J. Living Law of Democratic Society, (The Bobbs-Merrill
   Co., Inc., 1949), Part II: Savigny's postulate of a
   Volksgeist is considered as a criterion of valuation. This
   is followed by a consideration of the work of Bentham,
   Duguit and Pound.

5. ALLEN, C.K. Law in the Making, (7th ed., Oxford, 1964), pp.
   20-39: in the course of a general survey of jurisprudential
   thought the functional outlook is explained. The contributions of Ehrlich and Pound are outlined and critically
   appraised.

6. PATON, G.W. A Text-Book of Jurisprudence, (3rd ed., D.P.
   Derham, Oxford, 1964), pp. 21-36: distinction is drawn
   between sociological jurisprudence and legal sociology. The
   work of Ehrlich, Cairns, Pound and the general scope of
   functional study is discussed.

7. JONES, J.W. "Modern Discussions of the Aims and Methods of
   Legal Science", (1931), 47 L.Q.R., 62, at pp. 65, 72-78: in
   the course of a general review of the writings of various
   legal philosophers the work of Ihering, Duguit and Ehrlich
   is touched on. The article as a whole is useful in helping
   to place their contributions, and those of others, in
   perspective.

8. JOLOWICZ, H.F. Lectures on Jurisprudence, (ed. J.A. Jolowicz,
   The Athlone Press, 1963), chap. 13: this gives a general
   account of sociology and deals briefly with the theories of
   Ihering, Ehrlich, Pound and some others.

1. CASTBERG, F. Problems of Legal Philosophy, (2nd ed., Oslo
   University Press, Allen & Unwin, Ltd., 1957), chap. 3: the
   solving of problems according to the social purposes and
   functions of the law is considered. This is not an account
   of sociological jurisprudence, but a critical evaluation
   of it as a technique of decision.

2. CARDOZO, B.N. The Growth of the Law, (Yale University Press,
   1924), chaps. 4 and 5: there has to be a continuous
   re-adaptation of law so as to make it fulfil its purpose.
   When taking account of the ends of the law many factors
   have to be balanced.

3. CARDOZO, B.N. The Nature of the Judicial Process, (Yale
   University Press, 1921), chaps. 2 and 3: the method of
   sociology is to let the welfare of society fix the path,
   direction and distance to which rules are to be extended
   or restricted. The task of the judge in this connection
   is explained at length.

4. SETHNA, M.J. "The True Nature and Province of Jurisprudence
   from the Viewpoint of Indian Philosophy" in Essays in
   Jurisprudence in Honor of Roscoe Pound, (ed. R.A. Newman,
   The Bobbs-Merrill Co., Inc., 1962), 99: jurisprudence
   should combine analytical, historical, philosophical, and,
   above all sociological study. Sociological jurisprudence
   and the sociology of law are distinguished, and work of
   the chief supporters is outlined. Particular attention is
   paid to Pound's social engineering, and there is also
   mention of the American Realists.

5. HARVEY, C.P. "A Job for Jurisprudence" (1944) 7 M.L.R., 42:
   this is a plea that jurists should pay more attention to
   practical problems and the issues involved in them in the
   light of the social conditions of the day. W.B. KENNEDY:
   "Another Job for Jurisprudence" (1945) 8 M.L.R., 18:
   Harvey's proposals are criticised one by one; C.P. HARVEY:
   "A Job for Jurisprudence", ibid., p. 236: a reply to Kennedy.

6. ROBINSON, H.W. "Law and Economics" (1938-39), 2 M.L.R., 257:
   an economist dwells on the importance of the legal
   framework for the functioning of an economic system. Changes
   in the foundations of the economic system can only come
   through law. Therefore, economic ends are one of the factors
   to be taken into account in framing law.

7. ROSTOW, E.V. Planning for Freedom, (Yale University Press,
   1959): this work may be consulted as a work on sociology.
   It is an important contribution, written by one who is both
   a lawyer and an economist, but primarily from an economic

point of view. It concerns the function of law as an instrument of social change, and the mechanism for accomplishing it. (See review by W. FRIEDMANN: "Planning for Freedom" (1961), 24 M.L.R., 209).

1. McDOUGAL, M.S. "The Comparative Study of Law for Policy Purposes: Value Classification as an Instrument of Democratic World Order" (1952), 61 Yale L.J., 915: this article is an example of an application of sociological jurisprudence. A useful comparative study should begin, it is said, with an idea of what is being compared, the purpose of comparison and adequate techniques.

2. LASSWELL, H.D. and McDOUGAL, M.S. "Legal Education and Public Policy: Professional Training in the Public Interest" (1942-43), 52 Yale L.J., 202: this article is another example of the application of sociological jurisprudence. There should be an integration of law and other social sciences in the training of lawyers. This should be organised with reference to influence principles, value principles and skill principles. On similar lines, see M.S. McDOUGAL: "The Law School of the Future: from Legal Realism to Policy Science in the World Community" (1946-47), 56 Yale L.J., 1345).

3. LASSWELL, H.D. "The Interplay of Economic, Political and Social Criteria in Legal Policy" (1960-61), 14 Vand.L.R., 451: this is a difficult article. It enters into complex questions as to the criteria to be adopted towards economic activities.

4. SCHWARZENBERGER, G. "The Three Types of Law" (1949), 2 C.L.P., 103: this is an inquiry into the different functions of law in three types of society.

5. WEBER, M. On Law in Economy and Society, (ed. M. Rheinstein, trans. E.A. Shils and M. Rheinstein, Harvard University Press, 1954), especially chap. 1: this may be used for reference. The book envisages an idealised type of society with which actual societies might be compared.

6. MORRIS, C. "Law, Reason and Sociology" (1958-59), 107 U.Pa. L.R., 147: this article is based on M. Weber's analysis of the judicial process. A judge has to act on values when adapting the law. It is argued that some means should be found for discriminating between unjust rules, which should be remedied by legislation, and those which might be remedied by the courts.

7. COHEN, J. "The Value of Value Symbols in Law" (1952) 52 Col.

L.R. 893: the scientist starts with hypothetical symbols
and hopes to translate them into fact judgments; the lawyer
starts with facts and seeks normative judgments. Hence his
symbols are value-charged. They are instruments, not of
discovery, but of ordering society. In order to make them
effective instruments, emphasis should shift from the
search of the appropriate symbol to the actual fact-
situations, the values involved and the probable effect of
giving policy decisions.

1. COHEN, J., ROBSON, R.A.H., BATES, A. Parental Authority: The
    Community and the Law, (Rutgers U.P. 1958): this is an
    investigation into the moral sense of a community in a
    particular sphere. The kind of information obtained and
    significant facts are related to the law regarding the
    matter.

2. COWAN, T.A. "The Relation of Law to Experimental Science"
    (1948), 96 U.Pa.L.R., 484: there are many ways in which
    legal theory can be usefully related to other social
    sciences. But for this purpose the existing divisions of
    jurisprudence are inadequate.

3. COSSIO, C.S. "Jurisprudence and the Sociology of Law" (trans.
    P.J. Eder and F. Uno, 1952), 52 Col.L.R., 356, 479: this
    is a long and difficult article, but might be referred to
    for a critique of the demarcation between "dogmatic
    jurisprudence" and the sociology of law.

4. CARLSTON, K.S. Law and Structure of Social Action, (Stevens
    & Sons, Ltd., 1956), especially chap. 1: this is of general
    interest. It deals with organisations, which have become a
    feature of modern society. Old categories of thinking,
    which were adapted to take account of the relations of
    individuals, have had to be re-adapted to organisations,
    and this has proved to be inadequate. What is required is
    a new approach based on social realities.

5. REUSCHLEIN, H.G. Jurisprudence - Its American Prophets, (The
    Bobbs-Merrill Co., Inc., 1951), pp. 63-71, 103-53; 299-306:
    in the first section the work of Livingston and Field, two
    utilitarians in the Benthamite tradition, is considered.
    Their main preoccupation was with legislation and
    codification. In the second section, as a prelude to Pound
    the work of his forerunners, including Montesquieu, Ihering,
    Ehrlich and Duguit, is dealt with. Pound's own contribution
    is set out at length. In the final section the work of
    Seagle and Timasheff is dealt with.

6. SIMPSON, S.P. and STONE, J. Cases and Readings on Law and

Society, (West Publishing Co., 1949), II, chap. 4: this chapter deals mainly with the limits on law as a means of social control. The material has been collected from various sources.

1. HALL, J. *Readings in Jurisprudence*, (The Bobbs-Merrill Co., 1938), chaps. 4, 5, 17, 18, 22 and 23: chapter 4 deals with utilitarianism and contains extracts from Bentham, Mill, Ihering and Lorrimer. Chapter 5 deals with the doctrine of Duguit. Part III, which includes the remaining chapters mentioned above, deals generally with the scientific approach to social questions.

2. COWAN, T.A. *The American Jurisprudence Reader*, (Oceana Publications, 1956), pp. 135-156: the nature of sociological jurisprudence is explained and is followed by extracts from Pound, Cardozo, Cairns and Patterson.

3. LLOYD, D. *Introduction to Jurisprudence*, (2nd ed., Stevens & Sons, Ltd., 1965), chap. 5: modern sociology is introduced via brief accounts of the work of Bentham, Ihering, Weber, Ehrlich and Pound. There are extracts from Ihering, Ehrlich, Pound, The American Restatement of Torts and de Jouvenal.

4. LLOYD, D. *The Idea of Law*, (Penguin Books, Ltd., A 688, 1964), chap. 9, especially pp. 207-13: natural law theory was individualist. During the 18th. and 19th. centuries it assumed an economic pattern in the doctrine of laissez faire. The utilitarians provided a philosophy for society as a whole. In this brief account the views of Ihering, Weber, Ehrlich and Pound are mentioned.

5. LASSWELL, H.D. *Power and Personality*, (Norton & Co., New York, 1948): the unifying factor in modern society is power. This conclusion is derived empirically from an observation of political Man.

6. *Towards a General Theory of Action*, (ed. T. Parsons and E.A. Shils, Harvard University Press, 1954), especially Part I: this might be used for reference. Part I concerns the approach to a general theory of social action and the reasoning processes that are required in working one out. The various essays are not written from a legal point of view, but they open up possibilities of a theory of law which might fit in with a general theory of society.

7. SPROTT, W.J.H. *Science and Social Action*, (Watts & Co., 1954): in this book, which is of general interest, various problems of modern society are raised and discussed.

1. SPROTT, W.J.H. Sociology, (Hutchinson University Library, London, 1966): this book provides an introduction to sociology. It is useful for the lawyer in so far as the different types of study, pursuits and concerns of sociology are explained so that the lawyer might discern where his interests can be fitted in.

2. JOHNSON, H.M. Sociology: A Systematic Introduction, (Routledge & Kegan Paul, Ltd., 1961): this is a more detailed study of general sociology than that of W.J.H. Sprott. It is not a legal work, but it may usefully be consulted for the methods and aims of sociology.

3. Sociological Theory, (ed. L.A. Coser and B. Rosenberg, The Macmillan Co., New York, 1957): this is a book of readings, which might be used for general reference.

19

M O D E R N   R E A L I S M

American Realism

1. RUMBLE, W.E. American Legal Realism. Skepticism, Reform and the Judicial Process, (Cornell University Press, 1968): this lucid and easily-read book provides the first comprehensive review of the Realist movement. It covers the intellectual background from which it sprang, philosophical and especially sociological, and considers the views of all the leading Realists and their relationship to one another. Various criticisms are considered at various points and misunderstandings of the Realist position pointed out.

2. HOLMES, O.W. "The Path of the Law" in Collected Legal Papers, (Constable & Co., Ltd., 1920), 167: in this paper Holmes pioneers the view that law consists of prophecies of what courts will do and considers some of the implications of such a view. He also introduces his famous "bad man's" outlook on law.

3. LLEWELLYN, K.N. The Bramble Bush, (Tentative Printing and 2nd ed., Columbia University School of Law, 1930): Llewellyn's earlier and more robust "rule skepticism" is put forward. The principal point is that law is what officials do.

4. LLEWELLYN, K.N. Jurisprudence: Realism in Theory and Practice, (University of Chicago Press, 1962), chaps. 1-3, 5, 7, 8: various articles are reprinted in this volume. In chapter 1 the point is made that words are the centre of thinking about law and tend to obscure clear thought. Rules are not without importance, but they are less important than are traditionally supposed. In the course of a reply to Pound, the nine points of the Realist programme are set out. Chapter 3 lays emphasis on what officials do. The need for a temporary divorce of the "is" and the "ought" is explained and the point is repeated that ideas are of value. Chapter 7 amplifies that. The method of the new jurisprudence is to check doctrine against results and to take account of all crafts, traditions and ideas. To exclude the last would be to omit a vital factor. The judges' personalities are only one factor.

5. FRANK, J.N. Law and the Modern Mind, (English ed., Stevens & Sons, Ltd., 1949): The Preface is especially interesting in that Frank modifies certain views which are found in the text (written in 1930). This work might be regarded as one of the classic expositions of "fact skepticism".

6. LLEWELLYN, K.N. "The Normative, the Legal, and the Law-jobs:

the Problem of Juristic Method", (1939-40), 49 Yale L.J.,
1355: ethical considerations are only a part of what makes
up "legal". Beneath all doctrines lie problems. Five "law-
jobs" are considered. There has to be machinery for dealing
with actual situations. The problem of juristic method is
to make the machinery cope suitably with law-jobs and the
upkeep and improvement of method and machinery.

1. LLEWELLYN, K.N. "Law and the Social Sciences - especially
    Sociology", (1948-49), 62 Harv. L.R., 1286: law has moved
    away from other social disciplines because lawyers are
    obsessed with rules. The case is presented for re-estab-
    lishing useful contacts by taking account of the function
    of legal institutions, which brings in the individual who
    applies the law to a given situation.

2. LLEWELLYN, K.N. The Common Law Tradition. Deciding Appeals,
    (Little, Brown & Co., 1960), and Appendix B on "Realism":
    rules alone will not provide a basis for predicting
    decisions. But rules should be, and are to a large extent,
    applied according to the judge's "situation-sense", and
    this is the product of a number of far-reaching factors
    which do provide a workable basis for prediction. This book
    seeks to restore the lost confidence of the Bar in the pre-
    dictability of judicial decisions by showing the way in
    which they can be predicted. In Appendix B the author
    explains that this thesis is in fact a development of that
    originally propounded in The Bramble Bush.

3. TWINING, W. "Two Works of Karl Llewellyn", (1967), 30 M.L.R.,
    514; (1968) 31 M.L.R., 165: an insight into Llewellyn's
    thought, and through it into realism, is to be found in
    these accounts of two of his major works. The articles
    conclude with an assesment of their place in Llewellyn's
    thought and his contribution to jurisprudence.

4. CLARK, C.E. and TRUBEK, D.M. "The Creative Role of the
    Judge: Restraint and Freedom in the Common Law Tradition",
    (1961-62), 71 Yale L.J., 255: K.N. Llewellyn's thesis in
    The Common Law Tradition is criticised on the ground that
    it does not take adequate account of the subjective element.
    It is pointed out that no guidance is offered as to how
    judges are to exercise their "situation-sense" that will
    lead them to the "immanent law" in each situation. The
    omission of the subjective element removes one of the most
    important factors that should be taken into account in
    achieving what Llewellyn seeks to achieve, viz.,
    "reckonability".

5. FRANK, J.N. If Men were Angels: Some Aspects of Government in

a Democracy, (Harper & Bros., New York, 1942), especially
chaps. 6-8: this book marks a change in Frank's thought.
The emphasis shifts away from his anti-rule polemic to the
uncertainties in the fact-finding process. The charges of
Pound against the Realists are alleged to be misdirected
in respect of even one Realist.

1. FRANK, J.N. "Words and Music: Some Remarks on Statute
    Interpretation" (1947), 47 Col.L.R., 1259: the legislature
    composes the piece, but the judges play it, each according
    to his own interpretation in the light of the evidence
    before him.

2. FRANK, J.N. "Say it with Music" (1947-48), 61 Harv.L.R., 921:
    judicial reactions to oral evidence in trial-courts and
    the various influences at work there are examined.
    Suggestions are made for minimising the personal factor.

3. FRANK, J.N. "Short of Sickness and Death: a Study of Moral
    Responsibility in Legal Criticism" (1951), 26 N.Y.U.L.R.,
    545: this is a further lengthy investigation into the
    fallibilities of the fact-finding process.

4. FRANK, J.N. Courts on Trial, Myth and Reality in American
    Justice, (Princeton University Press, 1949): it is senseless
    to speak of rules creating rights or that rights can be
    known before they are tested in the courts. The chief
    concern of the book is with the fact-finding process and
    the factors that influence judges and juries.

5. FRANK, J.N. "What Courts do in Fact" (1932), 26 Ill.L.R.,
    645: this represents Frank's earlier view. Specific decisions
    are the essence of the law; all else is subsidiary. Rules
    are only "hunch producers". All such factors operate
    through the judge's personlity. Facts are what the court
    thinks happened. A judge often arrives at his decision
    before trying to explain it.

6. FRANK, J.N. "Are Judges Human?" (1932), 80 U.Pa.L.R., 17, 233:
    Frank continues his campaign against the belief that law
    consists of rules. The personal element in the judicial
    process is stressed and examined with a view to improving
    the process.

7. FRANK, J.N. "Cardozo and the Upper-Court Myth" (1948), 13 L.
    C.P., 369: this is a review of the Selected Writings of
    Benjamin Nathan Cardozo, (ed. M.E. Hall, Fallon Publications,
    1947). He accuses Cardozo of having by-passed what goes on in
    trial courts. Much space is devoted to an explanation of
    the distinction between "rule-skepticism" and "fact-
    skepticism".

1. RUTTER, I.C. "The Trial Judge and the Judicial Process"
   (1962-63) 15 J.L.E. 245: the author agrees with Judge Frank
   that far too little attention has been paid to what goes on
   in trial courts. Much of the scepticism has resulted from
   too much preoccupation with apellate courts. It is in trial
   courts that the great importance of rules can be seen.

2. THE HOLMES READER, (ed. J.J. Marke, Oceana Publications, 1955):
   selections from Holmes's writings and judgments are given.
   The concluding chapter appraises his contribution. For
   further tributes to Holmes's work the following might be
   consulted: (1930-31) 44 Harv.L.R., 677, (which includes a
   full list of his judicial opinions); W.H. HAMILTON: "On
   Dating Mr. Justice Holmes" (1941-42) 9 U.C.L.R., 1; M.de W.
   HOWE: "The Positivism of Mr. Justice Holmes" (1950-51) 64
   Harv.L.R., 529; H.M. HART: "Holmes's Positivism - an
   Addendum", ibid, 929; M.de W. HOWE: "Holmes's Positivism -
   a brief Rejoinder", ibid, 937; J.C.H. WU: "Justice Holmes
   and the Common Law Tradition" (1960-61) 14 Vand.L.R., 221;
   Mr. Justice Holmes, (ed. F. Frankfurter, Coward McCann, Inc.,
   1931); M. de W. HOWE: Justice Oliver Wendell Holmes. The
   Shaping Years, (Harvard University Press, 1951); Justice
   Holmes. The Proving Years, (1963).

3. LLEWELLYN, K.N., ADLER, M.J., COOK, W.W. "Law and the Modern
   Mind: a Symposium" (1931), 31 Col.L.R., 83: these represent
   three views on Frank's book. Llewellyn is adulatory, though
   he adheres to his view as to the importance of rules. Adler
   is critical; the book is, in his opinion, simply dogmatic
   and not an argument. Cook defends Frank against Adler's
   criticisms.

4. PAUL, J. The Legal Realism of Jerome N. Frank, (Matinus
   Nijhoff, The Hague, 1959), especially chaps. 2, 4 and 5:
   Frank's place in the Realist movement and his impact are
   considered in detail. A good deal about Realism in general
   can be gathered from the book, especially from chapter 6.

5. OLIPHANT, H. "A Return to Stare decisis" (1928), 14 Am.B.A.J.,
   71, 107, 159: the proposal is that attention should be paid
   to the non-vocal behaviour of judges, i.e., what they
   actually do. This attitude having now been lost, in order
   to recapture it there should be a study of the social
   structure and stare decisis can then be used effectively.

6. COHEN, F.S. "Transcendental Nonsense and the Functional
   Approach" (1935), 35 Col.L.R., 809: the traditional
   language of the law is a device for formulating decisions
   reached on other grounds. The methods that would be employed
   in a functional approach are explained. The point is made,

however, that the judicial "hunch" is in part the product
of the study of rules.

1. COHEN, F.S. "The Problems of a Functional Jurisprudence"
   (1937), 1 M.L.R. 5: the Realists are functional in their
   approach. This can be seen in what they set out to achieve
   and the types of results that are to be expected.

2. COHEN, F.S. "Field Theory and Judicial Logic" (1949-50), 59
   Yale L.J., 238: a dependable approach to the prediction of
   decisions can be worked out by observing the judge's use of
   precedents, which will reveal his value patterns. Even
   though the opinions of individual judges vary, certain
   lines of precedents are to be discovered.

3. YNTEMA, H.E. "The Rational Basis of Legal Science" (1931), 31
   Col.L.R., 924: thinking about law is referable to experience.
   The case for Realism is argued and defended.

4. YNTEMA, H.E. "American Legal Realism in Retrospect" (1960-61),
   14 Vand.L.R., 317: law, being a means to certain ends,
   should be correlated with other social and natural sciences.
   Legal research should be conducted on scientific lines and
   with factual data, such as statistics. A distinction is
   drawn between legal science, which should be descriptive,
   and the art of the judge, which is normative.

5. YNTEMA, H.E. "The Hornbook Method and the Conflict of Laws"
   (1927-28), 37 Yale L.J., 468, especially at p. 480: in the
   course of this review of a treatise on conflict of laws, the
   point is made that it is not symbols but habits of thought
   that control decisions. Decision is reached after an
   emotional experience by the judge in which logic and
   principles play a subsidiary part.

6. BINGHAM, J.W. "What is the Law?" (1912), 11 Mich.L.R., 1, 109:
   the lawyer studies external sequences with a view to
   forecasting sequences of the same sort. Rules and principles
   are not the law; law is what happens in a state, i.e., what
   courts do. The real field of study should include many
   factors other than rules, for it is such factors which
   provide the motives for decisions. See also "The Nature of
   Legal Rights and Duties" (1913) 12 Mich.L.R., 1.

7. KOCOUREK, A. Review of Bingham's two articles in (1913) 8 Ill.
   L.R., 138: Bingham's thesis is criticised on a number of
   points. See J.W. BINGHAM: "Legal Philosophy and the Law"
   (1914), 9 Ill.L.R., 98, for his reply to Kocourek's
   criticisms seriatim.

1. SCHROEDER, T. "The Psychological Study of Judicial Opinions", (1918), 6 Calif. L.R., 89: Judicial conduct is determined by a chain of causation running back to infancy. Every choice, conclusion, etc. is determined by some dominant personal motive.

2. HAINES, C.G. "General Observations on the Effects of Personal, Political, and Economic Influences on the Decisions of Judges", (1922), 17 Ill. L.R., 96: this is a most interesting investigation into the factors mentioned.

3. COOK, W.W. "The Logical and Legal Bases of the Conflict of Law", (1923-24), 33 Yale L.J., 457: the decision lies in the construction of the premises of the legal syllogism. Rules are useful tools, but they are not the premises. This point is developed with reference to the conflict of laws.

4. ULMAN, J.N. A Judge Takes the Stand, (Alfred A. Knopf, 1933): a judge writes on various aspects of the judicial process. Of the greatest interest is his treatment of the emotional factors that play on judges. He asserts emphatically that rules and precedents do exercise a decisive influence sometimes, even against the judge's own feelings.

5. HUTCHESON, J.C. "The Judgement Intuitive: the Function of the 'Hunch' in Judicial Decisions", (1929), 14 Corn. L.Q., 274: this develops the theme that the judicial decision is the produce of innumerable factors.

6. HUTCHESON, J.C. "Lawyer's Law, and the Little, Small Dice" (1932-33), 7 Tul. L.R., 1: this stresses the point that, whatever principles there may be, the judge has on occasions to make up his mind which way he wants to decide.

7. RADIN, M. "Legal Realism", (1931), 31 Col. L.R., 824: "Realism" signifies opposition to "Conceptualism" as an ideal itself. But conceptualism has its place. Moreover not all judges are "realists" and, therefore, the Realists should take account of how non-Realist judges behave.

8. RADIN, M. Law as Logic and Experience, (Yale University Press, 1940): law needs to be applied to facts, but the facts that reach the courts are past and "dead". The attempt to resurrect them is fraught with difficulties. Therefore, a new approach is suggested, namely, that the courts should work out the best solution for the future out of the situation that has arisen (cf. arbitral award).

9. GRAY, J.C. The Nature and Sources of the Law, (2nd ed.,

R. Gray, The Macmillan Co., New York, 1921), especially chap. 4: Gray's cardinal thesis is that law is what the courts do and that all else, including statutes, are only sources of law.

1. POUND, R. "Law in Books and Law in Action", (1910), 44 Am. L. R., 12: the divergence between legal principles and what actually occurs is illustrated. Particular attention is drawn to the fact that judicial thinking is out of touch with contemporary social and economic thinking.

2. MOORE, W.U. and HOPE, T.S. "An Institutional Approach to the Law of Commercial Banking", (1929), 38 Yale L.J., 703: the problem of predicting official decisions is developed along Realist lines. The thesis is that prediction will be aided if attention is paid, not only to judicial reactions to the individual cases, but also the reactions to "institutional" (repeated, usual) behaviour.

3. KALES, A.M. "'Due Process'. The Inarticulate Major Premise and the Adamson Act", (1916-17), 26 Yale L.J., 519: the "inarticulate major premise" behind the "due process" formula is examined in the light of social factors.

4. NELLES, W. "The First American Labor Case", (1931-32), 41 Yale L.J., 165: this is of general interest as showing the influences that were at work behind the decision in an industrial dispute primae impressionis.

5. NELLES, W. "Towards Legal Understanding", (1934), 34 Col L.R. 862, 1041: the factors underlying decisions that bring about changes and development in the law are subjected to detailed examination. Law is not independent of personal wills.

6. KEYSER, C.J. "On the Study of Legal Science" (1928-29), 38 Yale L.J., 413: the subject-matter of such a study is the conduct of the officials who answer questions as to what is just. The science of law consists of propositions concerning such conduct, the circumstances and stimuli behind it.

7. LERNER, M. "The Supreme Court and American Capitalism", (1932-33), 42 Yale L.J., 668: the Supreme Court has to work within the framework of a constitution and rules, but attention is also drawn to the social and cultural environment and the personalities of the judges.

8. SCHMIDHAUSER, J.R. "Stare Decisis, and the Background of the Justice of the Supreme Court of the United States", (1962), 14 Tor. L.J., 194: this is a statistical study of the

personal background of various judges of the Supreme Court.
The tentative conclusion is drawn that such factors do
affect judicial behaviour.

1. ARNOLD, T.W. Symbols of Government, (Yale University Press,
    1935), especially pp. 1-104, 199-288: the scientific
    approach is advocated, (but the differences between the
    subject-matter of social and physical sciences are not
    stressed). Lawyers use symbols which will give the result
    desired by the individual rather than by society. That is
    why legal science fails to adapt itself to society.

2. ROBINSON, E.S. Law and the Lawyers, (The Macmillan Go., New
    York, 1935), especially pp. 1-19, 46-121, 284-323: law is
    unscientific. It can only be made "naturalistic" (i.e.,
    realistic) with the aid of psychology, which all lawyers
    should study. What is required is a psychology that takes
    account of legal doctrines while not interpreting them
    literally. What a judge says is a sound starting point in
    the study of judicial deliberation, because this adds to
    the arguments that were present in arriving at the original
    conclusion. They serve to persuade himself as well as
    others. The discrepancy between legal values and those of
    common sense is brought about by rules. This is due to the
    need for consistency and rules are important.

3. ABRAHAM, H.J. The Judicial Process, (New York and Oxford
    University Press, 1962): this is not a "realist" book, but
    it gives useful insights into the sort of thing that goes
    on "behind the scenes" in the American administration of
    justice.

4. WEYRAUCH, W.O. The Personality of Lawyers, (Yale University
    Press, 1964): interviews with 130 German lawyers, represent-
    ing judges, attorneys, students etc., are analysed and
    evaluated. The results are set out in the form of general-
    isations about the prejudices and predilections peculiar to
    lawyers. The conclusions are admittedly unverified hypo-
    theses as yet, and are the result of an original line of
    research along the lines of realist doctrine.

5. ARNOLD, T.W. "The Jurisprudence of Edward S. Robinson", (1936-
    37), 46 Yale L.J., 1282: in this appraisal of Robinson's
    work particular emphasis is laid on the psychological
    approach to law, which Robinson viewed as a study in modern
    anthropology.

Mechanical aids to prediction

6. LOEVINGER, L. "Jurimetrics: the Next Step Forward", (1949), 33

Minn. L.R., 455: this article is of interest as introducing
the term "Jurimetrics" for a growing new discipline, which
applies the methods of mathematical and scientific investigation to legal problems.

1. BEUTEL, F.K. "Some Implications of Experimental Jurisprudence"
    (1934-35), 48 Harv. L.R., 169: the requirements of an
    experimental science are explained, and the possibility of
    their adaptation to legal science is discussed.

2. BEUTEL, F.K. Some Potentialities of Experimental Jurisprudence
    as a New Branch of Social Science, (University of Nebraska
    Press, 1957): this contains the results in detail, statis-
    tical and other data, which were obtained by putting the
    approach outlined above into operation.

3. NUSSBAUM, A. "Fact Research in Law", (1940), 40 Col. L.R.,
    189: the revolt against conceptualism on the Continent and
    in America is the background to the use of fact research
    and statistics in law. An account is given of fact research,
    followed by a discussion of the value of statistics. The
    latter, it is said, are of little value.

4. MOORE, W.U. and CALLAHAN, C.C. "Law and Learning Theory: A
    Study in Legal Control", (1943-44), 53 Yale L.J., 1: the
    authors set out factual evidence of the effect on human
    behaviour of enactments and administrative procedure on a
    matter of parking vehicles. The statistics are then analysed
    with a view to deriving a psychological and objective theory
    of behaviour. C.L. HULL: ibid. p. 331, reviews the results
    as a psychologist. H.E. YNTEMA, ibid. p. 338, in his review
    raises several objections.

5. KRISLOV, S. "Theoretical Attempts at Predicting Judicial
    Behaviour" (1965-66), 79 Harv. L.R., 1573: scientists value
    predictability because it tests theory. What is sought is
    understanding. There is a distinction between predicting
    and forecasting. The social scientist can do no more than
    forecast. Four techniques of achieving this are discussed.

6. SNYDER, E. "The Supreme Court as a Small Group", (1958), 36
    Social Forces, 232: over a period of 32 years the voting
    patterns in the Supreme Court revealed a liberal, conserv-
    ative and an uncommitted group. Judges often moved from the
    last to either of the former; no judge moved from the
    liberal to the conservative group; and rarely did a judge
    move from the conservative to the liberal group without
    some pause in the uncommitted group. New judges tended to
    join the uncommitted group.

1. MURPHY, W.F. "Courts as Small Groups", (1965-66), 79 Harv. L.
   R., 1565: how useful are theories and data about human
   behaviour in small groups ? Voting records are not enough;
   we need to consider interpersonal interaction. There is the
   role of "task leadership" in solving the problem efficiently,
   and "social leadership" in providing the atmosphere that
   facilitates co-operation. Some of the limitations of this
   kind of inquiry are indicated.

2. TANENHAUS, J. "The Cumulative Scaling of Judicial Decisions",
   (1965-66), 79 Harv. L.R., 1583: the object is to determine
   whether, e.g., votes cast by members of a court in a group
   of cases can be arranged in an ordinal scale. Cumulative
   scaling tries to determine whether persons who respond
   affirmatively to a weak stimulus do in fact respond affirmatively to stronger stimuli; and whether persons who
   respond negatively to a strong stimulus will respond
   similarly to all weaker ones. This approach is said to be
   useful in showing that a set of attitudes is shared by
   members of a court so that their probable behaviour in
   future cases might be predicted.

3. KORT, F. "Quantitative Analysis of Fact-patterns in Cases and
   their Impact on Judicial Decisions", (1965-66), 79 Harv. L.
   R., 1595: the relation between facts and decisions should
   be explored by statistical methods. In this connection the
   acceptance or rejection of facts by appellate courts from
   lower court records as well as the dependence by appellate
   court decisions on the accepted facts have to be considered.

4. DICKERSON, F.R. "Some Jurisprudential Implications of
   Electronic Data Processing", (1963), 28 L.C.P., 53:
   computerization is a help, not a substitute for the methods
   of lawyers. The chief objections to its use are considered
   in detail and shown to spring from uninformed or unreal
   fears.

5. DICKERSON, F.R. "Automation and the Lawyer", (1965), Res
   Gestae, 5: the various possible uses of computers to
   lawyers in their daily work and to legal researchers is
   outlined. Some indication is also given of the likely
   impact of such new techniques, principally in the law of
   evidence.

6. TAPPER, C.F. "The Uses of Computers for Lawyers", (1965), 8
   J.S.P.T.L.(N.S.) 261: the use of computers in law in Great
   Britain has been backward largely because the profession is
   unable to cope with the cost involved and because of the
   special problems involved in law. The possible uses of
   computerization to lawyers are enumerated. Of these

information storage and retrieval are paramount. How this could be made to work is discussed in detail.

1.   LAWLOR, R.C. "What Computers Can Do: Analysis and Prediction of Judicial Decisions" (1963) 49 Am.B.A.J. 337: computers could find and analyse the law and predict decisions. Predictability is possible not only in so far as there is "legal" stare decisis but also an element of personal stare decisis (consistency of attitude).

2.   WIENER, F.B. "Decision Prediction by Computers: Nonsense Cubed - and Worse" (1962) 48 Am.B.A.J. 1023: the claim that computers could be used to predict decisions rests on untenable assumptions. If one knows which rule a judge will apply and which way the facts will be found, then a computer is unnecessary; if these are not known a computer is useless. Even in the matter of information storage and retrieval, there might always be human error in programming. There is also the problem of classification and indexing.

3.   ROHNER, R.J. "Jurimetrics, No!" (1968) 54 Am.B.A.J. 896: this gives a dream of the future in which judges, lawyers and law-books will have been replaced by machines.

4.   BROWN, J.R. "Electronic Brains and the Legal Mind: Computing the Data Computer's Collision with Law" (1961-62) 71 Yale L.J. 239: computers are making an impact on the law. But the administration of the law involves an indispensable human element. Computers should be able to help in making good law, which no machine can do. It is not enough to sort out the bad.

5.   FREED, R.N. "Prepare Now for Machine - Assisted Legal Research" (1961) 47 Am.B.A.J. 764: legal research is a two-stage operation, collation of relevant information and analysis of it. Computers can help the former process, but their success will depend on indexing.

6.   J.T.E. "Computers and Discovery" (1967) 117 New L.J. 917: the existing rules governing judicial orders for discovery will have to be reconsidered in the light of computer techniques of storing and retrieving information.

7.   TAPPER, C.F. "The Solicitor and the Computer" (1968) 118 New L.J. 55: the solicitor has to provide an essentially human service to clients, which cannot be computerised. It is all the more important, therefore, to relieve him of routine work which can be computerised so that he may devote more time and energy to the human tasks. Suggestions are offered as to recording the legal histories of clients (cf. medical

records), registers and police records and how legal
information might be classified and stored according to the
concepts involved.

1. GOTTSCHALK, K. "The Computer and the Law" (1969) 66 L.S. Gaz.
    168: four problems are discussed. (1) At what stage should
    there be copyright protection for authors whose materials
    are computerized - at input or output stage ? (2) Should
    there be copyright or patent protection for programs ?
    (3) How may the individual's right to privacy be safeguarded
    when with the aid of computers a great deal of information
    can be collated easily ? (4) How far are computer data
    admissible as evidence ? Computers, it is said, can aid the
    law in three ways, namely by facilitating information
    retrieval, helping in the prevention and detection of crime
    and in performing everyday legal processes.

2. HOWELL, B.R. "Law and the Computer" (1968) 6 Legal Exec. 120:
    this short article reviews the developments that have taken
    place and the research that is being done in Britain and in
    America. The uses of computers to lawyers are outlined.

3. MICHAEL, D.N. "Speculations on the Relation of the Computer
    to Individual Freedom and the Right to Privacy" (1964-65)
    33 Geo.Wash.L.R. 270: the speculations are limited to the
    next twenty years, since after that people's values will
    have changed completely. Computers enable the easy and
    rapid collation of data which at present is scattered and
    open up possibilities of recording new data, keeping track
    of individuals, and generally making such data available.
    The impact of these possibilities on privacy and freedom
    are considered.

4. MILLER, A.R. "Personal Privacy in the Computer Age: the
    Challenge of a New Technology in an Information Oriented
    Society" (1969) 67 Mich.L.R. 1091: computers provide a new
    form of power. It can be beneficial, but it also has grave
    dangers to privacy, which is fundamental to democratic
    traditions of individual autonomy. It is necessay therefore
    to start now to solve the privacy problems. In this 155-page
    article the author examines in great detail the practice
    and use of computer techniques and the dangers which they
    pose.

5. HUDSON, C.A. "Some Reflections on Information Retrieval"
    (1968) 6 Os.H.L.J. 259: the article begins with a survey
    of the methods of information storage that have been used
    since pre-Norman times. Case-law depends not only on how a
    case happens to be reported, but also on what cases the
    reporter chooses to report. If every decision were

computerized the conception of case-law will alter. So, too, computerization of statute-law could reduce the human element between the source of information and its recipients.

1. KAYTON, I. "Can Jurimetrics be of Value to Jurisprudence ?" (1964-65) 33 Geo.Wash.L.R. 287: "jurimetrics" is the scientific investigation of legal problems. Its tools are symbolic logic and digital computers. After a detailed demonstration of their use the conclusion is that jurimetrics can be of limited value.

2. MEYER, P. "Jurimetrics: the Scientific Method in Legal Research" (1966) 44 Can.B.R. 1: this considers the value of jurimetrics in saving drudgery, analysing evidence, predicting judgments, drafting and law reform. Of special interest is the portion dealing with the use of behavioural models to predict the behaviour of members of a group, such as a court, and the use of models in stare decisis.

3. FULLER, L.L. "An Afterword: Science and the Judicial Process" (1965-66) 79 Harv.L.R. 1604: science works with simplified, hence abstracted, models. In the social sciences the difficulty is to know what to abstract and what correction to make when applying the model to life. The process of abstraction is governed by a personal element. Hence the results of such models is built into them from the outset. Predictive theories offer no guidance to discovery. We have to decide on the end and then find the best means for achieving it. Science can help with means, not with ends.

4. STONE, J. Legal System and Lawyers' Reasonings, (Stevens & Sons, Ltd., 1964), pp. 37-41; Social Dimensions of Law and Justice, (Stevens & Sons, Ltd., 1966), pp. 687-96: the value of computer techniques in the judicial process is considered in the first book, and in providing quantitative analyses of judicial behaviour in the second. While computers are useful for information retrieval, they cannot supplant the need to make creative decisions.

5. Symposium on "Jurimetrics", (1963) 28 L.C.P. 1-270: this collection of papers might be used for further reference. Various writers enlarge upon the new methods, possibilities and limitations of their use.

6. Modern Uses of Logic in Law (M.U.L.L.) 1959-1966: this journal is devoted to jurimetrics. Its contributions tend to be extremely technical, but may be consulted as to the sort of problems that are being tackled and methods of dealing with them.

General accounts and critiques of Realism

1. POUND, R. Jurisprudence, (West Publishing Co., Inc., 1959),
    I, pp. 247-54, 264-81: the place of the American Realists
    in the history of juristic thought is discussed and the
    forms which it has assumed are distinguished, explained
    and criticised.

2. PATTERSON, E.W. Jurisprudence, (The Foundation Press, Inc.,
    1953), chap. 17 and pp. 537-58: this provides a most
    valuable account of the background to the Realist movement,
    including the pragmatism of C.S. Peirce and William James.
    There is also a very good appraisal of the work of Holmes
    and of the Realists generally.

3. GOODHART, A.L. "Some American Interpretations of Law" in
    Modern Theories of Law, (ed. W.I. Jennings, Oxford
    University Press, 1933), chap. 1: the reasons for the
    growth of this movement in America are considered. The main
    points of the Realist case and its weaknesses are indicated.

4. LLOYD, D. Introduction to Jurisprudence, (2nd ed., Stevens &
    Sons, Ltd., 1965), chap. 7: Realism arose as part of the
    movement towards increased empiricism. There is a brief
    account of "fact-skeptics" and "rule-skeptics" and an
    appraisal of the work of Holmes and of the Realists
    generally.

5. LLOYD, D. The Idea of Law, (Penguin Books, Ltd., A 688, 1964),
    pp. 213-17: American Realism developed out of the reliance
    on science and technology as a key to solving problems as
    well as the rise of pragmatism.

6. GILMORE, G. "Legal Realism: its Cause and Cure" (1960-61) 70
    Yale L.J. 1037: realism is one response to the crisis in
    America produced by the growing multiplicity of cases and
    the changing role of legislation.

7. FRIEDMANN, W. Legal Theory, (5th ed., Stevens & Sons, Ltd.,
    1967), pp. 292-304: this is a valuable assessment of the
    work of the American Realists in the sociological field.

8. JONES, J.W. Historical Introduction to the Theory of Law,
    (Oxford, 1940), pp. 191-202: the American Realist movement
    is considered in the context of the psychological
    interpretation of law. The views of Frank are considered.
    It is pointed out that the Realists have not done more than
    stress the importance of intuition. The psychological
    approach as a whole is appraised.

328 Modern Realism

1. BODENHEIMER, E. Jurisprudence, (Harvard University Press, 1962), pp. 116-20: the work of the American Realists is set out briefly.

2. PATON, G.W. A Text-Book of Jurisprudence, (3rd ed., D.P. Derham, Oxford, 1964), pp. 21-28: the American Realists are regarded as being the left-wing of the sociological approach, and their contributions are assessed.

3. STONE, J. Social Dimensions of Law and Justice, (Stevens & Sons, Ltd., 1966), pp. 62-71; 680-87; 734-42: the contribution of American Realism is set in the context of a broad survey of sociological jurisprudence. The account centres on the work of Llewellyn, and it is said that the changes in his thought show how realism, shorn of its initial excesses, has come to reinforce a number of sociological insights. Much of the debate over realism in the 1930's was at cross purposes. The problems of fact-finding and law-finding are also dealt with, and Frank's programme is critically examined.

4. KEETON, G.W. The Elementary Principles of Jurisprudence, (2nd ed., Pitman & Sons, Ltd., 1949), pp. 21-24: this is a brief, general summary of the functional and Realist approaches.

5. JOLOWICZ, H.F. Lectures on Jurisprudence, (ed. J.A. Jolowicz, The Athlone Press, 1963), chap. 9: a simplified account is given of the main contentions of the movement and a criticism of these.

6. GARLAN, E.N. Legal Realism and Justice, (Columbia University Press, 1941): in the course of this important study it is shown that the Realists cannot avoid talking about law as it ought to be. It examines critically the implications of their contentions. The bibliography at the end is most comprehensive.

7. MECHEM, P. "The Jurisprudence of Despair" (1935-36), 21 Iowa L.R., 669: this is a critique of the views of Arnold and Robinson. The Realists wish to escape from the hampering restriction of law; hence the movement might be called "Lazy Jurisprudence".

8. FULLER, L.L. "American Legal Realism" (1934), 82 U.Pa.L.R., 429: W.U. Moore's behaviourism (supra) is criticised on the ground that mere observation of conduct without taking account of the ends that are being sought is inadequate. A judge's reaction is always to the situation as a whole, which includes many factors ignored by the Realists.

1. FULLER, L.L. Law in Quest of Itself, (The Foundation Press,
    Inc., 1940): throughout the book positivism from Hobbes
    onwards, and especially the Realist movement, is subjected
    to strong criticism. It is maintained that the "is" and the
    "ought" cannot be separated.

2. McDOUGAL, M.S. "Fuller vs. The American Realists: an
    Intervention" (1940-41), 50 Yale L.J., 827: this is
    principally a criticism of Fuller's advocacy of natural
    law on the ground of vagueness.

3. DICKINSON, J. "Legal Rules and their Function in the Process
    of Decision" (1931), 79 U.Pa.L.R., 833, 1052: rules do
    have influence, for in many cases they do govern the
    decision. It is important to appreciate how the rule-element
    and the discretion-element interact. The study of judicial
    psychology alone is not enough, for this can only operate
    within a given rule.

4. KANTOROWICZ, H.U. "Some Rationalism about Realism" (1934),
    43 Yale L.J., 1240: the Realists are criticised for
    confusing natural and cultural sciences; in the latter the
    question is not whether people do this or that, but whether
    they ought to have done what they did. The Realists also
    confuse explanation and justification and law and ethics. On
    the other hand, they fail to distinguish between realities
    and their meaning. Lawyers are concerned with meaning.

5. COHEN, M.R. "On Absolutisms in Legal Thought" (1936), 84 U.
    Pa.L.R., 681: in rejecting the mechanical function of rules
    one should not reject rules altogether. The argument that
    law does not correspond with fact loses some of its force
    when it is remembered that there always has to be some
    discrepancy between theory and practice.

6. COHEN, M.R. "Positivism and the Limits of Idealism in the
    Law" (1927), 27 Col.L.R., 237, especially pp. 249-30:
    positivism is itself an ideal. As soon as it is realised
    that law is not a closed system, ideals as to what ought
    to be come in. Yet the ideal and the actual are never
    completely identical. The need for abstract general rules
    is pointed out at pp. 249-50.

7. COHEN, M.R. Law and the Social Order, (Harcourt, Brace & Co.,
    1933), pp. 184-197, 198-267, 352-69: principles are needed
    in the development of the law. The law cannot abandon the
    striving towards consistency. It consists of norms regulat-
    ing conduct, rather than describing it. The contentions of
    the Realists are examined from a theoretical point of view.
    The work of Holmes, Gray and Frank is assessed.

1. CARDOZO, B.N. The Nature of the Judicial Process, (Yale
    University Press, 1921), pp. 124-30: the extreme Realist
    position is disavowed as containing the seeds of fallacy
    and error. The significance of law before it reaches the
    courts is pointed out.

2. CARDOZO, B.N. The Growth of the Law, (Yale University Press,
    1924), pp. 31-55: varying views as to the nature and origin
    of law can lead to varying decisions on the merits of a
    lawsuit. Law stands at some point behind actual adjudication.
    It is more than a collection of isolated judgments; it is a
    stock of rules and principles which will be enforced by
    courts.

3. KELSEN, H. General Theory of Law and State, (trans. A. Wedberg,
    Harvard University Press, 1949), pp. 165-78: it is said by
    some jurists that the task of legal science is to predict
    the behaviour of judges. But there is a difference between
    normative rules and rules deducible from observation. A
    sociological interpretation of law presupposes a normative
    interpretation.

4. POUND, R. "The Call for a Realist Jurisprudence" (1930-31),
    44 Harv.L.R., 697: a faithful portrayal of what courts do
    is not the whole task of a science of law. The aims and
    contentions of the Realists are critically appraised.

5. POUND, R. The Ideal Element in Law, (University of Calcutta,
    1958), chap. 10: the various brands of realism are
    classified and surveyed critically.

6. HART, H.L.A. The Concept of Law, (Oxford, 1961), pp. 132-44:
    the denial of rules is inconsistent with the authoritative
    character of a judicial decision, for it is authoritative
    by virtue of rules. The inadequacy of regarding law as
    simply predictions of what courts do is indicated.

7. ALLEN, C.K. Law in the Making, (7th ed., Oxford, 1964), pp.
    41-48: this is a somewhat denigratory account of the Realist
    movement in which the rise of it is attributed to the
    complex situation obtaining in America.

8. PATTERSON, E.W. "Can Law be Scientific ?" (1930), 25 Ill.L.R.,
    121: the advantages of mathematical symbols to make new
    hypotheses explicit is not available in law. The ways in
    which law might be made explicit and scientific are
    discussed. Legal rules are not myths; they mark the
    boundaries of judicial thought.

9. COOK, W.W. "Scientific Method and the Law" (1927), 13 Am.B.

A.J., 303: the task confronting the judge is considered.
Past judicial behaviour can be generalised into rules,
which are then used to forecast future decisions.

1. WADE, H.W.R. "The Concept of Legal Certainty. A Preliminary
   Skirmish", (1941), 4 M.L.R., 183, especially pp. 191-99:
   Frank's attack on certainty in law is critically considered.

2. BROWN, R.A. "Police-power - Legislation for Health and
   Personal Safety" (1928-29), 42 Harv. L.R., 866: this is an
   examination of judicial decisions on the "due process"
   clause by investigating the judges who made them. Personal
   prejudice is not the only factor; various others come in
   (p. 872). See also R.A. BROWN: "Due Process of Law, Police
   Power and the Supreme Court", (1926-27), 40 Harv. L.R., 943.

3. HARVEY, C.P. "A Job for Jurisprudence", (1944), 7 M.L.R., 42:
   jurisprudence has failed to cope with practical problems.
   The mistake has lain in elevating it into a science.

4. KENNEDY, W.B. "Another Job for Jurisprudence", (1945), 8 M.L.
   R., 18: this is a reply to Harvey and arguing against a
   purely factual approach. For C.P. Harvey's reply, see "A
   Job for Jurisprudence" (1945), 8 M.L.R., 236.

5. KENNEDY, W.B. "A Review of Legal Realism", (1940), 9 F.L.R.,
   362: Realism has failed to catch hold because of (a) a
   consistent adherence to the scientific technique in its
   approach to the criticism of traditional law; (b) submersion
   of rules by over-emphasis on fact-finding; (c) absence of
   skepticism regarding the hypothetical theories of the social
   sciences; (d) the creation of a new form of word-magic and
   verbal gymnastics.

6. CAVERS, D.F. "In Advocacy of the Problem Method", (1943), 43
   Col. L.R., 449, at pp. 453-54: it is alleged that the
   Realists secretly like legal concepts; they dissect them
   whereas "traditionalists" put them together. Their approach
   is unsuited to legal education.

7. HARRIS, R.C. "Idealism Emergent in Jurisprudence", (1935-36),
   10 Tul. L.R., 169: with reference to the rise of idealism
   in America, it is maintained that resort to the subjective
   psychological processes is itself a form of idealism.

8. JONES, H.W. "Law and Morality in the Perspective of Legal
   Realism", (1961), 61 Col. L.R., 799: there are greater
   affinities between realism and natural law tradition than
   between analytical and natural law tradition. The ethical
   theory to be drawn from realism is that the moral dimension

of the law is not to be found in rules and principles, but in the process of decision. Choice and decision are inevitable in the life of the law. This is guided by moral considerations.

1. KESSLER, F. "Theoretic Bases of Law", (1941-42), 9 U.C.L.R. 98, at pp. 109-12: the early Realists represented an early form of positivism, later they developed the functional approach. The Realist approach is said to achieve a synthesis between natural law philosophy and positivism.

2. HALL, J. "American Tendencies in Legal Philosophy and the Definition of 'Law'", (1956), 3 Comparative Law Review of Japan, 1: the chief contributions of the Realist movement are set out. Among other criticisms levelled at them it is pointed out that they resort to law in the traditional sense in order to discover who the officials are, and that separation of the "is" and the "ought" is not possible.

3. TAYLOR, R. "Law and Morality", (1968), 43 N.Y.U.L.R., 611: the realists are criticised for not going far enough. They focus attention too much on the judge. Commands as binding as those issued by judges emanate from other sources. These are all "laws".

4. DEWEY, J. "Logical Method and Law", (1924), 10 Corn. L.Q., 17: this deals generally with the instrumental nature of legal logic as distinct from syllogistic logic. He is, therefore, in a sense a spiritual father of the Realist movement. See also J.DEWEY: The Quest for Certainty, (G.P. Putnam's Sons, 1929).

5. My Philosophy of Law, (Boston Law Book Co., 1941): this contains views of J.W. Bingham, M.R. Cohen, W.W. Cook, J. Dewey, J. Dickinson, W.B. Kennedy, K.N. Llewellyn, U. Moore and E.W. Patterson (and others).

6. REUSCHLEIN, H.G. Jurisprudence - its American Prophets, (The Bobbs-Merrill Co., Inc., 1951), pp. 183-275: this work may usefully be consulted for studies of most of the American Realists and the principal features of their work.

Scandinavian Realism

7. HÄGERSTRÖM, A. Inquiries into the Nature of Law and Morals, (ed. K. Olivecrona, trans. C.D. Broad, Almqvist & Wiksell, Stockholm, 1953): the substance of Hägerström's teachings are contained in this volume. Many legal concepts, e.g., rights, duties, are dismissed as myths, and everything

which cannot be expressed either as fact or emotion is
condemned as metaphysical.

1. OLIVECRONA, K. Law as Fact, (Einer Munksgaard, Copenhagen;
   Humphrey Milford, London, 1939; reprinted Wildy & Sons,
   1962): law is a set of social facts, and its "binding force"
   is a myth. Obedience is due to people's psychological
   reactions to certain procedures and forms of expression.
   These propositions are developed with exemplary clarity. At
   pp. 213-15 there is a short critique of American Realism.

2. ROSS, A. On Law and Justice, (Stevens & Sons, Ltd., 1958),
   especially chaps. 1-9: in these chapters, especially in the
   earlier, Ross's views on the nature of law are set out. The
   last eight chapters of the book deal with the criteria for
   evaluating the law.

3. LUNDSTEDT, A.V. Legal Thinking Revised, (Almqvist & Wiksell,
   Stockholm, 1956): this is the most extreme rejection of
   everything metaphysical amongst the Scandinavian school.
   Nothing is valid, which cannot be proved as fact. The main
   distinction is between the science of law, which should
   have nothing to do with values, and valuations, which are
   necessary but individualistic.

4. OLIVECRONA, K. "Law as Fact", in Interpretations of Modern
   Legal Philosophies, (ed. P. Sayre, Oxford University Press,
   New York, 1947), chap. 25: the "binding force" of law is
   examined with the aid of the concept of duty. The connection
   between the idea of a rule and the feeling of being bound
   is a psychological one.

5. MERRILLS, J.G. "Law, Morals and the Psychological Nexus",
   (1969), 19 Tor. L.J., 46: the author considers critically
   and takes issue with Olivecrona's thesis that morality is
   shaped by legal enforcement. He thinks that Olivecrona fails
   to distinguish between acceptance of a rule as binding and
   the morality of it. He also criticises Olivecrona for
   grossly underestimating the influence of morals on law.

6. OLIVECRONA, K. "Legal Language and Reality" in Essays in
   Jurisprudence in Honor of Roscoe Pound, (ed. R.A. Newman,
   The Bobbs-Merrill Co., Inc., 1962), p. 151: the views of
   various groups of thinkers to find some realistic basis for
   rights are considered and rejected. There are also critical
   comments on the views of the American Realists, Hägerström
   and Lundstedt. The discussion then proceeds with the
   function of legal language.

7. OLIVECRONA, K. "The Legal Theories of Axel Hägerström and

Vilhelm Lundstedt" (1959), 3 Scand. S.L., 125: the views of
Hägerström and Lundstedt are explained. The illusory nature
of a right is further discussed. Right has a behaviourist
function.

1. ARNHOLM, C.J. "Olivecrona on Legal Rights. Reflections on the
Concept of Rights" (1962), 6 Scand. S.L., 11: Olivecrona's
views are explained. The difference between his views and
those of the American Realists is said to be the difference
between a juristic and a sociological concept.

2. STONE, J. Legal System and Lawyers' Reasonings, (Stevens &
Sons, Ltd., 1964), pp. 92-93: in the course of a discussion
of the imperative theory of law there is a passing reference to Olivecrona's idea of "independent imperative". It
is said that there are many situations in which there are
actual commands addressed to individuals, and for these the
idea of "independent imperative" is inappropriate.

3. ROSS, A. Towards a Realistic Jurisprudence, (trans. A.I.
Fausbøll, Einar Munksgaard, Copenhagen, 1946): the normative and factual aspects of law are inescapable. The former
are alleged to be rationalisations of emotional experiences.

4. HART, H.L.A. "Scandinavian Realism", (1959), C.L.J., 233:
this is a critical review of A. Ross's On Law and Justice.

5. CHRISTIE, G.C. "The Notion of Validity in Modern
Jurisprudence", (1963-64), 48 Minn. L.R., 1049: the views
of Kelsen and Ross as to the criterion of validity are
compared with reference to concrete situations, and the
former is preferred.

6. ARNHOLM, C.J. "Some Basic Problems of Jurisprudence", (1957),
1 Scand. S.L., 9: Ross's contention that the validity of a
norm depends on whether a judge will act on it is criticised.
Other interpretations of validity are also considered and
rejected.

7. JØRGENSEN, S. "Argumentation and Decision" in Liber Amicorum
in Honour of Professor Alf Ross, (Copenhagen, 1969), 261:
after pointing out that Ross does not deal with the problem
which faces the judge, the author discusses the approaches
of natural law theory, argumentation theory and decision
theory. The first proceeds a priori; the second makes it
possible to discuss values and the question is one of good
and bad argumentation; while the last takes account of
values themselves.

8. LUNDSTEDT, A.V. Superstition or Rationality in Action for

Peace ? (Longmans, Green & Co., 1925): this is a strongly expressed polemic against traditional views about legal concepts and an uncompromising rejection of everything metaphysical.

1. LUNDSTEDT, A.V. "Law and Justice: A Criticism of the Method of Justice" in Interpretations of Modern Legal Philosophies, (ed. P. Sayre, Oxford University Press, New York, 1947), chap. 21: the idea that justice underlies law and determines its content is attacked with illustrations drawn from criminal law and torts. Judgments of justice are expressions of feeling. Such evaluations should be made with reference to public welfare.

2. CASTBERG, F. Problems of Legal Philosophy, (2nd ed., Oslo University Press; Allen & Unwin, Ltd., 1957), especially pp. 27-37: a Norwegian writer takes issue with the Realists. The importance and indispensability of norms and values are the underlying theme.

3. MARSHALL, G. "Law in a Cold Climate. The Scandinavian Realism" (1956), 1 Jur.R.(N.S.), 259: this is a discussion in dialogue form of what the Scandinavians mean by positivism and some of their other doctrines.

4. REDMOUNT, R.S. "Psychological Views in Jurisprudential Theories" (1958-59), 107 U.Pa.L.R., 472: the psychological bases of the theories of the Scandinavian Realists and of Bentham and Petrazhitsky are examined. The dependance of human beings on their environment is stressed.

5. SMITH, J.C. "Law, Language, and Philosophy" (1968) 3 U.Br. Col.L.R. 59: in the course of reviewing the attitude to language of various legal philosophers, the attitudes of Hägerström and Olivecrona, among others, are explained and considered.

6. LLOYD, D. Introduction to Jurisprudence, (2nd ed., Stevens & Sons, Ltd., 1965), chap. 8: the work of Olivecrona, Lundstedt and Ross is briefly reviewed. See also D. Lloyd, The Idea of Law, (Penguin Books, Ltd., A. 688, 1964), pp. 217-19.

7. FRIEDMANN, W. Legal Theory, (5th ed., Stevens & Sons, Ltd., 1967), pp. 304-311: this is a brief account of the work and contribution of the Scandinavian Realist School.

8. BODENHEIMER, E. Jurisprudence, (Harvard University Press, 1962), pp. 120-25: this is another brief account of the work of the Scandinavian Realists.

20

NATURAL LAW

General

1. d'ENTREVES, A.P. Natural Law, (Hutchinson's University Library, 1951): this is the best and most convenient survey of the contributions of natural law doctrine to thought. The principal issues connected with naturalist philosophy are examined.

2. ROMMEN, H.A. The Natural Law, (trans. T.R. Hanley, B. Herder Book Co., 1947): the movement away from natural law is deplored. Natural law is said to be essential to a philosophy of social order and justice. Part I traces the history of natural law thought from Greek times down to the present. In Part II the content of natural law is examined.

3. HAINES, C.G. The Revival of Natural Law Concepts, (Harvard University Press, 1930): natural lawyers are said to fall into three groups. In the light of this division the doctrines of natural lawyers are examined from Greek times onwards. The modern revival of natural law theory and the reasons for it are considered in detail. Much of the book is concerned with natural law thinking in America.

4. SABINE, G.H. A History of Political Theory, (3rd ed., Harrap & Co. Ltd., 1963), chaps. 2-6, 8-9, 13, 21-23, 26-29: this book provides one of the best surveys of the history of thought from Greek times to the present.

5. POUND, R. The Ideal Element in Law, (University of Calcutta, 1958), chaps. 2-6: there is always an ideal element underlying the law; even analytical positivism is founded on an ideal. A survey of natural law doctrine and its contributions is followed by discussions of the relation between law and morals and the end of law.

6. FRIEDMANN, W. Legal Theory, (5th ed. Stevens & Sons, Ltd., 1967), chaps. 7-14: the first of these chapters deals generally with the functions which natural law theory has fulfilled. This is followed by a historical discussion of the various stages and forms of natural law thought.

7. JONES, J.W. Historical Introduction to the Theory of Law, (Oxford, 1940), chap. 4: the idea of a law of nature is ascribed to the belief that there are certain principles inherent in the scheme of things. The survey includes a fairly lengthy discussion of the work of Cicero, the Roman period, the Middle Ages and modern natural law.

1. BODENHEIMER, E. Jurisprudence, (Harvard University Press, 1962), chaps. 1-4, 9-14: in the first four chapters and chapter 9 there are accounts of the theories of philosophers and writers from Greek times down to the present time. The remaining chapters deal more generally with the need for order and justice and with law as the means of achieving these. In chapter 12 there is a discussion of the validity of an unjust law.

2. PATTERSON, E.W. Jurisprudence, (The Foundation Press, Inc., 1953), chaps. 13-14: six meanings of the expression "natural law" are distinguished. There are good accounts of the work of Aristotle, Cicero and Aquinas. Human nature as assumed in naturalist theory is critically appraised. In chapter 14 the work of Kant is dealt with at some length and there are slighter accounts of Stammler and some others.

3. STONE, J. Human Law and Human Justice, (Stevens & Sons, Ltd., 1965), chaps. 1-3: the first two of these chapters give an introduction to the natural law theory of the Greeks and Romans down to evolution of international law and natural law as a criterion of the validity of positive law. In the last chapter the work of Kant is dealt with and the part played by individual rights on English and American law is considered.

4. JOLOWICZ, H.F. Lectures on Jurisprudence, (ed. J.A. Jolowicz, The Athlone Press, 1963), chaps. 2-5: these chapters survey natural law theory from Greek times until the 18th century. It provides a perspective of the various movements in thought.

5. HOLLAND, T.E. The Elements of Jurisprudence, (13th ed., Oxford, 1924), pp. 31-40: natural law is said to be based on morality, and the interpretations of the Stoics, Cicero, Aquinas and Hobbes, inter alia, are also mentioned. The effects and implications of naturalist doctrine are enumerated.

6. PATON, G.W. A Text-Book of Jurisprudence, (3rd ed., D.P. Derham, Oxford, 1964), chap. 4: natural law theory concerns law in relation to purpose, the basis of law and the relation between law and justice. There is a brief survey of the views of the Greeks, Romans, Christian Fathers, 17th century and modern writers. Particular mention is made of the attitude of the common law.

7. VINOGRADOFF, P. Common-sense in Law, (3rd ed., H.G. Hanbury, Oxford University Press, 1959), chap. 9: rules have a two-fold justification - as authoritative commands and as

reasonable propositions. There is an account of the work
of the Greeks, Romans and early churchmen. The influence
of naturalist thinking on English case-law is mentioned
at some length.

1. VINOGRADOFF, P. Collected Papers, (Oxford, 1928), II, chap.
   18: the need to satisfy the desire for justice was met by
   appeal to natural law. The various stages in the development
   of this idea are developed.

2. SALMOND, J.W. "The Law of Nature" (1895), 11 L.Q.R., 121: the
   lack of interest on the part of common lawyers in legal
   philosophy is attributed to the separation of ideas of law
   and moral questions as preserved by the different words
   "right" and "law", whereas Continental jurists have one
   word to connote the two ideas. Both are said to go too far
   in their respective attitudes. There is a clear historical
   account of speculation about natural law and natural
   rights from Greek times down to the 19th century.

3. SALMOND, J.W. Jurisprudence, (7th ed., Sweet & Maxwell, Ltd.,
   1924), pp. 26-30; (12th ed., P.J. Fitzgerald, 1966), pp.
   15-25: it is significant that whereas Salmond's own
   treatment of natural law was cursory and "illustrated
   sufficiently" by a few sample quotations from very ancient
   writers, his latest editor sees fit to develop much more
   fully a theme which has sprung to life in recent years.

4. SEAGLE, W. The Quest for Law, (Alfred A. Knopf, 1941), chap.
   14: natural law is more than a matter of individual
   preference. It can be a dangerous and shattering force. In
   this chapter the uses to which natural law theory have been
   put are traced down to the 18th century.

5. CHLOROS, A.G. "What is Natural Law ?" (1958), 21 M.L.R. 609:
   the question What is natural law ? is still a fruitful one
   for considering the different types of order that will
   result from the application of natural law theory. It is
   said that there is little or no difference between natural
   law thinking and the sociological approach. A framework for
   jurisprudential study based on a broad classification of
   natural law theory is outlined.

6. CHROUST, A.H. "On the Nature of Natural Law" in Interpretations
   of Modern Legal Philosophies, (ed. P. Sayre, Oxford
   University Press, New York, 1947), chap. 5: natural law is
   opposed to positive law and to empiricism. It proceeds
   deductively from presuppositions and represents a quest for
   the absolute and ultimate meaning of law and justice.

1. POUND, R. An Introduction to the Philosophy of Law, (Yale
    University Press, 1922), chaps. 1-2: this is a readable
    account of the various functions which legal philosophy
    has fulfilled through the ages, natural law theory in
    particular.

2. POUND, R. "The Scope and Purpose of Sociological Juris-
    prudence", (1910-11), 24 Harv. L.R., 591, at pp. 604-11;
    (1911-12), 25 Harv. L.R., 140, at pp. 147-62: the philo-
    sophical approach is surveyed broadly. Among the 19th.
    century doctrines there is special mention of Stammler.

3. POUND, R. "Fifty Years of Jurisprudence", (1937-38), 51 Harv.
    L.R., 444, at pp. 463-72: the modern revival of natural
    law is dealt with.

4. POUND, R. "The End of Law as Developed in Juristic Thought",
    (1913-14), 27 Harv. L.R., 195, at p. 605; (1916-17), 30
    Harv. L.R., 201: this surveys thinking about law from
    Greek times down to the 19th. century. The theme which is
    stressed is the way in which legal theory has been used to
    satisfy the paramount social need of the age. The invest-
    igation is pursued into the 20th. century in "Twentieth-
    century Ideas as to the End of Law" in Harvard Legal Essays,
    (Harvard University Press, 1934), 357.

5. POUND, R. Interpretations of Legal History, (Cambridge
    University Press, 1923), chap. 2: the ethical interpretation
    of legal history is considered historically with reference
    to the part played by ideals.

6. POUND, R. Jurisprudence, (West Publishing Co., 1959), I, chaps
    2-4, 7-8; II, chap. 11: the above are collated and re-stated
    generally.

7. WINDOLPH, F.L. Leviathan and Natural Law, (Princeton Univer-
    sity Press, 1951): an attempt is made to construct a natural
    law theory on a positivist basis principally by separating
    politics from morality. But the upshot of the argument is
    that it is not necessary to introduce a moral element into
    the idea of the validity of law.

8. FRIEDRICH, C.J. The Philosophy of Law in Historical Perspec-
    tive, (The University of Chicago Press, 1958), chaps. 1-10,
    12-13, 19: the various theories of law are explained from
    the time of the Old Testament and the Greeks down to the
    present. Throughout the book the underlying theme is that
    an unjust law is not law.

9. MAINE, H.J.S. Ancient Law, (ed. F. Pollock, John Murray, 1906),

chaps. 3-4 and Notes F-G: in chapter 3 equity in Roman law, the origin of the _jus gentium_ and the influence of Greek philosophy on the Romans is considered. In chapter 4 the modern history of natural law is dealt with. Its influence in giving rise to international law is stressed. In the Notes Pollock comments on and questions some of Maine's contentions.

1. POUND, R. "Natural Natural Law and Positive Natural Law", (1952), 68 L.Q.R., 330; (1960), 5 Nat. L.F., 70: the contrast is between a rationally conceived ideal relation between men, on the one hand, and universal precepts that are logically derived from actual experience, on the other. The functions of "natural natural law" are explained.

2. SILVING, H. _Sources of Law_, (Wm. S. Hein & Co., Inc., New York, 1968), "'Positive' or 'Natural Law' ?", p. 251: in these pages will be found a general discussion of the relation between positive and natural law. An interesting contention is that positivism has provided a new type of natural law, which is said to occur when courts decide, not according to what was understood by the legislators at the time the law was laid down, but according to contemporary legal science. Also of interest is the naturalist call for positivism in law as a guarantee of certainty and hence of justice, and the assertion that positivism is grounded in a basic assumption that the law and those who make it shall behave rationally. When this assumption breaks down, _e.g._, in Nazi Germany, the limit of the bindingness of law _is_ reached.

3. HARPER, F.V. "The Forces Behind and Beyond Juristic Pragmatism in America" in _Receuil d'Etudes sur les Sources du Droit en l'Honneur de F. Geny_, (Librairie du Receuil Sirey, 1934), II, 243: Philosophy has followed physical science, but it has led the social science by giving direction to it.

4. GOODHART, A.L. _English Law and the Moral Law_, (Stevens & Sons, Ltd., 1955), pp. 28-37: there is an "objective morality" which jurists should not ignore. This constitutes the "revived natural law". It has its basis in a sense of obligation: why do people regard moral law as obligatory ? The reasons are considered at length.

5. THAYER, A.S. "Natural Law", (1905), 21 L.Q.R., 60: moral ideas are described as ghosts of habit. They have become idealised and hence are thought to be perfect.

6. BRUNNER, E. _Justice and the Social Order_, (trans. M. Hottinger, Lutterworth Press, 1945), chap. 12: the author's aim is to

evolve a Protestant version of natural law. Three meanings
of natural law are contrasted, the objective interpretation
of pre-Christian times, the subjective individualist interpretation and the Christian interpretation. The chapter is
mainly concerned with showing how Christian theology came
to appropriate natural law theory.

1. WU, J.C.H. Fountain of Justice. A Study in Natural Law,
(Sheed & Ward, 1955): this book is written from a devoutly
Christian (Thomist) point of view. The common law of
England and America is the material on which the argument
is constructed.

2. BROWN, B.F. "Natural Law: Dynamic Basis of Law and Morals in
the Twentieth Century", (1957), 31 Tul. L.R., 491: this is
a vigorous re-statement of an essentially Thomist position.
Natural law is the common basis of law and morals. Law
bears an immutable relationship to Natural law; it has the
character of law only so far as it has this relation. The
separation of law and morals will undermine the common law.

3. Southern Methodist University Studies in Jurisprudence, (ed.
A.L. Harding, S.M.U. Press), II, (1955), chaps. 3-4: these
are respectively a critical appraisal of the value of the
natural law theory for the problems of today, and the
revived natural law of today. III, (1956), chap. 4: natural
law is discussed from a Christian point of view.

4. ELLUL, J. The Theological Foundation of Law, (trans. M. Wieser,
S.C.M. Press, Ltd., 1946, first British ed., 1961): divine
law is opposed to natural law. The latter became corrupt
after the Fall of Man and therefore no profitable theory
can be built on it. The true law is that revealed by God
through Christ.

5. NORTHROP, F.S.C. The Complexity of Legal and Ethical
Experience, (Little, Brown & Co., 1959): it is contended
that judgments of goodness and badness are scientifically
verifiable. If so, a normative discipline like law assumes
the character of a science. Law has three levels: positive
law, living law and natural law. The last is derived from
a true and, as far as possible, complete knowledge of Man.
Such knowledge comes from experimentally verified findings
of physics, biology and other natural science. Nature, as
thus interpreted by science, is the source of verification
for law. For an application of this approach to international law, see F.S.C. NORTHROP: "Naturalistic and
Cultural Foundations for a More Effective International
Law" (1949-50), 59 Yale L.J., 1430; "Contemporary Jurisprudence and International Law", (1952), 61 Yale L.J., 623.

1. WILD, J.D. Plato's Modern Enemies and the Theory of Natural
    Law, (University of Chicago Press, 1953): "value" and
    "existence" are intertwined. Fulfilment of existence is
    "good", and its frustration is "evil". Existence has a
    tendential character, and such tendency is fact on which
    certain norms are grounded. On this basis it becomes
    possible to construct a theory of natural law.

2. KELSEN, H. "A 'Dynamic' Theory of Natural Law", in What is
    Justice ? (University of California Press, 1957), 174:
    J.D. Wild's theory is subjected to criticism. Modern
    natural law takes a monistic view of "ought" and "is"; but
    this is mistaken. To show factual grounds for the content
    of the rules of natural law does not show why natural law
    is to be binding.

3. STONE, J. Human Law and Human Justice, (Stevens & Sons, Ltd.,
    1965), pp. 196-202: these pages contain an account of J.D.
    Wild's theory of natural law and criticism of it. The main
    comment is that the fact that people have a sense of obli-
    gation does not explain why they ought to obey this sense.
    Other criticisms are the vagueness of his terminology, and
    there are so many different opinions as to what constitutes
    "fulfilment" of "tendency" that it ceases to be objective
    fact.

4. LASERSON, M.M. "'Positive' and 'Natural' Law and their
    Correlation" in Interpretations of Modern Legal Philo-
    sophies, (ed. P. Sayre, Oxford University Press, New York,
    1947), chap. 20: positive law keeps up with ideas of what
    ought to be in a series of periodic jumps. Intuitive law is
    individually variable and socially adaptable. This is
    natural law.

5. HALL, J. Studies in Jurisprudence and Criminal Theory,
    (Oceana Publications Inc., 1958), chap. 2: current theories
    of natural law fail to take account of facts. Realism has
    paid too much attention to facts and too little to values.
    Positivism is too concerned with pure ideas. The author
    pleads for an "integrative jurisprudence" which will
    combine values, facts and ideals.

6. HALL, J. Living Law of Democratic Society, (The Bobbs-Merrill
    Co., Inc., 1949), chap. 2: various trends of thought
    throughout history are reviewed in the light of the need
    for values. The Stoic theory is praised as having contained
    an integrative view of law, i.e., made ideals part of the
    essence of positive law.

7. DEWEY, J. Philosophy and Civilisation, (G.P. Putnam's Sons,

1931), 166: "nature" and "reason" are ambiguous terms.
Their use as synonyms of "morality" has given rise to
different interpretations.

1. LLOYD, D. "Legal and Ideal Justice" in Legal Essays. A
   Tribute to Frede Castberg, (Universitetsforlaget, 1963),
   III: this begins by contrasting the kind of natural law
   that one gets by deriving it from nature as it is and from
   ideals of what ought to be. Instead of searching for
   absolute values it is thought to be more fruitful to
   explore how the values of a developing society may best be
   realised in the conditions of today.

2. Law and Philosophy. A Symposium, (ed. S. Hook, New York
   University Press, 1964), Part II: various versions of
   natural law theory are outlined by different authors, while
   others offer criticisms. The whole is of general interest.

3. COWEN, D.V. The Foundations of Freedom (Cape Town, O.U.P.
   1961), chap. 10: in the course of a general appraisal of
   a naturalist approach there is a brief review of the Greek
   and Roman periods, the Middle Ages and Renaissance.

Critical appraisals

4. BENTHAM, J. The Theory of Legislation, (5th ed., trans.
   R. Hildreth, Trubner & Co., Ltd., 1887): chap. 13, S 10:
   Bentham was a redoubtable opponent of natural law theory.
   His attacks are to be found in many other places in his
   writings.

5. AUSTIN, J. Lectures on Jurisprudence, (5th ed., R. Campbell,
   John Murray, 1885), II, pp. 567-75, chaps. 31-32:
   jurisprudence, as the science of positive law, should be
   kept distinct from what law ought to be. The different
   senses in which the term "natural law" is used are
   explained, and there is also a discussion of jus naturale
   in relation to jus gentium.

6. KELSEN, H. "The Metamorphoses of the Idea of Justice" in
   Interpretations of Modern Legal Philosophies, (ed.
   P. Sayre, Oxford University Press, New York, 1947), chap.
   18, especially pp. 395-97: the idea of justice is
   considered in relation to natural law. The assumption that
   what is just is natural assumes that a just regulation of
   human nature proceeds from nature. Natural law theories
   have so far failed to define the content of this just
   order. The article contains discussions of Aristotle's and
   Plato's views on justice.

1. KELSEN, H. What is Justice ? (University of California Press, 1957), pp. 137-97; 209: various criticisms of the traditional naturalist doctrine are developed in detail. Its vitality derives from the fact that it serves as justification. Natural law doctrine is said to stand or fall with the assumption that value is inherent in reality. Values of law determine whether conduct is lawful or unlawful; this is decided according to the validity of the norm. Values of justice determine whether the law is just or unjust. These cannot be objectively verified and a science of law has no place for them.

2. ROSS, A. On Law and Justice, (Stevens & Sons, Ltd., 1958), chaps. 10-11: natural law philosophy is the product of an infantile fear of life's inconsistencies. Its history is traced from Homeric times to the present. Chapter 11 subjects natural law doctrine to incisive criticism. The ideology does not exist that cannot be defended by appeal to natural law.

3. ROSS, A. Towards a Realistic Jurisprudence, (trans. A.I. Fausbøll, Einar Munksgaard, 1946), 21-32: the concept of natural law is considered in the course of a general survey of theories of law and is rejected.

4. KORKUNOV, N.M. General Theory of Law, (trans. W.G. Hastings, The Boston Book Co., 1909), chap. 3: there are elements common to various systems of law which are imposed by necessity. This has given rise to a belief in natural law which exists without human agency. Natural law in Roman law and in the 17th century, as well as the attacks upon it by the Historical School, are set out.

5. SHKLAR, J.N. Legalism, (Harvard University Press, 1964): "legalism" is the attitude of mind which makes a morality of rule following. Naturalist, no less than Positivist, legal theorists are tainted with it. But this morality is only one among many in a pluralist society. Hence the efforts of Naturalists, including their polemics against Positivism, are narrow and out of touch with social realities. Natural Law theory is said to be an ideology of agreement.

6. GOLUNSKII, S.A. and STROGOVICH, M.S. "The Theory of the State and Law" in Soviet Legal Philosophy, (trans. H.W. Babb, Harvard University Press, 1951), pp. 402-6: this gives a general explanation of what natural law and the Roman jus gentium are. The developments, which are commonly ascribed to natural law theory, are explained on Marxist lines.

1. BUCKLAND, W.W. Some Reflections on Jurisprudence, (Cambridge
   University Press, 1945), chap. 3: the old conception of
   natural law made the rightness and wrongness of law the
   criterion of its validity. There is a brief account of the
   use which has been made of naturalist theory.

2. HOLMES, O.W. "Natural Law" in Collected Legal Papers,
   (Constable & Co., Ltd., 1920), 310: There is a human
   tendency to demand the superlative in all things, which
   might account for the search for criteria of universal
   validity. The naturalist attitude of mind is dealt with.

3. LLEWELLYN, K.N. Jurisprudence. Realism in Theory and Practice,
   (The University of Chicago Press, 1962), chap. 5: the
   lawyer's natural law is an effort to harness the philosopher's
   natural law to the solution of specific problems. Guidance
   for a particular society should be rooted in it. Viewed in
   this way, there need not be any irreconcileable antinomy
   between natural law and realism.

4. KESSLER, F. "Theoretic Bases of Law" (1941-42), 9 U.C.L.R.,
   98, especially pp. 99-108: natural law philosophy believes
   in certain fundamental principles inherent in all ordered
   society. While giving credit to the achievements of natural
   law, the author criticises its claim to eternal validity.
   Positivism is also criticised. It is contended that realism
   enables the best in both to be combined.

5. KESSLER, F. "Natural Law, Justice and Democracy - Some
   Reflections on Three Types of Thinking about Law and
   Justice" (1944-45), 19 Tul.L.R., 32: the contributions of
   natural and positive law theory to the relationship
   between law, justice and democracy are assessed. Natural
   law philosophy is contrasted with the objective idealism
   of Plato on the one hand, and positive law on the other.

History of natural law thought

6. PLATO The Laws, (ed., E.B. England, Manchester University
   Press, 1921), I and II: the text and notes are provided.
   The main point in The Laws is that, in default of
   philosopher kings, a state ruled by law is second best.

7. POPPER, K.R. The Open Society and its Enemies, (5th ed.,
   Routledge & Kegan Paul, Ltd., 1966), I and II: the "open
   society" has set free the critical powers of Man. Both
   parts constitute a powerful argument against inevitability
   in evolution. Volume I provides a searching and stimulating
   examination of Plato's doctrine. It is one of the best
   critiques.

1. WILD, J. Plato's Modern Enemies and the Theory of Natural
   Law, (The University of Chicago Press, 1953): Plato is
   defended against the attacks of subsequent writers who, it
   is alleged, have misread his dialogues. A theory of natural
   law can be found in his works with which to appraise modern
   naturalist doctrine.

2. HALL, J. Studies in Jurisprudence and Criminal Theory,
   (Oceana Publications Inc., 1958), chap. 3: this gives an
   interesting account of Plato's attitude to law as evidenced
   by his works.

3. KELSEN, H. "Plato and the Doctrine of Natural Law" (1960-61),
   14 Vand.L.R., 23: observations of what "is" cannot be
   causally lined with what "ought to be". Plato's views are
   considered with reference to two recent expositions of
   them. See also H.KELSEN: What is Justice ? (University of
   California Press, 1957), 82.

4. VINOGRADOFF, P. Outlines of Historical Jurisprudence, (Oxford
   University Press, 1910), II: this contains a very good
   account of the Greek city-states.

5. ARISTOTLE Politics, (trans. J.E.C. Weldon, Macmillan & Co.,
   Ltd., 1912), I, chaps. 1-7: these contain Aristotle's
   views on the function of the state and the position of
   slaves.

6. ARISTOTLE Nichomachean Ethics, (3rd ed., trans. R. Williams,
   Longmans, Green & Co., 1879), V: this famous discussion of
   justice might usefully be referred to in the general
   context of natural law.

7. SHELLENS, M.S. "Aristotle on Natural Law" (1959), 4 Nat.L.F.,
   72: the accounts of natural law in the Rhetoric, Magna
   Moralia and Nichomachean Ethics are examined and their
   significance assessed.

8. KELSEN, H. What is Justice ? (University of California Press,
   1957), 110: this is a study in Aristotle's doctrine of
   Justice.

9. HAMBURGER, M. The Awakening of Western Legal Thought, (trans.
   B. Miall, Allen & Unwin, Ltd., 1942): this small and worth
   while book summarises the contribution of the Greeks to
   modern ideas of law. Part I deals with various writers,
   poets, dramatists and philosophers; Part II assesses what
   they can teach the world.

10. STONE, J. Human Law and Human Justice (Stevens & Sons, Ltd.,

1965), pp. 9-18: an account is given of the lines of
thought underlying early Greek philosophy, the relativism
of the Sophists, the absolute idea of Plato and the
interpretation of Aristotle. Natural law thinking is
entangled with ideas of justice.

1. CICERO, M.T. De Legibus, I-III; De Re Publica, III, (Loeb
   Classical Library ed., G.P. Putnam's Sons, 1928): Cicero
   is the best exponent of natural law doctrines among the
   Roman writers. These passages contain the essence of his
   views.

2. JOLOWICZ, H.F. Historical Introduction to Roman Law, (2nd ed.,
   Cambridge University Press, 1952), chap. 6: the origin of
   the Roman jus gentium and its connection with the jus
   naturale is explained.

3. BRYCE, J. Studies in History and Jurisprudence, (Oxford, 1901),
   II, pp. 112-71: the way in which the Greeks developed the
   ideas that underlie natural law are first examined. The
   emphasis is on the influence of natural law on Roman law
   and, through it, on international law.

4. CLARK, E.C. Practical Jurisprudence, (Cambridge University
   Press, 1883), I, chap. 10; II, chap. 13: natural law as a
   motive for obedience is first considered, and then the jus
   gentium of Roman law.

5. EMERTON, W. "Stoic Terminology in Roman Law" (1887), 3 L.Q.R.,
   64: this might be referred to for general information. See
   further P. von SOKOLOWSKI: Die Philosophie im Privatrecht
   (1902).

6. SILVING, H. "The Jurisprudence of the Old Testament" (1953),
   28 N.Y.U.L.R., 1129: the main features of the original
   Jewish state are explained with reference to some modern
   legal and political problems.

7. SILVING, H. Sources of Law (Wm. S. Hein & Co., Inc., New
   York, 1968), "The Origins of the 'Rule of Law'" p. 233: the
   doctrines enunciated in the English Magna Carta and the
   earlier Spanish Charta Magna Leonesa are traceable to the
   Bible.

8. ISAACS, N. "The Influence of Judaism on Western Law" in The
   Legacy of Israel, (edd. E.R. Bevan and C. Singer, Oxford,
   1927), pp. 377-406: the example of Jewish law is said to
   have predisposed western Europe towards the "better rule".
   How this is so is explained in detail.

1. COHN, H. "Praelegomena to the Theory and History of Jewish
    Law" in Essays in Jurisprudence in Honor of Roscoe Pound,
    (ed. R.A. Newman, The Bobbs-Merrill Co., Inc., 1962), 44:
    this explains the theoretical basis of Jewish law and the
    rules that are followed in interpretation.

2. KAGAN, K.K. Three Great Systems of Jurisprudence, (Stevens &
    Sons, Ltd., 1955), especially chap. 4: Jewish, Roman and
    English law are compared, and the superiority of Jewish law
    is asserted. Chapter 4 is of interest since it deals at
    length with the Jewish version of the social contract.

3. EPSTEIN, I. Judaism. A Historical Presentation, (Pelican Books,
    1959): the story of Israel is presented historically from
    the earliest times down to the present. The early chapters
    are especially useful in providing a background for the
    juristic theory. The rest of the book is of general interest.

4. STONE, J. Human Law and Human Justice, (Stevens & Sons, Ltd.,
    1965), pp. 18-30: this is a convenient account of the Jewish
    contribution to ideas of justice. The concept of equality of
    men derives from the fact of being God's children. It is
    pointed out that the lex talionis operated as a limitation
    on self-help. Explanation is also given as to why Jewish law
    never evolved a doctrine of natural law or equity superior
    to positive law.

5. LLOYD, D. The Idea of Law, (Penguin Books, Ltd., A 688, 1964),
    pp. 48-51: the attitude of the Hebrew prophets towards God's
    law and human law is outlined and is followed by an account
    of the Greek philosophers.

6. AQUINAS, St. T. Summa Theologica, (trans. Fathers of the
    English Dominican Province, R. & T. Washbourne, Ltd., 1915),
    I, 2, pp. 90-97: distinctions between different kinds of law
    are drawn and explained. The importance of promulgation is
    stressed.

7. DAVITT, T.E. "Law as a Means to an End - Thomas Aquinas",
    (1960-61), 14 Vand. L.R., 65: various features of God-made
    and Man-made law are explained and their interrelation con-
    sidered. This is a clear summary of Aquinas's views.

8. SLESSER, H. The Judicial Office and Other Matters, (Hutchinson
    & Co., Ltd.), chap. 5: the place which Aquinas occupies in
    relation to prior and subsequent thought is discussed at
    length.

9. COPLESTON, F.C. Aquinas, (Penguin Books, Ltd., 1955): the
    relationship between Aquinas's thought and that of the Greek

philosophers is considered. The value of his scheme is assesed at length, and there is also some account of modern Thomism.

1. NIELSEN, K. "An Examination of the Thomist Theory of Natural Law", (1959), 4 Nat. L.F., 44: the doctrines of Aquinas are considered with reference to the interpretations of Copleston (supra) and Maritain. The essence of the doctrine is outlined at pp. 52-56. The thesis of the article is to take issue with the conception of a natural moral law. For a critical commentary on Nielsen, see V.J. BOURKE: "Natural Law, Thomism - and Professor Nielsen" (1960), 5 Nat. L.F., 112.

2. NIELSEN, K. "The Myth of Natural Law" in Law and Philosophy. A Symposium, (ed. S. Hook, New York University Press, 1964), p. 122: the fact that human life is purposive is no evidence of the mind of God. "Purpose" may signify "function" or "aim". Men have aims, but these are no indication of Man's function.

3. HARDING, R.W. "The Evolution of Roman Catholic Views of Private Property as a Natural Right" (1963), 2 Sol. Q., 124: Aquinas's views about property are examined in order to show that for him the natural right of property was common ownership. The idea that private ownership is a natural right is said to be a later development and a departure from Aquinas's teachings.

4. BRODERICK, A. "The Radical Middle: The Natural Right of Property in Aquinas and the Popes" (1964), 3 Sol. Q., 127: Aquinas's doctrine of property is explained so as to remove what is alleged to be R.W. Harding's misconception. The last section on the jurisprudential value of natural rights deals with value as guides to just enactments.

5. STONE, J. Human Law and Human Justice, (Stevens & Sons, Ltd., 1965), pp. 51-55: in these pages there is a brief and very general account of Aquinas's thought relation to the development of Greek and Christian thinking.

6. Southern Methodist University Studies in Jurisprudence, (ed. A.L. Harding, S.M.U. Press), I, (1954), chaps. 1-2: these deal respectively with Cicero's and Aquinas's concepts of law.

7. ULLMANN, W. "Baldus's Conception of Law", (1942), 58 L.Q.R., 386: this is of general interest as giving the views of a 14th. century scholar of natural law.

1. LEWIS, J.U. "Sir Edward Coke (1552-1633): His Theory of 'Artificial Reason' as a Context for Modern Basic Legal Theory", (1968), 84 L.Q.R., 330: law enjoins obedience by virtue of being reasonable. It was on this basis that he argued in Bonham's Case that even Acts of Parliament, which offend common right and reason, could be avoided. Reason is not "natural reason", but "artificial perfection of reason, gotten by long study". Coke's views, it is said, enabled English Law to modernise itself for the future.

2. BERGER, R. "Doctor Bonham's Case: Statutory Construction or Constitutional Theory ?" (1969), 117 U.Pa. L.R., 521: what did Coke mean when he showed a readiness to avoid a statute which was "against reason" ? Was he simply interpreting a statute, or propounding a doctrine of judicial review ? The author considers the use that has been made of Coke's utterance, and he himself believes that by this phrase Coke meant "against natural law".

3. GROTIUS, H. De Jure Belli ac Pacis, (trans. F.W. Kelsey, Oxford, 1925), I, chap. 1, SS 10-17: Grotius sets out his views on the law of nature with the utmost clarity and vigour.

4. RUTHERFORD, T. Institutions of Natural Law, (2nd ed., Cambridge, 1779), chap. 1: the book represents a course of lectures on Grotius's masterpiece. Chapter 1 gives a general account of the nature of laws, divine, natural and positive.

5. RATTIGAN, W.H. "Hugo Grotius" in Great Jurists of the World, (edd. J. MacDonnell and E. Manson, John Murray, 1913), 169: an account of Grotius's life and career is given. The principal contentions of De Jure Belli ac Pacis are explained as part of his contribution to juristic thinking.

6. HOBBES, T. Leviathan, (ed. M. Oakeshott, Oxford, 1946),: the text provides the uncompromising Hobbesian version of the social contract. The editor in his introduction analyses Hobbes's thesis and relates it to philosophical and political thought. He believes, incidentally, that Hegel achieved harmony of reason and will.

7. BROWN, J.M. "A Note on Professor Oakeshott's Introduction to the Leviathan" (1953), 1 Pol. S., 53: Oakeshott's analysis of Hobbes is criticised on a number of important points and should be read as a corrective to Oakeshott's Introduction.

8. BALOGH, E. "Note on Thomas Hobbes" in Interpretations of Modern Legal Philosophies, (ed. P. Sayre, Oxford University Press, New York, 1947), chap. 2: Hobbes's work is considered

in relation to psychology and legal theory. He is said to
represent a reaction against both the Reformation and
Renaissance. Freedom of conscience had brought men to
anarchy.

1. de MONTMORENCY, J.E.G. "Thomas Hobbes" in Great Jurists of
   the World, (edd. J. MacDonnell and E. Manson, John Murray,
   1913), 195: the line of argument of the Leviathan is
   explained. This is followed by an assessment of Hobbes as
   a lawyer and jurist.

2. CAMPBELL, E. Thomas Hobbes and the Common Law", (1958), 1
   Tasm. L.R., 20: the views of Hobbes, not on political
   theory, but on the common law are explained, in particular
   his equation of "civil law" with natural law. From his
   basic norm of the need for self-preservation, he was led
   to the need for civil society, a determinate superior therein and for civil law to be the command of this superior. He
   has to translate natural law into positive law. The judges,
   who are the agents of the superior, should therefore apply
   natural law where necessary.

3. LOCKE, J. Two Treatises of Government, (ed. P. Laslett,
   Cambridge University Press, 1960): Book I is a refutation
   of Filmer's view of sovereign power. Book II contains
   Locke's theory of state and government. The editor's
   Introduction is important as providing a background to
   Locke's work and explaining its relation to that of Hobbes.

4. HAMILTON, W.H. "Property - According to Locke" (1931-32), 41
   Yale L.J., 864: the connection between Locke's view of
   "property" and the decision of the United States Supreme
   Court in Adkins v. Childrens' Hospital (1923), 261 U.S.,
   525, is considered. The use that has been made of Locke's
   doctrine in America is explained.

5. POLLOCK, F. Essays in the Law, (Macmillan & Co., Ltd., 1922),
   chap. 3: the background to Locke's Civil Government is
   examined and the views of Locke and Hobbes on the social
   contract are compared.

6. Southern Methodist University Studies in Jurisprudence, (ed.
   A.L. Harding, S.M.U. Press), II, (1955), chap. 2: the
   theory of Locke is outlined.

7. ROUSSEAU, J-J. Contrat Social, (Garnier Freres, Paris): the
   well-known theory is set out, in French, from p. 239
   onwards.

8. BLACKSTONE, W. Commentaries on the Laws of England, I, pp.

38-43: the law of nature is the will of the Maker. There is also the revealed or divine law as found in the Scriptures. Human law should not contradict these. But later Blackstone admitted that he knew of nothing that could invalidate an Act of Parliament (p. 91).

1. KANT, I. The Philosophy of Law, (trans. W. Hastie, T. & T. Clark, 1887): some of Kant's views, but not the full range of his thought on the subject, is to be found in this work.

2. COHEN, M.R. Reason and Law, (The Free Press, Glencoe, 1950), chap. 4: Kant's philosophy of law is explained. Kant accepts God, freedom and immortality. Law is a part of morality.

3. STONE, J. Human Law and Human Justice (Stevens & Sons, Ltd., 1965), pp. 82-88: this gives a clear and convenient account of Kant's doctrines and the incorporation of his concept of justice in his concept of Law. The rest of the Chapter (Chap. 3) discusses the development and weaknesses of the Kantian position.

4. HUME, D. A Treatise on Human Nature, in The Philosophical Works of David Hume, (edd. T.H. Green and J.H. Grose, Longmans, Green & Co., 1874): the idea of "reason" is considered with unrelenting logic and its ambiguities are exposed. He launched a devastating attack on the prevailing doctrines of natural law.

5. MORRIS, C. "Four 18th Century Theories of Jurisprudence" (1960-61), 14 Vand.L.R., 101: The views of Hume, Montesquieu and Kant are primarily dealt with, and there is mention of Bentham.

6. GIERKE, O. Natural Law and the Theory of Society, 1500-1800, (trans. E. Barker, Cambridge University Press, 1950), especially chap. 1, Sect. V, S. 14; chap. 2, Sect. 11, S. 17: not only is the natural law theory of associations important for its own sake, but so are the introduction by Barker and Appendix 1 by Troeltsch. The former gives a very good account of the part played by natural law throughout the ages. The latter discusses the differences between German and western European thought.

7. GIERKE, O. Political Theories of the Middle Age, (trans. F.W. Maitland, Cambridge University Press, 1900), especially chap. 9: the medieval theory is said to be dominated by the principle of unity and the supremacy of law.

8. POLLOCK, F. Essays in the Law, (Macmillan & Co., Ltd., 1922), chap. 2: the law of nature is an ultimate principle of

fitness with regard to the nature of man as a rational and
social being, which is, or ought to be, the justification
for every form of positive law. The doctrines of Aristotle,
the Stoics, the Romans and medieval writers are outlined.

1. STAMMLER, R. The Theory of Justice, (trans. I. Husik, The
   Macmillan Co., New York, 1925): as a neo-Kantian Stammler
   seeks to find a universally valid method of just law. This
   enables him to evolve a "natural law with a changing content".

2. GINSBERG, M. "Stammler's Philosophy of Law" in Modern Theories
   of Law, (ed. W.I. Jennings, Oxford University Press, 1933),
   chap. 3: this is a convenient summary of Stammler's doctrine
   and an evaluation of it.

3. ALLEN, C.K. "Justice and Expediency" in Interpretations of
   Modern Legal Philosophies, (ed. P. Sayre, Oxford University
   Press, New York, 1947), chap. 1: there has to be a compromise
   between extremes of intellectual abstraction and realism.
   The views of Stammler, together with those of Geny and
   Pound, are considered.

4. ALLEN, C.K. Law in the Making, (7th ed., Oxford, 1964), pp.
   8-27: the modern law of nature is relativistic. In the
   light of this, Stammler's "natural law with a variable
   content" is explained. There is mention also of J. Kohler,
   L. Duguit and the French Natural Law School.

5. STONE, J. Human Law and Human Justice, (Stevens & Sons, Ltd.,
   1965); pp. 167-181: this gives a clear account of Stammler's
   difficult doctrine and of its relation to Kant's philosophy.
   The critique brings out the unpractical character of
   Stammler's thought, but also stresses its importance in
   20th century thought.

6. STONE, J. Human Law and Human Justice, (Stevens & Sons, Ltd.,
   1965): Chap. 7. this is a difficult but useful account of
   the versions of naturalist thinking since World War II. Of
   particular interest are the accounts of certain modern
   attempts to base some sort of natural law on existential
   tendencies. Such tendencies are the "facts" on which values
   can be grounded.

7. Legal Philosophies of Lask, Radbruch and Dabin, (trans.
   K. Wilk, Harvard University Press, 1950), Parts 1 and 11:
   J. Dabin presents the modern Catholic doctrine of natural
   law. The view of G. Radbruch as contained here is not his
   final view. Since 1945 he has leaned towards a naturalist
   interpretation of law.

1. STONE, J. Human Law and Human Justice, (Stevens & Sons, Ltd., 1965), pp. 235-262: in these pages is to be found a full and sympathetic account of Radbruch's thought and its development. The earlier part of the chapter (Chap. 8) serves as a prologue to modern relativist thinking, for which Radbruch is noted. Despite the possibility that in certain repects his post-1945 position is reconcileable with his earlier position, it is pointed out that there remain fundamental shifts.

2. FRIEDMANN, W. "Gustav Radbruch" (1960-61), 14 Vand.L.R., 191: this is a penetrating and understanding account of the life of Radbruch and the development of his thought.

3. DEL VECCHIO, G. Formal Bases of Law, (trans. J. Lisle, The Boston Book Co., 1914): this is a forceful attempt to rehabilitate natural law. The question whether and under what conditions a universal definition of law is possible is discussed at length.

4. DEL VECCHIO, G. Philosophy of Law, (trans. T.O. Martin, The Catholic University of America Press, 1953): from pp. 23-243 various theories from Greek times to the present are reviewed. In the second part the concept of law is examined. It is maintained that there is an unchangeable element in it.

5. DEL VECCHIO, G. Justice, (trans. Lady Guthrie, ed. A.H. Campbell, Edinburgh University Press, 1952): the formal notion of justice is distinct from its content, the former can be universal, the latter is derived from the empirical data of social existence.

6. GOUGH, J.W. The Social Contract, (2nd ed. Oxford, 1957): the origins and various interpretations of the social contract are examined. As a historical explanation of government, the theory has been irretrievably discredited; as an explanation of political obligation it imports a relationship analogous to contract.

7. RUSSELL, B. History of Western Philosophy, (Allen & Unwin, Ltd., 1946): although this is not written from a juristic point of view, it is most useful for reference, for it gives a good picture of the movements in philosophical thought.

8. BOWLE, J. Western Political Thought, (Oxford University Press, New York, 1948): this provides a careful examination of philosophic thought from the earliest times down to Rousseau.

1. SABINE, G.H. A History of Political Theory, (3rd ed.,
   Harrap & Co., Ltd., 1963), Parts 1-11: Part 1 deals with
   the views of Plato, Aristotle and the Stoics and their
   influence on Christian theory; Part 11 deals with the
   Christian concepts of church and state.

2. CARLYLE, R.W. and CARLYLE, A.J. A History of Medieval
   Political Theory in the West, (3rd ed., Blackwood & Sons,
   Ltd., 1930-36), 1, chaps. 3 and 9; 11, Part 1, chap. 3,
   Part 11, chap. 3; 111, Part 11, chap. 1; V, Part 1, chaps.
   2 and 4: this monumental work need only be used for general
   reference.

3. CAIRNS, H. Legal Philosophy from Plato to Hegel, (John
   Hopkins Press, 1949): convenient accounts are given of the
   juristic contributions of some of the great thinkers of
   history.

4. HERON, D.C. An Introduction to the History of Jurisprudence,
   (J.W. Parker & Son, 1860), Parts 11-V: accounts are given
   of a large number of writers from Greek and Roman times
   down to the 19th century German philosophers.

5. MILLER, W.M. The Data of Jurisprudence, (Green & Sons, 1903),
   chap. 6: the aim of law is considered with reference to
   justice, equity, reason, morality, etc. These ideas are
   correlated with reference to the works of writers throughout
   the ages.

6. LLOYD, D. The Idea of Law, (Penguin Books, Ltd., A 688, 1964),
   chaps. 1 and 4: the first chapter considers generally views
   about the part played by Law, which derive from assumptions
   about the nature of Man - that Man is evil and Law is a
   means of curbing his passions; that Man is good but became
   spoiled through sin, so Law is an instrument for realising
   the goal of his good impulses; that Man is good, but his
   social environment is reponsible for his condition, so Law
   as an institution of society is a bad thing. Chapter 4
   reviews ideas about natural law from the Greek philosophers
   down to modern versions.

7. MORRIS, C. The Great Legal Philosophers, (University of
   Pennsylvania Press, 1959), chaps. 1-10, 19: extracts are
   given from the works of Aristotle, Cicero, Aquinas,
   Grotius, Hobbes, Locke, Montesquieu, Hume, Rousseau, Kant
   and Dabin.

8. HALL, H. Readings in Jurisprudence, (The Bobbs-Merrill Co.,
   1938), chaps. 1 and 3: the extracts include some from
   Aristotle, Cicero, Aquinas, Maine, St. German and Stammler.

Chapter 3 deals with transcendental idealism.

1. LLOYD, D. <u>Introduction to Jurisprudence</u>, (2nd ed., Stevens & Sons, Ltd., 1965), chap. 3: natural law theory has served to preserve the status quo as well as inspire revolution. A brief survey of its history is given. In addition to selected extracts from various writers there are portions of the United States Constitution and of judgments in decided cases.

2. COHEN, M.R. and COHEN, F.S. <u>Readings in Jurisprudence and Legal Philosophy</u>, (Prentice-Hall Inc., 1951), chaps. 5, 9 and 10: not all the extracts in chapter 5 are concerned with natural law, but there are portions of Aristotle, Cicero, Aquinas, St. German, Coke, Hobbes and Blackstone. Chapter 9 includes, <u>inter alia</u>, passages from Kant and Stammler. Chapter 10 deals with law and metaphysics.

3. COWAN, T.A. <u>The American Jurisprudence Reader</u>, (Oceana Publications, 1956), pp. 70-91: extracts are given from case-law and writings. The latter include those of Haines, Pound, Brown and Chroust.

<u>Practical contributions of natural law theory</u>

4. POUND, R. <u>The Spirit of the Common Law</u>, (Marshall Jones Co., 1921), chap. 4: the rights of Man are considered with reference to the needs of successive ages. In England there was a tendency to identify common law rights with natural rights.

5. RADCLIFFE, C.J. <u>The Law and its Compass</u>, (Faber & Faber, Ltd., 1961): Christianity has been abandoned as the source of common law ideology, but there has to be some compass by which the law guides its course. Contact with natural law theory should not be lost.

6. DOWRICK, F.E. <u>Justice According to the English Common Lawyers</u>, (Butterworths, 1961), chap. 4: the theological interpretation of natural law is explained first, and then its influence on English law. St. German's ideas follow Aquinas closely.

7. VINOGRADOFF, P. <u>Collected Papers</u>, (Oxford, 1928), 11, chap. 9: the first part deals with reason as discussed by St. German; the second part deals with conscience and equity.

8. KEETON, G.W. "Natural Justice in English Law" (1955), 8 C.L.P., 24: the influence of ideas about natural justice is illustrated with reference to case-law.

1. AMES, J.B. Lectures on Legal History and Miscellaneous Legal
    Essays, (Harvard University Press, 1913), 435: the old
    principle of strict responsibility is said to be "unmoral"
    (quaere, whether it seemed so at the time). The development
    towards the fault principle is regarded as following a
    moral principle.

2. ST. GERMAN, C. The Doctor and Student: Dialogue between a
    Doctor of Divinity and a Student in the Laws of England,
    (17th ed., W. Muchall, 1787), Dialogue I, chaps. 1, 2, 4,
    5 and 16: There is an initial account of the Thomist system.
    This is followed in chap. 5 by an explanation of the way in
    which reason operates in English law.

3. SLESSER, H. The Judicial Office and Other Matters,
    (Hutchinson & Co., Ltd., 1943), chap. 3: where there is no
    rule a judge applies a sociological and a transcendental
    method. He is influenced by Christianity and natural law.
    (See also H. SLESSER: The Administration of Law,
    (Hutchinson's University Library, 1949), chap. 4, for a
    shorter version).

4. O'SULLIVAN, R. "The Philosophy of the Common Law", (1949), 2
    C.L.P., 116: this purports to show that the common law has
    been nourished by Christian philosophy and theology.

5. Le FROY, A.H.F. "The Basis of Case-Law", (1906), 22 L.Q.R.,
    293, 416: the considerations underlying case-law are
    examined in detail. Among these are naturalist concepts,
    such as justice and reason.

6. HOLDSWORTH, W.S. A History of English Law, (Methuen & Co.,
    Ltd.,) II, 602: in this short Appendix the law of nature is
    discussed in relation to the common law.

7. STRAUSS, L. Natural Right and History, (University of Chicago
    Press, 1953): natural rights are classified as Socratic,
    Platonic, Aristotelian and Thomist. The history of natural
    rights is traced from the Stoic idea to the 19th century.
    The views of Hobbes, Locke, Rousseau and Burke are consid-
    ered in the latter part of the book.

8. JONES, J.W. "Acquired and Guaranteed Rights" in Cambridge
    Legal Essays, (edd. P.H. Winfield and A.D. McNair, Heffer
    & Sons, Ltd., 1926), 223: the basis and origins of natural
    right are considered historically.

9. RITCHIE, D.G. Natural Rights, (Allen & Unwin, Ltd.,1894):
    various systems of natural rights are discussed in detail.

Part I deals with the theory behind them; Part II with individual rights. The author warns that abstract theories are always open to divergent interpretations.

1. O'SULLIVAN, R. "The Bond of Freedom", (1943), 6 M.L.R., 177: this is a plea for a return to natural law theory. The great creative effort of the common law is said to have been the achievement of freedom - the creation of the <u>liber homo</u>.

2. O'MEARA, J. "Natural Law and Everyday Law", (1960), 5 Nat. L. F., 83: Natural Law is not an arbiter of legal validity, but it can provide ethical guidance in the day by day application of law. Judges should resort to fundamental ethical considerations in applying their discretion.

3. CORWIN, E.S. "The 'Higher Law' Background of American Constitutional Law" (1928-29), 42 Harv. L.R., 149, 365: the supremacy of the Constitution is partly due to the belief that it embodies certain principles of right and justice, which are entitled to prevail <u>ex proprio vigore</u>. The origin of these is examined at length with reference to the Greeks, Cicero, their development in the Middle Ages and in the common law. The work of Locke and Coke, in particular, is dealt with at length.

4. HUMPHREYS, R.A "The Rule of Law and the American Revolution", (1937), 53 L.Q.R., 80: the claim to omnipotence by the British Parliament was met by the argument that Parliament itself was subject to the rule of law, <u>i.e.</u>, natural law.

5. GRANT, J.A.C. "The Natural Law Background of Due Process", (1931), 31 Col. L.R., 56: the theme of this article is similar to the above, but it is concerned more specifically with judicial interpretation of "due process".

6. HOGAN, H.J. "The Supreme Court and Natural Law" (1968), 54 Am. B.A.J. 570: the old ideas of natural law are now discredited. This is the era of state power and there is now more than ever a need for the expression of social conscience. It is argued that the Supreme Court is the body best fitted to do this.

7. REUSCHLEIN, H.G. <u>Jurisprudence - Its American Prophets</u>, (The Bobbs-Merrill Co., Inc., 1951), pp. 5-28; 342-404: the Puritans brought to America the view that the true laws are God's laws, and this gave rise to the rights of Man as embodied in the Constitution. In the latter section the modern idea of a "higher" law is considered.

1. WRIGHT, B.F. American Interpretations of Natural Law,
   (Harvard University Press, 1931): the views of different
   American writers since the 17th century are surveyed. A
   distinction is drawn between natural law as a description
   of existing order and as a prescription for what ought to
   be.

2. WRIGHT, R.A. "Natural Law and International Law" in Interpretations of Modern Legal Philosophies, (ed. P. Sayre,
   Oxford University Press, New York, 1947), chap. 33: this
   article stresses the importance of viewing international
   law, not as positive law, but as based on fundamental
   principles.

The validity of unjust law

3. HART, H.L.A. "Positivism and the Separation of Law and
   Morals" (1957-58), 71 Harv. L.R., 593: the positivist case
   is clarified and certain misconceptions about it removed.
   The arguments of the naturalists are considered and
   rejected.

4. HART, H.L.A. The Concept of Law, (Oxford, 1961), chap. 9:
   the relationship between law and morality is considered
   point by point, and the positivist position is defended.

5. FULLER, L.L. "Positivism and Fidelity to Law - a Reply to
   Professor Hart", (1957-58), 71 Harv. L.R., 630: Fuller
   takes issue with Hart. In this detailed and spirited reply
   the points made by Hart are answered. It is one of the
   best expositions of the naturalist position.

6. FULLER, L.L. The Morality of Law, (Yale University Press,
   1964): "Law is the enterprise of subjecting human conduct
   to the governance of rules". On this basis eight conditions
   are laid down without which no system can continue as a
   system. These eight comprise the "inner" morality of law.
   The "external" morality concerns policies and ideals which
   guide the development of law, but there can be no "law" in
   the sense indicated unless the desiderata of its "inner"
   morality are present. This "inner" morality is largely
   indifferent to "external" morality, except where the aims
   tend to impair the "inner" morality.

7. JENKINS, I. "The Matchmaker, or Towards a Synthesis of Legal
   Idealism and Positivism", (1959-60), 12 J.L.E., 1:
   positivists and idealists are participants in a common
   enterprise and they differ only in the contributions which
   they respectively make. Positivists assert the distinctness
   of law, not its isolation or self-sufficiency. Idealists

stress the mutual relevance of the "is" and the "ought"
because law is a means to an end.

1. PAPPE, H.O. "On the Validity of the Judicial Decisions in the
   Nazi Era" (1960), 23 M.L.R., 260: this is primarily a
   demonstration of a misapprehension that underlies the Hart-
   Fuller controversy (supra). It is shown that they both
   proceed on a misreport of a decision by a German court: the
   court did not hold a certain enactment of the Nazi government to be void.

2. BODENHEIMER, E. "Significant Developments in German Legal
   Philosophy since 1945" (1954), 3 A.J.C.L., 379: since the
   collapse of the Nazi regime with its extremely positivist
   attitude, there has been a revival of a value philosophy.
   In this connection the alteration in Radbruch's views is
   discussed.

3. von HIPPEL, E. Note in (1959), 4 Nat. L.F., 106: the attitude
   of German courts both before and after 1945 is commented on.
   Radbruch is alleged to have turned "about face" since 1945.
   The rejection of positivism and the growth of naturalist
   principles is illustrated. See also Note by J. MESSNER,
   ibid, p. 101.

4. HOWE, M. de W. "The Positivism of Mr Justice Holmes" (1950-
   51), 64 Harv. L.R., 529: Holmes is defended against the
   charge that it is his type of positivism that enables
   regimes like Nazism to arise. Holmes, it is said, never did
   make a rigid separation of "is" and "ought". To him the
   ultimate source of law lay in the moral sentiments of the
   community.

5. CARPENTER, R.V. "The Problem of Value Judgments as Norms of
   Law" (1954-55), 7 J.L.E., 163: the thesis is that positivism
   gives rise to regimes like that of Nazi Germany. For a
   vigorous answer to this charge, see G.O.W. MUELLER: "The
   Problem of Value Judgments as Norms of the Law: the Answer
   of a Positivist", ibid., 567.

6. FULLER, L.L. Law in Quest of Itself, (The Foundation Press,
   Inc., 1940): the positivist separation of the "is" from the
   "ought" is not possible, for the moral "ought" enters into
   every legal activity. This is the underlying theme of the
   book.

7. FULLER, L.L. "American Legal Philosophy at Mid-century", (1953-
   54), 6 J.L.E., 457, at pp. 467 et seq.: purpose is a fact and
   a standard for judging facts. Therefore, the separation of
   the "is" and the "ought" and the idea that one cannot derive

a statement about what ought to be from a statement of what
exists are both said to be false assumptions. If a thing is
to achieve a certain end, it has to function in a certain
way. Therefore, ends and means are closely connected.

1. STONE, J. and TARELLO, G. "Justice, Language and Communication"
   (1960-61), 14 Vand. L.R., 331: this is a lengthy and difficult investigation into the function of legal language and
   into the relation between law and justice. The functions of
   language in the fields of law and justice differ and should
   not be merged.

2. MARITAIN, J. The Rights of Man and Natural Law, (Geoffrey
   Bles, The Centenary Press, 1944): this short essay reviews
   the position of the individual in society. One of its
   characteristics is its intrinsic morality and an unjust law
   is not "law".

3. COHEN, M.R. "Positivism and the Limits of Idealism in the Law"
   (1927), 27 Col. L.R., 237: the law cannot be divorced from
   what it ought to be. The ideal and the actual are inseparable, but never completely identifiable. The limits of
   idealism are considered.

4. COHEN, M.R. Reason and Nature, (Kegan Paul, Trench & Trubner
   & Co., Ltd., 1931), Part III, chap. 4: the above theme is
   developed in greater detail.

5. MacGUIGAN, M.R. "Law, Morals, and Positivism" (1961), 14 Tor.
   L.J., 1: the separation between law and morals is examined
   historically. It is not morals, but the law, that suffers
   from such a separation, for it removes the moral support
   behind law.

6. LUMB, R.D. "Natural Law and Legal Positivism" (1958-59), 11
   J.L.E., 503, 508-12: the relation between the legal and
   moral "ought" is considered. It is suggested that the
   theorist should rightly be concerned with the impact of
   morals on law and vice versa, but that he should concern
   himself, first, with law as it is and then with values.

7. CHLOROS, A.G. "Some Aspects of the Social and Ethical Element
   in Analytical Jurisprudence", (1955), 67 Jur. R., 79: the
   purpose of this article is to expose some of the arbitrary
   assumptions, which it is asserted, underlie Austin's analytical jurisprudence. There is an ethical principle beneath
   it in the form of an "intellectual natural law". A parallel
   is drawn between Platonic theory of Forms and certain
   aspects of Analytical Jurisprudence.

1. BRECHT, A. "The Myth of <u>Is</u> and <u>Ought</u>" (1940-41), 54 Harv. L.
   R., 811: the history of the separation between the "is" and
   the "ought" is first considered. But it is maintained that
   by examining one's own inner processes it is possible to
   discover some natural or biological "is" which directs one
   towards an ethical "ought". In this way it would be possible to establish a factual link between the "is" and the
   "ought". Phenomenology is the method of doing this. Feeling
   something as an "ought" is part of human equipment. This
   "ought" is a datum of the word "is".

2. STUMPF, S.E. "Austin's Theory of the Separation of Law and
   Morals", (1960-61), 14 Vand. L.R., 117: the article begins
   by explaining the positivist case and that Austin did not
   deny the influence of morals. But the very concept of law
   is meaningless until the nature of man is brought into
   consideration. It is alleged that Austin himself contemplated implicitly the moral characteristics of law and
   sovereignty.

3. SMITH, J.C. "Law, Language, and Philosophy", (1968), 3 U. Br.
   Col. L.R., 59: after reviewing the attitude to language of
   various legal philosophers, the linguistic background of
   the positivist-naturalist controversy is set out in its
   different aspects. The paper is explanatory rather than
   conclusive.

4. LAMONT, W.D. <u>The Principles of Moral Judgment</u>, (Oxford, 1946)
   chap. 6: the relation between morals and social justice is
   examined. There is a close connection between an ideal
   morality and justice, the differences being a matter of
   emphasis.

5. BODENHEIMER, E. "The Province of Jurisprudence", (1960-61),
   46 Corn. L.Q., 1: the view that all valuations are matters
   of personal opinion cannot be accepted. There are areas of
   uniform or near uniform valuation among different men or
   groups of men. These provide the bottom layer of human
   normative ordering. Jurisprudence should concern itself
   with schemes for improving social life.

6. HALL, J. <u>Living Law of Democratic Society</u>, (The Bobbs-
   Merrill Co., Inc., 1949), Part II: justice is an essential
   attribute of positive law. Value judgments can be true in
   an important sense. They are not nonsense because they
   cannot be proved. Many people act against their own
   desires because they want to do the right thing.
   Scientific perception is not the only source of knowledge.

7. CAHN, E.N. <u>The Sense of Injustice</u>, (New York University

Press, 1949): justice is what is needed to put right what would arouse a sense of injustice. The nature of law is discussed with reference to justice, power, freedom and order, security and change.

1. LLOYD, D. The Idea of Law, (Penguin Books, Ltd., A 688, 1964), pp. 102-105, 111-15: the question of the validity of law is discussed briefly in the context of a general discussion of positivism. Positivism is defended against the charge that it has fostered the growth of dictatorships, and the assertion that absolute moral values do exist is also considered.

2. BIENENFELD, F.R. Rediscovery of Justice, (Allen & Unwin, Ltd., 1947): this is of general interest. It seeks to achieve international justice by examining the development of nations. The parallels drawn from individuals are somewhat questionable. In conclusion a set of absolute values is propounded.

3. MEYER, P. "Justice in Politics" in Legal Essays. A Tribute to Frede Castberg, (Universitetsforlaget, 1963), 125: there is a middle way between positivism and natural law, depending upon the way in which values can be important in social administration.

4. CRABB, J.H. "Airing a Couple of Myths about Natural Law", (1964), 39 Notre Dame Lawyer 137: two misconceptions are considered. One is that natural law is a peculiarly Roman Catholic conception; the other is that natural law "exists" as some kind of law superior to statute and case-law.

5. TAYLOR, R. "Law and Morality", (1968), 43 N.Y.U.L.R., 611: in answering the question "what is a law?" the author insists on the separation between laws and morality. They can be re-united if one considers law as an activity, for then the end in view becomes relevant.

BIBLIOGRAPHICAL INDEX

Note:- References are to page numbers. Figures in brackets indicate the paragraph number on a particular page. Thus "24(3)" indicates paragraph (3) on page 24.

ANONYMOUS "A Trade Dispute?"
(1964) 235 L.T. 563... 146(7)
ANONYMOUS "'Corporate Entity' -
its Limitations as a Useful
Legal Conception" (1926-27) 36
Yale L.J. 254... 199(5)
ANONYMOUS "Exceptions to the Rule
of Stare Decisis" (1958) 92 I.L.
T. 131... 28(7)
ANONYMOUS "Expulsion of Member of
Club" (1926) 70 Sol. Jo. 828...
206(7)
ANONYMOUS "Headings and Marginal
Notes" (1960) 124 J.P.J. 247...
99(9)
ANONYMOUS "Injury to an Unborn
Child" (1939) 83 Sol. Jo. 185...
193(1)
ANONYMOUS "Intimidation and Trade
Unions" (1964) 98 I.L.T. 431,
437... 146(7)
ANONYMOUS "Judicial Precedents in
Criminal Law" (1958) 22 J.C.L.
155... 28(3)
ANONYMOUS "Legal Entities" (1964)
235 L.T. 578... 208(8)
ANONYMOUS "Local Authorities and
Parental Rights" (1961) 231 L.T.
342... 195(3)
ANONYMOUS "Precedent" (1967) 131
J.P. & L.G.R. 595... 30(8)
ANONYMOUS "Prospective Over-
ruling and Retroactive Appli-
cation in the Federal Courts"
(1961-62) 71 Yale L.J. 907...
51(8)
ANONYMOUS "Proximate and Remote
Cause" (1870) 4 Am. L.R. 201...
184(1)
ANONYMOUS "Residence of Companies"
(1959) 26 Solicitor 299, 305...
199(1)
ANONYMOUS "Responsibility of
Labor Unions for Acts of Members"
(1938) 38 Col. L.R. 454... 207(2)
ANONYMOUS "Stare Decisis" (1967)
101 I.L.T. 61... 30(5)
ANONYMOUS "Statutory Interpreta-
tion" (1967) S.L.T. 243...83(3)
ANONYMOUS "Strike on" (1964) 98
I.L.T. 421... 146(7)
ANONYMOUS "The Aged Precedent"
[1965] S.L.T. 53... 52(5)
ANONYMOUS "The Force of Precedent"
(1966) S.L.T. 157... 30(6)

ANONYMOUS "The State and the Judi-
ciary" (1897) 14 Cape L.J. 94...
79(6)
ANONYMOUS "Unions as Juridical
Persons" (1956-57) 66 Yale L.J.
712... 207(1)
ANSCOMBE, M. "Intention" (1956-57)
57 P.A.S. 321... 186(8)
ANSON, W.R. "The Government of
Ireland Bill and the Sovereignty
of Parliament" (1886) 2 L.Q.R.
427...72(7)
"AQUARIUS" "Causation and Legal
Responsibility" (1941) 58 S.A.L.J.
232... 185(7)
"AQUARIUS" "Causation and Legal
Responsibility" (1945) 62 S.A.L.J.
126... 185(8)
AQUINAS, St. T. Summa Theologica
(trans. English Dominican Fathers)
... 348(6)
ARGYLE, M., WALKER, N. and "Does
the Law affect Moral Judgments?"
(1964) 4 Br. J.C. 570... 137(1)
ARISTOTLE Nichomachean Ethics (3rd
ed., trans. R. Williams) V... 131
(3), 346(6)(7)
ARISTOTLE Politics (trans. J.E.C.
Weldon)... 346(5)
ARNHOLM, C.J. "Olivecrona on Legal
Rights. Reflections on the Concept
of Rights" (1962) 6 Scand. S.L. 11
... 164(4), 334(1)
ARNHOLM, C.J. "Some Basic Problems
of Jurisprudence" (1957) 1 Scand.
S.L. 9... 334(6)
ARNOLD, J.C. "The Control of a
Company" (1959) 26 Solicitor 167;
(1960) 27 Solicitor 13... 198(6)
ARNOLD, T.W. Symbols of Government
... 321(1)
ARNOLD, T.W. The Folklore of Capi-
talism ... 197(1)
ARNOLD, T.W. "The Jurisprudence of
Edwards S. Robinson" (1936-37) 46
Yale L.J. 1282... 321(5)
ARONSON, M.J. "The Juridical Evo-
lutionism of James Coolidge Carter"
(1953-54) 10 Tor. L.J. 1... 261(8)
ASHTON-CROSS, D.I.C. "Suggestion
Regarding the Liability of Corpo-
rations for the Torts of their
Servants" (1950) 10 C.L.J. 419...
203(3)

ASQUITH, C. "Some Aspects of the Work of the Court of Appeal" (1950) 1 J.S.P.T.L.(N.S.) 350 ... 29(1), 37(3)

ATIYAH, P.S. "A Re-examination of the Jus Tertii in Conversion" (1955) 18 M.L.R. 97... 229(7)

ATKINSON, C.M. Jeremy Bentham. His Life and Work... 296(3)

ATKINSON, S.B. "Life, Birth and Live-birth" (1904) 20 L.Q.R. 134... 192(4)

AUBERT, V. "Structure of Legal Thinking" in Legal Essays. A Tribute to Frede Castberg 41... 43(3)

AUERBACH, C.A. "On Professor Hart's Definition and Theory in Jurisprudence" (1956) 9 J.L.E. 39... 13(1), 167(8)

AUSTIN, J. Lectures on Jurisprudence (5th ed. R. Campbell) ... 2(6), 19(2), 45(5), 47(3), 53(5), 60(6), 88(4), 109(5), 155(2), 166(6), 179(1), 187(5), 189(7), 192(6), 219(8), 226(6), 238(2), 260(5), 295(1), 343(5)

AUSTIN, J. The Province of Jurisprudence Determined and the Uses of the Study of Jurisprudence (ed. H.L.A. Hart)... 2(6), 238(3)

AUSTIN, J.L. "A Plea for Excuses" (1956-57) 57 P.A.S. 1... 177(5)

Authority and the Individual... 251(3)

AYER, A.J. Language, Truth and Logic... 17(7)

BALLARD, F.A. "Retroactive Federal Taxation" (1934-35) 48 Harv. L.R. 592... 101(4)

BALOGH, E. "Note on Thomas Hobbes" in Interpretations of Modern Legal Philosohpies (ed. P. Sayre) chap. 2... 350(8)

BAMFORD, B.R. "Aspects of Judicial Independence" (1956) 73 S. A.L.J. 380... 150(3)

BARKER, E. "Introduction" to O. Gierke, Natural Law and the Theory of Society, 1500-1800 (trans. E. Barker)... 263(3)

BARLOW, A.C.H. "Gift Inter Vivos of a Chose in Possession by Delivery of a Key" (1956) 19 M.L. R. 394... 221(6)

BARNETT, J.D. "External Evidence of the Constitutionality of Statutes" (1924) 58 Am. L.R. 88 ... 71(3)

BARRACLOUGH, G. "Law and Legislation in Medieval England" (1940) 56 L.Q.R. 75... 62(6)

BARRIE, G.N. "Rhodesian U.D.I. - an Unruly Horse" (1968) 1 C.I.L. S.A. 110... 81(8)

BARRY, J.V. "Morality and the Coercive Process" (1962) 4 Syd. L.R. 28... 135(3)

BARRY, J.V. "The Child en ventre sa mere" (1940-41) 14 Austr. L.J. 351... 192(2)

BARTLETT, C.A.H. "The Sovereignty of the People" (1921) 37 L.Q.R. 497... 65(5)

BARWICK, G. "Courts, Lawyers, and the Attainment of Justice" (1958) 1 Tasm. L.R. 1... 122(6)

BATES, A., COHEN, J., ROBSON, R.A.H. Parental Authority: the Community and the Law... 311(1)

BATY, T. "The Rights of Ideas - and of Corporations" (1919-20) 33 Harv. L.R. 258... 212(5)

BAUMGARDT, D. Bentham and the Ethics of Today... 295(8)

BEALE, J.H. A Treatise on the Conflict of Laws... 168(6)

BEALE, J.H. "Recovery for Consequences of an Act" (1895-96) 9 Harv. L.R. 80... 183(3)

BEALE, J.H. "The Proximate Consequences of an Act" (1920) 33 Harv. L.R. 633... 183(3)

BEARD, C.A. An Economic Interpretation of the Constitution of the United States... 286(6)

BEINART, B. "Parliament and the Courts" (1954) B.S.A.L.R. 134... 77(2)

BEINART, B. "Sovereignty and the Law" (1952) 15 Tydskrif vir Hedensdaagse Romeins-Hollandse Reg 101... 77(1)

BEINART, B. "The South African Appeal Court and Judicial Review" (1958) 21 M.L.R. 587... 76(9)

BEINART, B. "The South African Senate" (1957) 20 M.L.R. 549... 76(8)

BENAS, B.B. "Problems for the Coveyancer. The Construction of Statutes" (1952) 102 L.J. 269 ... 103(4)

BENNION, F.A.R. "Copyright and the Statute of Westminster" (1961) 24 M.L.R. 355... 75(1)

BENTHAM, J. A Comment on the Commentaries (ed. C.W. Everett) ... 109(3)

BENTHAM, J. A Fragment on Government in Works (ed. J. Bowring)... 67(2), 294(4)

BENTHAM, J. An Introduction to the Principles of Morals and Legislation in Works (ed. J. Bowring)... 1(5), 178(7), 187 (5), 294(4), 295(8), 296(4), 297(7)

BENTHAM, J. "Nomography, or the Art of Inditing Laws" in Works (ed. J. Bowring)... 105(2)

BENTHAM, J. The Limits of Jurisprudence Defined (ed. C.W. Everett)... 109(4), 161(2), 169 (7), 218(3), 238(1), 239(4), 297(7)

BENTHAM, J. Theory of Fictions (2nd ed. C.K. Ogden)... 12(4)

BENTHAM, J. The Theory of Legislation (5th ed. trans. R. Hildreth)... 294(5), 343(4)

BENTHAM, J. Works (ed. J. Bowring)... 2(5), 67(2), 105(2), 161(3), 168(5), 218(4), 226(5), 294(4)

BENTWICH, N. "The Jurisdiction of the Privy Council" (1964) 114 L.J. 67... 31(8)

BERGER, R. "Doctor Bonham's Case: Statutory Construction of Constitutional Theory?" (1969) 117 U.Pa. L.R. 521... 350(2)

BERLE, A.A. "The Theory of Enterprise Entity" (1947) 47 Col. L. R. 343... 211(1)

BERLE, A.A. and MEANS, G.C. The Modern Corporation and Private Property... 195(6), 231(5)

BERMAN, H.J. "Commercial Contracts in Soviet Law" (1947) 35 Calif. L.R. 191... 282(7)

BERMAN, H.J. Justice in the U.S.S. R. An Interpretation of Soviet Law... 277(8)

BERMAN, H.J. "Principles of Soviet Criminal Law" (1946-47) 56 Yale L.J. 803... 282(4)

BERMAN, H.J. "Soviet Family Law in the Light of Russian History and Marxist Theory" (1946-47) 56 Yale L.J. 26... 283(2)

BERMAN, H.J. "Soviet Law and Government" (1958) 21 M.L.R. 19... 278(7)

BERMAN, H.J. The Nature and Functions of Law... 37(6)

BEST, W.M. "Codification of the Laws of England" (1856) Trans. Jur. S. 209... 61(2)

BEUTEL, F.K. "Some Implications of Experimental Jurisprudence" (1934-35) 48 Harv. L.R. 169... 322(1)

BEUTEL, F.K. Some Potentialities of Experimental Jurisprudence as a New Branch of Social Science... 322(2)

BEUTEL, F.K. "The Necessity of a New Technique of Interpreting the N.I.L. (Uniform Negotiable Instruments Law) - the Civil Law Analogy" (1931-32) 6 Tul. L.R. 1... 94(1)

BIENENFELD, F.R. Rediscovery of Justice... 363(2)

BIGELOW, M.M. The Law of Torts (3rd ed.)... 172(3), 188(6)

BIGGS, J.M. The Concept of Matrimonial Cruelty... 187(6)

BINGHAM, J.W. "Legal Philosophy and the Law" (1914) 9 III. L.R. 98... 318(7)

BINGHAM, J.W. "Some Suggestions Concerning 'Legal Cause' at Common Law" (1909) 9 Col. L.R. 16, 136... 127(1), 184(3)

BINGHAM, J.W. "The Nature and Importance of Legal Possession" (1915) 13 Mich. L.R. 534, 623... 216(2)

BINGHAM, J.W. "The Nature of Legal Rights and Duties" (1913) 12 Mich. L.R. 1... 318(6)

BINGHAM, J.W. "What is the Law?" (1912) 11 Mich. L.R. 1, 109... 318(6)

BIRNBAUM, H.F. "Stare Decisis vs. Judicial Activism. Nothing Succeeds like Success" (1968) 54 Am. B.A.J. 482... 31(1)

BISHOP, W.W. "The International Rule of Law" (1960-61) 59 Mich. L.R. 553... 142(7)

BLACK, M. Language and Philosophy ... 17(7)

BLACKSTONE, W. Commentaries on the Laws of England (16th ed.) ... 65(1), 98(4), 109(1), 194(2), 351(8)

BLOM-COOPER, L.J. and DREWRY, G.R. "The House of Lords: Reflections on the Social Utility of Final Appellate Courts" (1969) 32 M.L. R. 262... 30(1)

BOBER, M.M. Karl Marx's Interpretation of History (2nd ed.)... 274(4)

BOBERG, P.Q.R. "Reflection on the Novus Actus Interveniens Concept" (1959) 76 S.A.L.J. 280... 185(6)

BODENHEIMER, E. Jurisprudence... 8(1), 19(7), 88(1), 111(5), 132 (1), 237(1), 242(2), 254(8), 266 (1), 284(5), 307(3), 328(1), 335 (8), 337(1)

BODENHEIMER, E. "Law as Order and Justice" (1957) 6 J.P.L. 194... 132(2)

BODENHEIMER, E. "Modern Analytical Jurisprudence and the Limits of its Usefulness" (1955-56) 104 U. Pa. L.R. 1080... 13(5)

BODENHEIMER, E. "Power and Law: a Study of the Concept of Law" (1939-40) 50 Ethics, 127... 255 (1)

BODENHEIMER, E. "Significant Developments in German Legal Philosophy since 1945" (1954) 3 A.J.C.L. 379... 360(2)

BODENHEIMER, E. "The Impasse of Soviet Legal Philosophy" (1952-53) 38 Corn. L.Q. 51... 278(3)

BODENHEIMER, E. "The Province of Jurisprudence" (1960-61) 46 Corn. L.Q. 1... 362(5)

BOGGS, A.A. "Proximate Cause in the Law of Tort" (1910) 44 Am. L. R. 88... 184(2)

BOHLEN, F.H. "Fifty Years of Torts" (1936-37) 50 Harv. L.R. 725, 1225... 143(4)

BOHLEN, F.H. "Incomplete Privilege to Inflict Intentional Invasions of Interests of Property and Personality" (1925-26) 39 Harv. L.R. 307... 172(4)

BOHLEN, F.H. "Mixed Questions of Law and Fact" (1924) 72 U. Pa. L. R. 111... 143(3)

BOHLEN, F.H. Studies in the Law of Torts... 143(5), 183(2), 189(9), 287(2)

BOND, H. "Possession in the Roman Law" (1890) 6 L.Q.R. 259... 216(6)

BONNECASE, J. "The Problem of Legal Interpretation in France" (1930) 12 J.C.L. (ser. 3) 79... 95(1)

BORCHARD, E.M. "Governmental Responsibility in Tort" (1926-27) 36 Yale L.J. at pp. 774-780... 195(1)

BORCHARD, E.M. "Some Lessons from the Civil Law" (1916) 64 U. Pa. L.R. 570... 56(7)

BOURKE, J.P. "Damages: Culpability and Causation" (1956) 30 Austr. L.J. 283... 186(1)

BOURKE, V.J. "Natural Law, Thomism - and Professor Nielsen" (1960) 5 Nat. L.F. 112... 349(1)

BOWKER, W.F. "Basic Rights and Freedoms: What are they?" (1959) 37 Can. B.R. 43... 302(7)

BOWLE, J. Western Political Thought ... 354(8)

BRADLEY, F.E. "Modern Legislation in the United Kingdom" (1894) 10 L.Q.R. 32... 84(1)

BRANDEN, N. "Free Will, Moral Responsibility and the Law" (1969) 42 Southern Calif. L.R. 264... 178(5)

BRAYBROOKE, E.K. "Custom as Source of English Law" (1951) 50 Mich. L.R. 71... 108(2)

BRECHT, A. "The Myth of Is and Ought" (1940-41) 54 Harv. L.R. 811... 236(1), 362(1)

BRIERLEY, J.E.C., DAVID, R. and Major Legal Systems in the World Today... 274(3)

British Philosophy in Mid-Century (ed. C.A. Mace)... 16(6), 17(7)

BROADHURST, S. "Is Copyright a Chose in Action?" (1895) 11 L.Q. R. 64... 227(9)

BRODERICK, A. "Hauriou's Institutional Theory: an Invitation to Common Law Jurisprudence" (1965) 4 Sol. Q. 281... 210(6), 306(8)

BRODERICK, A. "The Radical Middle: The Natural Right of Property in Aquinas and the Popes" (1964) 3 Sol. Q. 127... 231(4), 349(4)

BROTHWOOD, M. "Parliamentary Sovereignty and U.K. Entry" (1968) 118 New L.J. 415... 70(1)

BROWN, B.F. "Natural Law: Dynamic Basis of Law and Morals in the Twentieth Century" (1957) 31 Tul. L.R. 491... 341(2)

BROWN, J.M. "A Note on Professor Oakeshott's Introduction to the Leviathan" (1953) 1 Pol. S. 53 ... 350(7)

BROWN, J.R. "Electronic Brains and the Legal Mind: Computing the Data Computer's Collision with Law" (1961-62) 71 Yale L.J. 239... 324(4)

BROWN, L.N. "Cruelty without Culpability or Divorce without Fault" (1963) 26 M.L.R. 625... 188(2)

BROWN, L.N. "The Offence of Wilful Neglect to Maintain a Wife" (1960) 23 M.L.R. 1... 188(1)

BROWN, L.N. "The Sources of Spanish Civil Law" (1956) 5 I.C. L.Q. 364... 60(4)

BROWN, R. "A Comment on L.J. Macfarlane's 'Justifying Rebellion: Black and White Nationalism in Rhodesia'" [1968] 6 J. Comm. P.S. 155... 82(2)

BROWN, R.A. "Due Process of Law, Police Power and the Supreme Court" (1926-27) 40 Harv. L.R. 943... 331(2)

BROWN, R.A. "Police Power - Legislation for Health and Personal Safety" (1928-29) 42 Harv. L.R. 866... 126(3), 331(2)

BROWN, W.J. "Jurisprudence and Legal Education" (1909) 9 Col. L.R. 238... 10(6)

BROWN, W.J. "Re-analysis of a Theory of Rights" (1924-25) 34 Yale L.J. 765... 165(6)

BROWN, W.J. The Austinian Theory of Law ... 2(6), 4(2), 109(6), 155(4), 167(1), 214(4), 239(6)

BROWN, W.J. "The Jurisprudence of M. Duguit" (1916) 32 L.Q.R. 168 ... 305(7)

BROWN, W.J. "The Personality of the Corporation and the State" (1905) 21 L.Q.R. 365... 214(3)

BROWN, W.J. "The Purpose and Method of a Law School" (1902) 18 L.Q.R. 78, 192... 10(5)

BROWNE, D. "Reflections on the Teaching of Jurisprudence" (1953) 2 J.S.P.T.L.(N.S.) 79... 10(1)

BRUNCKEN, E. "Interpretation of the Written Law" (1915) 25 Yale L.J. 129... 92(5)

BRUNNER, E. Justice and the Social Order (trans. M. Hottinger)... 286(1), 340(6)

BRYCE, J. Studies in History and Jurisprudence... 2(2), 68(6), 140 (6), 160(5), 236(7), 246(3), 262 (3), 347(3)

BRYCE, J. "The Interpretation of National Character and Historical Environment on the Development of the Common Law" (1908) 24 L.Q.R. 9... 259(5)

BUCKLAND, W.W. A Text-book of Roman Law from Augustus to Justinian (3rd ed. P.Stein)... 216(7), 229(9)

BUCKLAND, W.W. "Difficulties of Abstract Jurisprudence" (1890) 6 L.Q.R. 436... 4(1)

BUCKLAND, W.W. Some Reflections on Jurisprudence... 3(8), 111(3), 158(4), 167(6), 175(7), 243(6), 255(4), 306(3), 345(1)

BUCKLAND, W.W. "The Nature of the Contractual Obligation" (1944) 8 C.L.J. 247... 158(4)

BUKHARINE, N.I. Le Theorie du Materialisme Historique... 275(9)

BURDICK, F.M. "Are Defectively Incorporated Associations Partnerships?" (1906) 6 Col. L.R. 1... 206(1)

BURDICK, F.M. "Is Law the Expression of Class Selfishness?" (1911-12) 25 Harv. L.R. 349... 286(7)

BURNHAM, J. The Managerial Revolution... 195(7)

BURROW, J.W. Evolution and Society. A Study in Victorian Social Theory ... 268(6)

BURROWS, R. "Law Reporting" (1942) 58 L.Q.R. 96... 25(7)

CAHILL, F.V. Judicial Legislation ... 71(2)

CAHN, E.N. The Sense of Injustice ... 362(7)

CAIRNS, H. Law and the Social Sciences... 271(4), 285(3)

CAIRNS, H. Legal Philosophy from Plato to Hegel... 17(1), 264(1), 355(3)

CAIRNS, H. "Philosophy as Jurisprudence" in Interpretations of Modern Legal Philosophies (ed. P. Sayre) chap. 4... 6(4)

CAIRNS, H. The Theory of Legal Science... 16(7), 290(2)

CAIRNS, H. "The Valuation of Legal Science" (1940) 40 Col. L. R. 1... 120(1)

CALLAHAN, C.C., MOORE, W.U. and "Law and Learning Theory: A Study in Legal Control" (1943-44) 53 Yale L.J. 1... 322(4)

CALVERT, H. "The Vitality of Case-Law under a Criminal Code" (1959) 22 M.L.R. 621... 60(8)

Cambridge Legal Essays (edd. P.H. Winfield and A.D. McNair)... 108 (4), 357(8)

CAMERON, J.T. "Two Jurisprudential Case Notes" [1964] Jur. R. 155 ... 171(8)

CAMPBELL, A.H. "A Note on the Word 'Jurisprudence'" (1942) 58 L.Q. R. 334... 7(3)

CAMPBELL, A.H. "Fascism and Legality" (1946) 62 L.Q.R. 141... 264 (7)

CAMPBELL, A.H. "Some Footnotes to Salmond's Jurisprudence" (1939-40) 7 C.L.J. 206... 167(4), 172 (6), 228(1), 244(2)

CAMPBELL, E. "Legal Personality, Trade Unions, and Damages for Unlawful Expulsion" (1954-56) 3 U. Wes. Aus. A.L.R. 393... 208(4)

CAMPBELL, E. "Thomas Hobbes and the Common Law" (1958) 1 Tasm.L. R. 20... 351(2)

CAMPS, F.E. and HAVARD, J.D.J. "Causation in Homicide - a Medical View" (1957) Crim. L.R. 576 ...185(2)

Canadian Jurisprudence. The Civil Law and Common Law in Canada (ed. E. McWhinney)... 31(6)

CANFIELD, G.F. Corporate Responsibility for Crime" (1914) 14 Col. L.R. 469... 202(4)

CANFIELD, G.F. "The Scope and Limits of the Corporate Entity Theory" (1917) 17 Col. L.R. 128 ... 212(4)

CANNON, R.W. "Born Alive" [1964] Crim. L.R. 748... 192(10)

CARDEN, P.T. "Limitations on the Powers of Common Law Corporations" (1910) 26 L.Q.R. 320... 201(4)

CARDEN, P.T. "Loose Leaf Law Reports" (1910) 26 L.Q.R. 75... 56(5)

CARDOZO, B.N. "Jurisprudence" in Selected Writings of B.N. Cardozo (ed. M.E. Hall)... 51(2)

CARDOZO, B.N. The Growth of the Law... 20(2), 48(4), 54(7), 116 (1), 309(2), 330(2)

CARDOZO, B.N. The Nature of the Judicial Process... 40(7), 50(7), 54(6), 114(2), 121(2), 309(3), 330(1)

CARDOZO, B.N. The Paradoxes of Legal Science... 121(3)

CARLSTON, K.S. Law and Structure of Social Action... 285(2), 311 (4)

CARLYLE, A.J., CARLYLE, R.W. and A History of Medieval Political Theory in the West (3rd ed.)... 355(2)

CARLYLE, R.W. and CARLYLE, A.J. A History of Medieval Political Theory in the West (3rd ed.)... 355(2)

CARON, Y. "The Legal Enforcement of Morals and the so-called Hart-Devlin Controversy" (1969) 15 McGill L.J. 9... 138(2)

CARPENTER, C.E. "Concurrent Causation" (1935) 83 U. Pa. L.R. 941... 182(1)

CARPENTER, C.E. "Court Decisions and the Common Law" (1917) 17 Col. L.R. 593... 48(7)

CARPENTER, C.E. "De Facto Corporations" (1911-12) 25 Harv. L.R. 623... 205(7)

COING, H. "Bentham's Influence on the Development of Interessenjurisprudenz and General Jurisprudence" (1967) 2 Ir. Jur. (N.S.) 336... 296(1)

COLE, R.H. "Windfall and Probability: a Study of 'Cause' in Negligence Law" (1964) 52 Calif. L.R. 459... 182(6)

COLE, W.G. "Private Morality and Public Law" (1968) 54 Am. B.A.J. 158... 162(6)

COLLARD, D. "State Arbitration in the U.S.S.R." (1955) 18 M.L.R. 474... 283(1)

COMMONS, J.R. Legal Foundations of Capitalism... 174(1)

COMMONS, J.R. "Value in Law and Economics" in Law: A Century of Progress II, 332... 287(1)

COMTE, A. The Positive Philosophy (trans H. Martineau)... 237(7)

CONARD, A.F. "New Ways to Write Laws" (1947) 56 Yale L.J. 458... 106(2)

CONQUEST, R. Justice and the Legal System in the U.S.S.R.... 278(8)

COOK, W.W. "Act, Intention and Motive in the Criminal Law" (1916-17) 26 Yale L.J. 645... 179(4), 187(5)

COOK, W.W. "'Facts' and 'Statements of Facts'" (1936-37) 4 U.C.L.R. 233... 11(8)

COOK, W.W. "Hohfeld's Contribution to the Science of Law" in W.N. Hohfeld, Fundamental Legal Conceptions as Applied in Judicial Reasoning (ed. W.W. Cook)... 169(5), 175(3), 224(4)

COOK, W.W. Lectures on Legal Topics... 8(4), 173(2), 224(5)

COOK, W.W. "Note on the Associated Press Case" (1918-19) 28 Yale L.J. 387... 173(4)

COOK, W.W. "Privileges of Labor Unions in the Struggle for Life" (1917-18) 27 Yale L.J. 779... 173(3)

COOK, W.W. "Scientific Method and the Law" (1927) 13 Am. B.A.J. 303... 7(7), 330(9)

COOK, W.W. "Statements of Facts in Pleading under the Codes" (1921) 21 Col. L.R. 416... 11(8)

COOK, W.W. "The Alienability of Choses in Action" (1916) 29 Harv. L.R. 816... 173(5)

COOK, W.W. "The Alienability of Choses in Action: a Reply to Professor Williston" (1917) 30 Harv. L.R. 449... 173(5)

COOK, W.W. "The Logical and Legal Bases of the Conflict of Laws" (1923-24) 33 Yale L.J. 457... 17(2), 43(4), 319(3)

COOK, W.W. "The Utility of Jurisprudence in the Solution of Legal Problems" in Lectures on Legal Topics 338... 8(4), 173(2), 224(5)

COOK, W.W., LLEWELLYN, K.N., ADLER, M.J., ---, "Law and the Modern Mind: a Symposium" (1931) 31 Col. L.R. 83... 317(3)

COOPER, F.E. "The Executive Departments of Government and the Rule of Law" (1960-61) 59 Mich. L.R. 515... 142(7)

COOPER, H.H.A. "Ratio Decidendi" (1968) 118 New L.J. 1180... 57(2)

COOPER, T.M. "The Common Law and the Civil Law - a Scot's View" (1950) 63 Harv. L.R. 468... 55(8)

COOPERRIDER, L.K. "The Rule of Law and the Judicial Process" (1960-61) 59 Mich. L.R. 501... 142(7), 150(5)

COPLESTON, F.C. Aquinas... 348(9)

CORBIN, A.L. "Jural Relations and their Classification" (1920-21) 30 Yale L.J. 226... 175(1)

CORBIN, A.L. "Legal Analysis and Terminology" (1919-20) 29 Yale L.J. 163... 170(4)

CORBIN, A.L. "Offer and Acceptance, and Some of the Resulting Legal Relations" (1916-17) 26 Yale L.J. 169... 173(7)

CORBIN, A.L. "Rights and Duties" (1923-24) 33 Yale L.J. 501... 156(3), 173(6)

CORBIN, A.L. "The Judicial Process Revisited: Introduction" (1961-62) 71 Yale L.J. 195... 40(8)

CORRY, J.A. "Administrative Law and the Interpretation of Statutes" (1935-36) 1 Tor. L.J. 286... 83(2)

CORRY, J.A. "The Use of Legislative History in the Interpretation of Statutes" (1954) 32 Can. B.R. 624 ... 102(9)

CORWIN, E.S. "Judicial Review in Action" (1926) 74 U. Pa. L.R. 639... 142(5)

CORWIN, E.S. "The 'Higher Law' Background of American Constitutional Law" (1928-29) 42 Harv. L.R. 149, 365... 65(6), 358(3)

COSSIO, C.S. "Jurisprudence and the Sociology of Law" (trans. P.J. Eder and F. Uno, 1952) 52 Col. L.R. 356, 479... 311(3)

COUTTS, J.A. Note in (1937-38) 1 M.L.R. 166... 99(3)

COUTTS, J.A. Note in (1950) 71 L. Q.R. 24... 36(10)

COUTTS, J.A., J.C.H.M., R.E.M. and --- Notes in (1948) 64 L.Q.R. 28, 29, 193, 454, 463... 36(9)

COWAN, T.A. "Legal Pragmatism and Beyond" in Interpretations of Modern Legal Philosophies (ed. P. Sayre) chap. 7... 7(2)

COWAN, T.A. The American Jurisprudence Reader... 175(6), 312 (2), 356(3)

COWAN, T.A. "The Relation of Law to Experimental Science" (1948) 96 U. Pa. L.R. 484... 311(2)

COWEN, D.V. "An Agenda for Jurisprudence" (1964) 49 Corn. L.Q. 609... 1(2)

COWEN, D.V. "Legislature and Judiciary I and II" (1952) 15 M.L.R. 282; (1953) 16 M.L.R. 273... 76(5)

COWEN, D.V. Parliamentary Sovereignty and the Entrenched Sections of the South Africa Act... 76(4)

COWEN, D.V. "The Entrenched Sections of the South Africa Act" (1953) 70 S.A.L.J. 243... 76(6)

COWEN, D.V. The Foundations of Freedom... 76(7), 343(3)

COWEN, Z. "Parliamentary Sovereignty and the Limits of Legal Change" (1952-53) 26 Aust. L.J. 236... 77(3)

COX, A. "Judge Learned Hand and the Interpretation of Statutes" (1946-47) 60 Harv. L.R. 370... 86(5), 92(1), 103(7)

CRABB, J.H. "Airing a Couple of Myths about Natural Law" (1964) 39 Notre Dame Lawyer 137... 363(4)

CRAIES, W.F. Statute Law (6th ed. S.G.G. Edgar)... 98(1)

CROSS, A.R.N. "Larceny and the Formation of a Felonious Intent after Taking Possession" (1949) 12 M.L.R. 228... 223(4)

CROSS, A.R.N. Precedent in English Law (2nd ed.)... 19(6), 22(1), 26 (8), 32(5), 35(2), 36(5), 38(1), 87(2), 104(5), 112(1), 241(1), 255(5)

CROSS, A.R.N. "Recent Developments in the Practice of Precedent - the Triumph of Common Sense" (1969) 43 A.L.J. 3... 56(1)

CROSS, A.R.N. "Stare Decisis in Contemporary England" (1966) 82 L.Q.R. 203... 29(10)

CURTIS, C.P. "A Better Theory of Legal Interpretation" in Jurisprudence in Action 135... 84(4)

DANIEL, W.T.S. The History and Origin of 'The Law Reports'... 24(2)(11)

DAUBE, D. Biblical Law... 273(3)

DAUBE, D. Forms of Roman Legislation... 157(4)

DAVID, R. and BRIERLEY, J.E.C. Major Legal Systems in the World Today... 274(3)

DAVID, R. and DeVRIES, H.P. The French Legal System... 57(5)

DAVIDSON, C.G. "Stare Decisis in Louisiana" (1932-33) 7 Tul. L.R. 100... 59(9)

DAVIES, D.J.Ll. "The Interpretation of Statutes in the Light of their Policy by the English Courts" (1935) 35 Col. L.R. 519... 90(6)

DAVIS, K.C. "Legislative History and the Wheat Board Case" (1953) 31 Can. B.R. 1... 102(8)

DAVITT, T.E. "Law as a Means to an End - Thomas Aquinas" (1960-61) 14 Vand. L.R. 65... 348(7)

DEÁK, F. "The Place of the 'Case' in the Common and Civil Law" (1933-34) 8 Tul. L.R. 337... 58(7)

de BUSTAMANTE y MONTORO, A.S. "Kelsenism" in Interpretations of Modern Legal Philosophies (ed. P. Sayre) chap. 3... 252(4)

DEISER, G.F. "The Juristic Person" (1919) 57 U.Pa.L.R. 131, 216, 300 ... 214(6)

GILMOUR, D.R. "The Sovereignty of Parliament and the European Commission of Human Rights" [1968] P.L. 62... 69(8)

GINSBERG, M. On Justice in Society... 131(4), 136(3), 286 (6)

GINSBERG, M. Reason and Unreason in Society... 255(7), 290(5)

GINSBERG, M. "Stammler's Philosophy of Law" in Modern Theories of Law (ed. W.I. Jennings) chap. 3... 353(2)

GINSBERG, M., HOBHOUSE, L.T., WHEELER, G.C., ---. The Material Culture and Social Institutions of the Simpler Peoples... 269(4)

GLASSON, E., LYALL, A.C., ---, HOLTZENDORFF, F. von, COGLIOLO, P. "Sir Henry Maine" (1884) 4 L.Q.R. 129... 270(2)

GLUCKMAN, M. Politics, Law and Ritual in Tribal Society... 270(8)

GLUCKMAN, M. The Judicial Process among the Barotse of Northern Rhodesia... 270(6)(7)

GOBLE, G.W. "A Redefinition of Basic Legal Terms" (1935) 35 Col. L.R. 535... 170(6)

GOBLE, G.W. "The Sanction of a Duty" (1927-28) 37 Yale L.J. 426 ... 156(4), 174(5)

GODDARD, R. "Working of the Court of Criminal Appeal" (1952) 2 J. S.P.T.L.(N.S.) 1... 28(5)

GOLD, J. "Common Employment" (1937) 1 M.L.R. 225... 288(2)

GOLDING, M.P. "Principled Decision-making and the Supreme Court" in Essays in Legal Philosophy (ed. R.S. Summers) 208... 126(1)

GOLDSCHMIDT, H.W. English Law from a Foreign Standpoint... 55(2)(3)

GOLUNSKII, S.A. and STROGOVICH, M. S. "The Theory of the State and Law" in Soviet Legal Philosophy (trans. H.W. Babb) 351... 256(5), 267(2), 293(4), 306(5), 344(6)

GOODERSON, R.N. Note in (1955) 33 Can. B.R. 612... 37(1)

GOODERSON, R.N. "Ratio Decidendi and Rules of Law" (1952) 30 Can. B.R. 892... 34(4)

GOODERSON, R.N. "Young v. Bristol Aeroplane Co. Ltd." (1950) 10 C. L.J. 432... 29(3)

GOODEVE, L.A. Modern Law of Personal Property (9th ed. R.H. Kersley)... 220(4)

GOODHART, A.L. "An Apology for Jurisprudence" in Interpretations of Modern Legal Philosophies (ed. P. Sayre) chap. 12... 6(2)

GOODHART, A.L. "Case Law - a Short Replication" (1934) 50 L.Q.R. 196 ... 53(2)

GOODHART, A.L. "Case Law in England and America" in Essays in Jurisprudence and the Common Law chap. 3... 55(7)

GOODHART, A.L. "Corporate Liability in Tort and the Doctrine of Ultra Vires" in Essays in Jurisprudence and the Common Law chap. 5... 202(7)

GOODHART, A.L. "Cruelty, Desertion and Insanity in Matrimonial Law" (1963) 79 L.Q.R. 98... 187(9)

GOODHART, A.L. "Determining the Ratio Decidendi of a Case" in Essays in Jurisprudence and the Common Law chap. 1... 34(2)

GOODHART, A.L. English Law and the Moral Law... 134(4), 153(1), 340 (4)

GOODHART, A.L. Essays in Jurisprudence and the Common Law... 34(2), 55(7), 127(3), 202(7), 220(8)

GOODHART, A.L. "Freedom under the Law" (1960) 1 Tasm. L.R. 375... 130(3)

GOODHART, A.L. Note in (1950) 66 L.Q.R. 314... 100(6)

GOODHART, A.L. "Precedent in English and Continental Law" (1934) 50 L.Q.R. 40... 52(7)

GOODHART, A.L. "Precedents in the Court of Appeal" (1947) 9 C.L.J. 349... 29(2)

GOODHART, A.L. "Reporting the Law" (1939) 55 L.Q.R. 29... 56(3)

GOODHART, A.L. "Roscoe Pound" (1964-65) 78 Harv. L.R. 23... 302(3), 304(7)

HART, H.L.A. "The Ascription of Responsibility and Rights" in Logic and Language (ed. A.G.N. Flew) I, 145... 123(5), 177(6)

HART, H.L.A. The Concept of Law ... 12(6), 19(3), 68(2), 89(5), 109(7), 153(4), 172(5), 238(3), 240(3), 244(7), 245(4), 256(6), 330(6), 359(4)

HART, H.L.A. "The Use and Abuse of the Criminal Law" (1961) 4 Oxford Lawyer , 7... 136(5)

HART, H.L.A. "Varieties of Responsibility" (1967) L.Q.R. 346 ... 178(1)

HART, H.L.A. and HONORÉ, A.M. "Causation in the Law" (1956) 72 L.Q.R. 58, 260, 398... 182(2)

HART, H.L.A. and HONORÉ, A.M. Causation in the Law... 182(2)

HART, H.M. "Holmes's Positivism - an Addendum" (1950-51) 64 Harv. L.R. 929... 317(2)

HART, H.M. "The Time Chart of the Justices" (1959-60) 73 Harv. L. R. 84... 125(6)

HART, W.G. "The Place of Trust in Jurisprudence" (1912) 28 L.Q.R. 290... 228(8)

HART, W.G. "What is a Trust?" (1899) 15 L.Q.R. 294... 228(7)

Harvard Legal Essays... 96(3), 339 (4)

Harvard Studies in the Conflict of Laws... 210(3)

HARVEY, C.P. "A Job for Jurisprudence" (1944) 7 M.L.R. 42; (1945) 8 M.L.R. 236... 10(2), 309(5), 331(3)(4)

HARVEY, W.B. "A Value Analysis of Ghanaian Legal Development since Independence" (1964) 1 U.G.L.J. 4... 120(5)

HARVEY, W.B. "The Challenge of the Rule of Law" (1960-61) 59 Mich. L.R. 603... 142(7)

HARVEY, W.B. "The Rule of Law in Historical Perspective" (1960-61) 59 Mich. L.R. 487... 142(7)

HASTIE, W. "Introduction" to G.F. Puchta and Others, Outlines of the Science of Jurisprudence (trans. W. Hastie)... 244(3)

HAVARD, J.D.E., CAMPS, F.E. and "Causation in Homicide - a Medical View" (1957) Crim.L.R. 576... 185(2)

HAVIGHURST, A.F. "James II and the Twelve Men in Scarlet" (1953) 69 L.Q.R. 522... 64(5)

HAVIGHURST, A.F. "The Judiciary and Politics in the Reign of Charles II" (1950) 66 L.Q.R. 62, 229... 64(5)

HAWKINS, F.V. "On the Principles of Interpretation with Reference especially to the Interpretation of Wills" (1858-63) 2 Trans. Jur. S. 298... 90(5)

HAZARD, J.N. "Cleansing Soviet International Law of anti-Marxist Theories" (1938) 32 A.J.I.L. 244 ... 279(7)

HAZARD, J.N. Law and Social Change in the U.S.S.R.... 232(4), 274(7)

HAZARD, J.N. "Socialism, Abuse of Power and Soviet Law" (1950) 50 Col. L.R. 448... 279(2)

Hazard, J.N. "Soviet Codifiers Release the First Drafts" (1959) 8 A.J.C.L. 72... 279(6)

HAZARD, J.N. "Soviet Government Corporations" (1942-43) 41 Mich. L.R. 850... 279(6)

HAZARD, J.N. "Soviet Law: an Introduction" (1936) 36 Col. L.R. 1236... 277(5)

HAZARD, J.N. and WEISBERG, M.L. Cases and Materials on Soviet Law ... 280(3)

HAZO, R.G. "Montesquieu and the Separation of Powers" (1968) 54 Am. B.A.J. 665... 291(7)

HEARN, W.E. The Theory of Legal Duties and Rights... 155(6), 168(4), 170(3), 227(5), 242(7), 247(6)

HEARNSHAW, F.J.C. The Social and Political Ideas of some Representative Thinkers of the Age of Reaction and Reconstruction (ed. F.J.C. Hearnshaw)... 239(7)

HEATH, P.L., PASSMORE, J.A. and "Intentions" (1955) Aristotelian Society Supp. Vol. 29, 131... 186(6)

HEGEL, G.W.F. Philosophy of Rights (trans. T.M. Knox)... 263(5), 267(6)

HEMMING, G.W. "The Law Reports" (1885) 1 L.Q.R. 317... 25(1)

HENKIN, L. "Morals and the Constitution: the Sin of Obscenity" (1963) 63 Col. L.R. 393... 137(6)

ISAACS, N. "Judicial Review of Administrative Findings" (1921) 30 Yale L.J. 781... 11(8)

ISAACS, N. "The Influence of Judaism on Western Law" in The Legacy of Israel (edd. E.R. Bevan and C. Singer) 377... 347 (8)

ISAACS, N. "The Law and the Facts" (1922) 22 Col. L.R. 1... 11(8)

ISAACS, N. "The Schools of Jurisprudence" (1917-18) 31 Harv. L.R. 373... 2(1)

ISON, P.G. "The Enforcement of Morals" (1967) 3 U. Br. Col. L. R. 263... 137(5)

ISRAELS, C.L. "Implications and Limitations of the 'Deep Rock Doctrine'" (1942) 42 Col. L.R. 376... 211(1)

JACKSON, R.H. "Decisional Law and Stare Decisis" (1944) 30 Am. B. A.J. 334... 54(10)

JACKSON, R.H. "The Meaning of Statutes: what Congress Says or what the Court Says" (1948) 34 Am. B.A.J. 535... 103(8)

JACKSON, R.M. "Absolute Prohibition in Statutory Offences" in Modern Approach to Criminal Law (edd. L. Radzinowicz and J.W.C. Turner) 262... 100(1)

JACKSON, R.M. Note in (1939) 55 L.Q.R. 488... 103(3)

JAMES, F. "Accident Liability Reconsidered. The Impact of Liability Insurance" (1947-48) 57 Yale L.J. 549... 145(2)

JAMES, F. "Accident Liability: Some Wartime Developments" (1945-46) 55 Yale L.J. 365... 145(2)

JAMES, F. and PERRY, R.F. "Legal Cause" (1951) 60 Yale L. J. 761... 181(5)

JANZEN, H. "Kelsen's Pure Theory of Law" (1937) 31 Am. Pol. Sc.R. 205... 257(5)

JENKINS, I. "Rudolph von Ihering" (1960-61) 14 Vand. L.R. 169... 292(7)

JENKINS, I. "The Matchmaker, or Towards a Synthesis of Legal Idealism and Positivism" (1959-60) 12 J.L.E. 1... 359(7)

JENKS, E. "English Civil Law" (1916-17) 30 Harv. L.R. 1... 49(1)

JENKS, E. "Recent Theories of the State" (1927) 43 L.Q.R. 186... 285(4)

JENKS, E. The New Jurisprudence... 3(5), 156(1), 167(5), 192(1), 243(3), 247(7)

JENNINGS, J. "The Growth and Development of Automatism as a Defence in Criminal Law" (1961-62) 2 Os. H.L.J. 370... 180(2)

JENNINGS, W.I. "A Plea for Utilitarianism" (1938) 2 M.L.R. 22... 297(3)

JENNINGS, W.I. Constitutional Laws of the Commonwealth (3rd ed.)... 73(1)

JENNINGS, W.I. "Courts and Administrative Law - the Experience of English Housing Legislation" (1935-36) 49 Harv. L.R. 426... 93(1)

JENNINGS, W.I. "Judicial Process at its Worst" (1937-39) 1 M.L.R. 111... 93(2)

JENNINGS, W.I. Parliament (2nd ed.) ... 67(5)

JENNINGS, W.I. "The Institutional Theory" in Modern Theories of Law (ed. W.I. Jennings) chap. 5... 306(6)

JENNINGS, W.I. The Law and the Constitution (5th ed.)... 67(3), 160(7)

JENNINGS, W.I. "The Statute of Westminster and Appeals to the Privy Council" (1936) 52 L.Q.R. 173... 73(6)

JENSEN, O.C. The Nature of Legal Argument... 39(2)

Jeremy Bentham and the Law. A Symposium, (edd. G.W. Keeton and G. Schwarzenberger)... 294(7)

JEWELL, R.E.C. "Education and Deprived Children: statute and prergative" (1962) 125 J.P.J. 320, 356... 195(4)

JEWKES, J. "The Nationalisation of Industry" (1953) 20 U.C.L.R. 615 ... 233(2)

JOHNSON, H.M. Sociology: A Systematic Introduction... 313(2)

JOHNSTON, W.J. "The English Legislature and the Irish Courts" (1924) 40 L.Q.R. 91... 72(8)

KOCOUREK, A. Jural Relations (2nd
ed.)... 159(5), 171(3)(4), 175(1),
178(2), 212(1), 217(3), 224(6)

KOCOUREK, A. "Libre Recherche in
America" in Recueil d'Etudes sur
les Sources du Droit en l'Honneur de F. Geny II, 459... 119(2)

KOCOUREK, A. "Plurality of Advantage and Disadvantage in Jural
Relations" (1920) 19 Mich. L.R.
47... 171(2)

KOCOUREK, A. "Preface to Science
of Legal Method: Select Essays
by Various Authors (trans. E.
Bruncken and L.B. Register)...
83(5)

KOCOUREK, A. "Retrospective Decisions and Stare Decisis and a
Proposal" (1931) 17 Am. B.A.J.
180... 51(1)

KOCOUREK, A. "Review" of J.W
Bingham (1913) 8 Ill. L.R. 138
... 318(7)

KOCOUREK, A. "Roscoe Pound as a
Former Colleague Knew Him" in
Interpretations of Modern Legal
Philosophies (ed. P. Sayre) chap.
19... 304(6)

KOCOUREK, A. "Sanctions and
Remedies" (1924) 72 U. Pa. L.R.
91... 159(5)

KOCOUREK, A. "Tabulae Minores
Jurisprudentiae" (1920-21) 30
Yale L.J. 215... 159(5)

KOCOUREK, A. "The Alphabet of
Legal Relations" (1923) 9 Am. B.
A.J. 237... 171(3)

KOCOUREK, A. "The Century of
Analytic Jurisprudence since
John Austin" in Law: A Century
of Progress II, 194... 171(1),
234(6)

KOCOUREK, A. "The Hohfeld System
of Fundamental Legal Concepts"
(1920) 15 Ill. L.Q. 23... 174(7),
175(1)

KOHLER, J. "Judicial Interpretation of Enacted Law" in Science
of Legal Method: Select Essays
by Various Authors (trans. E.
Bruncken and L.B. Register)...
94(2)

KORAH, V.L. "The Restrictive
Practices Court" (1959) 12 C.L.
P. 76... 145(8)

KORKUNOV, N.M. General Theory of
Law (trans. W.G. Hastings)...
17(6), 113(5), 160(3), 168(7),
211(5), 260(6), 344(4)

KOROVIN, E.A. "The Second World
War and International Law" (1946)
40 A.J.I.L. 742... 278(8)

KORT, F. "Quantitative Analysis of
Fact - patterns in Cases and their
Impact on Judicial Decisions"
(1965-66) 79 Harv. L.R. 1595...
323(3)

KORZYBSKI, A. Science and Sanity
(2nd ed.)... 17(7)

KOTZÉ, J.G. "Judicial Precedent"
(1917) 34 S.A.L.J. 280; (1918)
144 L.T. 349... 59(4)

KRISLOV, S. "Theoretical Attempts
at Predicting Judicial Behaviour"
(1965-66) 79 Harv. L.R. 1573...
322(5)

KRUSE, L.F. VINDING The Foundations
of Human Thought (trans. A.
Fausbøll and I. Lund)... 17(7)

KRUSE, L.F. VINDING The Right of
Property (trans. P.T. Federspiel)
... 227(7)

KUNZ, J.L. "On the Theoretical
Basis of the Law of Nations"
(1925) 10 Trans. Gro. S. 115...
257(1)

KUNZ, J.L. "The Vienna School of
Law and International Law" (1936)
11 N.Y.U.L.Q. 370... 257(1)

LAIRD, D.H. "The Doctrine of Stare
Decisis" (1935) 13 Can. B.R. 1...
27(6)

LAMBERT, E. "Codified Law and Case
Law: their Part in Shaping the
Policies of Justice" in Science
of Legal Method: Select Essays by
Various Authors (trans. E.
Bruncken and L.B. Register)...
49(3)

LAMBERT, E. and WASSERMAN, M.J.
"The Case Method in Canada and
the Possibilities of its Adaptation to the Civil Law" (1929) 39
Yale L.J. 1... 58(2)

LAMONT, W.D. The Principles of
Moral Judgment... 12(1), 132(3),
158(5), 362(4)

LAMONT, W.D. The Value Judgment...
120(6)

McDOUGAL, M.S. and REISMAN, W.M.
"Rhodesia and the U.N.: the
Lawfulness of International
Concern" (1968) 62 A.J.I.L. 1...
82(5)

McDOUGAL, M.S., LASWELL, H.D. and
"Legal Education and Public
Policy: Professional Training in
the Public Interest" (1942-43)
52 Yale L.J. 202... 310(2)

McDOUGAL, W. The Group Mind...
214(7)

McILWAIN, C.H. Constitutionalism
and the Changing World... 65(7),
247(8)

McILWAIN, C.H. The High Court of
Parliament and its Supremacy...
62(5), 95(4)

McKEAN, F.G. "The Rule of Precedents" (1928) 76 U. Pa. L.R. 481
... 54(1)

McLAUGHLIN, J.A. "Proximate Cause"
(1925-26) 39 Harv. L.R. 149...
183(7)

McLOUD, J.W. "The Value of Precedents" (1894) 28 Am. L.R. 218...
55(6)

McNAIR, A.D. "The National Character and Status of Corporations"
(1923-24) 4 B.Y.I.L. 44... 199(8)

McWHINNEY, E. "Court versus Legislature in the Union of South
Africa: the Assertion of a Right
of Judicial Review" (1953) 31
Can. B.R. 52... 78(2)

McWHINNEY, E. Judicial Review in
the English-speaking World (2nd
ed.)... 31(5), 69(4), 78(5),
142(1)

McWHINNEY, E. "La Crise Constitu-
tionelle de l'Union Sud-
Africaine" (1953) Revue Internationale de Droit Comparè, 542...
78(6)

McWHINNEY, E. "Legal Theory and
Philosophy of Law in Canada" in
Canadian Jurisprudence. The
Civil Law and Common Law in
Canada (ed. E. McWhinney)... 31
(6)

McWHINNEY, E. Note on Collins v.
Minister of the Interior (1957)
35 Can. B.R. 1203... 78(4)

McWHINNEY, E. Note on the "High
Court Case" (1952) 30 Can. B.R.
734... 78(3)

McWHINNEY, E. "'Sovereignty' in
the United Kingdom and the Commonwealth Countries at the Present
Day" (1953) 68 Pol. Sc. Q. 511...
74(1)

McWHINNEY, E. "The Supreme Court
and the Bill of Rights - the
Lessons of Comparative Jurisprudence" (1959) 37 Can. B.R. 16...
125(1)

McWHINNEY, E. "The Union Parliament, the Supreme Court and the,
'Entrenched Clauses' of the South
Africa Act" (1952) 30 Can.B.R.
692... 78(1)

MEANS, G.C., BERLE, A.A. and The
Modern Corporation and Private
Property... 195(6), 231(5)

MECHEM, P. "The Jurisprudence of
Despair" (1935-36) 21 Iowa L.R.
669... 328(7)

MEGARRY, R.E. "Decisions by
Equally Divided Courts as Precedents" (1954) 70 L.Q.R. 318, 471
... 32(7)

MEGARRY, R.E. "Fair Wear and Tear
and the Doctrine of Precedent"
(1958) 74 L.Q.R. 33... 29(5)

MEGARRY, R.E. "Precedent in the
Court of Appeal: How Binding is
'Binding'?" (1958) 74 L.Q.R. 350
... 29(6), 36(1)

MEGARRY, R.E. and WADE, H.W.R. The
Law of Real Property (3rd ed.)...
225(9)

von MEHREN, A.T. "Roscoe Pound and
Comparative Law" (1964-65) 78
Harv. L.R. 1585... 302(3)

von MEHREN, A.T. The Civil Law
System: Cases and Materials...
44(5), 47(6), 59(1), 124(5)

MENDELSON, W. "The Judge's Art"
(1960-61) 109 U. Pa. L.R. 524...
124(4)

MENZIES, D. "Australia and the
Judicial Committee of the Privy
Council" (1968) 42 A.L.J. 79...
32(1)

MERRIAM, C.E. History of the
Theory of Sovereignty since
Rousseau... 66(1), 247(2)

MERRILLS, J.G. "Law, Morals and
the Psychological Nexus" (1969)
19 Tor. L.J. 46... 134(9), 333(5)

MESSNER, J. Note in (1959) 4 Nat.
L.F. 101... 360(3)

RENNER, K. The Institutions of Private Law and their Social Functions (trans. A. Schwarzchild, ed. O. Kahn-Freund)... 232(3), 276(6)

Report of the Committee on Ministers' Powers... 91(3)

Report of the Lord Chancellor's Committee on Law Reporting... 25(8)

REUSCHLEIN, H.G. Jurisprudence - its American Prophets... 175(8), 286(5), 311(5), 332(6), 358(7)

RHEINSTEIN, M. "Education for Legal Craftsmanship" (1944-45) 30 Iowa L.R. 408... 8(6)

RICHARDS, I.A., OGDEN, C.K. and The Meaning of Meaning (10th ed.) ... 17(7)

RIDEOUT, R.W. "Protection of the Right to Work" (1962) 25 M.L.R. 137... 147(3)

RIDEOUT, R.W. "Rookes v. Barnard" (1964) 3 Sol. Q. 193... 147(4)

RIESMAN, D. "Possession and the Law of Finders" (1939) 52 Harv. L.R. 1105... 221(9)

RITCHIE, D.G. Natural Rights... 357(9)

ROBERTSON, L.J. "The Judicial R Recognition of Custom in India" (1922) 4 J.C.L. (ser. 3) 218... 115(5)

ROBINSON, E.S. Law and Lawyers... 43(6), 321(2)

ROBINSON, H.W. "Law and Economics" (1939) 2 M.L.R. 257... 286(4), 309(6)

ROBINSON, R. Definition... 12(2)

ROBSON, R.A.H., COHEN, J., ---, BATES, A. Parental Authority: the Community and the Law... 311(1)

ROBSON, W.A. Justice and Administrative Law (3rd ed.)... 127(2)

ROBSON, W.A. "Sir Henry Maine Today" in Modern Theories of Law (ed. W.I. Jennings) chap. 9... 269(6)

ROBSON, W.A. "The Public Corporation in Britain Today" in Problems of Nationalised Industry (ed. W.A. Robson) chap. 1... 203(4)

ROGERS, J.G. "A Scientific Approach to Free Judicial Decision" in Recueil d'Etudes sur les Sources du Droit en l'Honneur de F. Gény II, 552... 119(2)

ROGERS, S. "On the Study of Law Reports" (1897) 13 L.Q.R. 250... 26(2)

ROHNER, R.J. "Jurimetrics, No!" (1968) 54 Am. B.A.J. 896... 324(3)

ROMMEN, H.A. The Natural Law (trans. T.R. Hanley)... 336(2)

ROSEN, L. "Legal Cruelty and Cruelty" (1964) 108 S.J. 887... 188(2)

ROSS, A. Directives and Norms... 17(4), 158(2)

ROSS, A. On Law and Justice... 17(3), 20(9), 57(8), 69(5), 87(1), 111(4), 158(1), 164(5), 253(3), 261(5), 284(6), 295(4), 303(3), 333(2), 334(4), 344(2)

ROSS, A. Review of Kelsen's What is Justice? (1957) 45 Calif. L. R. 564... 253(2)

ROSS, A. Towards a Realistic Jurisprudence (trans. A.I. Fausbøll) ... 334(3), 344(3)

ROSS, A. "Tu-tu" (1956-57) 70 Harv. L.R. 812... 224(7)

ROSTOW, E.V. Planning for Freedom ... 309(7)

ROSTOW, E.V. "The Democratic Character of Judicial Review" (1952-53) 66 Harv. L.R. 193... 70(4)

ROSTOW, E.V. "The Enforcement of Morals" (1960) C.L.J. 174... 136(6)

"Round Table Discussion: 'What should be the Relation of Morals to Law?'" (1952) 1 J.P.L. 259... 134(8)

ROUSSEAU, J-J. Contrat Social... 351(7)

RUEFF, J. From the Physical to the Social Sciences: Introduction to a Study of Economic and Ethical Theory (trans. H. Green); "Introduction" by H. Oliphant and A. Hewitt, in J. Hall, Readings in Jurisprudence 355... 43(2)

Rules of Drafting (1948) 26 Can. B. R. 1231... 105(4)

continued

SAWER, G. "Injunction, Parliamentary Process, and the Restriction of Parliamentary Competence"
(1944) 60 L.Q.R. 83... 74(4)
SAWER, G. Law in Society...
261(3), 272(7), 277(1), 290(1),
294(3), 304(4)
SAWER, G. "Referendum to Abolish
the Upper House in New South
Wales" (1961) P.L.' 131... 74(6)
SAWER, G. in The Commonwealth of
Australia (ed. G.W. Paton) 38...
74(5)
SAWER, G., PATON, G.W. and "Ratio
and Obiter Dictum in Appellate
Courts" (1947) 63 L.Q.R. 461...
36(11)
SCAMMELL, E.H. "Nationalisation
in Legal Perspective" (1952) 5
C.L.P. 30... 233(1)
SCARMAN, L.G. "Codification and
Judge-made Law. A Problem of
Co-existence" (University of
Birmingham Faculty of Law, 1966)
... 61(9)
SCHAPIRA, I. "Malinowski's
Theories of Law" in Man and
Culture (ed. R.W. Firth) 139...
269 (3)
SCHECHTER, F.I. "Popular Law and
Common Law in Medieval England"
(1928) 28 Col. L.R. 269... 114(1)
SCHLESINGER, R.B. "A Glance at
Soviet Law" (1949) 65 L.Q.R. 504
... 280(4)
SCHLESINGER, R.B. Comparative Law:
Cases, Text, Materials (2nd ed.)
... 59(2)
SCHLESINGER, R.B. Marx, His Time
and Ours... 277(2)
SCHLESINGER, R.B. "Recent Devel-
opments in Soviet Legal Theory"
(1942) 6 M.L.R. 21... 278(1)
SCHLESINGER, R.B. Soviet Legal
Theory (2nd ed.)... 274(2)
SCHLOSBERG, H.J., KENNEDY, W.P.M.
and The Law and Custom of the
South African Constitution...
79(5)
SCHMIDHAUSER, J.R. "Stare Decisis,
and the Background of the
Justice of the Supreme Courts of
the United States" (1962) 14 Tor.
L.J. 194... 151(7), 320(8)
SCHMIDT, F. "Construction of
Statutes" (1957) 1 Scand.S.L. 157
... 104(2)

SCHMITTHOF, C.M. "The Growing
Ambit of the Common Law" (1951)
29 Can. B.R. 469; (1952) 30 Can.
B.R. 48... 54(9), 118(9)
SCHROEDER, T. "The Psychologic
Study of Judicial Opinions"
(1918) 6 Calif. L.R. 89... 319(1)
SCHULMAN, H. "The Standard of Care
Required of Children" (1927-28)
37 Yale L.J. 618... 144(8)
SCHWARTZ, B. "The Changing Role of
the United States Supreme Court"
(1950) 28 Can. B.R. 48... 125(2)
SCHWARTZ, M.L., MUELLER, A. and
"The Principle of Neutral Prin-
ciples" (1960) 7 U. Ca. L.A.L.
571... 125(8)
SCHWARZ, A.B. "John Austin and the
German Jurisprudence of his Time"
(1934-35) 1 Politica, 178...
239(2)
SCHWARZENBERGER, G. "The Forms of
Sovereignty" (1957) 10 C.L.P. 264
... 248(7)
SCHWARZENBERGER, G. "The Three
Types of Law" (1949) 2 C.L.P. 103
... 310(4)
Science of Legal Method: Select
Essays by Various Authors (trans.
E. Bruncken and L.B. Register)...
6(1), 40(1), 49(3), 50(8), 53(10),
55(3)(4), 83(5), 87(3), 94(2)(3)
(4), 119(1)
SCOTT, A.W. "Pound's Influence on
Civil Procedure" (1964-65) 78
Harv. L.R. 1568... 302(3)
SCOTT, A.W. The Law of Trusts (3rd
ed.)... 228(2)
SCOTT, A.W. "The Nature of the
Rights of the Cestui que Trust"
(1917) 17 Col. L.R. 269... 228(3)
SCOTT, W.C. "Judicial Logic as
Applied in Delimiting the Concept
of Business 'Affected with a
Public Interest '" (1930) 19 Ken.
L.J. 16... 126(4)
SCRUTTON, T.E. "The Work of the
Commercial Court" (1921-23) 1 C.
L.J. 6... 122(3)
SEABORNE DAVIES, D. "Child-killing
in English Law" in Modern
Approach to Criminal Law (edd. L.
Radzinowicz and J.W.C. Turner)...
192(9)

STAMMLER, R. "Fundamental Ten-
dencies in Modern Jurisprudence"
(1923) 21 Mich. L.R. 623...
260(3)
STAMMLER, R. The Theory of Jus-
tice, (trans. I. Husik)... 353(1)
STEIN, P. "Justice Cardozo, Marcus
Terentius Varro and the Roman
Juristic Process" (1967) 2 Ir.
Jur. (N.S.) 367... 41(1)
STEINER, H.A. "The Fascist Con-
ception of Law" (1936) 36 Col.
L.R. 1267... 264(7)
STEPHEN, J.F. Commentaries on the
Laws of England (21st ed. L.C.
Warmington)... 65(2), 109(2)
STEPHEN, L. The English Utilita-
rians... 239(1)
STERN, K. "Either-or or Neither-
nor" in Law and Philosophy. A
Symposium (ed. S. Hook) 247...
237(6)
STERN, W.B. Note on "Kelsen's
Theory of International Law"
(1936) 30 Am. Pol. Sc. R. 736...
257(4)
STEVENS, E.G. "Christianity and
the Law" (1915) 49 Am. L.R. 1...
140(3)
STEVENS, R. "Justiciability: the
Restrictive Practices Court Re-
examined" (1964) P.L. 221...
146(1), 151(2)
STEVENS, R. "The Final Appeal:
Reform of the House of Lords and
Privy Council, 1867-1876" (1964)
80 L.Q.R. 343... 29(11)
STEVENS, R. "The Role of a Final
Appeal Court in a Democracy: the
House of Lords Today" (1965) 28
M.L.R. 509... 122(7)
STEVENS, R.S. "A Proposal as to
the Codification and Restatement
of the Ultra Vires Doctrine"
(1926-27) 36 Yale L.J. 297...
201(10)
STEWART, R.D.C. "The Difference
Between Possession of Land and
Chattels" (1933) 11 Can. B.R.
651... 220(3)
STJERNQUIST, P. "How are Changes
in Social Behaviour Developed
by Means of Legislation?" in
Legal Essays. A Tribute to Frede
Castberg 153... 160(6)

STOCKS, J.L. Jeremy Bentham,
1748-1832... 296(10)
STOLJAR, S.J. "The Logical Status
of a Legal Principle" (1952-53)
20 U.C.L.R. 181... 11(4), 39(3)
STONE, F.F. "Ultra Vires and
Original Sin" (1939-40) 14 Tul.
L.R. 190... 201(1)
STONE,H.F. "Some Aspects of the
Problem of Law Simplification"
(1923) 23 Col. L.R. 319... 61(6)
STONE, H.F. "The Nature of the
Rights of the Cestui que Trust"
(1917) 17 Col. L.R. 467... 228
(6)
STONE, J. "A Critique of Pound's
Theory of Justice" (1934-35) 20
Iowa L.R. 531... 302(1)
STONE, J. Human Law and Human
Justice... 292(5), 295(6),
302(4), 337(3), 342(3), 346(10),
348(4), 349(5), 352(3), 353(5)(6),
354(1)
STONE, J. Legal System and
Lawyers' Reasonings... 1(1),
33(6), 39(6), 86(4), 119(4),
169(6), 241(7), 253(6), 256(7),
292(4), 326(4), 334(2)
STONE, J. "Mystery and Mystique
of the Basic Norm" (1963) 26 M.
L.R. 34... 254(1)
STONE, J. "Reason and Reasoning
in Judicial and Juristic Argu-
ment" in Legal Essays. A Tribute
to Frede Castberg 170... 39(5)
STONE, J. "'Result-orientation'
and Appellate Judgment" in Per-
spectives of Law. Essays for
Austin Wakeman Scott (edd. R.
Pound, E.N. Griswold, A.E.
Sutherland) 347... 126(2)
STONE, J. "Roscoe Pound and
Sociological Jurisprudence"
(1964-65) 78 Harv. L.R. 1578...
302(3)
STONE, J. Social Dimensions of
Law and Justice... 52(2), 129(1),
138(6), 211(3), 232(2), 265(5),
268(5), 284(4), 290(3), 302(5),
307(1)(2), 326(4), 328(3)
STONE, J. "The Golden Age of
Pound" (1962) 4 Syd. L.R. 1...
302(2)
STONE, J. "Theories of Law and
Justice of Fascist Italy" (1937)
1 M.L.R. 177... 264(7)

WRIGHT, R.A. "Public Policy" in Legal Essays and Addresses chap. 3... 133(7)

WRIGHT, R.A. "The Common Law in its Old Home" in Legal Essays and Addresses 338... 53(8), 60(11)

WRIGHT, R.S., POLLOCK, F. and An Essay on Possession in the Common Law... 219(1)

WU, J.C.H. Fountain of Justice. A Study in Natural Law... 341(1)

WU, J.C.H. "Justice Holmes and the Common Law Tradition" (1960-61) 14 Vand. L.R. 221... 317(2)

WULFSOHN, J.G. "Separation of Church and State in South African Law" (1964) 81 S.A.L.J. 90, 226... 141(2)

WURZEL, K.G. "Methods of Juridical Thinking" in Science of Legal Method: Select Essays by Various Authors (trans. E. Bruncken and L.B. Register)... 6(1)

WYLIE, J.C.W. "Adverse Possession: an Ailing Concept?" (1965) 16 N.I.L.Q. 467... 223(8)

YALE, D.E.C. Lord Nottingham's Chancery Cases... 22(9)

YNTEMA, H.E. "American Legal Realism in Retrospect" (1960-61) 14 Vand. L.R. 317... 318(4)

YNTEMA, H.E. "Review" of "Law and Learning Theory" (1943-44) 53 Yale L.J. 338... 322(4)

YNTEMA, H.E. "The Hornbook Method and the Conflict of Laws" (1927-28) 37 Yale L.J. 468... 318(5)

YNTEMA, H.E. "The Rational Basis of Legal Science" (1931) 31 Col. L.R. 924... 318(3)

YOUNG, E.H. "The Legal Personality of a Foreign Corporation" (1906) 22 L.Q.R. 178... 215(2)

YOUNG, E.H. "The Status of a Foreign Corporation and the Legislature" (1907) 23 L.Q.R. 151, 290... 215(3)

ZANE, J.M. "Bentham" in Great Jurists of the World (edd. J. Macdonell and E. Manson) 532... 297(2)